The Art of Family
Theory and Practice

Third Revised Edition

The Art of Family Mediation
Theory and Practice

A Foundational Text for Mediation Training

Third Revised Edition

Lynn E. MacBeth

VANDEPLAS PUBLISHING
UNITED STATES OF AMERICA

The Art of Family Mediation: Theory and Practice

A Foundational Text for Mediation Training

Third Revised Edition

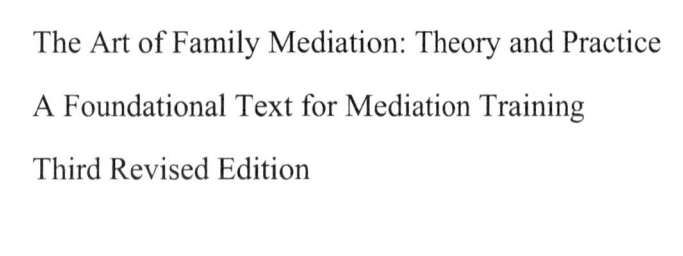

MacBeth, Lynn E.

Names and descriptions identifying individuals have been changed to preserve anonymity. Circumstances, places, people, quotations, and statements have been altered to protect confidentiality and to teach principles. Examples are alterations of cases and fictional.

Published by:

Vandeplas Publishing, LLC – December 2022

801 International Parkway, 5th Floor
Lake Mary, FL. 32746
USA

www.vandeplaspublishing.com

Copyright © 2022 by Lynn E. MacBeth
All rights reserved.

No part of this book may be reproduced, stored in a retrieval system, or transmitted by any means, electronic, mechanical, photocopying, recording, or otherwise, without written permission from the author.

ISBN 978-1-60042-551-6

Table of Contents

The Author vii

Acknowledgments vii

Chapter 1- Evolution of Family Mediation in America 1

Chapter 2- Legal and Social Landscape 19

Chapter 3- Conflict Systems and Dynamics 43

Chapter 4- The Standards of Practice 63

Chapter 5- The Art of Mediation: How Does a Mediator
            Inspire Change? (Mediation 101) 175

Chapter 6- Mediation Procedures 203

Chapter 7- Child Custody 253

Chapter 8- Divorce Primer 277

Chapter 9- High Conflict 293

Chapter 10- Reflective Practice 325

Chapter 11- Communication and Mediation 329

Chapter 12- Mediation Skills (Mediation 102) 349

Chapter 13- The Science of Mediation 363

Chapter 14- Role Plays and Case Scenarios 371

References 391

Index 401

The Author

Lynn MacBeth is a professor, mediator, attorney, licensed professional counselor, and teacher of mediation. She is on the faculty of Duquesne University School of Law. She has served as director, officer, chair, speaker, and practitioner member of various mediation and legal organizations. She is an advanced practitioner member of the Academy of Family Mediators of the Association for Conflict Resolution, which also approved her basic family mediation trainings conducted in Pittsburgh and other cities. She serves as a founder, officer, and board member of the Pennsylvania non-profit Parenting Institute, a court-appointed custody mediator in the Generations court-connected custody mediation program of the Allegheny County Court of Common Pleas, a court-connected and private licensed professional counselor, and as a contract mediator for the U.S. Postal Service REDRESS Mediation Program and formerly a mediator for the U.S. Equal Employment Opportunity Commission Mediation Program. For more information, visit LynnMacBeth.com.

Acknowledgments

I am grateful to the Generations program of the Court of Common Pleas of Allegheny County for its continued support of the mediation model for resolving child custody disputes. I have worked as a mediator in this program together with other distinguished mediators, since 1997, and have come to love and appreciate the value of this work more than anything else I do. I know my colleagues feel the same. Through the pandemic and lockdowns, our leader Amy Ross transitioned our program to online mediation with barely a hiccup.

The institutions of higher learning that have supported my work deserve my deepest gratitude. Duquesne University School of Law, has made my course *The Art of Mediation* available at the law school for the last 15 years. The late Professor Harry Gruener and his successor Bill Congelio have allowed me access to the University of Pittsburgh School of Law Family Law Clinic to teach mediation and conduct simulations with his students. These role plays have provided many hours of valuable instruction, experimentation, investigation, and testing of mediation techniques. I am grateful to them for their support and belief in the process.

Lynn MacBeth

Pittsburgh, PA

2022

Chapter One

"Peace cannot be kept by force; it can only be achieved by understanding." –Albert Einstein

Evolution of Family Mediation in America

The Peace Movement

The peace movement influenced American culture from 1954 through the seventies, beginning with the Cold War between the U.S. and Soviet Union. The two superpowers held opposing worldviews about communist totalitarianism, the Soviets propagating messianic communism[1] and the U.S opposing it in favor of democracy and individual civil liberties. Although they never engaged in all-out war, each took a side in major military conflicts in Vietnam, Korea, and Afghanistan. The war in Vietnam had a particularly strong effect on the peace movement in America, mostly on college campuses.[2]

The U.S. had nuclear weaponry by 1945 when it defeated Japan in World War II by bombing the Japanese cities of Nagasaki and Hiroshima. Both were devastated with an estimated 200,000[3] people killed, one-third of them instantly,[4] and many others severely wounded. In 1949 the Soviet Union detonated its first atomic bomb,[5] and both countries amassed nuclear stockpiles totaling 77,000 warheads between them at the height of nuclear proliferation from 1966 to 1986.[6] The world had suddenly become gravely dangerous, the only assurance of peace being the promise of "mutually assured destruction" if either side initiated war. In the 1950s American school children were famously shown the film *Duck and Cover* to reduce effects of thermonuclear radiation in the event of a strike.[7]

October of 1962 marked what many believe was America's greatest threat of direct nuclear war with the Soviets when President John F. Kennedy, in only his second year of office, was thrust into the Cuban Missile Crisis. The Soviet Union had delivered ballistic missiles to Cuba capable of delivering nuclear weapons directly to the U.S. capital and beyond. While President Kennedy and Soviet leader Nikita

---

[1] Zubok, V. (2007). A failed empire: The Soviet Union in the Cold War from Stalin to Gorbachev. University of North Carolina Press.
[2] Lefkowitz, J. (2005). Movement outcomes and movement decline: The Vietnam War and the anti-war movement. *New Political Science, 27*(1), 1-22.
[3] Richardson, D. (2012). Lessons from Hiroshima and Nagasaki: The most exposed and the most vulnerable. *Bulletin of the Atomic Scientists, 68*(3), 29-35.
[4] Cullen, L. (2003). Unleashing an era of dread. *Time, 161*(13), A24.
[5] Harrison, K. & Hughes, M. (2013). Mushroom clouds in the Arctic. *History Today, 63*(8), 18-20.
[6] Pappalardo, J. (2008). Ever-present arsenals. *Popular Mechanics, 185*(11), 24.
[7] Ringstad, A. (2012). The evolution of American civil defense film rhetoric. *Journal of Cold War Studies, 14*(4), 93-121.

Khrushchev made dangerous moves and countermoves to maintain their positions, America was held in suspense for 13 days, fearing nuclear war at its doorstep.

As the missile crisis deepened, President Kennedy gripped the nation in a televised speech broadcast on all three major television networks warning of, "a series of offensive missile sites....now in preparation on that imprisoned island [Cuba]," declaring, "The purposes of these bases can be none other than to provide a nuclear strike capability against the Western Hemisphere."[8] In the months leading up to the crisis, the Soviet Union made repeated public assurances that the build-up was for defensive purposes only. In schools and at family dinner tables, American children learned about nuclear war and its threat to human survival. It became commonplace for households to store up canned goods, water, and survival supplies, with grocery stores placing a limit on purchases of canned food.[9]

Over the next several decades, the American cultural response was a pervasive peace movement that brought about bilateral arms reductions, anti-war sentiment, and even government sponsored community mediation centers where local conflicts between neighbors and parties to legal disputes could be talked through. At the same time, court reform efforts were calling for alternative dispute resolution in interpersonal conflicts, noting the waning role of traditional institutions such as churches and the extended family in resolving interpersonal conflict in communities.[10] Of most significance for family mediation, however, was the onslaught of divorce cases brought about by the sharp rise in divorces between 1963 and1975, setting up the need for an alternative to the divorce courtroom as the method to resolve difficult issues and disputes brought about by divorce.

The Mediation Explosion

It is well documented that the U.S. divorce rate doubled between the years 1963 and 1975, from 2.3 per thousand to 4.9 per thousand.[11] More recently, it has hovered around 2.6.[12] Paired with the marriage rate of 6.1(now steadily declining), the divorce rate has recently decreased to 42.6%, from around 53% in 2014[13], according to statistics from the U.S. Centers for Disease Control. In 1973, legalized abortion

---

[8] JFK Library (2014) Retrieved from http://microsites.jfklibrary.org/cmc/oct22/doc5.html
[9] George, A.L. (2003). *Awaiting Armageddon: How Americans faced the Cuban Missile Crisis.* Chapel Hill: University of North Carolina Press.
[10] Hedeen, T. & Coy, P. (2000). Community mediation and the court system: The ties that bind. *Mediation Quarterly, 17*(4), 351-367.
[11] Vital Statistics of the United States, 1975, Volume III, Marriage and Divorce. Retrieved 2/1/2014 from http://www.cdc.gov/nchs/data/vsus/mgdv75_3.pdf
[12] The Hive Law. (2021). Divorce Rate in America (2000 to 2020). https://www.thehivelaw.com/blog/divorce-statistics-us-divorce-rate-in-america/
[13] Vital Statistics of the United States. 1975, Volume III, Marriage and Divorce. http://www.cdc.gov/nch/nvss/marriage_divorce_tales.htm Retrieved February 1, 2014.

contributed to the sexual revolution,[14] and, coupled with the emergence of No-Fault Divorce laws beginning with California in 1970, brought on relaxed sexual mores and greater acceptance of divorce.

Throughout the country, courtrooms across America were inundated with litigants filing for divorce, custody, and support. The ordeal of divorce received the attention of mental health and social work professionals, and in 1963 the Association of Family and Conciliation Courts, known as the AFCC, was formed. This and other national efforts resulted in modern family courts found today in nearly every U.S. jurisdiction with day care (no more crying babies in the hallways of justice), smoke-free facilities, metal detectors, trained court staff, mandatory parenting education, domestic violence laws, and court-connected mediation.

Formal family mediation originated with two men, O.J. Coogler and John Haynes, around 1975. O.J. Coogler is considered by many to be the father of family mediation. He wore multiple hats— attorney, state legislator, family and marriage counselor, consul to Mexico, counsel to the Consulate of Germany, and member of the bar of the state of Georgia.[15] Perhaps the most important label he sported, though, was that of a twice-divorced husband and father. After his contentious second divorce, he claimed that his life, his wife's life, and his children's lives were "unnecessarily embittered."[16] He decided to turn his frustration and anger into something that would create a more "humane world," creating a blueprint for family mediation in his 1978 book *Structured Mediation in Divorce Settlement*.

Coogler's mediation blueprint is based on forty-five rules comprising a system of family mediation. Although mundane considerations such as payment of fees, cancellation of appointments, preparation of budgets, and tape recording of sessions are addressed, the book tackles other important aspects of the family mediation process, some of which survive today, while others have been rejected.

Coogler's model applied the no-fault provisions of the Uniform Divorce Act since, at the time, not all states had no-fault divorce. He provided a detailed nine-hour mediation template, a description of the mediator's impartiality, a rule against separate communications or caucuses (as we now call them) with the mediator, and an "Advisory Attorney" who would somehow neutrally advise both parties of their rights and duties under their mediated agreement, prepare the agreement, and execute its contents. In the event the parties failed to agree, Coogler's rules called for arbitration of the disputed issues following mediation, at the election of the parties.

Few of Coogler's original rules survive today, as distinct mediation styles have emerged and evolved. In particular, the use of an advisory attorney is prohibited by the conflict of interest rules applicable

---

[14] Klick, J., Avraham, D., & Stratmann, T. (2003). The effect of abortion legalization on sexual behavior: Evidence from sexually transmitted diseases. *Journal of Legal Studies, 32*(2), 407-433.
[15] Grebe, S. (1988). Structured mediation and its variants: What makes it unique. In Folberg, J. & Milne, A. (Eds). *Divorce Mediation: Theory and practice*. New York: Guilford Press, 225-248.
[16] Coogler, O.J. (1978). *Structured mediation in divorce settlement: A handbook for marital mediators*. Lexington, MA: D.C. Heath and Company, xv.

to attorneys, forbidding dual representation of parties on opposite sides of a case. Today's family mediators are obligated to advise both parties to seek separate counsel, and, although the mediation process is designed to save time and money, the use of separate attorneys is not bypassed, but is curtailed by sparing the attorneys' fees involved in communication and negotiation of the agreement. These costly tasks are performed directly between the parties in the presence of the mediator, saving significant money for the parties by limiting attorneys' tasks to providing separate legal advice, filing papers, and executing the terms of the final agreement reached in mediation. The attorneys are not hired and paid for endless hours of negotiation, letter writing, posturing, bluffing, and making proposals and counter-proposals, let alone conducting court trials. All of these tasks are performed by the parties face-to-face with the assistance of the mediator. The parties are often in communication with their attorneys between mediation sessions and are still able to save vast amounts of money in attorneys' fees.

What was missing from Coogler's mediation blueprint, by his own admission, was a description of the methods to be used by the mediator in conducting the mediation. In contrast, today's mediator *methods* are virtually the only focus of interest for mediation professionals. Coogler offered Transactional Analysis, or TA, a school of pop psychology of his day, to address psychological needs and interpersonal communication difficulties. He believed the mediator should be trained in the "rules of communication" and game analysis, features of TA. He suggested that the mediator could first "get the parties to cooperate"[17] by complimenting cooperative behavior and giving them tasks that required input from the other, such as having the husband help the wife figure out her car expense and the wife help the husband with food and grocery costs. He also believed that catching the parties shortly after separation, before hostilities escalated, was beneficial.[18] In the event conflict erupted, his advice was to "simply stop the conflict."[19] This advice left mediators with few tools to facilitate natural disagreements that are bound to erupt when parties negotiate face to face, especially over highly emotional conflicts inherent in family break-ups.

Contemporary family mediators have developed strong tools to enable effective communication, manage conflict, and promote understanding and cooperation between disputing parties. Today's mediators would not attempt to take advantage of parties' vulnerability immediately after separation by catching them early before they could even comprehend what is happening to them. Today, mediators don't limit their work to cases where parties are cooperative and, instead, expect at least some lack of cooperation that can be eased with contemporary methods that encourage cooperation and productive conflict resolution. Today's mediation models tend not to prohibit private caucuses or separate meetings with a party, depending upon the model used. When caucuses are used only to prevent arguing between the parties, this reveals potential weakness on the part of the mediator. Today, mediators first administer techniques for managing the conflict before resorting to caucus for the sole purpose of establishing order. Caucus, although

---

[17] Coogler, 1978, p. 81
[18] Id. p. 82
[19] Id. p. 83

effective for stemming argument, also prevents parties from interacting in ways that can lead to resolution of the dispute.

Coogler admitted that, "Demonstrated techniques for conflict resolution upon which a marital mediator can rely must await the outcome of future in-depth longitudinal research."[20] In other words, he punted. Nevertheless, Coogler's blueprint was valuable for formalizing family mediation by establishing a structure, "centers" where mediation was performed, and by founding the Family Mediation Association, leaving mediation methodology to be discovered by his successors. Coogler died in 1982, only four years after his book was first published.

British born Canadian university professor John Haynes, the other founder of family mediation, had a methodology that drew on his experience in labor mediation and as a social work educator.[21] Haynes initially saw divorce mediation as an expansion of clinical practice for therapists and counselors, advocating the use of therapy to deal with emotional issues, stating, "When the emotional blocks are severe…the mediator calls for a "time-out" from the mediation for a specified number of sessions. I usually ask for a three-session time-out and the couple understands that during that time my role will switch from mediator to therapist and the focus of the session will be on an examination of feelings rather than on problem solving." [22] Haynes later disavowed this practice[23] as the role of mediator became a distinct role from that of therapist, and ethical considerations required a professional not to mix these roles. Like Coogler, Haynes first struggled to create a model of mediation and "define a field"[24] from scratch. Today, Haynes is best known and appreciated for his ability to understand the psychological foundations of interpersonal conflict. He saw the mediator's role as one of encouragement and empowerment of the parties.[25] In this, he was ahead of his time, presaging the Transformative Mediation movement that later came along in the mid-1990s, establishing the parties' empowerment and recognition as the principal goals of mediation.

Haynes's many videotaped mediation sessions survive, and in them viewers can observe his style. Gentle and reverent, his well-known response to clients who obsessively focused on past wrongs was, "I don't want to rehash your past; I want to reshape your future." Although today's mediators recognize the need for parties to process their past experiences in a mediation session, Haynes's intervention worked for him, probably because he was singularly able to form a near-spiritual connection with clients. In his Foreword to Haynes's posthumous book *Mediation: Positive Conflict Management,*[26] Robert Benjamin, who knew Haynes, recalls, "Few who had the opportunity to observe John Haynes mediate disputes would

---

[20] Id. p. 79
[21] Haynes, J. (1981). *Divorce mediation: A practical guide for therapists and counselors.* New York: Springer Publishing Company, p. xi.
[22] Haynes, 1981, p. 10
[23] Schneider, C.D. (2010). The works of John Haynes. Retrieved from http://www.mediationmatters.com/review_the_works_of_john_haynes.php
[24] Id.
[25] Haynes, 1981, p. 134.
[26] Haynes, J., Haynes, G., & Fong, L. (2004). *Mediation: Positive conflict management,* New York: SUNY Press.

deny his artistry. His elegant presence, accented by bow tie and the British accent, and supported by subtle hand motions, were suggestive of a shaman drawing out evil spirits." Haynes himself explained in his second book that he drew on his relationship with God and viewed his clients as reflecting the goodness of God. According to Haynes, the mediator, "searching for goodness," can find "that of God" in everyone.[27] Haynes and Coogler joined forces until they split up in 1981 and Haynes founded the Academy of Family Mediators, the predecessor of today's Association for Conflict Resolution. Haynes died in 1999, survived by his wife Gretchen Haynes who appeared as co-author of his later books.

Beyond Haynes and his soothing, genuinely loving style, the 1970s found hundreds of mediators discovering their own styles and writing about communication techniques,[28] emotional needs,[29] theoretical mediation models,[30] power dynamics,[31] and conflict management.[32] Yet, no commanding theory of the "how" of mediation missing from Coogler's model emerged until 1994 when Robert A. Baruch Bush and Joseph P. Folger stunned the mediation community with their pivotal book *The Promise of Mediation,* introducing transformative mediation style. However, before style could be meaningfully addressed, the mediation community had more pressing hurdles to overcome. For a while in the 1970s and eighties there was a question of whether mediation would gain recognition as a legitimate profession. Mediation faced opponents who questioned the ethics, effectiveness, and even the safety of divorce mediation.[33]

Some members of the legal profession were against divorce mediation, accusing mediators (whether they were attorneys or not) of engaging in the unauthorized practice of law. Coogler devoted the entire last chapter of his book responding to thirteen criticisms made by the legal profession. In his defense of mediation, he pointed out safeguards provided by the reviewing attorney (albeit the single attorney whose role would not pass muster today due to conflict of interest) and the fact that labor and federal non-lawyer mediators were already the industry standard for settling many legal disputes. His chief justification for mediation was what he called "The Do-It-Yourself Movement," holding that individuals should be in control of their own divorce and not at the mercy of professionals who are incentivized to perpetuate the conflict at great expense to clients who feel they have "no way out."[34] Coogler's view of party self-determination was based on the constitutional right of every American to have the "freedom to contract" provided in Section 10, Article I of the U.S. Constitution. In fact, Sarah Childs Grebe, a strong proponent and early student of Coogler's had this very section of the Constitution inscribed in her own handwriting

---

[27] Haynes, J., Haynes, G. (1989). *Mediating divorce: Casebook of strategies for successful family negotiations.* San Francisco: Jossey-Bass, p. 18.
[28] Donohue, W.A., Allen, M., Burrell, N. (1985). Communication strategies in mediation. *Mediation Quarterly, 10,* 75-89.
[29] Barsky, M. (1983). Emotional needs and dysfunctional communication as blocks to mediation. *Mediation Quarterly, 7*(2), 55-66.
[30] Lind, D. (1992). On the theory and practice of mediation: The contribution of seventeenth-century jurisprudence. *Mediation Quarterly, 10*(2), 119-128.
[31] Mayer, B. (1987). The dynamics of power in mediation and negotiation. *Mediation Quarterly, 16,* 75-85.
[32] Bartunek, J.M. & Bowe, B.E. (1988). The transformational management of conflict: A perspective from the early Christian Church. *Employee Responsibilities and Rights Journal, 1*(2), 151-162.
[33] Silberman. L. (1982). Professional responsibility problems of divorce mediation. *Family Law Quarterly, 16*(2), 107
[34] Coogler, 1978, p. 6

on the front inside cover of her personal copy of Coogler's book (See Figure 1). This section of the Constitution forbids states from impairing the obligations of contracts. A fundamental premise of American law and freedom, this "right to contract" was evidently the last line of defense for pioneers of the mediation movement that included Coogler, Haynes, and Grebe, among many others.

Another early opponent of divorce mediation was the women's movement, particularly advocates for victims of domestic violence. Both groups lobbied against mediation, claiming it favored men with superior bargaining power, lacked checks and balances for full financial disclosure, and lacked the thoroughness of a case reviewed by two attorneys and a court.[35] Some even went so far as to declare that women are inherently weaker than men, arguing that women *per se* have unequal power in mediation.[36]

The mediation profession did the only thing it could. Proponents of the movement went about legitimizing the profession by focusing on ethics. The first standards of professional conduct for mediators were created by the Association of Family and Conciliation Courts (AFCC) in 1984, together with the American Bar Association's Task Force on Mediation and the Academy of Family Mediators (now part of the Association for Conflict Resolution). Early ethical concerns included the mediator's response to known or suspected child or spousal abuse, dealing with full disclosure of assets and income, preventing fraud, disclosure by clients of illegal activity, extended or lengthy mediation, use of compulsory arbitration in the event of impasse, unlicensed and unqualified mediators, bias, and mental health or substance abuse issues.[37] In addition, mediation advocates lobbied for legislation to protect confidentiality of mediation with privilege statutes,[38] and, in some states, gained licensure, certification, or legislated minimum qualifications for mediators.[39] Overcoming objections of family mediation opponents by the mid-1990s, the movement turned its attention to style and methodology.

---

[35] Pearson, J., (1997). Mediating when domestic violence is a factor: Policies and practices in court-based divorce mediation programs. *Mediation Quarterly*, 14(4), 319-335.
[36] Dingwall, R., Greatbatch, D., Ruggerone, L. (1998). Gender and interaction in divorce mediation. *Mediation Quarterly*, 15(4), 277-285.
[37] Grebe. S. (1989). Ethical issues in conflict resolution: Divorce mediation. *Negotiation Journal*, April 1989, 179-190.
[38] e.g., 42 Pa.C.S.A. §5949 (Pennsylvania)
[39] e.g., F.S.A. Mediator Rule 10.100 (Florida).

Contract.

U.S.
Constitution
Article I
Section 10
#1

Figure 1: Inside front cover of Sarah Childs Grebe's personal copy of OJ Coogler's book

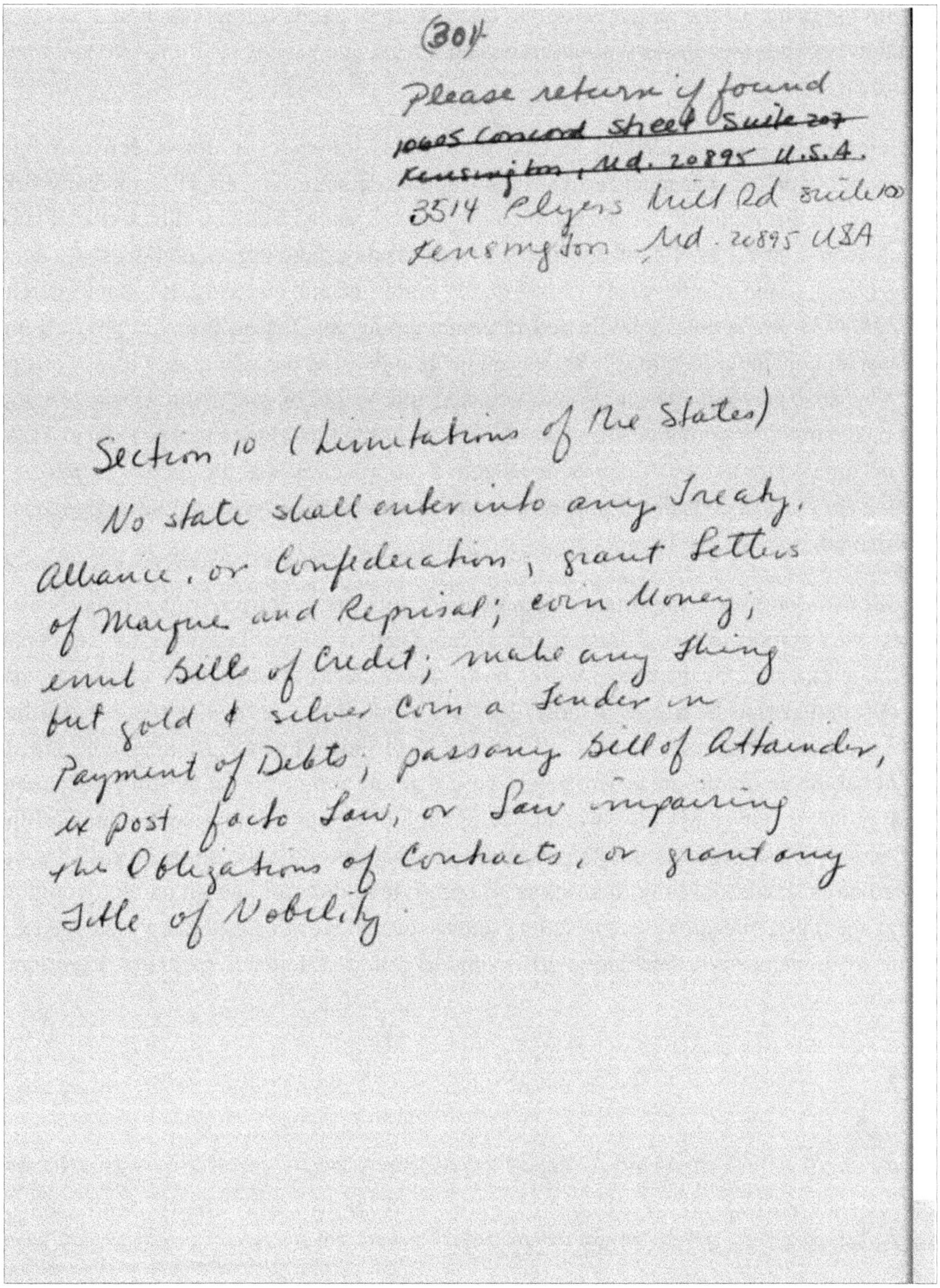

(30)¢

Please return if found
~~10605 Concord Street Suite 207~~
~~Kensington, Md. 20895 U.S.A.~~
3514 Plyers Mill Rd Suite 100
Kensington, Md. 20895 USA

Section 10 (Limitations of the States)

No state shall enter into any Treaty, Alliance, or Confederation; grant Letters of Marque and Reprisal; coin Money; emit Bill of Credit; make any thing but gold & silver Coin a Tender in Payment of Debts; pass any Bill of Attainder, ex post facto Law, or Law impairing the Obligations of Contracts, or grant any Title of Nobility.

Mediation Styles

Mediation style refers to the "how" of mediation that was missing in O.J. Coogler's model. Early on, mediators labeled their styles evaluative or facilitative to indicate whether or not they acted as judges do, evaluating the merits of the parties' case vs. taking a more hands off approach and merely facilitating communication between the parties without imposing a legal analysis or solution, but enabling the parties to find their own solution.

Alternatively, some mediators labeled their styles directive or non-directive to indicate how authoritative their approach was in terms of structure and leadership. The directive mediator (like Coogler) dictated a structure that required the parties to follow the mediator. The non-directive mediator used less structure and would, at times, follow the parties' lead. Today, labeling mediation styles has become a moving target because the number of styles is virtually unlimited and evolving. It is not a stretch to say that as many as 25 styles are regularly addressed in contemporary mediation literature,[40] while many others receive at least an honorable mention.[41] Styles can be thought of as a continuum with various extremes on either side. One such paradigm places process-oriented approaches on one extreme and substance-oriented approaches on the other.[42] Another continuum, the Style Continuum® (see Figure 2) places Transformative mediation on one extreme vs. Evaluative/Directive approaches on the other extreme, where the transformative approach is considered process oriented and the evaluative/directive approach is considered substance oriented.

Style labels have some importance because mediators can be judged (rather unfairly and unwisely) by what style they purport to use. Commercially, a label can develop a following among consumers who believe that a certain style of mediation works best. Consumers have the right to choose whatever style they want but should also be aware of how the style works for a particular type of conflict and how mediation participants might react to its use. By being pigeon-holed into a particular style, a mediator could limit his or her ability to obtain work. Moreover, there is ample authority[43] suggesting mediators should not limit their approach to any one style. Instead, styles should be viewed on a continuum and the mediator given the freedom to use professional judgment to use whatever style the situation calls for at any given moment. Mediators should not limit themselves to one style in the same way a painter would not limit his style to using one brush, one stroke, or one color. Artists, even if working within a style or genre, eventually develop their own unique style. Mediation art is similarly fluid. A talented mediator, experienced enough

---

[40] Wall, J.A., Dunne, T.C., Chan-Serafin, S. (2011). *Conflict Resolution Quarterly,* 29(2), 127-150.
[41] e.g., Benjamin, R. (2012). The natural history of negotiation and mediation: The evolution of negotiative behaviors, rituals, and approaches (Updated). Retrieved from: http://www.mediate.com/articles/NaturalHistory.cfm (naturalist style); Kressel, K. (2007). The strategic style in mediation. *Conflict Resolution Quarterly,* 24(3), 251-283. (strategic style)
[42] Amadei, R.N., Lehrburger, L.S. (1996). The world of mediation: A spectrum of styles. *Dispute Resolution Journal, 51*(4), 62-86.
[43] Holland, E. (2020). Understanding the top 3 styles of mediation with ADR Times. https://www.adrtimes.com/styles-of-mediation/

to act from instinct, will glide back and forth across the continuum to use techniques from the entire range of styles as they are needed, to produce a finished product of a completed mediation.

A style label means little by itself because its use is dictated by the type of conflict. Insured liability claims (as in car accidents) tend to be the most easily settled cases because insurers reserve money for this purpose, and the adjuster, whose job it is to settle the case, is not personally funding payment.[44] Uninsured contract and workplace disputes tend to be more difficult to settle because funding presents an added challenge. Family and workplace conflicts tend to be the most emotion-laden conflicts again because of funding but also due to the added challenges presented by parties' existing interpersonal relationships, making them the most difficult to settle. A discussion of style alone without consideration of the type of conflict yields little, if any, information about the likelihood of settlement using a particular style, since various types of disputes have varying inherent degrees of difficulty.

Another important aspect of style choice is the mediation parties' reaction to a particular style. After all, the parties' reactions to a style should be the most reliable determinant of its appropriateness. A 2002 study of mediation participants' satisfaction with their mediator found that party dissatisfaction was most likely the result of two distinct causes: the mediator's failure to address or respond to expressions of emotion and (conversely) the mediator's failure to maintain order in the session.[45] Presumably, a perceived lack of order in a session would result from a mediator allowing emotions to go unchecked. Many mediators find the tension between these two goals of allowing expression of emotions vs. reining in negative emotions to be the essence of "managing" conflict. Mediators often feel unable to accomplish both of these goals simultaneously. Therefore, styles that purport to provide a method of responding effectively to expressions of emotion while not creating a chaotic, uncomfortable environment are the most appealing.

In 1981, an important book on negotiation offered mediators some guidance on how to manage the "people problem" that obstructs negotiations when emotions run high. *Getting to Yes*[46] by Roger Fisher and William Ury of the Harvard Negotiation Project advised negotiators, "Don't argue over positions." Citing the nuclear testing ban negotiations between the former Soviet Union and the United States, they demonstrated that most negotiations do not go beyond the positions stage, and fail. The U.S. had insisted on ten "inspections" within Soviet borders, while the Soviets agreed to only three. Talks broke down, but reportedly, no one ever discussed in detail what an inspection would actually be. For instance, how many inspectors would there be? How often? What would they do? If the parties had gone beyond the positions (number of inspections) and explored interests (verification, minimal intrusion), their discussions may have been more fruitful. The negotiators never got beyond the surface of positions to the underlying interests. Other classic examples of going beyond positions to the underlying interests are the orange and librarian examples. In the orange example, there is only one orange and two people claiming possession of it. The

---

[44] Wall, J. Chan-Serafin, S. (2014). Friendly persuasion in civil case mediation. *Conflict Resolution Quarterly*. 285-304.
[45] Gale, J., Mowery, R., Herrman, M. & Hollett, N. (2002). Considering effective divorce mediation: Three potential factors. *Conflict Resolution Quarterly, 19*(4), 389-420.
[46] Fisher, R. & Ury, W. (1991). *Getting to yes: negotiating agreement without giving in*. (2nd ed). New York: Penguin Books.

negotiations break down because the problem seems to have an all-or-nothing solution impossible to resolve. A consideration of the interests of the claimants, however, resolves the problem. One party desires the orange for its juice while the other is interested only in the orange peel. If a negotiator (or mediator) explores the parties' interests, the parties can find a solution to share the orange. In the librarian example, a dispute exists between two library patrons, one of whom wants the window open and the other who insists it be closed. The librarian, who knows the importance of interests over positions, finds out the reasons for the parties' positions. The first party wants the window open for fresh air, while the other wants it closed to avoid a draft. By opening a window in a nearby room, the librarian is able to satisfy the interests of both parties. Positions are defenses. Parties instinctively know that if they reveal the reasons for their positions, they open themselves up to attempts by their opponent to persuade them away from their positions. A skilled mediator goes beyond the position by exploring underlying interests. In family mediation, positions are often declared as, "I want 50/50 custody," "I want alimony for 5 years," or "I want the house." When asked for their reasons, parties almost invariably reply, at least at first, with another position (something else humans seem to do instinctively), such as, "Because it's fair," or "Because it's my right."

Assertive or Pressing Style

In formal mediation settings such as mandatory, court-connected programs, the style least likely to rub parties the wrong way should be the style used. Obviously, parties who are forced to use mediation should not be subjected to an unpleasant process. One style perceived as potentially unpleasant is the assertive, "pressing" style where the mediator has a strong settlement-driven agenda and uses caucus and shuttle mediation to collect data, make suggestions, lower aspirations, and "close" the deal, similar to a sales pitch.[47] In observing 100 civil mediations, Wall et al. (2011) found that pressing techniques resulted in a high settlement rate and did not offend disputants, while other studies conclude disputants are decidedly unhappy when they feel pressed and challenged by the mediator.[48] In theory, it seems that parties would bristle at being pressed or persuaded off of their positions, but sometimes, the benefit of applying this technique to both parties equally and reaching a settlement invites acceptance of these tactics because parties expect the mediator to work towards settlement.[49] Again, it depends on the content of the conflict, the parties' feelings, and the parties' expectations, and the mediator should always be wary of aggressive tactics.

---

[47] Wall, Dunne, & Chan-Serafin, 2011.
[48] Wissler, R. (2002). Court-connected mediation in general civil cases: What we know from empirical research. *Ohio State Journal on Dispute Resolution, 17,* 641-680; McDermott, E.P. & Obar, T. (2004). What's going on in mediation: An empirical analysis of the influence of a mediator's style on party satisfaction and monetary benefit. *Harvard Negotiation Journal, 9,* 75-113.
[49] Wall, Dunne, & Chan-Serafin, 2011.

Evaluative, Facilitative, and Neutral Styles

Evaluative style is another assertive style where the mediator analyzes the case from both perspectives, pronounces conclusions regarding each side's strength and weakness, and gives opinions and suggestions, but in a balanced way. Some commentators recommend giving evaluative style a different name so as not to confuse it with early neutral evaluation, an ADR process that is not mediation, but an actual case evaluation.[50] Wall, et al. (2011) found evaluative style to yield the greatest number of settlements in civil cases. Neutral style, on the other hand, where the mediator refrains from evaluating or attempting to persuade, yielded the fewest civil case settlements. The neutral mediator is committed to keeping both sides talking in an attempt to lead the parties to find their own solutions. Another type of style that is perceived as neutral is facilitative style. Facilitative style means that the mediator takes a less hands-on approach to the process and allows parties to lead the process with facilitation or help from the mediator. It is a less directive approach that recognizes the parties' input into resolving their own dispute and a precursor to the transformative model. These styles offer less risk of offending participants by seeming biased or pushy. However, where there are fewer settlements, there can also be less satisfaction with mediation.

Transformative Style

The style that offers the most advice for managing emotions while maintaining order is transformative style, which pays particular attention to expressions of emotions. Transformative mediation, introduced by Bush and Folger[51] in 1994, created a serendipitous style that begins with a newly-defined approach or "orientation" by the mediator. Instead of focusing on settlement as the goal of the mediation, the mediator focuses on specific goals that relate to feelings, and this focus serendipitously brings about settlement. The specific goals are empowerment of the parties individually and recognition between the parties.

Bush and Folger observed that traditional mediators tended to focus on problem-solving, emphasizing resolution of the conflict as the primary goal, and noticed that in doing so, mediators were missing golden opportunities, presented by the parties (but too often ignored by the mediator) to accomplish other, more satisfying and important tasks that resulted in transforming not just the conflict, but the parties. They found that mediation could do much more than merely resolve conflict and had the potential to

---

[50] Coltri, L. (2010). *Alternative Dispute Resolution: A Conflict Diagnosis Approach.* Upper Saddle River, NJ: Pearson Education.
[51] Bush, R.A.B. & Folger, J.P. (1994). *The promise of mediation: Responding to conflict through empowerment and recognition.* San Francisco: Jossey Bass.

engender moral growth[52] and transform human character.[53] If mediators listened closely and caught these golden opportunities, moments could occur when parties experienced what Bush and Folger called "empowerment" and "recognition," that could transform the parties, their relationship, and their conflict.

Empowerment is defined as "the restoration to individuals of a sense of their own value and strength and their own capacity to handle life's problems."[54] In other words, empowerment occurs when a party, with or without the mediator's assistance, becomes introspective and accesses their own internal power, often for the first time. This can be as simple as a party becoming aware of a long-held personal value or resource they hadn't previously been aware of, or as complex as understanding a past hurt in a new context or frame that makes it less painful. These moments are personally empowering because they bring parties from a feeling of disempowerment to a feeling of greater personal power.

Recognition is defined as "the evocation in individuals of acknowledgment and empathy for the situation and problems of others."[55] Therefore, empowerment occurs within an individual, while recognition occurs between parties. Recognition is seen in understanding the other party's struggles for the first time, believing the other party for the first time, or even forgiving or refusing to forgive the other party. The process is cyclical because recognition, the grandchild of empowerment, is actually very empowering itself. As individuals, we are empowered when our own introspection raises our awareness of self, but we are all the more empowered when we are able to recognize another in a new way because seeing the other differently transforms not only the individual but the conflict the individual has with another.

To accomplish these moments, the mediator follows the parties, instead of requiring the parties to follow the mediator. To the transformative mediator, "the action is in the room."[56] The parties provide the grist for the mill by bringing their raw feelings, thoughts, beliefs, and expressions into the process. Instead of avoiding conflict (as OJ Coogler advocated, "Simply stop the conflict."), the transformative mediator uses the conflict to solve the problem. The mediator allows expressions of feelings and responds to them, encouraging the introspection that brings about empowerment and recognition. Nevertheless, the mediator is not merely a follower of the parties but has a powerful leadership role in the process. In some ways, transformative mediation is almost a pedagogical process, much like a teacher and students, although these roles are often reversed because the mediator learns much in the teaching process (as teachers often do, too).

Transformative mediation was, and still is, misunderstood by some as focusing too much on feelings at the expense of practical goals of problem-solving and settlement. Yet, this style can be most valuable where conflict is intractable and settlement has not been attainable. Its ability to transform

---

[52] Id., p. 4.
[53] Id., p. 27.
[54] Id., p. 2.
[55] Id.
[56] Folger, J.P. & Bush, R.A.B. (1996). Transformative mediation and third-party intervention: Ten hallmarks of a transformative approach to practice. *Mediation Quarterly, 13* (4), 263-278.

relationships and promote recognition between battling parties who may have long failed to hear, believe, and understand each other is truly revolutionary. Its creators and adherents acknowledge its serendipitous dimension.[57] Parties trying to find a solution to a legal dispute serendipitously find something else: forgiveness, healing, change, and personal power. Mediators who seek empowerment and recognition for their clients find something unexpected more often than not: settlement. Paradoxically, by not focusing on settlement, this method works (perhaps better than traditional problem-solving methods) to settle cases. Moreover, its techniques solve mediators' age-old problem of needing to simultaneously respond to and allow difficult emotional expression while maintaining order. Transformative techniques are discussed in greater depth in Chapter 5. Clearly, this style lends itself particularly to family mediation because of the strong emotions clients bring to the family mediation table. Nevertheless, the family mediator will also need to borrow techniques from other styles, particularly at the point where the parties are discussing distributive matters such as division of property and payment of alimony or support. These discussions tend to lend themselves to the assertive style of most distributive negotiations where finding a discrete number is the singular goal of the process.

Adaptive or Integrative Style

With so many styles to choose from within a large variety of conflicts, mediators should feel free to label their personal style as adaptive, meaning the mediator, like the artist, adapts his or her style to the conflict presented. It would be silly to apply an approach out of loyalty to a prescribed label when a different style is called for in a conflict situation. It is widely known that in actual practice, regardless of what style a mediator purports to use, mediators regularly shift styles within a mediation session.[58] Pressing mediators lighten their touch. Facilitative mediators ask a leading question to steer the discussion. Transformative mediators problem solve. Neutral mediators express an opinion. When asked what style I use by a potential new client, I have come to use the term adaptive or integrative style to describe my craft. The two labels can be used interchangeably because they both mean the mediator views style as fluid, something to be applied when the problem calls for it.

The freedom to adapt or self-select my style comes from my role as a leader in the mediation process. A mediator is a leader who values conflict and "leverages it for change…."[59] A mediator possesses many of the characteristics of the prototypical modern leader: innovative, motivating, risk-taking, and empowering of others.[60] A mediator is comfortable with suspending judgments and living with

---

[57] Bush & Folger, 1994, p. 83.
[58] Wall & Chan-Serafin, 2014.
[59] Kuttner, R. (2011). Conflict specialists as leaders: Revisiting the role of conflict specialist from a leadership perspective. *Conflict Resolution Quarterly,* 29(2), 101-126.

[60] Id.

uncertainty.[61] Unlike traditional leadership style, the modern mediator leads others by empowering and supporting them, rather than by commands, orders, and rules. By modeling respectful behavior, the modern mediator commands respect and secures obedience to behavioral norms smoothly, without use of didactic tools such as demanding rote ground rules. Today's mediator is both a leader and client-led. The parties provide the raw material of conflict that the mediator works, like a sculptor, to assist them in finding a solution to their problem and resolution of the dispute. The mediator follows the clients to discover their unique disagreement and all of its facets, but the mediator also leads the parties to find not just what they want, but what they need. Parties *want* the mediator to intervene and suggest not only possible solutions to the dispute, but remedies and balms the mediator knows to be helpful to their unique situation.[62]

The goal of any mediation should be the same: **change**. A successful mediation is defined as whether or not the mediator was able to bring about change in the parties or their perspectives from beginning to end. Clearly, the parties are hiring the mediator because change is needed. Ideally, the parties want the dispute resolved. This can happen only if one or both parties have a change in perspective. It is not necessary (although it is certainly desirable) that both parties experience a change, but it is necessary for at least one party to undergo a change of some kind in order for movement in the direction of resolution to occur.

A Final Note on Mediation Styles

The Style Continuum (Figure 2) shows where styles fit within the extremes of Assertive to Transformative styles and how a mediator might respond from a particular orientation, style, or mediator goal. Assertive represents any of a number of styles (Directive, Pressing, Evaluative, etc.) wherein the mediator controls the process, emphasizes substance (the content of the dispute) over process, and focuses primarily on settlement using persuasion (whether it be subtle or overt). Transformative style is any style where emphasis is not on settlement but on empowerment and recognition, process is emphasized over substance, and the process is client-led. In the middle rests Facilitative style. Both extremes are characterized underneath each heading. The purpose of the chart is to allow the mediator to visualize the extremes. The mediator has the freedom to glide back and forth from one side to the other, avoiding extremes for the most part, but also enjoying the benefits of each extreme by selecting strategies from any style as the conflict warrants.

---

[61] Id.
[62] Id.

	The Style Continuum®	
Transformative	**Facilitative**	**Assertive** **Pressing, Evaluative, Directive**
	Process	
Freedom		Oppression
Autonomy		Tyranny
Empowerment and Recognition		Settlement is the Main Goal
Relationship and the Self Changed		Mediator's Ego is Satisfied
Unconscious Mind, Love Higher Self		Conscious Mind, Fear, Ego
	Mediator Goals	
"Where would you like to begin?"	**Creating a Comfortable Environment**	"This is the agenda."
Follower	**Structure**	Leader
"Where would you like to go from here?"	**Identifying Issues**	"The issues are a, b, c."
Empowers Parties	**Power**	Empowers Mediator
"I" and "You"	**Boundaries**	"We"
Parties Responsible for Own Feelings/Behavior Mediator Responsible for Own Needs	**Managing the Conflict**	Mediator Controls Parties' Behavior With Ground Rules
Parties Take Responsibility for Process and Outcome	**Self-Determination of Parties/Autonomy**	Mediator Sets Ground Rules and Directs Outcome
Belongs Solely to Parties	**Ownership of the "Problem"**	Ambiguous Boundary/Mediator is a Helper
No Forbidden Topics/Negative Emotions and Arguing Allowed/Free Dialogue Encouraged	**Maintain Order**	Avoid Conflict by Discouraging Argument/ Avoid Negative Emotions Emphasize the Substantive
What is happening "now" is focus even if it involves discussion of the past. Parties determine what is relevant	**Staying Focused**	Discussion of past discouraged/relevance determined by mediator.
On request of party, to gain clarity, to protect privacy, infrequent	**Caucus**	To break up conflict, not give up bottom line/deceive
Trust parties to find outcome	**Neutrality**	Impose optimal solution

Figure 2: The Style Continuum®

Chapter Two

"*A family in harmony will prosper in everything.*" –Chinese Proverb

Legal and Social Landscape

The Changing Family

Marital Attachment Theory

The opening chapter to Diane Vaughan's 1986 book *Uncoupling*[63] contains a profound sentence, "*Uncoupling begins with a secret.*" In this simple statement lies the drama of family mediation. Most people marry intending to remain forever coupled. When the first seed of doubt takes hold in the mind of the initiator (the person who wants to leave), it is preceded by numerous troubling thoughts and emotions that must be pushed aside in favor of the status quo, staying together. The initiator may sit with doubt for years before taking action to leave. Fear of autonomy, fear of financial hardship, and fear of rejection by loved ones become obstacles for making the break.[64] It is not unusual for the decision to leave to take three or more years.[65] In my experience as a divorce mediator, I have not yet encountered a divorcing couple who took the decision lightly; everyone I've met has in some way agonized over the decision, even after the die is cast.

Douglas Darnell describes the main difference between men and women's appraisals of what makes a marriage happy.[66] When asked the question, students often guess, incorrectly, that men gauge the marriage by sexual standards while women do not. The answer actually has little to do with sex. According to Darnell, women judge the quality of marriage in terms of "emotional closeness" while men judge a marriage as happy when there is "lack of hassle." Uniformly, my students, both male and female, give an enthusiastic nod of recognition to this pronouncement. I am sure Darnell makes the observation mostly tongue-in-cheek, and yet it crystalizes the disparity between men and women's thoughts about intimate relationships and their endings. It may be a stereotype, but it does help explain the state of mind of divorcing parties, especially when one party is blindsided by the other's decision to leave. A husband stunned by the seemingly sudden end to his marriage finds himself confused because the marriage seemed happy, while

---

[63] Vaughan, D. (1986). *Uncoupling: Turning points in intimate relationships.* New York: Oxford University Press.
[64] Applewhite, A. (1997). *Cutting loose: Why women who end their marriages do so well.* New York: Harper Collins, 25-32.
[65] Willen, H., Montgomery, H. (2006). From marital distress to divorce: the creation of new identities for spouses. *Journal of Divorce and Remarriage,* 45(1/2), 125-147; Kitson, G.C., Babri, K.B., Roach, M.J. (1985). Who divorces and why: a review. *Journal of Family Issues,* 6, 255-293.
[66] Darnell, D. (2003). Workshop on Parental Alienation: Its Impact on Children and Managing High Conflict Families, Rivers Club, Pittsburgh, PA; Darnell, D. (1998). *Divorce Casualties.* National Book Network, 1998.

the exiting wife knows that the lack of emotional closeness was what finally caused her to stop complaining and move on.

Family mediators are acutely familiar with the differing mental states of divorcing spouses. It is usually evident that the initiating spouse has had the opportunity to detach from the marriage, while the non-initiator, sometimes blindsided, is just beginning to deal with the break-up. After all, the exiting spouse has had the deliberation stage before separation to plan and adjust. There is an advantage to having the luxury of time to detach emotionally from the other, to be weaned from emotional dependence and find support outside of marriage for friendship and emotional attachment, to adjust to the idea and lifestyle of singlehood, and, in short, to *uncouple*. The non-exiting spouse, on the other hand, is taken by surprise when what was at worst theoretical becomes reality. The non-initiator may have had warning signals along the way, but ignored, minimized, or denied them for as long as possible. When the finality of the initiator's decision is sprung on him, this party is thrust into an all-out crisis with the usual grief, shock, and depression that accompany a break-up.

This information is of much value to the divorce mediator. Understanding differences between the initiator and the non-initiator helps the mediator respond to parties' emotions expressed in mediation and assess the parties' capacity to mediate. When parting spouses or parents come to a family mediator, it is a virtual certainty they will be in different stages of loss.

Many believe that divorce can be compared to death. Grief in divorce is caused by loss of the marital attachment. This attachment is comparable to a parent-child attachment and can be as strong. In fact, children may have greater defenses against loss of a parent than an adult has against loss of an intimate partner.[67] The classic model for grief stages is offered by Elisabeth Kübler-Ross in her timeless work *On Death and Dying.*[68] The stages are Denial, Anger, Bargaining, Depression, and Acceptance. Earlier, in 1961, John Bowlby developed studies of loss focusing on attachment theory. His loss stages were the wish to recover the lost object, disorganization, and reorganization. Researchers have applied these grief models to the trauma of divorce, and with good reason.[69] In divorce, parties undergo a grieving process, and those who are able to move successfully through all of the stages to a healthy acceptance of the marriage ending are the most successful in coping with the loss.[70]

Another grief process model introduced by Scott and Jaffe,[71] designed primarily for employment loss during the 1980s, is simpler, less negative, and applies more suitably to marital grief than other models.

---

[67] Ehmke, R. (2010). Helping children deal with grief. Retrieved from http://www.childmind.org/en/posts/articles/2010-10-12-helping-children-deal-grief
[68] Kubler-Ross, E. (1973). *On death and dying.* Routledge.
[69] Gray, C., Koopman, E., Hunt, J. (1991). The emotional phases of marital separation. *American Journal of Orthopsychiatry,*6(1), 138-143.
[70] Mazor, A., Baptiste-Hamel, P., Gampel, Y. (1998). Divorcing spouses' coping patterns, attachment bonding, and forgiveness processes in the post-divorce experience. *Journal of Marriage and the Family,* 29(3/4), 65-81.
[71] Scott, C. & Jaffe, D.T. (1989). *Managing personal change: Self-management skills for work and life transitions.* Los Altos, CA: Crisp Publications.

The stages are Denial, Resistance, Exploration, and Commitment. Visualizing these stages as a curve, beginning with Denial and ending with Commitment, the path, intersected by a midline, can be represented by Figure 3.

Figure 3: The Transition Curve

The stages of Denial, Resistance, Exploration and Commitment occur in a counterclockwise direction, beginning with Denial.

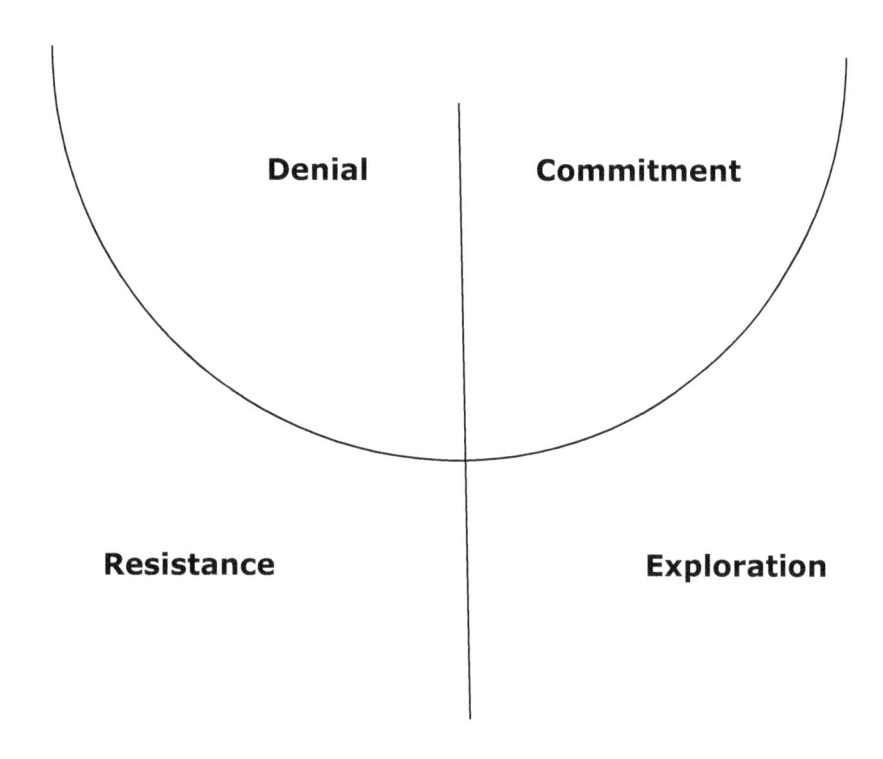

Denial	**Commitment**
Resistance	**Exploration**

Adapted by Lynn MacBeth from Scott & Jaffe, 1989.

Denial

Denial is pretending that something doesn't exist. It's the coping mechanism most commonly used to escape reality. It can be a natural, healthy, and logical reaction to an unwanted event. Its purpose is to challenge, and perhaps change, reality. As an initial reaction, it makes sense. Often an unwanted situation will change. When denial persists past the inevitability of an event, it becomes unhealthy and no longer protective. Defensive denial refuses to acknowledge both reality and personal responsibility in a situation in ways that may tend to blame others.[72] Denial that persists is often rooted in shame. Most people experiencing loss can move past denial and recognize reality. However, some go to extremes to continue denying reality. Continuing with denial in the face of reality can be unhealthy and even dangerous because it deprives the sufferer of the ability to take protective, corrective action. When the alternative to denial is severe psychological distress, denial provides a buffer between trauma and acceptance of the unwanted event. As a temporary coping mechanism, denial is a powerful comfort, but it can only be useful during a limited window of time because it acts as a mental block.[73] In order to gain insight into oneself and learn from the situation, denial must yield to the next stage.

Resistance

The next phase, resistance, is a way to let go of denial without letting go of it completely. Since denial can give the sufferer a sense of control, letting go of denial can lead to loss of control and, worse, being controlled by circumstances. When reality persists and denial becomes difficult to maintain, a perceived loss of control invites stress and negative emotions and behaviors. This phase is characterized by anger, fear, pain, and irritability. Blame is directed at others and, less clearly, at self in the form of shame and regret. A fixation on the past, feelings of victimization, the inability to take responsibility for one's part in the break-up, and a desire for retribution are some of the destructive tendencies in the resistance stage. Some remain in this stage throughout their lives. This is often the stage in which a non-initiating spouse in divorce enters the legal process. Resistance consumes a great deal of energy because it requires constant effort to go against the natural flow of life, truth, and reality. This stage can be disempowering for the sufferer because it consumes immense effort, hindering positive growth. Resistance to change creates inertia at best and a pattern of destructive behavior, at worst. Because a mediator's goal is to empower parties, knowledge of behaviors associated with this stage, their root cause, and attendant feelings helps the mediator respond appropriately to resistance. In addition, when resistance and its attendant feelings are severe, the mediator must be equipped to assess client capacity to mediate.[74] Debilitating feelings or coping patterns (such as substance abuse) could also affect capacity to mediate.

Exploration

The next phase in the transition curve is more grounded in reality. In the exploration stage, anger may still be present, but it subsides and is replaced with at least a glimmer of hope for the future. Although exploration is a positive stage of growth and forward movement, it can also be accompanied by confusion and disorientation. The reality of change sets in, and exploration opens up a world of choices that were previously hidden from view. The diversity of life's choices becomes apparent. Sometimes the multiplicity

---

[72] Lannin, D.G., Bittner, K.E., Lorenz, F.O. (2013). Longitudinal effect of defensive denial on relationship instability. *Journal of Family Psychology, 27*(6).
[73] Nelson, S.D. (2011). The posttraumatic growth path: An emerging model for prevention and treatment of trauma-related behavioral health conditions. *Journal of Psychotherapy Integration,21*(1), 1-42.
[74] An ethical prescription. See Chapter 4.

of options seems overwhelming. I remember cycling through the phases after my mother died of lung cancer following a three-month illness. When I entered the exploration phase, it seemed overwhelming to notice that life had gone on during those dark three months, and that out of nowhere I had many choices before me that included a new office, new opportunities, friends who wanted to catch up, a new computer I'd purchased right before she became sick and hadn't even taken out of the box, and so on. While exhilarating, the stage also felt confusing, unfamiliar, and even surprising. Thanks to my experience, I can relate to parties who find themselves in the exploration stage. I have known them to lose items, leave things behind in my office, be clumsy, and even have car accidents during this disorienting time. I hope I've been able to avert a disaster or two by reminding them to be extra careful during this distracting time when they are spending most of their waking hours rediscovering life and contemplating the many issues and alternatives facing them. It can be an exciting, empowering time, but being overwhelmed can also be disempowering. Exploration brings on feelings of hope and optimism sometimes interrupted with feelings of frustration and confusion. Because the stages are diffuse, most people go back and forth a few times before leaving a stage. In order to cope, a party could leave exploration to return to resistance for a time, if only temporarily. It is in this stage, or, in some cases, the next stage, that the initiating party typically enters the mediation or legal process.

Commitment

The final stage of commitment restores stability. A person's commitment is to new beginnings, reality, and an acceptance of what has happened, free from overpowering remorse, regret, blame, and denial. In commitment choices are made, situations change, and life flows naturally. Emotional growth has taken root, and a rebirth, of sorts, has occurred. Life has changed and the world seems different. A feeling of having survived (and perhaps thrived) after a disaster takes hold. Awareness that one is forever changed dominates. Of course, these stages will repeat themselves in a different context later when another loss of any magnitude occurs.

Mediator Interventions and Client Readiness

Being alert to the parties' passages through these stages is of great value to the family mediator because it helps the mediator assess for client readiness and informs the mediator's responses to parties' expressions of feelings.

In a 1998 study[75] of 20 family mediators and their styles of intervention (or lack thereof), parties presented negative feelings (anger, sadness, bitterness) relating to unresolved marital attachment. It was observed that mediator behaviors in response to these expressions of negative emotions fell into five categories:

---

[75] Kruk, E. (1998). Deconstructing family mediation practice via the simulated client technique: The case of unresolved marital attachment. *Mediation Quarterly, 15*(4), 321-332.

Anticipating/preempting during opening statement;

Normalizing

Acknowledging, then quickly redirecting

Use of challenge, including reality testing

Working on settlement of at least one issue in the first session

By using these interventions, the mediators thought they were appropriately reacting to the non-initiating spouse's troubling emotions. Most likely the spouse was in the denial or resistance stage. The study concluded that the mediator's behavior exhibited a settlement-driven mentality as opposed to therapeutic listening, and that this served the needs of the mediator and the initiating party, but did not serve the needs of the non- initiating party who wanted more acknowledgment and understanding of the feelings that were relevant to them. This created a feeling of partiality toward the initiating spouse and "placed the non-initiator at a distinct disadvantage in subsequent negotiation."[76] Whether the partiality is real or perceived makes no difference from the party's point of view. To be dismissive of a party's real, expressed emotions creates the appearance of partiality or favoritism. Ethically, a mediator must maintain neutrality.

Another ethical duty the mediator has is to assess parties' capacity to mediate. The standards of conduct are explored in depth in Chapter 4. Most of the time, parties are ready (or ready enough) to mediate. However, there are unusual circumstances when a party simply is not capable of making important, permanent life decisions for a variety of reasons. Mental illness, substance abuse, and lack of emotional readiness can be obstacles to an effective, fair mediation process. Early in my mediation practice, I had a couple who drove 200 miles to my office. I really wanted to make their visit worthwhile, but the wife was unable to stop sobbing and crying during our sessions. In addition to using nearly a whole box of Kleenex, she wanted to cry on my shoulder, permanently staining my favorite navy pinstriped suit with heavy makeup and tears. I sensed that my listening and empathizing skills were merely being challenged and that if I just used the correct technique, I would be able to set this mediation aright. After the second session, I realized that her sadness was debilitating, and she lacked the capacity to mediate. I asked her to tell her doctor about it, hoping to find a solution to the incessant sobbing and waterworks. A few weeks later, she called to say that her medications were interacting, and the doctor had now corrected the conflicting prescriptions. When the couple returned to mediation, her state was improved, and the mediation was able to go on.

Sometimes a readiness problem can escape detection. I met Janis and Don when I was a new mediator and welcomed the challenges their case presented. Unfortunately, what I now know to be "red flags" went unnoticed. Now, their case provides a perfect example of a lack of emotional readiness. As you read the case, try to identify what stages along the transition curve the parties might be in. Also, don't

---

[76] Id. p. 331.

be quick to judge the new mediator. Theory is great, but mediators learn most by doing. The good news is we are not brain surgeons.

Janis and Don: A Case Study in Client Readiness

After twenty years of marriage, Janis and Don separated. Janis initiated a call to the mediator stating she no longer wanted to live with Don's lack of employment and "addictions." Since he refused to move out, she found an apartment for herself but remained worried about being away from their two teenagers. She hoped they could get back together, but felt hopeless because Don would not acknowledge his behaviors and how much they bothered her. They had tried marriage counseling and individual counseling for several years, but nothing seemed to change.

The parties came to mediation seemingly eager to work out a settlement agreement relating to custody, support and property division. Don was annoyed at having to do mediation because he did not initiate the separation and did not want a divorce. He often complained about spending money on "getting this divorce." However, he was well acquainted with the economic consequences of friends' divorces and was certain that mediation was preferable to going to court with lawyers. After five or six sessions, they arrived at a comprehensive settlement of all issues. Up to this point, the mediation was going smoothly and seemed to the mediator to be deceptively easy. In fact, there was no rage, no tears, no despair, and no anger. The mediator was unsure what Don's "addictions" were since neither party addressed that concern again. A comprehensive Memorandum of Understanding was prepared and sent to the parties. A few days later, the bottom fell out.

Don went into a deep depression and began calling the mediator with repeated and desperate pleas for help. He finally realized he was losing Janis. He acted as if the written Memorandum was a surprise to him. He was completely unwilling to enter into any agreement. He was ready to get a lawyer and fight about all of the issues. In the alternative, he sought more mediation, and wanted to begin the process all over from scratch. Janis told the mediator that Don had been in denial all along and never took her demands seriously. She recognized his feelings of despair as the same feelings she had eighteen months ago when she realized the marriage was in trouble. This successful mediation had unraveled.

Questions for Discussion and Analysis

1. **Much can be learned from this "failed mediation." The mediator, a novice, failed to recognize and respond to several red flags. What were they?**

Answer: The red flags (alarm bells) were:

- *Addiction*-- The mediator never explored Janis's concerns about Don's addictions. The mediator was too "client-led" and could have, instead, taken the initiative to explore this red flag. This information could have been useful to assess the parties' capacity to mediate. If Don was an active addict, he may have been too impaired to make decisions in his own interests. If Janis was in denial about Don's addiction (which seems apparent by her failure to address it again after the first phone call) she may have had readiness issues as well.

♛ *Don's statements revealing denial about the impending divorce*-- The mediator did not address Don's statements that he did not want the divorce. Don's denial of Janis's seriousness about divorce kept him in the Denial stage where he could not make decisions about divorce because he did not really think it was going to happen.

♛ *Lack of emotion*-- The lack of emotion was an indicator that there was a world of unspoken thoughts and feelings. This is not always the case; however, given the parties' statements about the difficulties of their situation, strong emotions would normally accompany loss of a 20-year marriage and a mother having to leave her teenage children.

♛ *Janis's initial statement that she hoped the parties could get back together*-- Janis's statement that she hoped they could get back together was incongruous. It didn't fit the situation. She had left and was leading the charge toward divorce. Why would she even say she hoped they could get back together? This statement could be part of her denial, or, worse, it could be a defense against Don's resistance. In other words, sometimes a party will lead the other to believe there is a chance of reconciliation so that the other party will be generous in a divorce settlement.

2. In what stage of the transition curve was Don? Janis?

Answer: Don was in denial.

The shock of receiving tangible, undeniable evidence of reality in the form of the written Memorandum of Understanding was the event that moved him to resistance. His resistance was evident when he called the mediator with threats to get a lawyer and fight in court. Janis was in the exploration stage; however, she seemed to revisit the denial stage when it suited her. Janis, as the initiator, would normally have moved beyond denial. Her occasional sojourns back to denial probably threw the mediator. When both parties are in denial, it is more convincing. Janis's denial was evident in her failure to bring up the addictions and her lack of emotion, particularly anger, which would be normal after a twenty-year marriage to an addict. She was pretending that a divorce could really be this easy, even though she suspected all along that Don was himself in denial. She recognized his behavior as similar to her own when she first began thinking about ending the marriage. After all, she has known Don for at least twenty years. Her impressions of his behavior would be reliable.

3. Why did the agreement unravel?

Answer: Don was not mediating in good faith.

He was mediating under the belief that none of this would ever take place. He pretended that Janis did not really want a divorce. Everything was fantasy until Don received the papers in the mail. This was an expensive mistake, and if the mediator could have caught it early it would have been a great service to the clients. Nevertheless, the mediator is not entirely to blame because the game the parties were playing was exceptionally convincing.

4. What might the mediator have done to assist the parties in recognizing important issues?

Answers:

☼ *Transparency:* The mediator could have asked Janis's permission to state in joint session what Janis told her in confidence in the initial phone call. If Janis consented (which she likely would have because she did not say it was a secret) the issue of Don's addictions would have been on the table from the beginning. This would have given the mediator the opportunity to explore with the parties upfront whether or not they were ready to mediate. The mediator could have shared with the parties her bewilderment over the fact that they did not seem to be sad or angry about ending a twenty-year marriage. This could have led to more openness and honesty about what was happening. It could have cracked the denial.

☼ *Assessment and Intervention for Readiness:* The mediator could have done what many mediators do routinely and instinctively: assess for readiness. Parties are almost always on opposite sides of the transition curve (page 23), one being on the *right* side, in Exploration or Commitment, and the other being on the *left* side in Denial or Resistance. If a party seems stuck in denial (like Don) or resistance (evident in angry, shaming or blaming behavior—Don had not yet gotten there) it is appropriate for the mediator to intervene by pointing out to them that, on occasion, parties are in different stages of adjustment to the idea of divorce, and that the mediator recommends that the parties consider whether or not they are truly ready to tackle these issues and make decisions that will affect the rest of their lives. This could also be referred to as "reality testing." The decision about readiness is ultimately theirs. The mediator's duty is to place the information and the question before them. Incidentally, I do not show them the transition curve; I simply explain the stages as I observe them.

A Final Note on Client Readiness

This case demonstrates what can happen when parties are in significantly different stages in the grief process. Don's denial was undoubtedly a reaction to signs he saw, perhaps as far back as eighteen months ago when Janis revealed she first started to think about ending the marriage. The stages are not static and parties can move from stage to stage, often revisiting a previously completed phase. Janis still found denial to be, occasionally, an appropriate tool for her in dealing with Don. Referring back to the diagram on page 23, something significant can be observed about everything that happens on the *left* side of the curve. **The entire focus of the left hand side of the curve is the *past*, while the focus on the right side of the dividing line is on the *present* and *future*.** In mediation, while clients may need to focus on the past in order to process through the grieving cycle, most of their stated goals involve the present and future; therefore, the mediator's job is to assist clients in becoming aware of what their focus is so that they receive value for the time and money they invest in mediation. If clients are acting on beliefs about which they are unaware, they could be setting themselves up for a situation like Janis and Don's where a mediated agreement crumbles. When they say they are interested in discussing the present and future, but demonstrate a preoccupation with the past, there isn't anything wrong with the mediator pointing out the disparity between stated goals and current actions. Mediators will often point out incongruous statements to help parties become clear about their own thoughts and feelings.

Myths That Operate in the Divorce Culture

Myth #1: License to Misbehave

Beyond stages of grief, the mediator must be aware of behavior inspired by a "divorce culture" and its effects on parents and litigants in the family law system. With marriage declining and out-of-wedlock births on the increase, divorce may also be on the decline. Nevertheless, there will always be families and break-ups, whether or not they are, technically, *divorces*. From the child's perspective, parents and siblings are the family regardless of the legal structure.

The divorce culture refers to attitudes and behaviors that seem unique to divorce or break-ups. Hollywood is astute at characterizing and dramatizing weird behavior brought on by divorce. Gwyneth Paltrow and Chris Martin will always be known for their strange euphemism for divorce, "conscious uncoupling."[77] Demi Moore was described by People magazine as "desperate and alone" when her marriage to Ashton Kutcher, 16 years her junior, ended, and she was hospitalized for "convulsions and lack of consciousness."[78] Nora Ephron made a name for herself with her 1986 screenplay *Heartburn* dramatizing her divorce from journalist Carl Bernstein, played in the movie by Jack Nicholson. During a dinner party, Streep, playing Ephron, realizes she can no longer tolerate marriage to a philandering spouse and smashes a cream pie into Jack Nicholson's face, then leaves the party. In divorce, society considers this behavior acceptable, even expected. Divorced people, at least in the beginning, practically have their own culture. I

---

[77] Tauber, M., McNeil, E., Morrisey, S., et al. (2014). Gwyneth and Chris: The truth about their split. *People, 81*(15), 64.
[78] Tauber, M., Nahas, A., Cedenheim, P., Dodd, J., Jones, O., Garcia, J., et al. (2012) Desperate and alone. (Cover Story) *People, 77*(6), 64-70.

knew a fellow who went to his first Alcoholics Anonymous meeting for help with a drinking problem. His wife had left him, and the marriage was over. Devastated, he went to AA at the suggestion of friends, introducing himself as, "Hi, my name is Jack, and I'm divorced."

Adjusting from married to single life can take years, and, to avoid unhappiness, individuals are known to adopt negative approaches that range from finding a new partner immediately, to adopting a libertine lifestyle, to continuing a combative relationship with the ex, or even vowing never to trust enough to marry again.[79] The divorce culture excuses behaviors that, absent divorce, would not be accepted. This kind of behavior, also known as a "license to misbehave"[80] can be compared to the phenomenon of aggressive driving that induces folks who rarely commit overtly hostile acts to somehow feel empowered behind the wheel to say and do things they would not normally do in public. Road rage is common among men and women. Most of the time the behavior is harmless, consisting of "verbal assaults, obscene gestures, honking the horn…,"[81] and it often surprises the driver more than anyone. The driver knows the behavior would be completely unacceptable anywhere but behind the wheel of a car. Divorce behavior is similarly **contextually bound**, sometimes harmless, and atypical but for the painful break-up.

There are numerous theories for what drives this phenomenon of selective misbehavior. It could be testosterone,[82] but that would only account for half of the divorce population. It's possible that fear of ending up alone in life causes divorcing spouses to take irrational, self-defeating risk and to engage in unhealthy behaviors.[83] The examples set by Hollywood (as in Meryl Streep smashing a pie into Jack Nicholson's face) might account for this type of unrestrained behavior,[84] but some argue that cultural norms (of which the divorce culture is certainly a part) are more strongly affected by the realities of life than by Hollywood.[85] Whatever the cause, family lawyers and family mediators are very familiar with the phenomenon of outrageous behavior by family law clients who go outside the norm as if their divorce and accompanying feelings give them a license to misbehave.

Clients may come to expect a degree of tolerance for divorce misbehavior on the part of their lawyers, mediators, and even judges. In one court case, the husband destroyed all of the family video tapes of the parties' young daughter. When mother and her attorney brought this to the attention of the male judge during trial, the husband, on cross examination, had a ready explanation, "Well, your Honor, it was the Super Bowl, and I couldn't find any other tape; I guess I slipped it into the VCR." Alas, the judge,

---

[79] Portnoy, S.M. (2006). The psychology of divorce: A lawyer's primer part I—the effects of divorce on adults. *American Journal of Family Law, 20*(2), 73-79.
[80] MacBeth, L. (2010). *The art of family mediation: Theory and practice, 1st edition.* Lake Mary, FL: Vandeplas Publishing, p. 38.
[81] Arkowitz, H., Lilienfeld, S.O. (2009). Road rage. *Scientific American Mind, 22*(2), 64-65.
[82] Mazur, A., Michalek, J. (1998). Marriage, divorce, and male testosterone. *Social Forces, 77*(1), 315-330.
[83] Twenge, J., Catanese, K., Baumeister, R. (2002). Social exclusion causes self-defeating behavior. *Journal of Personality and Social Psychology, 83*(3), 606-615.
[84] Fine, G.A. (1997). Scandal, social conditions and the creation of public attention: Fatty Arbuckle and the problem of Hollywood. *Social Problems, 44*(3), 297-323.
[85] Sternheimer, K. (2008). Hollywood does not threaten family values. *Contexts, 7*(4), 44-48.

husband's attorney, and the husband simultaneously laughed at the wife's misfortune. Every family lawyer can recount at least one *War of the Roses*-type incident where the desire to one-up the other spouse is exhibited in a spouse's desperate behavior. In the movie, Barbara, played by Kathleen Turner, pretends to have killed Bennie, the family dog, serving him up for dinner for Oliver, her hated soon-to-be ex. In a prior scene, Oliver "accidentally" ran over Barbara's cat in the driveway. In real life, clients commonly hire private detectives, place sophisticated spyware on each other's computers, record phone conversations, destroy property, make public scenes, and brainwash the children. I was once involved in a case where the wife convincingly feigned mental illness as a way to obstruct the case and get as much money from husband as possible for as long as possible.

Family mediators should never accept the myth that divorce gives one a license to misbehave and must reject it outright. Instead of excusing, overlooking, accepting, or finding it humorous (except in private), mediators should actively dispel the myth that a license to misbehave is granted to those who find themselves in the throes of divorce, and instead, should compassionately promote personal responsibility and respectful behavior. If parties perceive that the mediator is willing to excuse destructive behavior, it will affect the mediation process. Parties instinctively know that negative feelings and behaviors towards their former loved one are destructive, and a part of them wants to stop. The mediator should support that part. The mediator should offer the solution, not perpetuate the problem. When clients first sense that I do not abide destructive behavior, character assassination, revenge, blame, or even victimhood, I notice a sense of surprise followed by relief when I gently signal that such behaviors are not encouraged, and are, in fact, self-destructive. I do this not by judging or condemning, but by empathizing with the painful feelings that lie at the root of such behavior.

I use several techniques, which will be explored in greater depth later in this book, to let parties know that overt negative behaviors and words are not helpful to the process and that I am not comfortable with behavior that intentionally causes pain to anyone in the room during the mediation process. I do this by using "I" statements, so that I am taking ownership of my feelings. "I" statements tend to be much less threatening than "you" statements, and more effective because they relate to feelings, and one's feelings are not up for debate. I may also mention that what a party says to his or her child's mother or father is the same as saying it directly to the child. This is not the same as setting ground rules. This is information. The following chart shows the deeper meaning behind negative behaviors and helps the mediator to immediately access parties' feelings on a deep level, beneath the behavior.

Figure 4. Statement and Message

To help me be compassionate…..

Statement	Possible Message
1. "You did this. I don't want a divorce."	If I accept any responsibility for this, my feelings of shame will be overwhelming and painful.
2. "But we were happy."	I am in denial because this hurts too much. I feel like a fool for believing everything was fine. I should have paid attention to the signals the marriage was ending.
3. "You are a liar and a cheat." (Or any other attack on character).	I am afraid that I may have contributed to this situation in some way, and I cannot face that.
4. "You will never see my children as long as you are with that tramp."	I feel so abandoned, I will say anything, however desperate and ridiculous it sounds, to get you to come back.
5. "You don't show good enough judgment to have unsupervised time with your children."	I feel so rejected by you that I have to act superior to you in order to live with my feelings of humiliation.
6. "I believe in being honest with my child. We are very close and she needs to know the kind of father she has—one who leaves his family for some home wrecker."	I feel so rejected that the only way I can handle the pain is by displaying anger. I am so lonely that the only person I have is my child.

When I hear even the most offensive, triggering words from a perspective of wounding, they lose their sting, and I want to understand the speaker rather than challenge the behavior and feelings. I think parties are grateful when the mediator lets them know that, notwithstanding divorce, they are still responsible for their behavior, and that includes working to resolve legal conflicts and custody battles. As parents, clients owe their children certain fundamental resources: food, clothing, shelter. In divorce or separation, there is one more basic need they are obligated to supply their child: a custody arrangement upon which both agree. From a child's perspective, it is not healthy for a parent to take a leave of absence from personal responsibility to grieve a divorce. Children need order and peace, not chaos and war. Their needs cannot be put on hold.

Myth #2: Suitability of the Litigation Model for Resolving Family Conflict

Another myth that operates in the divorce culture is the suitability of courts for resolving the situation. Somehow, by default, the same courts that hear commercial disputes, crimes, and car accidents are set up to hear divorce cases. Fortunately, state courts today have domestic relations divisions, but the courts themselves operate under the same principles and rules as any other courtroom.

After divorce, separation, or death, a family has to be restructured. This does not always have to be a court case, although it usually is. A court is the place people think of first for restructuring a family. Although mediation is making inroads to shatter this myth, the operative belief of most of society and Hollywood, is that the go-to for handling divorce is court. Indeed, one can hardly be divorced without a court.

The litigation model is a **warfare model**. The prescribed steps are **attack and defend**; that is why there is a *plaintiff* and a *defendant*. Parties should know that the dictionary definition of the word *trial* is *subjection to suffering or grievous experiences; a distressed or painful state.*[86] Rules of evidence obscure and obstruct the **truth.** Courts do not always seek the truth, nor do they claim to. Courts seek competent, relevant evidence. Courts decide credibility of competent, relevant, legal evidence. This is because there are other considerations besides the truth that govern courts. For example, if police shirk their responsibility to obtain a legal search warrant and obtain evidence illegally, the evidence is thrown out and the defendant can be set free. The constitutional protections against illegal searches and seizure trump the goal of punishing every guilty person. To guarantee freedom, a few guilty people get to walk free. This is as it should be. Even though the evidence was unassailably incriminating beyond any reasonable doubt, the truth of the defendant's guilt was not the goal of the system. Courts only decide credibility of competent, relevant, legal evidence, which is different from seeking the truth.

Lawyers with an appetite for litigation are not paid to seek justice; rather they work to persuade a court to find in favor of their side, regardless of which side they are on. A very effective lawyer I once knew told me that each side in a courtroom must tell a story. The lawyer is often the one, much like a public relations professional, who first spins that story for the client and artfully tells it in the courtroom. The client may have trouble even recognizing his own story. That same lawyer told me that the winner will always be the one who was able to tell the most compelling story. Sadly, the court's emotions are thus exploited to gain an advantage for the best storyteller. This is by no means intended as an indictment of the American justice system, which I believe is the best in the world. Nevertheless, it is a warfare model, limited in its ability to determine truth, and, therefore, to dispense ultimate justice.

---

[86] *Webster's Encyclopedic Unabridged Dictionary of the English Language.* (1996). New York, Gramercy Books, 1511.

Is Mediation Based on Truth?

In a weird way, yes, mediation is based on truth. Nothing turns me off more than mediators who say truth doesn't matter in mediation. There are many mediators who say this, suggesting that truth is relative or subjective. To me, they seem cynical at best, and at worst, foolish. The mediation model of resolving disputes *is* founded on truth. Those who argue it is not maintain that there can be two or more different versions of objective reality, and that this is perfectly fine. That's nonsense. Any philosopher worth his salt will tell you that A can *never* be "not A." It's not allowed by the rules of logic. Therefore, this argument is illogical and every consumer knows it. This argument damages the image of mediation because it sounds irrational. Parties don't want opposing versions of the facts to go unchallenged. That's why they seek a court judgment. They have a strong need for their side to be declared right.

Thankfully, from the mediator's perspective, there are two different factual accounts presented, but the mediator does *not* accept as truth two opposing realities. Mediation is based on truth because there is only one objective reality, and the parties typically know exactly what that reality is. Even if they differ in their selective memory, their perspectives, or the conclusions they drew from the situation, they know what happened. No one has yet discovered how to erase the hard drive of the human brain. They know. They were there. It is the mediator, who does not share their history, who does not know the truth, and does not need to know. In mediation, parties do not get the satisfaction of having a fact finder declare who is right, who is wrong, who is telling the truth, and who is lying. However, they get something much more valuable because that fact-finder is often wrong. In an imperfect system, the findings of "fact" made by a court nearly always contain some untruth. In mediation, there is no proclamation of truth; therefore, there is no chance for error, and the truth is not compromised. This is valuable because truth is valuable. A mediator who states that what really happened is not important and that both parties can be right sounds like a fool. A wise mediator says, "I don't know what happened. I wasn't there." The mediator says what she does know, "I do know it's possible for you to move forward with an agreement even if you don't agree about what happened." The mediator can tell the parties how he knows this, "I also know that both of you know what happened because you were there." This statement has power because it challenges both parties to look inward without threatening or judging them.

At the heart of any mediator's misguided statement that truth doesn't matter is the mediator's wish that the inability of the mediation process to determine the truth (because it has no jury or fact-finder like a courtroom does) can be forgiven by proclaiming the truth to be unimportant. It's an attempt to sell the mediation process to those who doubt its efficacy. I am all in favor of selling the mediation process because it is in need of selling. Hollywood has not helped the mediation profession by offering mediation drama and role models the way it promotes the legal profession. If mediation were regularly depicted by Hollywood, mediators would not have to painstakingly explain what mediation is to every prospective client. Lawyers do not have to explain to clients what a lawyer is. I long for the day when mediators don't have to explain what they do, and everyone automatically knows.

For now, mediators have to explain mediation and promote it as "safe and effective"[87] for public use. Perhaps no one has done this for mediation as much as courts have. By mandating mediation as many courts now do, courts have begun to send the message to the public that mediation is an effective and desirable alternative to court.

A long-term study reported in 2001 out of the University of Virginia[88] studied families twelve years after divorce, comparing parties who litigated with parties who mediated. It found that in families who mediated, the non-custodial parent was more involved with the children, and the families had more flexible custody arrangements. Participants were randomly assigned to mediate or litigate, so that characteristics lending themselves to amicability did not affect the results. Another study out of Indiana University[89] found that divorce mediation that helps parents focus on children's needs and interests benefits them by helping parents focus on the child's basic needs rather than on adult concerns. I have found the warfare system unable to focus on the child's needs for the parents to work together. By the time parties reach trial in a custody dispute and the gloves come off, maligning the other parent at all costs takes precedence over protecting the ability of parents to develop healthy co-parenting habits.

Using a warfare model to restructure a family can be destructive because there are always spoils of every war, and what is usually left of a family after a full-blown divorce or custody trial is a barely recognizable set of badly battered individuals. The legal system drains the family finances. Courtroom machinations require parents to demonize each other or risk losing. The battle become a contest of which parent is best, as if a child should only be with the best parent, while the second best, even if a very close second, should be discarded. Every past sin is dredged up; every mistake revisited; every misstep resurrected; every word misspun. Parents drag in neighbors, teachers, soccer coaches, guidance counselors, and therapists. Expert witnesses materialize (for a fee). Almost anyone passes for an expert in today's courtrooms. The chart below gives just some examples of what passes for "facts" that can be glorified by so-called experts. If these expensive facts cannot be "controverted" by an opposing expert, they are allowed to glide into the record as established evidence.

---

[87] Benjamin, R.D. (2007). Jim Melamed is 2007 recipient of ACR John Haynes Distinguished Mediator Award: A tribute and lament on the field of mediation. Retrieved from http://www.mediate.com/mobile/article.cfm?id=3147
[88] Emery, R.E., Lauman-Billings, L., Waldron, M.D., Sbarra, D.A., Dillon, P. (2001). Child custody mediation and litigation: Custody, contact, and co-parenting 12 years after initial dispute resolution. *Journal of Consulting and Clinical Psychology, 69*(2), 323-332.
[89] Holtzworth-Munroe, A., Applegate, A.G., D'Onofrio, B., Bates, J. (2010). Child Informed Mediation Study (CIMS): Incorporating the children's perspective into divorce mediation in an American pilot study. *Journal of Family Studies, 16*, 116-129.

FIGURE 5. EXPERT FORENSIC TESTIMONY

EXPERT TESTIMONY	TYPE OF EXPERT
What job a person is capable of securing and how much income he/she is capable of producing	Vocational Expert
What a person's thoughts, beliefs, and personality traits are, a person's tendency to lie or tell the truth	Psychological Expert
What a child thinks and why	Psychological Expert
What the economy will do	Economic Expert
What interest rates will be in the future	Financial Expert
How long a person will live	Actuarial Expert
Money value of damages to a person's reputation	Advertising Expert
The selling price of a house before it is sold	Real Estate Appraiser
The selling price of every object in a home before they are sold	Household Goods Appraiser
How an accident happened	Reconstruction Expert
Whether or not a person sincerely seeks asylum	Immigration Expert

    For every expert's testimony, there is typically an opposing expert with a polar opposite opinion. Then, there are the jury consultants who help parties find the best jurors to give credibility to one side's expert. Eyewitness testimony, infamously unreliable,[90] is accepted as truth if it is not opposed with conflicting evidence.

---

[90] Well, G.L., Olson, E. A., Charman, S.D. (2003). Distorted retrospective eyewitness reports as functions of feedback and delay. *Journal of Experimental Psychology: Applied*, 9(1), 42-52.

If the ideological arguments against the warfare model are not convincing, the practical realities are. The average cost of the litigated divorce is estimated at $37,200 and up,[91] although this estimate is conservative in light of reported legal bills in the millions of dollars.[92] Attorneys' fees commonly exceed several hundred thousand dollars per party. Father's rights groups have formed over issues of unfairness in the courts and have had success in influencing changes in custody laws.[93] The naïve expectation that justice will prevail and that the judge will listen, agree, and find in one's favor is almost never satisfied, and has been called a myth.[94] Too often, parties who cling to the warfare model find themselves left with the spoils of that war. In other words, parents who fail to see a "custody trial" from their child's perspective risk making an indelible mark on their child's life and leaving permanent painful memories if not permanent scars.

Ray and Patricia: A Case Study in the Warfare Model

Ray and Patricia are the parents of fifteen-year-old Casey. They never married each other, but both are now married with children to new spouses. Casey is truly a lost child. She is doing poorly in school and may drop out. She has low self-esteem and "anger issues." Casey has been suspended from school almost weekly and is now ordered by the school to take anger management class. Casey's parents are in court-ordered mediation prior to a custody hearing, and this is the fourth custody action brought by Casey's parents in her short life. These actions have led to three major, full-blown custody trials. Custody litigation over Casey began when she was two years old.

Casey's parents tell the mediator that Casey was recently raped by a 36 year-old man who was their next-door neighbor. The man has since moved. Casey is seeing a therapist to deal with the rape. The only issue in the current custody dispute is what anger management class Casey should take. Father also initially sought a slightly different schedule for his time with Casey (who resides primarily with Mother), but that issue settled in the first few minutes of mediation with Mother agreeing to Father's requested change.

Mother wants Casey to take anger management offered by the school. Father wants her to take a class through his church. Father is adamant about his choice and states that he has no qualms about taking his case to trial. The mediator asks both parties what they think Casey is so angry about. The

---

[91] Danois, Diane L. (2012). The cost of mediation versus litigation in family law. *The Huffington Post*. Retrieved from: http://www.huffingtonpost.com/diane-l-danois-jd/post_4201_b_2318483.html
[92] Divorce bill 11 million so far. *Sunday Tasmanian* (Australia), November 1, 2009, 5.
[93] Rhoades, H., Boyd, S. B. (2004) Reforming custody laws: A comparative study. *International Journal of Law, Policy and the Family*, 18, 119.
[94] Benjamin, R.D. (1998). Negotiation and evil: The sources of religious and moral resistance to the settlement of conflicts. *Mediation Quarterly*, 15(3), 245-266.

mediator senses that Casey's problems stem from lifelong exposure to her parents' war with each other, and that the rape, a terrible crime, symbolizes the depths to which her existence has sunk. It sounds as if she is one step away from self-destruction, possibly suicide. Judging by their behavior in mediation, the mediator imagines that Ray and Patricia have interacted with each other in an unproductive, cyclical dance of blame, shame, and anger throughout Casey's life. Their consistent behavior towards each other appears to have created a static system that has changed little over the thirteen-year battle over Casey. The mediator observed that Mother appeared tired of it all and exhibited an air of hopelessness and resignation. Father, on the other hand, appeared invigorated, energized, and hopeful about getting the result he wanted from the judge.

Father held in his hand a greeting card he presented to the mediator. It was tattered and frayed, as if it had been read and re-read repeatedly. Father says that this Father's Day card, sent to him by Casey, is what is motivating him to "fight for" his daughter. Inside the card, Casey's handwritten note reads, "Dad, I love you so much. You are an awesome father. Love you, Casey." Father's response to the mediator's question about what Casey is so angry about is, "I don't know." He shakes his head and says that all he knows is that this card is proof that he is right and Mom has always been the one trying to keep him from his daughter.

The mediator then asks Mother the same question. Mother says, "Oh I know what Casey is mad about. She tells me every day. This morning she said, "'Mom, if Dad goes through with this, I am not responsible for what I do.'" Mother is fearful that if Father continues with this fourth custody trial that Casey could commit suicide. The mediator asks both parties if they would be willing to put aside the disputed issue of the anger management class for a moment and, instead, explore what they might be able to do now, as parents, to help Casey. Both parents say yes. The mediator then tells the parties that there is research on children who experience high conflict between parents and that they might be interested in knowing about the link between parental conflict and depression and anxiety in children.[95] The parties appear interested. The mediator tells them that these children are at risk for severe depression as adults. This means that they must struggle with severe depression their entire lives. There is no cure for severe depression, and not all treatments are effective. This could be a life or death situation. Severe depression is life ruining. It is preventable.

This information is troubling to the parties. The mediator reminds them that Casey is only fifteen, and will be a minor for three more years. This may be their window of opportunity to change their parenting communication and possibly change Casey's experience of living in a war zone. Both parties resist such a suggestion, saying they have tried to change their behavior, but it never works because the other party will not change. The mediator tells them there are ways to change this relationship beginning

---

[95] Kelly, J., Emery, R.E. (2003). Children's adjustment following divorce. *Family Relations, 52*(4), 352-362.

with one person changing. The mediator tells them that she has seen very combative parties change their dynamic, but that it takes time, work and commitment, and begins with only one person making a change. The two-hour mandated mediation session is coming to an end, and Mother is considering asking for another session. The parties begin fighting. The content of their fight revolves around who is right and who is wrong. Mother maintains that Father has destroyed their daughter's life with his constant custody battles. Father responds that Mother has forced him to do this because she always tries to keep Casey from him. They are yelling at each other now, not listening to each other or the mediator. The mediator ends the session, thanking the parties for coming, and encouraging them to come back to work on these issues in mediation instead of going to trial. Mother says she would like to come back. Father says his lawyer is ready for the trial scheduled for one month from now, and he would rather go that route.

Questions for Discussion and Analysis:

1. What was the effect of the mediator asking the parties what they thought Casey was so angry about?

Answer: This question placed the parties' focus squarely on Casey and her present struggle. Sadly, the parent seeking court intervention did not seem interested in exploring this question.

2. Are there any other effects? What else might the mediator have done?

Answer: The mediator could have asked Mother what she intended to do going forward.

Father's intentions were clearly expressed. He was going to court. It might have been productive for Mother to speak about her intentions. Which anger management class Casey goes to seems inconsequential in the grand scheme of things, yet these parents are willing to risk her suicide to fight about who is right and who is wrong. Mother may intend to back off to avoid a trial. This would seem to be "caving" to some, yet it could be a healthy choice and recognition of how absurd the battle has become. In other words, it could be an empowering choice for Mother to step up and protect her daughter.

On the other hand, perhaps the choice of anger management class is not trivial. After all, the parties are heavily invested in their individual choices. Even Mother, who caved on the issue of the schedule, is holding fast to her choice of anger management class. These "positions" could be explored to identify the underlying interests that motivate them. (See Chapter 1). A discussion of the reasons for each party's choice of anger management class will keep the focus on Casey and will enable the parties, with any luck, to see each other's genuine desire to do what is best for her.

3. Did the mediator's mini-lecture about research on children of high-conflict parents have any effect? Was it improperly directive or did it show any bias?

Answer: From a purist's point of view, it could be said the mediator's neutrality was in question because the mediator was now advocating her own opinion and pushing a particular theory on the parties.

The mediator's motivation, however, was to benefit the child. Most family mediators will tell clients in their opening statement that, even though they are neutral and do not favor one party over the other, they do favor the child's best interests. This directive step was ethically acceptable. In addition to shaping the mediation to promote the child's best interests (Standard 8 of the Model Standards of Family Mediators, Chapter 4), family mediators often have a teaching role. The mediator's knowledge of family systems and changing families can benefit clients. This is part of what clients pay for when they hire a family mediator. The mediator must, nevertheless, always respect the boundaries of the mediator's role and be careful not to overstep the teaching role, but to teach respectfully and in a limited manner, as this mediator did.

The mediator's words did seem to have a direct effect on the parties. They went from behaving in a somewhat subdued, although still combative way, to beginning a robust fight. It is possible the mediator's words sank in on some level. The parties obviously became more emotional. The mediator's words may have inspired healthy fear or guilt. It is possible this mediation session, although ostensibly not successful, could have induced a change in the family dynamic and been helpful to Casey and her plight.

4. If the parties had agreed to work on their parenting relationship, what help could the mediator have offered?

Answer: The only way for the parties to change their relationship is to change their behavior towards each other.

The mediator hoped that having information about the dangerous consequences their conflict could have for Casey would motivate them to try to do this. Although Father appeared to be the parent driving the conflict, Mother was equally involved in the dance of conflict. In the brief time she knew Ray and Patricia, the mediator could see that Ray was begging to be heard by Patricia. There was something he wanted from her, that he thought he could prove with the card signed by Casey, that Mother would not acknowledge for him. He so wanted recognition of something (never revealed during the mediation) and was willing to continue moving along this destructive path to seek acknowledgment from a judge. The mediator's guess is that Ray would have been satisfied with almost any positive acknowledgment from Patricia. After all, the smallest acknowledgment from Casey in the form of the tattered card with a one-line message written in it seemed to hold great meaning for him.

Patricia appeared tired of engaging with Ray and seemed to be at a point where she was willing to try anything to improve the situation. Unfortunately, she waited too long, and now Ray is unwilling to work with her. The mediator did see a ray of hope (if you'll excuse the pun) in Ray's continuous attempts to get through to Patricia. By working with the parties for a few more sessions, the mediator could have helped the parties to see what the mediator was able to observe: that change was possible. This is not therapy. The mediator is not doing couple's or co-parenting therapy on the clients. The mediator is not exploring the parties' feelings. If feelings are expressed, the mediator will accept and acknowledge them, but it is inappropriate for the mediator to intrude on the clients' psyches and elicit their feelings. In mediation, the mediator is an observer and reporter, interventions that are helpful because the parties are unable to see themselves from the mediators' point of view (or that of any third party).

5. Can you add any more insights into how Ray and Patricia could work to change their harmful dynamic?

A Final Note on Effects of Litigation on Children

This case is a tragic example of how children become the spoils of war when their parents insist on waging a protracted battle for custody. In many states, custody can be modified any time[96] without a showing of "changed circumstances," which one would need to modify an order for child support. An allegation that a change is needed for the best interests of the child is sufficient, as it should be to protect children. Unfortunately, this rule is abused by people who want to keep going back to court. Casey's tortured life brought tears to my eyes. Family mediation is not a profession for the faint of heart.

Myth #3: Divorce is Bad and Obliterates a Family

Myths always contain truth and this myth is certainly an example of a truism. Much is lost when a family divides into two homes, but the myth takes a tragedy and turns it into a catastrophe. Children are told they are from a "broken home." Parents are told their family is destroyed. These messages, coming from the media and culture, are perpetuated by family courts. One court-mandated custody education program in Pennsylvania[97] is called C.H.I.L.D., which stands for Children Hurt in Loss through Divorce. The clever acronym comes at the cost of hurting, or at least offending, participants. Some might go so far as to call it destructive. Adults and children are required to attend the C.H.I.L.D. class to receive information about children's adjustment to divorce and separation. Clearly, children who read will learn much more: how hurt they are and just how much loss they have experienced. This can be damaging to a child on several levels. First, the child is receiving a negative message. In mandatory parenting education, the message should always be positive. The title of the mandated custody education program should not have the word "hurt" or any other negative word in its title. Second, many, if not most, of the families attending the program are not divorced because they were never married. Use of the word "divorce" in the title marginalizes these families and makes them feel different or less than. This is simply not necessary or advisable in a public program. Third, what if the child doesn't feel hurt? Some children are relieved when divorce comes, and they find themselves in a better environment. If a child does not feel hurt before

---

[96] See Chapter 7.
[97] Westmoreland County Court of Common Pleas, Greensburg, Pennsylvania.

attending the class, she will likely feel hurt or at least confused by the end of the class, if only because of its painful name. This mandatory class with its misguided title is an example of a court system unwittingly using its position of power to spread shame and negative stereotypes about custody litigants in the name of helping.

When a family divides into two homes, that singular unit is gone and it is important to acknowledge that something has been lost; however, no one has died. Children can thrive in two loving homes. There is nothing unnatural about a child actually having two parents. In fact, it is nature's model: a mother and a father. To place a child with one parent for the sake of "stability" is no different from saying that a child should only ever have one parent, the equivalent of saying that two parents make life unstable. No reasonable person would agree with such a statement. Society's negative characterizations of shared custody as "bouncing a child back and forth" and "treating a child like a Ping-Pong ball" miss the point that the child's ability to perpetuate residential, familial relationships with both parents is more important than avoiding inconvenience that will inevitably exist with living in two homes. The emphasis should be on minimizing the inconvenience by shifting that burden onto the adults wherever possible.

In fact, shared custody, meaning equal time with both parents, has been found to be advantageous to children because it promotes positive involvement with both parents.[98] In studies of grown children who have lived through their parents' divorce and are now adults, children themselves approve of shared custody.[99] Instead of divorce, per se, being harmful to children, Kelly and Emery suggest that parents' involvement of children in the conflict and their behavior towards each other are what hurts the family.[100] Children can thrive in two homes. Parents who oppose this model in favor of primary/partial custody are sometimes stuck in a vision of two homes from their own point of view and are unable to understand that, to children, there is nothing unnatural about shared custody. In fact, children seem to instinctively prefer shared custody because they understand the concept of fairness and sharing from an early age. When children see their parents acting fairly and sharing custody equally, it gives them a feeling of safety and security. They do not have to worry about a parent getting the short end of the stick and are free to concentrate on being children. When children are in situations of conflict or perceived unfairness between their parents, they inevitably become preoccupied with the problem and internalize the unfairness by attempting to compensate. These behaviors in children manifest themselves as taking sides, placating their parents with statements ("I want to live with you, Dad,"), and otherwise compensating to achieve a sense of balance within the family system. The child's compensating actions diminish the child's sense of self and self-worth. The message the child receives is that adult problems take precedence over the child's

---

[98] Bauserman, R. (2002). Child adjustment in joint custody versus sole custody arrangements: A meta-analytic review. *Journal of Family Psychology, 16*(1), 91-102.
[99] Fabricius, W.V. & Hall, J.A. (2000). Young adults' perspectives on divorce living arrangements. *Family and Conciliation Courts Review, 38*(4), 446-461.
[100] Kelly & Emery, 2003.

needs. The child's needs are not met in this unbalanced system. A fourth "sub-myth" evolves from this third myth: that divorce damages children.

Although divorce is typically not good news for a child, it pales in comparison to the damage that results from destructive, ongoing conflict between parents, and a failure to restructure the family in a healthy configuration that includes, whenever possible, shared, equal custody. In society, divorce has become a predictable life event. It can happen to anyone, and, indeed, does happen to roughly 50% of the married population. When divorce is viewed as a foreseeable, normal life passage, parents are able to see it as a fact of life, easing their transition through the grief process. The advantages and disadvantages of shared custody are discussed more fully in Chapter 7.

Parent Education

In the 1990s courts across the country recognized the need for education among divorcing families.[101] Mandatory classes of some kind were formed in virtually every jurisdiction to inform parents about the need for cooperation and co-parenting after divorce. The gist of parent education is to teach parents how to behave towards each other after divorce to minimize the conflict to which the children are subjected. Parents are taught, among other things, to treat co-parenting as a business. In a business relationship, being fond of one's co-worker is not required. Most adults can relate to being forced to work with someone they do not like or get along with. Parents are taught to see their restructured family from their child's point of view. Parents are often surprised when they put themselves in their child's shoes and notice that, from the child's perspective, the family has not disappeared, and there is still a family. In essence, parents are reprogrammed to change their way of thinking from the myths propagated by society. In jurisdictions that have mandatory custody mediation, the parenting class precedes the mediation so that the clients are "prepped" before they enter mediation. This relieves the mediator from some of the responsibility of teaching clients about the realities of their new world. In cases where clients enter mediation without first having received parent education, the mediator has a teaching role and must work to shatter myths and assist clients to view their families and their co-parenting relationships in a more constructive way.

---

[101] Whitehurst, D.H., O'Keefe, S.L., & Wilson, R.A., (2008). Divorced and separated parents in conflict: Results from a true experiment effect of a court mandated parenting education program. *Journal of Divorce and Remarriage, 48 (3/4)*, 127-134. See also, Arbuthnot, J., Kramer, K. (1998). Effects of divorce education on mediation process and outcome. *Mediation Quarterly, 15(3)*, 199-213.

Chapter Three

"A system is a network of interdependent components that work together to try to accomplish the aim of the system. A system must have an aim. Without an aim, there is no system. ...A system must be managed." --Michael Dell

Conflict Systems and Dynamics

Systems

To understand humans is to understand the systems in which they are born, grow, and thrive. No human develops alone. It may not exactly take a village to raise a child, but it certainly takes a family. Families, in turn, create larger systems, or cultures. A culture emerges from human relationships where beliefs, meaning, art, language, values, practices, identity, and belonging are expressed. Conflict can occur anywhere including in families, cultures, and within a single individual. Most often, conflict is caused by a threat to meanings and identities, the things a culture holds dear.[102] Therefore, it is said that culture and conflict are inseparable.

Family Systems Theory

Family systems theory provides a way for a mediator to understand human behavior because it is the study of human behavior at its starting point. It also helps a mediator to use **systems thinking** as a tool for resolving conflict. Systems thinking is the mediator looking beyond the individuals in the room, and considering what other systems affect the conflict. When the mediator recognizes the impact of systems upon the conflict being expressed in the room, the mediator discovers a world of new tools that can perhaps be wielded in service to the parties. For these reasons, it is beneficial for mediators of every discipline (not just family mediators) to learn systems theory beginning with family systems, perhaps the most familiar of systems.

Traditional psychotherapy has focused on the individual as containing within his mind all of the secrets of his psyche. The therapist worked alone with the individual in treatment. In the mid-twentieth century, Murray Bowen, a physician, challenged that paradigm with his family systems theory he called Bowen Systems Theory.[103] Bowen died at the age of 77 in 1990. At the time, it was hypothesized that schizophrenia was caused by faulty communication between mother and child. In observing behavior of schizophrenic young people, often with mothers and other family members, Bowen noticed that the family served as an "emotional unit" and that every member was a discrete part of a system in which each member

---

[102] LeBaron, M. (2003). *Bridging cultural conflicts: A new approach for a changing world.* San Francisco: Jossey Bass.
[103] Gilbert, R. (1992). *Extraordinary relationships: A new way of thinking about human interactions.* Minneapolis: Chronimed Publishing.

was influenced by every other member, and in which the whole sought balance in the management of anxiety. Bowen saw systems in nature and thought it was only logical that humans would follow the rest of nature and operate within systems. For instance, in a herd of animals, fear spreads almost instantaneously despite the obvious communication limitations, as shown by the uniform behavior of the entire herd.[104] Although it is only a theory, Bowen's systems theory can be applied and observed in families. In actual practice, professionals working with families find it to be useful for identifying root causes of behavior in families and individuals.

Other common examples of systems in nature are schools of fish and flocks of birds where the group appears to behave as one unit. Roberta Gilbert, who studied with Bowen, calls such a system "an emotional unit," because when it exhibits uniform behavior, the behavior is motivated by a uniform emotion like fear. "In animals, there is a tendency for anxiety to ripple instantaneously through a herd when there is danger. The herd functions as an emotional unit."[105]

There are systems everywhere. The body is a system of organs working separately and in concert. Individual body cells work independently to develop and survive as well as interdependently to support an organism (or system). Bowen's family system was governed by two opposing forces. The force of *togetherness* draws the members together, while the force of *differentiation* focuses on the development of the individual.[106] In order for any system to function optimally, these forces must be complementary. In a healthy system there is balance between the two forces so that one force does not dominate the other. In a family, the system serves the individual by fostering its development of the self, while the individual serves the system by being part of a group. In human evolution, togetherness was necessary for survival. No human could survive the natural habitat without the protection and resources of the group. Bowen found that his theory signaled two important truths: (1) that the emotional functioning of every family member plays a part in the occurrence of a medical, psychiatric, or social illness in one family member, and (2) treatment need not be directed at the symptomatic person.[107] In other words, what happens to any member of a family system will affect all other members, even if cause and effect are not obvious (or are deliberately hidden) because the family is an emotional unit, and nothing can happen to one member without affecting every other member. To a mediator, these implications have great significance.

There is a slogan among family therapists that when parents seek therapy for one member of the family, the **designated patient**, ironically and counter-intuitively, tends to be the *healthiest* member of the family. In other words, the family member who epitomizes the problematic family dysfunction by acting out or being mentally or physically ill is taking on a disproportionate amount of the anxiety within the system so that the other members are relieved from taking their share. In fact, the other members could be the problem because they may be exploiting this member and creating the imbalance in the system. When

---

[104] Id.
[105] Id., p.13.
[106] Id., p.12.
[107] Id., p.vii.

there is an imbalance in the system created by one member taking on more than an equal share of the anxiety, the system compensates in its attempt to restore balance. This tends to happen with some frequency.

Systems are created around common goals. When the goal of each individual member of a system is the same-- to differentiate (or individuate) -- there can be some competition. Differentiation in a family system means growing. For children, it means becoming mature by developing a fully actualized self. This occurs as a result of the individual living life in the natural environment, while receiving the support and resources provided by the system. The natural environment brings on anxiety. This is not good or bad, just a fact of life. Anxiety enters the system through the individuals, children and adults. An individual who manages anxiety poorly uses other members to manage his anxiety. This process involves a loss of self by the co-opted individual. In every family system, there are members who experience a diminishment of self. An example is a family in which abuse occurs. Often, the abused member does little to resist or avoid the abuse. The victim experiences a loss of self. If the self is not restored by the time the individual leaves the system (at full maturity), it is virtually impossible to become a whole self. "Most people remain at the level of differentiation attained by the time they left home. However, adults can improve upon that level with hard work."[108] According to Gilbert, the most one can hope for to regain self is a small increase, even with hard work. There is, however, a way for the individual to compensate with a *functional self*.

The **functional self** is an adaptation that allows the broken, undifferentiated self to function in the environment. An example often seen is the workaholic. This person, to all the world, is high-achieving and well-functioning. The anxiety level of the workaholic, however, is high. The functional self does well when the environment is cooperating. When things do not go well, the functional self has a way of dissolving. This is the difference between the self and the functional self. The differentiated (whole) self remains intact under stress. The functional self copes poorly under stress and reverts to poor decision-making, poor relationship choices, and problematic physical and mental symptoms. The functional self is ruled by emotions; whereas, the differentiated self is ruled by principle.[109]

A healthy family system supports the well-being of each individual, and does not stand for any giving or taking of the self. It has healthy one-on-one relationships (dyads) between every member. Every member is autonomous (in an age-appropriate way). There are boundaries that are semi-permeable, allowing for openness where appropriate while being intact for purposes of the separateness (allowing for autonomy) of the individual. There is equality in terms of "potential and basic humanness."[110] When one member is out of balance, the entire system compensates, and is changed. A system will always seek balance, even if it is attained at the expense of one or more of its members. The reason a system always seeks balance is for survival of the system. A lack of equilibrium, or balance, is a threat to the existence of the system. For example, if a member is impaired, the other members compensate to protect the system,

---

[108] Id., p. 25.
[109] Id., p. 23.
[110] Id., p.152.

taking on disproportionate responsibilities. If Father is a functioning alcoholic, the system protects his ability to provide for the family's economic needs by enabling his coping mechanism of drinking. Although the coping mechanism itself creates problems, the other members absorb these problems in order to keep the system functioning financially. In this unhealthy system, other members are being exploited by taking on disproportionate responsibility to compensate for the unhealthy needs of a parent. Part of that responsibility is to keep quiet and not complain about or try to change Father's behavior. Secrets and forbidden topics of conversation are one of many signs of a dysfunctional family system. Unhealthy family systems are known to use certain adaptations as ways of compensating for an imbalanced system. Commonly known adaptations are Fusion, Triangulation, Rigidity of Roles, and Scapegoating.

Fusion

Fusion, (also called enmeshment), is the taking or giving up of self in a relationship that results from a lack of differentiation. When an individual is required to give up self to create balance in the system, that self is incomplete. Two incomplete selves will attempt to merge to form a whole.[111] A diminished self is always in search of another to make him whole. This is seen in the family mediation setting, as well as in everyday life. In fused relationships people are heard to say, "We don't need to say I'm sorry to each other. It's understood," or "We don't know where he begins and I end." I once had a father in custody mediation tell me that he "told his children everything" and actually said of his preschooler son, "He's me." In fused families, it may not be acceptable to bring a "stranger" into the group. Even a member who wants to introduce a potential new spouse to the group encounters difficulty with acceptance of the new member. In one family, the bridal shower was boycotted by the groom's family because it only seemed natural to them to have a separate shower exclusive to their group. In a highly fused family, it is very difficult for members to differentiate and even harder to leave. One man, who worked in a home office, coped with his fused state by becoming agoraphobic (unable to leave his home). This fact came to light when his pregnant wife asked him to do an errand, and he could not operate his car because it had sat idle so long in the garage that mice had built nests in the engine. These individuals repeat the fusion from their family of origin in adult relationships where they fuse with another in an attempt to form a whole self. However, as noted by Gilbert, "Since trying to make a self out of a relationship cannot work, the attempt itself creates a certain amount of anxiety."[112] Fusion is an uncomfortable state. Because fused individuals derive their sense of self from others, they crave acceptance from others. Criticism from a loved one is intolerable.[113] Fused partners develop unhealthy relationship patterns; many thrive on high conflict. Many high-conflict parties in the family legal system (Keith and Suzanne, Chapter 9) are working out relationships that were formed by fusion, which never works to create a whole self. These parties are highly focused on the other, often physically and emotionally abusive towards each other due to lack of boundaries. They typically lack the ability to see their own dynamic and how their pattern is a product of the behaviors and reactions of both

---

[111] Id., p. 13.
[112] Id., p. 41.
[113] Id., p. 24.

parties. A mediator or other third party is often able to identify patterns and unhealthy coping mechanisms adopted by fused couples.

Triangulation

Triangulation occurs where a dyad (a one-on-one relationship of two people) needs a third person to tolerate the relationship due to inability of the dyad to manage anxiety (or conflict). A good example is an affair. Affairs are entered into as a coping mechanism with, and often without, the intention to jettison the marriage. The affair makes the marriage tolerable. Without taking the risks and enduring the stress of addressing the unresolved problems in the marriage, or dyad, the partner who undertakes the affair is avoiding the pain involved with repairing the relationship with the spouse, but is at least able to preserve the married state. The affair is a way of avoiding responsibility and substitutes for the personal growth an individual might experience if he chose, instead, to work on the marriage. The marriage was unhealthy because the married partners lacked the will to confront dissatisfaction with the relationship. If they had been willing to address the problem directly instead of triangulating, the relationship might have been repaired or terminated. Either way, confronting a relationship head-on addresses a problem directly, while triangulating circumvents a problem by going around it, leaving the problem unaddressed, and in some cases, festering.

Another example of triangulation is using a third party to make one's partner jealous. In order to get the attention wanted from her partner, a woman flirts with an attractive man hoping to make her husband jealous. Or, a man who feels disregarded by his wife may form excessive attachments to women friends at work or at a bar or club in order to get the attention and regard he misses at home. Again, the principal problem is ignored in favor of the band aid cure of going outside of the dyad to use a third party to get what was wanted from the dyad. The result is a half-measure that provides some relief, but leaves the original problem unresolved.

Perhaps one of the most common, and unfortunate, examples of triangulation occurs when a parent co-opts the children to take a side against the other parent. In one family, Kathy, the mother, routinely aired all of her complaints about her husband Dan to their three children. When Dan initiated divorced after 26 years of marriage, all of the children took Kathy's side and refused to talk to Dan. The oldest child, a 26 year old adult daughter, began to miss her father and initiated a meeting with him. At the meeting, Dan, for the first time, saw an opportunity to explain his side of the many stories the kids had been told about him. His daughter, with the help of her husband, came to understand Dan's perspective and learned that her mother was not the perfect wife, but that her parents' marriage had two imperfect members. Sadly, although the two adult daughters came to understand and heal from their part in Kathy's triangulation of her children, the youngest child, a 15 year-old son, was unable to detach from his mother's control and endured a troubled relationship with his father, at times erupting in violent confrontations between them. Later, when Kathy remarried, she repeated her triangulation of the son with her new husband, creating so much conflict between her young son and new husband that the son was forced to go live with his oldest sister, having been evicted from Kathy's home by her new husband. Triangulation prevents differentiation by offering a substitute for full individual expression and autonomy, and is thereby destructive.

Rigidity of Roles

Rigidity of roles is a way of controlling a member by labeling him or his conduct. It also places responsibility on the labeled member, relieving other members of responsibility. A rigid role can also be imposed on the self, as a way of assuming an identity that meets with the approval of others. When Mom is the "worrier" in the family, she gets attention because everyone tells her their problems. Mom worries for everyone and others can be carefree, or even irresponsible. The youngest child, the "baby," is not allowed to grow up, thought of as the "cute" one well into adulthood. This child could become the family "mascot" whose role never allows her to be taken seriously as an adult. When Grandma is labeled as the devout one or a "saint," attending church daily, others rely on her prayers, possibly stunting their own spiritual growth. Oddly, the saint can sometimes be anything but. This is because the role of saint can involve a certain amount of martyrdom. When the saint does not receive the appreciation or gratitude she believes is due her, she can act like more like a villain towards those who fail to give her the respect she demands.

When Dad is the "late one," the rest of the family compensates by telling him dinner is at 6:00 p.m. even though the true time is 7:00 p.m. The "cheerleader" is the person who is known to put her attention on others before herself, sacrificing her individuality and self-care to meet the needs of others. Sometimes a child is chosen as a parent's unabashed "favorite" or "pet." This can be very destructive to the child, creating jealousy among siblings, resentment, and a sense of personal inadequacy, since favoritism is often arbitrary. The parent choosing a favorite does so out of emotional emptiness, thinking, if I show favor to this child, she'll love me the most. Rigidity of roles stunts individual growth and sacrifices autonomy.

Scapegoating places blame and shame on one member, relieving others of their role in a situation. The designated patient is a scapegoat, assigned responsibility for the dysfunction of the whole system. The scapegoat role can be a self-fulfilling prophecy causing the scapegoated member to become a member of the prison system. All of these devices are unconscious adaptations to create balance in a system that encounters difficulty managing anxiety brought on by the environment.

Intervention in Family Systems

The usefulness of family systems theory is captured in the truths Bowen articulated above. *"The emotional functioning of every family member plays a part of every occurrence of a medical, psychiatric, or social illness in one family member and treatment need not be directed at the symptomatic person."* The experienced family mediator knows that families with at-risk children who hope to "fix" their child by sending the child into therapy alone are going down the wrong path. It is not possible for the child's symptoms to change unless the system is addressed because the cause of the child's behavior is in response to the demands of the unbalanced system. The therapist can most efficiently address the system when all members participate in therapy. In other words, one ninety-minute family therapy session that includes all members of the family is likely to accomplish as much as or more than numerous individual therapy sessions on the designated patient. Yet, families, and some therapists, resist this idea. As soon as parents are implicated, they reflexively fear they will be confronted and blamed as the cause of the child's behavior.

Unfortunately, therapists all too often support this defensive belief and fail to insist that the entire system enter into the process.

Application to Mediation

Knowing that the behavior of adult clients is the product of the level of differentiation accomplished in their family of origin, and that the marriage may have been the scene of fusion and the unsuccessful search of self, allows the mediator to understand behavior. This assists the mediator in being nonjudgmental as well as possibly helpful. If appropriate, the mediator's theory of lack of differentiation could lead the mediator to ask questions or make suggestions that bring into awareness behavior the parties engage in unconsciously, if the parties are ready for such awareness. The mediator never needs to engage in persuasion or argument because all of the behavior the mediator would spotlight is in full view in session. The mediator's approach is a light touch, as light as merely observing and responding. Parties are sometimes surprised to find out they are capable of becoming aware of something they have hidden from themselves since early childhood, in a productive mediation environment. The potential for human change is remarkable. I believe it is far beyond what Gilbert expressed-- that humans could only improve, with much work, slightly above the level of differentiation reached when they left home. In mediation, I have seen parties grow more than what I would characterize as slight. Such a limit need not be imposed on anyone. Here is an example of a man who was schooled by the threat of losing his wife and son. No doubt, his lesson was painful, but I came to admire him for pushing through the pain to find himself changed substantially.

The Case of Vince and Julie

Case Study in Family Systems

Vince and Julie have been married for 23 years. They have one child, their son Zachary. Zach is almost 17. They have been separated for two months. About eighteen months ago, their family life began to deteriorate.

Vince's description: "In May of last year, I realized that the marriage was not good and I asked Julie repeatedly to go to counseling. She refused and I became frustrated, and, yes, hostile when I realized I was losing my marriage and there was nothing I could do about it and she would not agree to get help. Yes, okay, I did call her bad names and I regret that. I regret being so mean and hostile. But I did not call Zach any names and I was not hostile towards him, I don't believe. But, okay, he now says I was and sides with his mother. We had terrible holidays and a lot of unhappiness in our home. There was no communication. Then I had the shock of my life. In February, after the holidays were over, I returned home from a business trip and Julie and Zachary had left. Most of the furniture was gone. Julie left a note saying they will now be living at her parents' house and that this was best for everyone. I never thought that would happen. On the advice of my attorney, I filed for custody and tried to get an emergency interim order to make Julie let me see Zach. The judge denied me and said if my son doesn't want to see me, she won't force a 17 year old and sent us to the mandatory custody mediation. Now Julie will not communicate with me. I have called and emailed her hundreds of times. She is taking Zach away from me and won't even let me see Spunky, our dog. Zach will only see me for four hours every Friday and is calling the shots. He does not respect my authority as a parent and will not forgive me even though I have apologized for anything I may have done, although I do not recall saying anything to hurt him. I don't understand why Julie won't try to get him to forgive me. We attended church and, as a family, we have values of forgiveness and love. He needs to know that forgiving me is what he is supposed to do."

Vince has many demands, requests, complaints, and grievances which he would like Julie to work on resolving. They are:

1. He wants a co-parenting agreement with Julie with a definite schedule for his time with Zach, for more than four hours every Friday.

2. He wants a commitment from Julie that there will be family meetings to discuss vacations and holidays with Zach.

3. He wants a commitment that there will not be more litigation (even though he is the only one who has introduced litigation into the system to date) and that they will work out all differences without attorneys and judges.

4. He wants a parenting plan that will promote:

   a. an equal and loving relationship with Zach

   b. a guarantee that Zach has consistent, frequent and continuous contact with both parents.

5. He wants a meeting with Julie, Zach and Vince to go over the "Children's Bill of Rights" and the "Parents' Bill of Rights" from a father's rights group he found online. He wants both parents to be vocal in promoting to Zach that they both agree to and support these rights.

He also has a list of "Professional Research" he cites, some of which is:

a. Children need to have a block of unbroken, significant time with each parent, including overnights.

b. Children needs parents to be PARENTS and should not be allowed to call the shots.

c. "When a child is able to call the shots about where they (sic) spend time with parents, many things can deteriorate over a period of time. Teenagers must learn to check their plans with the other parent as automatically as putting on a pair of shoes because of their *responsibility* to be with the other parent. This strengthens the relationship with BOTH parents because *it teaches the child how to work things out*." Vince found this information on the Internet. He believes it to be the authority on "how to co-parent."

Vince has documented all of his research and demands and hands a large pile of papers to the mediator.

Julie's description: "For 23 years, Vince has been very controlling, rigid and demanding. I spent all my energy trying to help him, trying to make him see how he comes off to people. When I realized I would never change him and that his actions were affecting Zach, I stopped trying to change him and started seeking help from friends and advisers who told me to leave, which I finally did. The problems did not begin 18 months ago, but 23 years ago! Vince has done terrible damage, calling Zach horrible names—using profanity and hurting Zach beyond repair. I let it happen. I also let him emotionally and mentally abuse me over many years. He now expects everyone to forgive him instantly and takes no responsibility for his behavior. He has apologized, yes, but he doesn't realize that forgiveness takes time. When we left, he did not even call us for four days. This hurt my son, although we were also relieved because we expected an angry, hostile phone call. Zach is only willing to see his dad once a week, and complains that that is too much time away from his schoolwork and friends. Zach is furious that his dad is pursuing a court action and has told his dad so. He says his dad does not listen to him. I have not been uncommunicative with Vince and I certainly have not "taken" Zach from him. Vince has not emailed or called one hundred times. He has called and emailed a few times, and I respond to him, but not when he is just complaining, demeaning and making demands. Those messages I try to ignore. If he is willing to limit communication to only what is really necessary to get us through this, I have no problem communicating and I certainly don't mind him seeing our dog (which I have offered) but he never responded. I want Zach to have a good relationship with his dad, but there is too much damage to expect this to happen overnight. Vince has to build trust over time with Zach and repair the damage himself. I can't do it for him."

Vince's response: "How can you help me with my relationship with Zach?"

Julie's response: "I can't- that's between you and Zach."

Mediator: "Vince, you seem to recognize that Julie is in a position to help you. Julie, I heard you say you want Zach and Vince to have a relationship. I heard you say it's up to Vince to reach out to Zach and try to repair the damage he has done, but I am wondering if perhaps you do have some insight as a mother you could share with Vince to help him do that."

     Julie agrees with the mediator that she does have insight into Vince's situation with Zach. She gives him a suggestion. Her suggestion is that instead of apologizing to Zach by saying, "I'm sorry **if** I called you names. I don't remember doing that. I don't think I did call you names, only your mother. But I am sorry," Vince needs to give a real apology. She says that all she has heard so far has been a half-hearted apology, not taking responsibility or even acknowledging what Julie and Zach both heard and witnessed. Vince needs to step up and come clean with a real apology so Zach can respect his dad for taking responsibility. Also, she told him to "Back off and stop calling Zach twice a day and pressuring him to spend more time with you." She said that's too much pressure for a kid. The mediator took a big risk and told Vince that the "Bill of Rights" might sound like pressure to a teenager. Vince agreed. Mother agreed. The mediator then asked Vince if Julie's insight about pressure and apologizing to Zach was helpful. He said, "Not really." The mediator used this opportunity to point out to Vince an inconsistency in what he was saying, "Help me understand," she said. "I heard you say you want to communicate with Julie, you see her (correctly) as a key person who can help you mend your relationship with Zach, yet you won't acknowledge her when she offers her insight?" He got it. His face totally changed; his body relaxed. He was quiet for a minute and then said to Julie, "I want you to know that I am a different person than I was when we were together. I have suffered emotional anguish. I don't want to say what thoughts I had or what I might have done to myself when you guys left me alone in that empty house. This whole situation has made me learn a lot and change. I am not going to be that mean person anymore. I am going to listen, and I am going to be different." Julie said, "Well that's good, I'll believe it when I see it." The mediator acknowledged both parties--acknowledged Vince for taking in the information the mediator risked offering to him. The mediator told Vince that she noticed a complete change in his facial expression and body language. His face looked tense and stressed at first, and now, his face looked totally relaxed and peaceful. His body at first seemed tense, arms crossed, and now he appeared more open and relaxed. His face beamed even brighter. The mediator acknowledged Julie for her willingness to leave the door open just a crack in spite of all the hurt and damage she described earlier. "It takes a lot for a person to do that and I appreciate it."

In this case, Vince tried to get Julie to do the parenting work for him. He was weak as a parent and obviously felt that Julie was his connection to Zach. When that didn't work he even tried to get God to do his job by using the family's church attendance to make the case that he deserved forgiveness from Zach. The mediator's task was to help Vince see that he has to do the work of relating to his son and that no one can do it for him. The mediator had to offer this information in the most gentle and non-confrontational way possible. The mediator could only observe and express what she saw and heard in session.

Once the parties began to talk to each other, getting past their initial anger, Vince asked the mediator, "Do you have kids?" The mediator said, "Yes." Vince asked, "Are you married?" The mediator said, "Well, it's not helpful to you for me to talk about my situation."

Vince: "Well, wouldn't you say in every family every kid always prefers one parent over the other?"

Mediator: (IN SHOCK) Vince had just revealed an important aspect of his family of origin. He left that system with this belief. Obviously, in his family of origin, this was the rule. One parent is the preferred parent. He assumed it was that way in EVERY family. He really believed this. Why wouldn't he?

Mediator: (Kindly, with great caring and empathy) "No, I have to say that is not my experience." Then, adding, "I'm sorry, that must be hard."

For Vince, family life was a competition, and there was a clear winner and loser. The mediation ended with Vince wanting to mediate more. Julie said she would think about it.

By applying family systems thinking, the mediator was able to understand that Vince's competitiveness (perceived by Julie as his meanness) during the marriage came from the belief he formed in his family of origin. In mediation, he became aware that his belief was unfounded, possibly freeing him to let go of his competitiveness as a parent, and form a healthier relationship with his son.

Questions for Discussion and Analysis:

1. **Why would a party bring notes, documents, and "expert research" to custody mediation?**

Answer: He sees it as a way to control and get what he wants. Julie said Vince was rigid, controlling, and demanding. His behavior offered insight into the personality traits that contributed to his current struggles.

2. **What is the mediator's response?**

Answer: Not to resist Vince's effort at control (even though it is a challenge to the process and to the mediator) because that would set up a power struggle between Vince and the mediator and would reinforce Vince's controlling behavior, which the mediator knew was not serving Vince's best interests. In his competitive family of origin, this behavior probably served him. Unfortunately, in the real world, he was finding that it caused him problems and cost him his marriage. The mediator simply never read his papers. Fortunately, he was more interested in talking, and barely noticed that his paperwork went unread. If he had become angry at the mediator for not reading it, she would have said, "Okay, but I can't talk and read at the same time, so excuse me while I read." Here, Vince never asked mediator to read it.

3. **Where are Vince and Julie in their respective positions on the transition curve of Denial, Resistance, Exploration and Commitment?**

Answer: Julie is obviously very far along. After spending an inordinate amount of time (at least 23 years by her account) being fused to Vince and "trying" to help him become a whole person by trying to make him see how his behavior was wrong, she finally gave up on Vince and placed her focus where it always need to be, on herself. She must have found this rewarding, because she seemingly had lost all interest in her former role as Vince's codependent helper. Even when Vince told her he had changed, and convincingly demonstrated some changed behavior, Julie was only mildly interested, reserving judgment until some time had passed. Julie appeared to be in the stages of exploration and commitment.

Vince appeared to have endured a torturous several months after separation. The mediator imagined his having been in anguish as he looked at himself, alone, abandoned, and undeniably at fault. His shame and anguish placed him in a position of denial (evidenced by his failed attempt to get the court to force Zach to live with him), with intermittent glimpses of reality. He still denied behaviors that Julie and Zach insisted occurred. He wanted forgiveness without taking responsibility for his actions, which is a form of denial. Vince's denial was unraveling, however, and he was gradually moving from the stages of denial and its protective anger and resistance into exploration of himself and his need to change.

4. **What were the mediator's interventions and how were they helpful?**

Answer: The mediator simply observed what she saw and repeated the parties' words back to them. This was effective because it did not create a conflict between the mediator and the parties. If the mediator had instead stated her own thoughts or beliefs to attempt to convince the parties to behave or think differently, it would have created conflict. When the mediator creates conflict by trying to persuade, the focus of the mediation becomes the conflict between the mediator and the parties instead of the conflict presented by the parties. In attempting to get Julie to offer Vince insight into his problem with Zach, the mediator used Julie's words that she wanted Vince and Zach to have a relationship. This is very different from a mediator saying, "Well, Julie, don't you want your son to have a relationship with his father?" There is judgment in such a question. Merely restating Julie's words is done without judgment. The mediator's statement to Vince that the Bill of Rights seemed like pressure to Zach was risky because it was judgmental and may have caused Vince to be defensive. If Vince had to put his energy into defending himself against the mediator, he would have missed the opportunity to see himself more clearly, as he ultimately did in this session. Fortunately for this mediator, Vince agreed with the statement and apparently did not feel the need to defend himself. This one risky move by the mediator could have thwarted Vince's opportunity to learn about himself in this mediation session. This expression of her opinion by the mediator did not seem to produce any helpful result to the parties, and probably should have been avoided. The mediator's observation of Vince's facial expression and body language appears to have been the most helpful intervention. By becoming aware of his body language, Vince was able to become more acutely aware of what was going on inside. The mediator's observation of his body confirmed for him that something important had happened, and that it was beneficial to him.

The Conley Family
Case Study in Family Systems

Bill Conley, a 57-year-old man, called asking for help with a family business problem. He explained that he and his wife Barbara had run a small electronics company all of their married lives and were now ready to turn the company over to their son Chip, 23. This had been their plan for years. Barbara was the office manager and Bill worked out in the field.

Chip, their son, was recently engaged to Tracy, his college girlfriend. Tracy came to upstate New York from St. Louis after Chip proposed. They wanted to spend their engagement living and working in the same town. Tracy and Chip both have master's degrees in business from the university they attended together. Tracy worked in a corporate accounting department and has decided to leave her employment to work for Chip's family company. Chip began working for Conley Electronics right out of college and is happy his parents agreed to create a position for Tracy, especially since it is a small company with only eight employees.

Unfortunately, after a few months, the family realized that the work situation was problematic and that family relationships were deteriorating due to the work environment. Barbara and Bill, accustomed to running their business like a well-oiled machine, and having total authority over all their employees, recognized that having their son work for them presented problems. Chip lacked the organization Barbara demanded. His office was messy, his desk disorganized, and, although he was excellent at cultivating new business and pleasing customers, he often neglected important paperwork. Barbara requested neatness, organization, and promptness with paperwork from Chip, but all she got were promises and excuses. Chip's behavior never seemed to change. Barbara noticed that Tracy was efficient and timely in her work (payroll and billing), so she solicited Tracy's help in getting Chip to change his habits. Initially, Tracy went along with Barbara's plan; however, Tracy soon began to feel "in the middle" and told Barbara that she could no longer help Barbara enforce the rules with Chip and that Barbara would have to deal with Chip herself. This conversation led to bad feelings between Barbara and Tracy. Barbara began to find fault with Tracy's work and, in an effort to "help" Tracy, would be found searching through Tracy's computer and appointment books, looking for mistakes and missed deadlines. She found several items she believed Tracy did not complete properly and reprimanded Tracy, leading to even worse feelings between them. Tracy and Chip's relationship became strained as Tracy shared her frustration with Chip. Ultimately, Chip, angered with his mother, decided that Tracy should leave the strained work environment and that he would spend as little time in the office as possible, working primarily in the field. This added to the deficiency in his paperwork. Not knowing what else to do, Barbara and Bill decided to officially fire Tracy and sent her a letter of termination. Since that letter was written to Tracy, neither Tracy nor Chip has spoken to either of Chip's parents.

Bill called the mediator to set up mediation. Tracy and Chip agreed to attend. Other than that conversation, there has been no communication for three weeks.

At the mediation, the parties immediately requested a caucus (a private meeting with the mediator) since Bill had the opportunity to speak to the mediator already while Chip and Tracy did not, although the mediator did attempt to reach them by phone.

In caucus, Tracy explained that she was very hurt by Barbara's harsh tone in the work environment and could not believe that Barbara would treat anyone the way she treated Chip and herself, especially her own relatives. She stated that in her family it is not okay to yell, make demands, and create drama with statements such as, "I am at the end of my rope with you." She could not believe that after such a terse and cold move as firing her future daughter-in-law by letter, that, to make matters worse, Barbara never called or tried to find out how she was. Tracy's family, who is paying for the wedding that will take place in two months, is considering not inviting Chip's parents because of how much they have hurt Tracy. Although Tracy is having a bridal shower in St. Louis, the New York (where the family now lives and Conley Electronics is located) shower she and Barbara initially discussed is now not going to happen because Barbara has abandoned the plan. Chip is completely supportive of Tracy and states that he disagrees with his parents' way of using negative reinforcement to motivate employees and prefers methods he learned in business school—using positive reinforcement and written disciplinary steps to modify employees' behavior. He loves his parents but does not believe they are creating a happy family. Asked by the mediator what they would like to get out of the mediation session, Chip stated he would like to continue taking over the business, which he has expedited by applying for a bank loan to buy out his parents outright and will take about four months for approval. In mediation, he wants to smooth hurt feelings so that his parents know he loves them and do not feel pushed out. Tracy wants to get through the wedding and celebrations with family harmony and to focus on having a happy family and marriage. She does not want to engage in conflict and does not want to return to work at the company any time in the foreseeable future. She does not feel she can easily forgive Chip's parents for what they have done but does have that as a long-term goal.

Barbara and Bill then had a caucus. Barbara's stated goal in mediation was to understand what it was she did that bothers Tracy and Chip so much. She wanted to make them understand that the whole reason there is a successful business to transfer to Chip is that, for 27 years, she has been demanding excellence of herself, Bill and every employee. Bill agrees that it is Barbara's organizational skills and accuracy that have made the business what it is today. They are not comfortable allowing Chip to relax those standards just because he is their son. Bill's goal is to keep the family together and not damage relationships.

In joint session, Chip asks to speak first. He tells his mother that he feels hurt when she gets extremely emotional and hostile towards him for failing to turn in a three-dollar receipt. It makes him feel like three dollars is more important to her than her love for him, or her desire for him to feel loved. Barbara does not understand this. She says, "I do love you Chip." She is not able to acknowledge his pain. She is not able to see his pain. She goes into a long explanation of how important it is to collect every receipt when you are running a business. For two hours, the parties each explain what it is like for them. After a long time, the parties decide that it is best to move away from the past and begin talking about the current plan of how to work together while Chip obtains his financing. Everyone agrees to change something about what they are currently doing to make life easier for all of them. Chip agrees to spend more time at the office. Bill agrees to yell less. Barbara agrees, reluctantly, not to ask Chip for his work, but to let Bill handle enforcement of the rules with Chip. She is dubious about how this plan will work, since it is so important to count every receipt and she does not believe she will get them all. It has been a long session, and the mediator checks in with each party to make sure they have paid attention to getting what they wanted out of the session. Chip apologizes to his mother, saying, "I am sorry that my lack of organization has made you suffer. I love you and I wish I could be more organized for you." Barbara says, "Thank you." Chip states, to the mediator, "I was hoping to get more of a response than that." (The mediator knows he means an apology) but Barbara does not see this, and merely says, "I said thank you." Barbara states that she "feels like a criminal" because of how she has been made out to be the bad guy. The mediator thanks her for saying that and asks if she would like to take a few minutes to see if there is anything else she can say or ask of the others in order to ease her discomfort. She is at a loss. The mediator asks (going out on a big limb) if she feels she needs to be forgiven. She says no. The mediator then asks if she feels like she has been accused or attacked, or does she feel that way because she feels she has done something wrong. She says it is because she has been accused.

The mediator (again) asks if it would make Barbara feel better if she asked Chip and Tracy if they could forgive her. She then says, yes. But she cannot come up with any words, and asks the mediator for help. The mediator helps her, saying, well based on what you and Chip already said to each other, you could just repeat that part, like this: "Chip I am sorry you felt hurt when I asked you for receipts in an angry way and that it made you feel that a three dollar receipt is more important than you." (Not risky because mediator used exact words). She said it and then said, "Do you forgive me?" Chip said yes. That was easy. Mediator waited to see what Barbara would do next. Barbara turned to Tracy and said, "Tracy do you forgive me for…whatever?" Then, in frustration, Barbara said, "It's confusing, I don't know what I did, I don't understand this, I don't know why it is not okay to just run a business like I have been for 27 years." Tracy, graciously, explained that she does forgive- but it will take a while for her to forget because she was hurt and she would just like to have some time to do that. Mediator suggested that the two women come back to work on just their relationship because they are embarking on a lifetime mother-in-law/daughter-in-law relationship and it might be important to clear the way for a better understanding at this juncture. Mediator explained what a complex relationship it is and that most are not successful. Then, Barbara described how wonderful her relationship was with her mother-in-law and how that relationship has been a huge success, and that she thought that would be how she and Tracy would get along, until all this happened. She reiterated, "I'm good at that relationship," implying that she is not the one who is coming up short in this current relationship. Mediator said, "Well you were the daughter-in-law then, now you are going to be the mother-in-law. It will be different."

Questions for Discussion

1.   In this family, what "roles" does each member take on?

Answer: It's clear that Barbara's role is the organized one. It's possible that this role is so rigid that it causes others (Chip) to be disorganized as a way to balance the system. Bill seems passive, deferring to Barbara, whose control he happily defers to. Similarly, Chip also defers to Barbara's control, only passively/aggressively rebelling against it.

2.   **What is the effect of the new member, Tracy, on this family?**

Answer: Barbara attempts to triangulate by using Tracy to control Chip, whom Barbara has tried and failed to control. Failing that, Barbara and Bill unite to oust Tracy from the company, and possibly from the family, although that is not clear.

3.   **What imbalances exist in this system?**

Answer: The rigid roles taken on by Chip and Bill are an attempt to balance the system against Barbara's rigid and demanding control of the business, its employees, and her family members. Chip is the "irresponsible" or "disorganized" one. Bill is the submissive one, although he seems to take out his frustrations by yelling at people in the office (perhaps to appear not so submissive), and Barbara is the controlling, super-responsible one. Tracy has upset the family balance by naming Barbara's cruelty and not overlooking it as Bill and Chip have for years. Tracy introduces the idea that people have feelings, and that their feelings should be respected by all family members, even Barbara, and not subordinated to the success of the business. Tracy does not buy into Barbara's belief that family members can be treated hurtfully if they do anything to disrupt the perfect functioning of the business. The family is out of balance with Barbara's rigidity and control. Chip compensates by being irresponsible and becoming coupled with a woman who seems the opposite of his mother. Bill compensates by being weak, submissive, passive-aggressive (cooperating in the mistreatment of Tracy) and yelling at people in the office. The designated patient is Chip, and, true to Bowen theory, he is arguably the healthiest member, having adapted to the imbalances in his family, being happy and well coupled. Barbara, the "perfect" member is arguably the unhealthiest with her rigidity and high anxiety creating imbalances in the system.

Culture and Family Systems

Daniel Lieberman, an evolutionary biologist, views culture as a distinct evolutionary force. He defines culture as "a set of learned knowledge, beliefs, and values that cause groups to think and behave differently...."[114] He believes that culture is *Homo sapiens'* most distinctive characteristic. Meanwhile, Marilynn Brewer argues that the human tendency to prefer one's own group or culture is perhaps the most well-established phenomenon in social psychology.[115] She concluded that our preference for our own group, which is ethnocentric, and leads to exclusion of outside groups is based on the universal need for belonging

---

[114] Lieberman, D. (2013). *The story of the human body: Evolution, health, and disease.* New York: Random House.
[115] Brewer, M.B. (2007). The importance of being we: Human nature and intergroup relations. *American Psychologist,* 62(8), 728-738.

and distinctiveness. Interestingly, she found that humans' attitudes towards out-groups are most positive when these needs are well satisfied within the in-group. Applying her work to family systems, the more functional the family system, the more positively its members will behave towards others outside of the system. Therefore, the family system is the best opportunity to optimize human potential.

A Final Note on Family Systems

As Bowen points out, his family systems theory exposes a paradox of human existence. "If one wants to work on a relationship, one must work on oneself. If one wants to work on individuality, it is best done in relationship to others."[116] As will be seen in subsequent chapters, mediation is full of paradoxes and seemingly counter-intuitive principles. To the untrained lay person, mediation is a complicated process requiring persuasion, manipulation, and control by the mediator. To the experienced mediator, the most effective interventions are devoid of judgment, persuasion, or control by the mediator. The trained mediator knows that attempts at control yield the opposite result. The mediation session, with at least three participants, becomes its own system with roles and balancing. When the mediator becomes judgmental or opinionated, the system compensates, often in a way that is detrimental to the mediation process. For this reason, part of the mediation system includes a code of ethics, the focus of the next chapter.

---

[116] Id., p. 169

Chapter Four

"*Live one day at a time emphasizing ethics, not rules.*" –Wayne Dyer

The Standards of Practice for Family Mediators

The Model Standards

Mediation ethics are governed by the Model Standards of Conduct for Mediators of the American Bar Association. For family mediators, there are separate standards set forth in the Model Standards of Practice for Family and Divorce Mediation promulgated by a symposium of major mediation organizations including the Association of Family and Conciliation Courts, the American Bar Association Family Section, and the Association for Conflict Resolution.

In addition to standards of conduct, there are laws governing mediators found in rules and statutes describing particular court-connected or mandatory mediation programs, as well as statutes addressing concerns such as reporting child abuse, privilege, and confidentiality of the process.

The Model Standards of Conduct for Family and Divorce Mediation are printed with permission on the following pages with "Overview and Definition," comments and "Appendix" in their original form as promulgated. Students should become familiar with the thirteen rules and comments. The Model Standards of Conduct for Mediators in general are also printed herein with comments. In the discussion that follows the family standards beginning on page 95, the "Omega" Ω symbol indicates a family standard that differs or is additional to the standards of conduct for mediators in general.

The fact that family mediators have a separate set of rules that differ, in part, from the general rules for all mediators underscores the point made throughout this book that family mediation has special characteristics that require the mediator to have specialized knowledge and skills. The practice of family mediation requires training and expertise in addition to what is learned in general mediation training. Knowledge of the substantive area is, of course, also needed as well as desirable for the sake of the clients' comfort and confidence in the mediator, and, occasionally, for the mediator to identify issues and details.

Model Standards of Practice for Family and Divorce Mediation

STANDARD I: A family mediator shall recognize that mediation is based on the principle of self-determination by the participants.

STANDARD II: A family mediator shall be qualified by education and training to undertake the mediation.

STANDARD III: A family mediator shall facilitate the participants' understanding of what mediation is and assess their capacity to mediate before the participants reach an agreement to mediate.

STANDARD IV: A family mediator shall conduct the mediation process in an impartial manner. A family mediator shall disclose all actual and potential grounds of bias and conflicts of interest reasonably known to the mediator. The participants shall be free to retain the mediator by an informed, written waiver of the conflict of interest. However, if a bias or conflict of interest clearly impairs a mediator's impartiality, the mediator shall withdraw regardless of the express agreement of the participants.

STANDARD V: A family mediator shall fully disclose and explain the basis of any compensation, fees and charges to the participants.

STANDARD VI: A family mediator shall structure the mediation process so that the participants make decisions based on sufficient information and knowledge.

STANDARD VII: A family mediator shall maintain the confidentiality of all information acquired in the mediation process, unless the mediator is permitted or required to reveal the information by law or agreement of the participants.

STANDARD VIII: A family mediator shall assist participants in determining how to promote the best interests of children.

STANDARD IX: A family mediator shall recognize a family situation involving child abuse or neglect and take appropriate steps to shape the mediation process accordingly.

STANDARD X: A family mediator shall recognize a family situation involving domestic abuse and take appropriate steps to shape the mediation process accordingly.

STANDARD XI: A family mediator shall suspend or terminate the mediation process when the mediator reasonably believes that a participant is unable to effectively participate or for other compelling reason.

STANDARD XII: A family mediator shall be truthful in the advertisement and solicitation for mediation.

STANDARD XIII: A family mediator shall acquire and maintain professional competence in mediation.

Overview and Definitions

Family and divorce mediation ("family mediation" or "mediation") is a process in which a mediator, an impartial third party, facilitates the resolution of family disputes by promoting the participants' voluntary agreement. The family mediator assists communication, encourages understanding and focuses the participants on their individual and common interests. The family mediator works with the participants to explore options, make decisions and reach their own agreements.

Family mediation is not a substitute for the need for family members to obtain independent legal advice or counseling or therapy. Nor is it appropriate for all families. However, experience has established that family mediation is a valuable option for many families because it can:

- increase the self-determination of participants and their ability to communicate;
- promote the best interests of children; and
- reduce the economic and emotional costs associated with the resolution of family disputes.

Effective mediation requires that the family mediator be qualified by training, experience and temperament; that the mediator be impartial; that the participants reach their decisions voluntarily; that their decisions be based on sufficient factual data; that the mediator be aware of the impact of culture and diversity; and that the best interests of children be taken into account. Further, the mediator should also be prepared to identify families whose history includes domestic abuse or child abuse.

These Model Standards of Practice for Family and Divorce Mediation ("Model Standards") aim to perform three major functions:

1. To serve as a guide for the conduct of family mediators;

2. To inform the mediating participants of what they can expect; and

3. To promote public confidence in mediation as a process for resolving family disputes.

Model Standards are aspirational in character. They describe good practices for family mediators. They are not intended to create legal rules or standards of liability.

The Model Standards include different levels of guidance:

- Use of the term "may" in a Standard is the lowest strength of guidance and indicates a practice that the family mediator should consider adopting but which can be deviated from in the exercise of good professional judgment.

- Most of the Standards employ the term "should" which indicates that the practice described in the Standard is highly desirable and should be departed from only with very strong reason.

- The rarer use of the term "shall" in a Standard is a higher level of guidance to the family mediator, indicating that the mediator should not have discretion to depart from the practice described.

Standard I

A family mediator shall recognize that mediation is based on the principle of self-determination by the participants.

A. Self-determination is the fundamental principle of family mediation. The mediation process relies upon the ability of participants to make their own voluntary and informed decisions.

B. The primary role of a family mediator is to assist the participants to gain a better understanding of their own needs and interests and the needs and interests of others and to facilitate agreement among the participants.

C. A family mediator should inform the participants that they may seek information and advice from a variety of sources during the mediation process.

D. A family mediator shall inform the participants that they may withdraw from family mediation at any time and are not required to reach an agreement in mediation.

E. The family mediator's commitment shall be to the participants and the process. Pressure from outside of the mediation process shall never influence the mediator to coerce participants to settle.

Standard II

A family mediator shall be qualified by education and training to undertake the mediation.

A. To perform the family mediator's role, a mediator should:

1. Have knowledge of family law;

2. Have knowledge of and training in the impact of family conflict on parents, children and other participants, including knowledge of child development, domestic abuse and child abuse and neglect;

3. Have education and training specific to the process of mediation;

4. Be able to recognize the impact of culture and diversity.

B. Family mediators should provide information to the participants about the mediator's relevant training, education and expertise.

Standard III

A family mediator shall facilitate the participants' understanding of what mediation is and assess their capacity to mediate before the participants reach an agreement to mediate.

A. Before family mediation begins a mediator should provide the participants with an overview of the process and its purposes, including:

1. Informing the participants that reaching an agreement in family mediation is consensual in nature, that a mediator is an impartial facilitator, and that a mediator may not impose or force any settlement on the parties;

2. Distinguishing family mediation from other processes designed to address family issues and disputes;

3. Informing the participants that any agreements reached will be reviewed by the court when court approval is required;

4. Informing the participants that they may obtain independent advice from attorneys, counsel, advocates, accountants, therapists or other professionals during the mediation process;

5. Advising the participants, in appropriate cases, that they can seek the advice of religious figures, elders or other significant persons in their community whose opinions they value;

6. Discussing, if applicable, the issue of separate sessions with the participants, a description of the circumstances in which the mediator may meet alone with any of the participants, or with any third party and the conditions of confidentiality concerning these separate sessions;

7. Informing the participants that the presence or absence of other persons at a mediation, including attorneys, counselors or advocates, depends on the agreement of the participants and the mediator, unless a statute or regulation otherwise requires or the mediator believes that the presence of another person is required or may be beneficial because of a history or threat of violence or other serious coercive activity by a participant.

8. Describing the obligations of the mediator to maintain the confidentiality of the mediation process and its results as well as any exceptions to confidentiality;

9. Advising the participants of the circumstances under which the mediator may suspend or terminate the mediation process and that a participant has a right to suspend or terminate mediation at any time.

B. The participants should sign a written agreement to mediate their dispute and the terms and conditions thereof within a reasonable time after first consulting the family mediator.

C. The family mediator should be alert to the capacity and willingness of the participants to mediate before proceeding with the mediation and throughout the process. A mediator should not agree to conduct the mediation if the mediator reasonably believes one or more of the participants is unable or unwilling to participate.

D. Family mediators should not accept a dispute for mediation if they cannot satisfy the expectations of the participants concerning the timing of the process.

Standard IV

A family mediator shall conduct the mediation process in an impartial manner. A family mediator shall disclose all actual and potential grounds of bias and conflicts of interest reasonably known to the mediator. The participants shall be free to retain the mediator by an informed, written waiver of the conflict of interest. However, if a bias or conflict of interest clearly impairs a mediator's impartiality, the mediator shall withdraw regardless of the express agreement of the participants.

A. Impartiality means freedom from favoritism or bias in word, action or appearance, and includes a commitment to assist all participants as opposed to any one individual.

B. Conflict of interest means any relationship between the mediator, any participant or the subject matter of the dispute that compromises or appears to compromise the mediator's impartiality.

C. A family mediator should not accept a dispute for mediation if the family mediator cannot be impartial.

D. A family mediator should identify and disclose potential grounds of bias or conflict of interest upon which a mediator's impartiality might reasonably be questioned. Such disclosure should be made prior to the start of a mediation and in time to allow the participants to select an alternate mediator.

E. A family mediator should resolve all doubts in favor of disclosure. All disclosures should be made as soon as practical after the mediator becomes aware of the bias or potential conflict of interest. The duty to disclose is a continuing duty.

F. A family mediator should guard against bias or partiality based on the participants' personal characteristics, background or performance at the mediation.

G. A family mediator should avoid conflicts of interest in recommending the services of other professionals.

H. A family mediator shall not use information about participants obtained in a mediation for personal gain or advantage.

I. A family mediator should withdraw pursuant to Standard IX if the mediator believes the mediator's impartiality has been compromised or a conflict of interest has been identified and has not been waived by the participants.

Standard V

A family mediator shall fully disclose and explain the basis of any compensation, fees and charges to the participants.

A. The participants should be provided with sufficient information about fees at the outset of mediation to determine if they wish to retain the services of the mediator.

B. The participants' written agreement to mediate their dispute should include a description of their fee arrangement with the mediator.

C. A mediator should not enter into a fee agreement that is contingent upon the results of the mediation or the amount of the settlement.

D. A mediator should not accept a fee for referral of a matter to another mediator or to any other person.

E. Upon termination of mediation a mediator should return any unearned fee to the participants.

Standard VI

A family mediator shall structure the mediation process so that the participants make decisions based on sufficient information and knowledge.

A. The mediator should facilitate full and accurate disclosure and the acquisition and development of information during mediation so that the participants can make informed decisions. This may be accomplished by encouraging participants to consult appropriate experts.

B. Consistent with standards of impartiality and preserving participant self-determination, a mediator may provide the participants with information that the mediator is qualified by training or experience to provide. The mediator shall not provide therapy or legal advice.

C. The mediator should recommend that the participants obtain independent legal representation before concluding an agreement.

D. If the participants so desire, the mediator should allow attorneys, counsel or advocates for the participants to be present at the mediation sessions.

E. With the agreement of the participants, the mediator may document the participants' resolution of their dispute. The mediator should inform the participants that any agreement should be reviewed by an independent attorney before it is signed.

Standard VII

A family mediator shall maintain the confidentiality of all information acquired in the mediation process, unless the mediator is permitted or required to reveal the information by law or agreement of the participants.

A. The mediator should discuss the participants' expectations of confidentiality with them prior to undertaking the mediation. The written agreement to mediate should include provisions concerning confidentiality.

B. Prior to undertaking the mediation the mediator should inform the participants of the limitations of confidentiality such as statutory, judicially or ethically mandated reporting.

C. As permitted by law, the mediator shall disclose a participant's threat of suicide or violence against any person to the threatened person and the appropriate authorities if the mediator believes such threat is likely to be acted upon.

D. If the mediator holds private sessions with a participant, the obligations of confidentiality concerning those sessions should be discussed and agreed upon prior to the sessions.

E. If subpoenaed or otherwise noticed to testify or to produce documents the mediator should inform the participants immediately. The mediator should not testify or provide documents in response to a subpoena without an order of the court if the mediator reasonably believes doing so would violate an obligation of confidentiality to the participants.

Standard VIII

A family mediator shall assist participants in determining how to promote the best interests of children.

A. The mediator should encourage the participants to explore the range of options available for separation or post-divorce parenting arrangements and their respective costs and benefits. Referral to a specialist in child development may be appropriate for these purposes. The topics for discussion may include, among others:

1. Information about community resources and programs that can help the participants and their children cope with the consequences of family reorganization and family violence;

2. Problems that continuing conflict creates for children's development and what steps might be taken to ameliorate the effects of conflict on the children;

3. Development of a parenting plan that covers the children's physical residence and decision-making responsibilities for the children, with appropriate levels of detail as agreed to by the participants;

4. The possible need to revise parenting plans as the developmental needs of the children evolve over time; and

5. Encouragement to the participants to develop appropriate dispute resolution mechanisms to facilitate future revisions of the parenting plan.

B. The mediator should be sensitive to the impact of culture and religion on parenting philosophy and other decisions.

C. The mediator shall inform any court-appointed representative for the children of the mediation. If a representative for the children participates, the mediator should, at the outset, discuss the effect of that participation on the mediation process and the confidentiality of the mediation with the participants. Whether the representative of the children participates or not, the mediator shall provide the representative with the resulting agreements insofar as they relate to the children.

D. Except in extraordinary circumstances, the children should not participate in the mediation process without the consent of both parents and the children's court-appointed representative.

E. Prior to including the children in the mediation process, the mediator should consult with the parents and the children's court-appointed representative about whether the children should participate in the mediation process and the form of that participation.

F. The mediator should inform all concerned about the available options for the children's participation (which may include personal participation, an interview with a mental health professional, the mediator interviewing the child and reporting to the parents, or a videotaped statement by the child) and discuss the costs and benefits of each with the participants.

Standard IX

A family mediator shall recognize a family situation involving child abuse or neglect and take appropriate steps to shape the mediation process accordingly.

A. As used in these Standards, child abuse or neglect is defined by applicable state law.

B. A mediator shall not undertake a mediation in which the family situation has been assessed to involve child abuse or neglect without appropriate and adequate training.

C. If the mediator has reasonable grounds to believe that a child of the participants is abused or neglected within the meaning of the jurisdiction's child abuse and neglect laws, the mediator shall comply with applicable child protection laws.

1. The mediator should encourage the participants to explore appropriate services for the family.

2. The mediator should consider the appropriateness of suspending or terminating the mediation process in light of the allegations.

Standard X

A family mediator shall recognize a family situation involving domestic abuse and take appropriate steps to shape the mediation process accordingly.

A. As used in these Standards, domestic abuse includes domestic violence as defined by applicable state law and issues of control and intimidation.

B. A mediator shall not undertake a mediation in which the family situation has been assessed to involve domestic abuse without appropriate and adequate training.

C. Some cases are not suitable for mediation because of safety, control or intimidation issues. A mediator should make a reasonable effort to screen for the existence of domestic abuse prior to entering into an agreement to mediate. The mediator should continue to assess for domestic abuse throughout the mediation process.

D. If domestic abuse appears to be present the mediator shall consider taking measures to insure the safety of participants and the mediator including, among others:

1. Establishing appropriate security arrangements;

2. Holding separate sessions with the participants even without the agreement of all participants;

3. Allowing a friend, representative, advocate, counsel or attorney to attend the mediation sessions;

4. Encouraging the participants to be represented by an attorney, counsel or an advocate throughout the mediation process;

5. Referring the participants to appropriate community resources;

6. Suspending or terminating the mediation sessions, with appropriate steps to protect the safety of the participants.

E. The mediator should facilitate the participants' formulation of parenting plans that protect the physical safety and psychological well-being of themselves and their children.

Standard XI

A family mediator shall suspend or terminate the mediation process when the mediator reasonably believes that a participant is unable to effectively participate or for other compelling reason.

A. Circumstances under which a mediator should consider suspending or terminating the mediation, may include, among others:

1. The safety of a participant or well-being of a child is threatened;

2. A participant has or is threatening to abduct a child;

3. A participant is unable to participate due to the influence of drugs, alcohol, or physical or mental condition;

4. The participants are about to enter into an agreement that the mediator reasonably believes to be unconscionable;

5. A participant is using the mediation to further illegal conduct;

6. A participant is using the mediation process to gain an unfair advantage;

7. If the mediator believes the mediator's impartiality has been compromised in accordance with Standard IV.

B. If the mediator does suspend or terminate the mediation, the mediator should take all reasonable steps to minimize prejudice or inconvenience to the participants which may result.

Standard XII

A family mediator shall be truthful in the advertisement and solicitation for mediation.

A. Mediators should refrain from promises and guarantees of results. A mediator should not advertise statistical settlement data or settlement rates.

B. Mediators should accurately represent their qualifications. In an advertisement or other communication, a mediator may make reference to meeting state, national or private organizational qualifications only if the entity referred to has a procedure for qualifying mediators and the mediator has been duly granted the requisite status.

Standard XIII

A family mediator shall acquire and maintain professional competence in mediation.

A. Mediators should continuously improve their professional skills and abilities by, among other activities, participating in relevant continuing education programs and should regularly engage in self-assessment.

B. Mediators should participate in programs of peer consultation and should help train and mentor the work of less experienced mediators.

C. Mediators should continuously strive to understand the impact of culture and diversity on the mediator's practice.

Appendix

Special Policy Considerations for State Regulation of Family Mediators and Court Affiliated Programs

The Model Standards recognize the National Standards for Court Connected Dispute Resolution Programs (1992). There are also state and local regulations governing such programs and family mediators. The following principles of organization and practice, however, are especially important for regulation of mediators and court-connected family mediation programs. They are worthy of separate mention.

A. Individual states or local courts should set standards and qualifications for family mediators including procedures for evaluations and handling grievances against mediators. In developing these standards and qualifications, regulators should consult with appropriate professional groups, including professional associations of family mediators.

B. When family mediators are appointed by a court or other institution, the appointing agency should make reasonable efforts to insure that each mediator is qualified for the appointment. If a list of family mediators qualified for court appointment exists, the requirements for being included on the list should be made public and available to all interested persons.

C. Confidentiality should not be construed to limit or prohibit the effective monitoring, research or evaluation of mediation programs by responsible individuals or academic institutions provided that no identifying information about any person involved in the mediation is disclosed without their prior written consent. Under appropriate circumstances, researchers may be permitted to obtain access to statistical data and, with the permission of the participants, to individual case files, observations of live mediations, and interviews with participants.

Only the Model Standards, not the Commentary, were approved by the American Bar Association in February 2001.

MODEL STANDARDS OF CONDUCT FOR MEDIATORS

AMERICAN ARBITRATION ASSOCIATION

(ADOPTED SEPTEMBER 8, 2005)

AMERICAN BAR ASSOCIATION

(APPROVED BY THE ABA HOUSE OF DELEGATES AUGUST 9, 2005)

ASSOCIATION FOR CONFLICT RESOLUTION

(ADOPTED AUGUST 22, 2005)

SEPTEMBER 2005

The Model Standards of Conduct for Mediators 2005[117]

The Model Standards of Conduct for Mediators was prepared in 1994 by the American Arbitration Association, the American Bar Association's Section of Dispute Resolution, and the Association for Conflict Resolution. A joint committee consisting of representatives from the same successor organizations revised the Model Standards in 2005. Both the original 1994 version and the 2005 revision have been approved by each participating organization.

Preamble

Mediation is used to resolve a broad range of conflicts within a variety of settings. These Standards are designed to serve as fundamental ethical guidelines for persons mediating in all practice contexts. They serve three primary goals: to guide the conduct of mediators; to inform the mediating parties; and to promote public confidence in mediation as a process for resolving disputes.

Mediation is a process in which an impartial third party facilitates communication and negotiation and promotes voluntary decision making by the parties to the dispute.

Mediation serves various purposes, including providing the opportunity for parties to define and clarify issues, understand different perspectives, identify interests, explore and assess possible solutions, and reach mutually satisfactory agreements, when desired.

Note on Construction

These Standards are to be read and construed in their entirety. There is no priority significance attached to the sequence in which the Standards appear.

The use of the term "shall" in a Standard indicates that the mediator must follow the practice described. The use of the term "should" indicates that the practice described in the standard is highly desirable, but not required, and is to be departed from only for very strong reasons and requires careful use of judgment and discretion.

The use of the term "mediator" is understood to be inclusive so that it applies to co-mediator models.

These Standards do not include specific temporal parameters when referencing a mediation, and therefore, do not define the exact beginning or ending of a mediation.

---

[117] Footnotes omitted. http://www.mediate.com/articles/model_standards_of_conflict.cfm

Various aspects of a mediation, including some matters covered by these Standards, may also be affected by applicable law, court rules, regulations, other applicable professional rules, mediation rules to which the parties have agreed and other agreements of the parties. These sources may create conflicts with, and may take precedence over, these Standards. However, a mediator should make every effort to comply with the spirit and intent of these Standards in resolving such conflicts. This effort should include honoring all remaining Standards not in conflict with these other sources.

These Standards, unless and until adopted by a court or other regulatory authority do not have the force of law. Nonetheless, the fact that these Standards have been adopted by the respective sponsoring entities, should alert mediators to the fact that the Standards might be viewed as establishing a standard of care for mediators.

STANDARD I. SELF-DETERMINATION

A. A mediator shall conduct a mediation based on the principle of party self-determination. Self-determination is the act of coming to a voluntary, uncoerced decision in which each party makes free and informed choices as to process and outcome. Parties may exercise self-determination at any stage of a mediation, including mediator selection, process design, participation in or withdrawal from the process, and outcomes.

1. Although party self-determination for process design is a fundamental principle of mediation practice, a mediator may need to balance such party self-determination with a mediator's duty to conduct a quality process in accordance with these Standards.

2. A mediator cannot personally ensure that each party has made free and informed choices to reach particular decisions, but, where appropriate, a mediator should make the parties aware of the importance of consulting other professionals to help them make informed choices.

B. A mediator shall not undermine party self-determination by any party for reasons such as higher settlement rates, egos, increased fees, or outside pressures from court personnel, program administrators, provider organizations, the media or others.

STANDARD II. IMPARTIALITY

A. A mediator shall decline a mediation if the mediator cannot conduct it in an impartial manner. Impartiality means freedom from favoritism, bias or prejudice.

B. A mediator shall conduct a mediation in an impartial manner and avoid conduct that gives the appearance of partiality.

1. A mediator should not act with partiality or prejudice based on any participant's personal characteristics, background, values and beliefs, or performance at a mediation, or any other reason.

2. A mediator should neither give nor accept a gift, favor, loan or other item of value that raises a question as to the mediator's actual or perceived impartiality.

3. A mediator may accept or give de Minimis gifts or incidental items or services that are provided to facilitate a mediation or respect cultural norms so long as such practices do not raise questions as to a mediator's actual or perceived impartiality.

C. If at any time a mediator is unable to conduct a mediation in an impartial manner, the mediator shall withdraw.

STANDARD III. CONFLICTS OF INTEREST

A. A mediator shall avoid a conflict of interest or the appearance of a conflict of interest during and after a mediation. A conflict of interest can arise from involvement by a mediator with the subject matter of the dispute or from any relationship between a mediator and any mediation participant, whether past or present, personal or professional, that reasonably raises a question of a mediator's impartiality.

B. A mediator shall make a reasonable inquiry to determine whether there are any facts that a reasonable individual would consider likely to create a potential or actual conflict of interest for a mediator. A mediator's actions necessary to accomplish a reasonable inquiry into potential conflicts of interest may vary based on practice context.

C. A mediator shall disclose, as soon as practicable, all actual and potential conflicts of interest that are reasonably known to the mediator and could reasonably be seen as raising a question about the mediator's impartiality. After disclosure, if all parties agree, the mediator may proceed with the mediation.

D. If a mediator learns any fact after accepting a mediation that raises a question with respect to that mediator's service creating a potential or actual conflict of interest, the mediator shall disclose it as quickly as practicable. After disclosure, if all parties agree, the mediator may proceed with the mediation.

E. If a mediator's conflict of interest might reasonably be viewed as undermining the integrity of the mediation, a mediator shall withdraw from or decline to proceed with the mediation regardless of the expressed desire or agreement of the parties to the contrary.

F. Subsequent to a mediation, a mediator shall not establish another relationship with any of the participants in any matter that would raise questions about the integrity of the mediation. When a mediator develops personal or professional relationships with parties, other individuals or organizations following a mediation in which they were involved, the mediator should consider factors such as time elapsed following the mediation, the nature of the relationships established, and services offered when determining whether the relationships might create a perceived or actual conflict of interest.

STANDARD IV. COMPETENCE

A. A mediator shall mediate only when the mediator has the necessary competence to satisfy the reasonable expectations of the parties.

1. Any person may be selected as a mediator, provided that the parties are satisfied with the mediator's competence and qualifications. Training, experience in mediation, skills, cultural understandings and other

qualities are often necessary for mediator competence. A person who offers to serve as a mediator creates the expectation that the person is competent to mediate effectively.

2. A mediator should attend educational programs and related activities to maintain and enhance the mediator's knowledge and skills related to mediation.

3. A mediator should have available for the parties' information relevant to the mediator's training, education, experience and approach to conducting a mediation.

B. If a mediator, during the course of a mediation determines that the mediator cannot conduct the mediation competently, the mediator shall discuss that determination with the parties as soon as is practicable and take appropriate steps to address the situation, including, but not limited to, withdrawing or requesting appropriate assistance.

C. If a mediator's ability to conduct a mediation is impaired by drugs, alcohol, medication or otherwise, the mediator shall not conduct the mediation.

STANDARD V. CONFIDENTIALITY

A. A mediator shall maintain the confidentiality of all information obtained by the mediator in mediation, unless otherwise agreed to by the parties or required by applicable law.

1. If the parties to a mediation agree that the mediator may disclose information obtained during the mediation, the mediator may do so.

2. A mediator should not communicate to any non-participant information about how the parties acted in the mediation. A mediator may report, if required, whether parties appeared at a scheduled mediation and whether or not the parties reached a resolution.

3. If a mediator participates in teaching, research or evaluation of mediation, the mediator should protect the anonymity of the parties and abide by their reasonable expectations regarding confidentiality.

B. A mediator who meets with any persons in private session during a mediation shall not convey directly or indirectly to any other person, any information that was obtained during that private session without the consent of the disclosing person.

C. A mediator shall promote understanding among the parties of the extent to which the parties will maintain confidentiality of information they obtain in a mediation.

D. Depending on the circumstance of a mediation, the parties may have varying expectations regarding confidentiality that a mediator should address. The parties may make their own rules with respect to confidentiality, or the accepted practice of an individual mediator or institution may dictate a particular set of expectations.

STANDARD VI. QUALITY OF THE PROCESS

A. A mediator shall conduct a mediation in accordance with these Standards and in a manner that promotes diligence, timeliness, safety, presence of the appropriate participants, party participation, procedural fairness, party competency and mutual respect among all participants.

1. A mediator should agree to mediate only when the mediator is prepared to commit the attention essential to an effective mediation.

2. A mediator should only accept cases when the mediator can satisfy the reasonable expectation of the parties concerning the timing of a mediation.

3. The presence or absence of persons at a mediation depends on the agreement of the parties and the mediator. The parties and mediator may agree that others may be excluded from particular sessions or from all sessions.

4. A mediator should promote honesty and candor between and among all participants, and a mediator shall not knowingly misrepresent any material fact or circumstance in the course of a mediation.

5. The role of a mediator differs substantially from other professional roles. Mixing the role of a mediator and the role of another profession is problematic and thus, a mediator should distinguish between the roles. A mediator may provide information that the mediator is qualified by training or experience to provide, only if the mediator can do so consistent with these Standards.

6. A mediator shall not conduct a dispute resolution procedure other than mediation but label it mediation in an effort to gain the protection of rules, statutes, or other governing authorities pertaining to mediation.

7. A mediator may recommend, when appropriate, that parties consider resolving their dispute through arbitration, counseling, neutral evaluation or other processes.

8. A mediator shall not undertake an additional dispute resolution role in the same matter without the consent of the parties. Before providing such service, a mediator shall inform the parties of the implications of the change in process and obtain their consent to the change. A mediator who undertakes such role assumes different duties and responsibilities that may be governed by other standards.

9. If a mediation is being used to further criminal conduct, a mediator should take appropriate steps including, if necessary, postponing, withdrawing from, or terminating the mediation.

10. If a party appears to have difficulty comprehending the process, issues, or settlement options, or difficulty participating in a mediation, the mediator should explore the circumstances and potential accommodations, modifications or adjustments that would make possible the party's capacity to comprehend, participate and exercise self-determination.

B. If a mediator is made aware of domestic abuse or violence among the parties, the mediator shall take appropriate steps including, if necessary, postponing, withdrawing from or terminating the mediation.

C. If a mediator believes that participant conduct, including that of the mediator, jeopardizes conducting a mediation consistent with these Standards, a mediator shall take appropriate steps including, if necessary, postponing, withdrawing from, or terminating the mediation.

STANDARD VII. ADVERTISING AND SOLICITATION

A. A mediator shall be truthful and not misleading when advertising, soliciting or otherwise communicating the mediator's qualifications, experience, services and fees.

1. A mediator should not include any promises as to outcome in communications, including business cards, stationery, or computer-based communications.

2. A mediator should only claim to meet the mediator qualifications of a governmental entity or private organization if that entity or organization has a recognized procedure for qualifying mediators and it grants such status to the mediator.

B. A mediator shall not solicit in a manner that gives an appearance of partiality for or against a party or otherwise undermines the integrity of the process.

C. A mediator shall not communicate to others, in promotional materials or through other forms of communication, the names of persons served without their permission.

STANDARD VIII. FEES AND OTHER CHARGES

A. A mediator shall provide each party or each party's representative true and complete information about mediation fees, expenses and any other actual or potential charges that may be incurred in connection with a mediation.

1. If a mediator charges fees, the mediator should develop them in light of all relevant factors, including the type and complexity of the matter, the qualifications of the mediator, the time required and the rates customary for such mediation services.

2. A mediator's fee arrangement should be in writing unless the parties request otherwise.

B. A mediator shall not charge fees in a manner that impairs a mediator's impartiality.

1. A mediator should not enter into a fee agreement which is contingent upon the result of the mediation or amount of the settlement.

2. While a mediator may accept unequal fee payments from the parties, a mediator should not allow such a fee arrangement to adversely impact the mediator's ability to conduct a mediation in an impartial manner.

STANDARD IX. ADVANCEMENT OF MEDIATION PRACTICE

A. A mediator should act in a manner that advances the practice of mediation. A mediator promotes this Standard by engaging in some or all of the following:

1. Fostering diversity within the field of mediation.

2. Striving to make mediation accessible to those who elect to use it, including providing services at a reduced rate or on a pro bono basis as appropriate.

3. Participating in research when given the opportunity, including obtaining participant feedback when appropriate.

4. Participating in outreach and education efforts to assist the public in developing an improved understanding of, and appreciation for, mediation.

5. Assisting newer mediators through training, mentoring and networking.

B. A mediator should demonstrate respect for differing points of view within the field, seek to learn from other mediators and work together with other mediators to improve the profession and better serve people in conflict.

End of Model Rules

Overview and Analysis of Model Standards for Family and Divorce Mediators

In this discussion, the **Model Standards for Family and Divorce Mediation** are examined. In some cases, these rules are compared to the second set of standards printed in the preceding pages, applicable to mediators in general. The first set applies to *family and divorce mediators*. The second set shall be referred to as the "general" rules because they apply to mediators in general.

Family Standard I

A family mediator shall recognize that mediation is based on the principle of self-determination by the participants.

Standard One addresses client self-determination, and, indirectly, mediator neutrality. Appropriately, this standard is listed first and is, according to the comment, the "fundamental principle of family mediation." Highly directive mediation where the mediator gives advice or tries to persuade parties to make decisions in line with the mediator's opinion of what is the best outcome is not only poor mediation (or, more accurately, not mediation, but some coercive process, such as conciliation or a settlement conference) but is unethical. Exceptions to this rule would be areas in which the mediator's bias is acceptable, as in advocating against decisions that would obviously not be in a child's best interests. An example of a gray area for mediator "bias" would be corporal punishment, considered acceptable in moderation by much of society. When clients admit they administer corporal punishment as a form of discipline, the mediator may feel compelled to intervene. I personally believe that hitting a child in anger is harmful to the parent-child relationship. There are more civilized and wholesome ways to modify behavior. If it becomes the topic of conversation in mediation, the mediator has a range of acceptable responses beginning with refraining from offering an opinion where parents agree to the practice and it is not "excessive," to the mediator giving a non-judgmental opinion such as, "I do not hit my children, even though there are undoubtedly times when I have had the urge. I find that it just is not effective as a form of discipline and that there are more effective and lasting measures, such as withholding privileges. Because studies[118] show there can be harmful effects from hitting, I'd rather err on the side of not hitting." This response validates the parents' values and feelings, while imparting information that is helpful to their family. If a mediator would rather not make the comment personal, she could speak about hitting children in general. By respecting the parties' "ability...to make their own voluntary and informed decisions," as comment A states, the mediator will resist the urge to impose the mediator's solutions onto the parties. When children are harmed by their parents, however, mediators is likely required to make a report of abuse.

---

[118] Gershoff, E. T., & Bitensky, S. H. (2007). The case against corporal punishment of children: Converging evidence from social science research and international human rights law and implications for U.S. public policy. *Psychology, Public Policy, And Law, 13*(4), 231-272.

Family Standard 2

A family mediator shall be qualified by education and training to undertake the mediation.

Untrained individuals who practice mediation professionally may be violating this standard when they hold themselves out as mediators. Exceptions are mediators who were self-trained in the 1970's when the profession was developing and training was scarce, although these mediators still have the duty to obtain continuing education. In addition, this standard requires family mediators to have knowledge of family law. Because divorce can be complex and require extensive knowledge of tax law, real estate law, divorce codes, civil procedure, and financial expertise, lawyers and non-lawyers must obtain this knowledge before undertaking divorce mediation. The decisions individuals make in divorce, such as retaining or distributing a pension, retaining or transferring title to real estate, signing permanent documents affecting alimony and support, and making decisions that affect future taxation of income, can be monumental and impact the rest of their lives. These decisions should only be made with the help of an attorney and other experts in these matters. A mediator who does not have technical knowledge does a disservice to divorcing clients. Without such knowledge, the mediator cannot identify legal, tax, and financial issues. Unable to identify these issues, the mediator cannot address them in mediation. Even though the parties have attorneys who, presumably, will identify the issues before an official agreement is signed, the mediator wastes clients' time and money by failing to facilitate a comprehensive agreement. This is malpractice. Therefore, complex divorce issues should be undertaken by attorney mediators or non-attorney mediators only when they have obtained extensive knowledge in the financial and legal aspects of divorce, have professional malpractice insurance covering mediation of divorce and all related claims, and the parties have separate counsel.

Family Standard 3

A family mediator shall facilitate the participants' understanding of what mediation is and assess their capacity to mediate before the participants reach an agreement to mediate.

This standard has two parts. The first part addresses the mediator's duty to explain the mediation process to clients and test that understanding by discerning whether or not parties appreciate the unique role of mediator. The mediator role must often be explained in stages because it is a novel concept for the average person to grasp. There is nothing in the environment to which clients can compare it. There are currently no Hollywood productions or network series about "The Mediator," (although this would create an intriguing television show). Clients typically learn something about the mediator role from websites, conversations with others, and their attorneys. At that point they understand that the mediator is a quasi-legal professional who understands the intricacies of divorce and will help in bringing about a settlement, but few understand at this initial point that the mediator is genuinely neutral and will not impose or direct a settlement. At this point, parties typically think the mediator is an arbitrator or decision-maker. When the initial phone call is made the mediator has an opportunity to add to this knowledge by explaining the mediator role further. During the mediation, the mediator has another opportunity to explain the mediator role and process during the mediator's opening statement (see Chapter 6). In the opening statement, the mediator also explains procedural steps such as consulting other experts, the possibility of caucusing, the role of attorneys or other individuals, confidentiality, the memorandum of understanding, etc. Throughout mediation, the mediator's role is often revisited. In fact, as will be seen in Chapter 12, addressing the mediator's role can even be a way to break impasse or deal with resistance. The definition of the mediator's role never loses its importance throughout the process because it creates the mediator/client boundary, an important aspect of the mediation process explored in Chapter 5. Some would say that without a clear mediator/client boundary, the mediation process cannot be effective.

Ω This standard is unique to the standards for family mediators, and is not found in the general standards. In the general standards, Standard VI A 5-8 defines the role of mediator and how it differs from other "professional roles." The standard advises a mediator not to mislabel the role of mediator, but does not specifically direct the mediator to explain the process of mediation to the parties. *Query,* why do the family standards specifically address the mediator's duty to explain the process to the clients, while the general rules omit this obligation?

The second part of this standard, assessing parties' capacity to mediate, relates to client readiness as well as client competence. The mediator is expected to address both parts of this standard before the parties reach an agreement to mediate. Capacity to mediate may arise from readiness (or lack thereof) in the form of grief issues, denial, extreme resistance to the process, unwillingness to voluntarily engage in the process, or domestic violence. Capacity may also arise from competency (or lack thereof) affected by mental illness, substance abuse, or medication. Any deterrent to conducting a safe, voluntary mediation in which clients are capable of making decisions in their own best interests constitutes a capacity issue under this standard. Moreover, the obligation to assess capacity is an ongoing duty that last throughout the process.

Family Standard 4

A family mediator shall conduct the mediation process in an impartial manner. A family mediator shall disclose all actual and potential grounds of bias and conflicts of interest reasonably known to the mediator. The participants shall be free to retain the mediator by an informed, written waiver of the conflict of interest. However, if a bias or conflict of interest clearly impairs a mediator's impartiality, the mediator shall withdraw regardless of the express agreement of the participants.

This standard defines the mediator's impartiality and duty to disclose all actual or potential conflicts of interest. Appearance of partiality is as important as actual or potential partiality or bias. Therefore, even if there is no potential or actual conflict of interest whatsoever, the mediator is obligated to avoid any appearance of a conflict. Conversely, if clients agree in writing to waive any perceived conflict of interest while the mediator continues to be impaired by the conflict of interest (by being biased), the mediator is obligated to override the parties' waiver and decline the case. A mediator is directed to resolve all doubts in favor of disclosure, which is a continuing duty. This standard also addresses recommendations of other professionals by the mediator, directing the mediator to consider whether or not such referrals could create a conflict of interest. For example, if the mediator makes a referral that favors one of the parties or their attorneys, it could be perceived as a conflict of interest. The standard also addresses the mediator acting outside of role in comment H, "A family mediator shall not use information about participants obtained in mediation for personal gain or advantage." This rule makes it clear that it is not appropriate for a mediator to ask clients for favors, nor would it be appropriate for the mediator to exploit the special relationship he has with clients for another purpose. An example of such a practice would be calling a realtor friend to inform him of people he knows who are thinking about selling their house.

Ω Interestingly, the general standards, but not the family standards specifically recognize that parties sometimes give *de Minimis* "gifts" to the mediator. Comment B 2 to Standard II of the general standards states the mediator should not accept gifts from parties, while Comment B 3 recognizes that *de Minimis* gifts given or received to facilitate mediation or respect cultural norms sometimes come with the territory.

Family Standard 5

A family mediator shall fully disclose and explain the basis of compensation, fees and charges to the participants.

This standard makes it clear in comment C it is not ethical for a mediator to take a case on a contingent fee or to accept referral fees (comment D). A contingent fee is permitted in certain litigation cases handled by attorneys. For instance, when attorneys represent an individual in car accidents, product liability, or medical malpractice cases, clients typically cannot afford legal fees or fees involved in retaining the services of expert witnesses. Attorneys take these cases on a contingent fee basis, paying the costs and then recovering all funds advanced as well as the attorney's fees by receiving a percentage of the total recovery, typically in the neighborhood of forty percent. If the case is lost, the attorney loses the money that was advanced and the client owes nothing. This is considered perfectly acceptable and fair because it allows access to the justice system by injured parties who cannot otherwise afford legal fees and costs. The attorneys' interests (getting as much money as possible) and the client's interests are identical. In mediation, however, the mediator must be paid hourly or at a flat rate and never with a contingent fee. Any contingency would likely be based on settlement of the case, which gives the mediator a stake in the outcome and compromises neutrality.

The prohibition against referral fees sometimes seems counter-intuitive to attorneys who are accustomed to paying and accepting referral fees in their law practices. When an attorney refers a client to another attorney to take the client's case, it is acceptable and ethical for the referring attorney to receive a portion of the fee as a referral fee, so long as the arrangement is explained to the client and the client consents. There is no conflict of interest because the client's interests are not affected by the sharing of fees. For a mediator to accept a referral fee the appearance of a conflict could be created. The mediator's interests would be intertwined with the interests of the referring professional.

Family Standard 6

A family mediator shall structure the mediation process so that the participants make decisions based on sufficient information and knowledge.

Ω This standard places an obligation on the family mediator that is not imposed on other mediators in the general rules. If a mediator sees clients making decisions without sufficient information, the mediator is ethically bound to do something ("structure the mediation process") to protect them. This standard implies an evaluative role of the mediator to know the pertinent information that supports decisions in divorce, and to assess whether or not the parties have considered that information in making decisions. Typically the "information" is the law as well as, arguably, information about children and families. This standard recognizes the unique conditions of family mediation: participants in divorce and custody mediation frequently do not possess the information they need. This is why custody courts require parent education prior to mediation. Parents are empowered with information from the parent education session that they can use to make decisions in the mediation session. It is important for parents to attend these classes. If the parents are not able to do so, then it is up to the mediator to either provide information about child development or "structure" the process so that the parties obtain the information. In divorce, clients rarely know the intricacies of the laws of equitable distribution and alimony. They rely on their attorneys to advise them, but often do not take their attorneys with them to the mediation session, relying on the mediator to be aware of the "information" that is necessary for the decisions concerning property, finances, income, child schedules, and support. This does not mean that the mediator gives them legal advice, which would be a clear conflict of interest since the clients have opposing legal interests and is not the mediator role. The mediator must, at a minimum, pay attention to what information is needed by the clients in order to make decisions. An example is the mediator who, in an attempt to be purely "transformative" allowed parties to set the agenda and identify all of the issues. The question of alimony never came up, and the mediator, being purely client-led, did not think it appropriate to bring it up. When the agreement reached the wife's attorney, it was discovered that wife had not effectively waived alimony because she did not know that the law provided for it. This forced the parties to return to a different mediator, and the entire agreement had to be re-worked because alimony is often related to property distribution in several respects. Therefore, by virtue of this standard, mediators are ethically bound to be directive and evaluative in assessing whether or not clients have sufficient information to make decisions. This requires a sophisticated thought process on the part of the mediator, who must make a judgment based on knowledge and information possessed by the mediator. The standard does not require the mediator to give the parties the information. The mediator is merely required to "structure" the mediation so that the clients make decisions with sufficient information and knowledge. The general rules impose a similar duty on the mediator, but stop short of requiring the mediator to make an assessment. The general rules (Standard VI, 10) state that if a party *appears* to have difficulty with the process, the mediator should explore what can be done to make possible the party's capacity to comprehend and participate. In the above example, the wife clearly may not have "appeared" to have had difficulty. On the contrary, when she left the mediator's office the first time, she thought (inaccurately) she had a comprehensive, satisfactory agreement.

Family Standard 7

A family mediator shall maintain the confidentiality of all information acquired in the mediation process, unless the mediator is permitted or required to reveal the information by law or agreement of the parties.

The obligation of confidentiality extends to everyone outside of the mediation process. The mediator cannot communicate about the mediation with the parties' attorneys without the permission of both clients. It is not acceptable for the mediator to even communicate with just one party's attorney without the consent of both parties. The duty of confidentiality extends to relationships and chance encounters outside of mediation. If the mediator sees a client in a restaurant or ends up involved in other business or social relationships with a client, the mediator must not acknowledge the mediator/client relationship without consent of the client, or, arguably, both clients.

If a mediator is served with a subpoena to testify in court, the mediator should not automatically divulge privileged and confidential mediation information without first giving clients notice of the subpoena and an opportunity to file a motion to quash the subpoena, blocking the mediator's testimony. If the parties do nothing after receiving notice of the subpoena, the mediator should comply with the subpoena but still must assert any privilege of mediation communications.

Family Standard 8

A family mediator shall assist participants in determining how to promote the best interests of children.

Ω This rule does not appear in the general rules. Children are silent parties in every family mediation from a needs and interests perspective. Typically, children are not present and do not have a voice in the mediation unless the parents advocate for them or they attend the mediation by meeting separately with the mediator. Therefore, in a typical case, the mediator is a silent partner with the child and, in a sense, represents the child's interests in the mediation. This is not a conflict of interest because the child's interests are not in conflict with the parents' interests, and, even if they were, the child's interests must come first. It is important for the mediator to explain to parties that although the mediator is neutral, the mediator does have an interest in promoting the best interests of the child. This applies in custody cases as well as in divorce, property division, child support, alimony, and any other related claims. *Query,* Does the issue of payment for college education fall under the mediator's obligation "…to promote the best interests of children?"

Family Standard 9

A family mediator shall recognize a family situation involving child abuse or neglect and take appropriate steps to shape the mediation process accordingly.

Ω The general rules address domestic abuse or violence in one rule, VI 10 B. The family mediator rules address the subject in two rules, Standard IX and Standard X. This standard applies to child abuse or neglect and, again, directs the mediator to "shape" the process. The prescribed actions for the mediator are to obtain appropriate training on the subject, to comply with applicable child protection (including reporting) laws, to recommend appropriate services for the family, and to consider suspending or terminating the mediation process "in light of the allegations." *Query,* how might suspending or terminating the process help the parties or the mediation process?

Family Standard 10

A family mediator shall recognize a family situation involving domestic abuse and take appropriate steps to shape the mediation process accordingly.

Ω The mediator clearly has an ongoing duty to ascertain whether or not domestic violence is present in a case. The mediator is not required to decline the mediation of a case where domestic violence is present. There are six duties imposed on the mediator who detects the existence of domestic violence. It is the mediator's obligation, as a professional serving consumers, to provide a safe workplace. Security and physical safety are the responsibility of the mediator who is aware of a domestic violence issue. Other measures suggested in the comments are caucus, the use of third parties in the mediation, the use of other professionals such as attorneys or advocates, referral to community resources, and the possible suspension or termination of mediation.

Family Standard 11

A family mediator shall suspend or terminate the mediation process when the mediator reasonably believes that a participant is unable to effectively participate or for other compelling reason.

The mediator is obligated to suspend or terminate mediation (in other words, end the process) under certain conditions. Collectively, these conditions are beyond the control of the mediator, with no chance that the mediator can influence the situation to remove the conditions. Harm to a child, lack of safety, an unconscionable agreement, illegal conduct, unfair exploitation of a party, irreversible compromising of the mediator's impartiality are examples given in the comments. An unconscionable agreement is a term meaning that the agreement is so unfair as to be egregiously inequitable without any justification. This issue arises when clients appear in mediation to be "giving away the farm." An example would be a retired couple in their late 60's who had already been separated for five years and wanted to finalize a divorce. The husband was giving virtually everything they had accumulated to the wife. He was also assigning to her the majority of his income. The mediator questioned this seeming over-generosity, as was her duty. The husband had a good explanation and clearly understood and intended what he was doing. He had remarried a wealthy woman and had a prenuptial agreement to protect his financial interests. He felt that he now had more than adequate means to live out the rest of his years. In this case, the agreement did not turn out to be unconscionable, although it did initially appear to be unconscionable, and further exploration was needed.

If the mediator determines that the mediation should be suspended or terminated, the additional obligation of doing so gracefully is imposed on the mediator. This may be more difficult than making the decision to terminate in the first instance. For example, if a mediator ends mediation because of illegal conduct, spousal abuse, or harm to a child, the mediator's actions could, conceivably, aggravate the danger by stirring up more drama. The abuser may take his anger out on the spouse or child. The mediator is directed to "minimize prejudice or inconvenience to the participants." This burden can be quite heavy. At a minimum, the mediator must take care to maintain confidentiality, promote safety, and involve authorities where necessary. If a party reveals abuse or illegal conduct in caucus, the mediator must not reveal confidentialities unless permitted by law. This can make it awkward for the mediator. If wife reveals abuse in caucus but does not want the mediator to reveal her disclosure in joint session, the mediator must think of a way to end the mediation without stating the real reason. This problem is explored later in Chapter 9 regarding high conflict and domestic violence.

Family Standard 12

A family mediator shall be truthful in the advertisement and solicitation for mediation.

Interestingly, the comment to Standard XII adds an important proscription not addressed in the standard itself. The mediator "should not advertise statistical settlement data or settlement rates." This is similar to the proscription against attorneys' advertising that they are the best lawyers. The reason for this prohibition is that laymen do not typically have an understanding about what settlement rates mean and the advertising could be deceptive if settlement rates are advertised. Professional mediators know that a mediator could do a very good job, consistently, and not settle cases for reasons that are individual to each case. Conversely, a mediocre mediator could have a track record for settlements by coincidence or a light case load. In other words, settlement rates alone do not reflect the quality of the mediation. Rates are relative. To take advantage of the ignorance of the public about the complexities of mediation is deceptive advertising.

Family Standard 13

A family mediator shall acquire and maintain competence in mediation.

As with any profession, competence is an obligation of the individual to self-regulate. Most mediation programs and organizations have basic training, advanced training, and continuing education requirements. For instance, the Association for Conflict Resolution has levels of competence that can be conferred as "Practitioner" status or "Advanced Practitioner" status. In order to attain these titles, a mediator must submit documentation of training, experience, work product, and consultation hours. However, since mediation is largely an unlicensed profession, technically, anyone can call himself a mediator in most states. A person practicing mediation without training, education, experience, and competence is violating this standard.

A Final Note on the Standards of Practice

One of the hallmarks of any professional, whether doctor, lawyer, psychotherapist, accountant, or other, is the attribute of judgment. The standards provide guidance and values; it is up to the individual professional to use judgment in determining what actions are appropriate. The actions to take are not prescribed by the standards. This is a heavy responsibility that involves a great deal of public trust being given to the professional. Given this reality, state legislatures are negligent when they do not take action to license mediators within their borders. Mediators come into contact with the public and provide an increasingly important service to consumers as mediation becomes more widespread. Their services are no less important than those of licensed professionals such as accountants, doctors, and lawyers.

Mediation Legislation

There is, fortunately, a good deal of legislation governing mediation procedures, most of which has come into being in recent decades. Laws regarding confidentiality of mediation communications materialized relatively quickly with the mediation explosion. These laws are referred to as "confidentiality" or "privilege" statutes. Generally, they provide that communications and documents generated within the confines of mediation are not admissible in court, and cannot be compelled or required as part of discovery or any other process. Exceptions to the general rule may apply where a crime or threat of bodily injury or property damage exists. Other exceptions pertain to fraudulent communications or documents that exist independently and not generated exclusively by mediation. In addition, reporting statutes could apply to mediators in certain cases. Reporting statutes are laws that mandate reporting by certain professionals of suspected child abuse, information that would otherwise be confidential. Other laws that affect mediators are laws passed to establish mediation programs. These programs typically have their own requirements and definitions of mediation practice, applicable to mediators who mediate in that program, such as a court-connected mediation program. Some examples of these types of laws follow.

I.   CONFIDENTIALITY AND PRIVILEGE STATUTES

PENNSYLVANIA

42 PA.C.S.A. §5949 Confidential mediation communications and documents

(a) **General Rule.**—except as provided in subsection (b), all mediation communications and mediation documents are privileged. Disclosure of mediation communications and mediation documents may not be required or compelled through discovery or any other process. Mediation communications and mediation documents shall not be admissible as evidence in any action or proceeding, including, but not limited to, a judicial, administrative or arbitration action or proceeding.

(b) **Exceptions.**—

(1) A settlement document may be introduced in an action or proceeding to enforce the settlement agreement expressed in the document, unless the settlement document by its terms states that it is unenforceable or not intended to be legally binding.

(2) To the extent that the communication or conduct is relevant evidence in a criminal matter, the privilege and limitation set forth in subsection (a) does not apply to:

(i) a communication of a threat that bodily injury may be inflicted on a person;

(ii) a communication of a threat that damage may be inflicted on real or personal property under circumstances constituting a felony; or

(iii) conduct during a mediation session causing direct bodily injury to a person.

(3) The privilege and limitation set forth under subsection (a) does not apply to a fraudulent communication during mediation that is relevant evidence in an action to enforce or set aside a mediated agreement reached as a result of that fraudulent communication.

(4) Any document which otherwise exists, or existed independent of the mediation and is not otherwise covered by this section, is not subject to this privilege.

(c) **Definitions**.—as used in this section, the following words and phrases shall have the meanings given to them in this subsection:

"Mediation." The deliberate and knowing use of a third person by disputing parties to help them reach a resolution of their dispute. For purposes of this section, mediation commences at the time of initial contact with a mediator or mediation program.

"Mediation communication." A communication, verbal or nonverbal, oral or written, made by, between or among a party, mediator, mediation program or any other person present to further the mediation process when the communication occurs during a mediation session or outside a session when made to or by the mediator or mediation program.

"Mediation document." Written material, including copies, prepared for the purpose of, in the course of, or pursuant to mediation. The term includes, but is not limited to, memoranda, notes, files, records and work product of a mediator, mediation program or party.

"Mediation program." A plan or organization through which mediators or mediation may be provided.

"Mediator." A person who performs mediation.

"Settlement document." A written agreement signed by the parties to the agreement.

Questions for Discussion:

1. **Where in the body of the above statute is the term "confidentiality" located?**

2. **What are the exceptions to "privilege" and what is the purpose of each exception?**

3. **Discuss the difference between privilege and confidentiality. Hint: "Privilege means not subject to disclosure in a court of law. "Confidentiality" means keeping secret communications and not divulging to anyone with possible exceptions.**

CALIFORNIA

Cal. Evid.Code §1119

§1119. Written or oral communications during mediation process; admissibility

Except as otherwise provided in this chapter:

(a) No evidence of anything said or any admission made for the purpose of, in the course of, or pursuant to, a mediation or a mediation consultation is admissible or subject to discovery, and disclosure of the evidence shall not be compelled, in any arbitration, administrative adjudication, civil action, or other noncriminal proceeding in which, pursuant to law, testimony can be compelled to be given.

(b) No writing, as defined in Section 250 [defining what constitutes a "writing"] that is prepared for the purpose of, in the course of, or pursuant to, a mediation or a mediation consultation, is admissible or subject to discovery, and disclosure of the writing shall not be compelled, in any arbitration, administrative adjudication, civil action, or other noncriminal proceeding in which, pursuant to law, testimony can be compelled to be given.

(c) All communications, negotiations, or settlement discussions by and between participants in the course of a mediation or a mediation consultation shall remain confidential.

Questions for Discussion:

1. What exception to confidentiality is made in subsection (a)? How is this exception similar to Pennsylvania's statute?

2. How does subsection (c) of the California statute differ from the Pennsylvania statute?

3. What other differences are found between the California and Pennsylvania laws?

4. For purposes of confidentiality by and between participants, which of the two states (Pennsylvania or California) makes the mediator's job easier? Why? In what way could California's approach be inconvenient for the mediator? For the parties? For the parties' attorneys?

II. SUSPECTED CHILD ABUSE REPORTING LAWS

Pennsylvania's child abuse reporting laws underwent a major overhaul after the 2011 Penn State University scandal involving former assistant football coach Jerry Sandusky's numerous acts of sexual abuse upon underage boys. According to the Freeh report,[119] university officials knew about the abuse and failed to report it to authorities. Sandusky was found guilty of 45 counts of sexual abuse and sentenced to 30 to 60 years in prison. Other high level officials resigned or were dismissed and the university's athletic program was severely sanctioned by the National College Athletic Association (NCAA).[120]

---

[119] Freeh, L. (2012). The Freeh report on Pennsylvania State University. Retrieved from http://progress.psu.edu/the-freeh-report

[120] Glenn, C. (2013). Introduction to Symposium on the legal implications of the Sandusky scandal. *Widener Law Journal*, 22, 551.

Reforms included changing the definition of abuse, redefining mandated reporters, and requiring the report to be made directly to ChildLine. Reporters are no longer defined as those who come into contact with a child, but also include those who receive a second-hand report of abuse. Attorneys, per se, are still not mandated reporters due to attorney-client privilege, but attorneys affiliated with an agency, institution, or other entity involved in the care, guidance, control, or supervision of children are mandated reporters. Definition of abuse is greatly expanded with examples. The statute has been revised several times already, and as of the date this edition went to print, there are proposed amendments under consideration.

PENNSYLVANIA

23 Pa.C.S.§§6303 et seq.

Effective: June 12, 2018

§ 6303. Definitions

(a) General rule.--The following words and phrases when used in this chapter shall have the meanings given to them in this section unless the context clearly indicates otherwise:

"Accept for service." Decide on the basis of the needs and problems of an individual to admit or receive the individual as a client of the agency or as required by a court order entered under 42 Pa. C.S. Ch. 63 (relating to juvenile matters).

"Adult." An individual 18 years of age or older.

"Adult family member." A person 18 years of age or older who has the responsibility to provide care or services to an individual with an intellectual disability or chronic psychiatric disability.

"Bodily injury." Impairment of physical condition or substantial pain.

"Child." An individual under 18 years of age.

"Child-care services." Includes any of the following:

(1) Child day-care centers.

(2) Group day-care homes.

(3) Family child-care homes.

(4) Foster homes.

(5) Adoptive parents.

(6) Boarding homes for children.

(7) Juvenile detention center services or programs for delinquent or dependent children.

(8) Mental health services for children.

(9) Services for children with intellectual disabilities.

(10) Early intervention services for children.

(11) Drug and alcohol services for children.

(12) Day-care services or programs that are offered by a school.

(13) Other child-care services that are provided by or subject to approval, licensure, registration or certification by the department or a county social services agency or that are provided pursuant to a contract with the department or a county social services agency.

The term does not apply to services provided by administrative or other support personnel unless the administrative or other support personnel have direct contact with children.

"Child protective services." Those services and activities provided by the department and each county agency for child abuse cases.

"Children's advocacy center." A local public agency in this Commonwealth or a not-for-profit entity incorporated in this Commonwealth which:

(1) is tax exempt under section 501(c)(3) of the Internal Revenue Code of 1986 (Public Law 99-514, 26 U.S.C. § 501(c)(3)); and

(2) operates within this Commonwealth for the primary purpose of providing a child-focused, facility-based program dedicated to coordinating a formalized multidisciplinary response to suspected child abuse that, at a minimum, either onsite or through a partnership with another entity or entities, assists county agencies, investigative teams and law enforcement by providing services, including forensic interviews,

medical evaluations, therapeutic interventions, victim support and advocacy, team case reviews and a system for case tracking.

"Cooperation with an investigation or assessment." Includes, but is not limited to, a school or school district which permits authorized personnel from the department or county agency to interview a student while the student is in attendance at school.

"County agency." The county children and youth social service agency established pursuant to section 405 of the act of June 24, 1937 (P.L. 2017, No. 396),1 known as the County Institution District Law, or its successor, and supervised by the department under Article IX of the act of June 13, 1967 (P.L. 31, No. 21),2 known as the Public Welfare Code.

"Department." The Department of Human Services of the Commonwealth.

"Direct contact with children." The care, supervision, guidance or control of children or routine interaction with children.

"Direct volunteer contact." The care, supervision, guidance or control of children and routine interaction with children.

"Education enterprise." An educational activity in this Commonwealth:

(1) for which college credits or continuing education units are awarded, continuing professional education is offered or tuition or fees are charged or collected; and

(2) that is sponsored by a corporation, entity or institution that is incorporated or authorized by other means in a state other than this Commonwealth and is approved and authorized to operate in this Commonwealth under 15 Pa.C.S. Pt. II Subpt. B (relating to business corporations)3 or C (relating to nonprofit corporations)4 and 24 Pa.C.S. Ch. 65 (relating to private colleges, universities and seminaries).

"Electronic technologies." The transfer of information in whole or in part by technology having electrical, digital, magnetic, wireless, optical, electromagnetic, photo-electronic or photo-optical systems, or similar capabilities. The term includes, but is not limited to, e-mail, Internet communication or other means of electronic transmission.

"Expunge." To strike out or obliterate entirely so that the expunged information may not be stored, identified or later recovered by any mechanical or electronic means or otherwise.

"Family child-care home." A residence where child day care is provided at any time to no less than four children and no more than six children who are not relatives of the caregiver.

"Family members." Spouses, parents and children or other persons related by consanguinity or affinity.

"Founded report." A child abuse report involving a perpetrator that is made pursuant to this chapter, if any of the following applies:

(1) There has been a judicial adjudication based on a finding that a child who is a subject of the report has been abused and the adjudication involves the same factual circumstances involved in the allegation of child abuse. The judicial adjudication may include any of the following:

(i) The entry of a plea of guilty or nolo contendere.

(ii) A finding of guilt to a criminal charge.

(iii) A finding of dependency under 42 Pa.C.S. § 6341 (relating to adjudication) if the court has entered a finding that a child who is the subject of the report has been abused.

(iv) A finding of delinquency under 42 Pa.C.S. § 6341 if the court has entered a finding that the child who is the subject of the report has been abused by the child who was found to be delinquent.

(2) There has been an acceptance into an accelerated rehabilitative disposition program and the reason for the acceptance involves the same factual circumstances involved in the allegation of child abuse.

(3) There has been a consent decree entered in a juvenile proceeding under 42 Pa.C.S. Ch. 63 (relating to juvenile matters), the decree involves the same factual circumstances involved in the allegation of child abuse and the terms and conditions of the consent decree include an acknowledgment, admission or finding that a child who is the subject of the report has been abused by the child who is alleged to be delinquent.

(4) A final protection from abuse order has been granted under section 6108 (relating to relief), when the child who is a subject of the report is one of the individuals protected under the protection from abuse order and:

(i) Only one individual is charged with the abuse in the protection from abuse action;

(ii) Only that individual defends against the charge;

(iii) The adjudication involves the same factual circumstances involved in the allegation of child abuse; and

(iv) The protection from abuse adjudication finds that the child abuse occurred.

"General protective services." Those services and activities provided by each county agency for cases requiring protective services, as defined by the department in regulations.

"Health care facility." As defined in section 802.1 of the act of July 19, 1979 (P.L. 130, No. 48),5 known as the Health Care Facilities Act.

"Health care provider." A licensed hospital or health care facility or person who is licensed, certified or otherwise regulated to provide health care services under the laws of this Commonwealth, including a physician, podiatrist, optometrist, psychologist, physical therapist, certified nurse practitioner, registered nurse, nurse midwife, physician's assistant, chiropractor, dentist, pharmacist or an individual accredited or certified to provide behavioral health services.

"Immediate vicinity." An area in which an individual is physically present with a child and can see, hear, direct and assess the activities of the child.

"Independent contractor." An individual who provides a program, activity or service to an agency, institution, organization or other entity, including a school or regularly established religious organization, that is responsible for the care, supervision, guidance or control of children. The term does not apply to administrative or other support personnel unless the administrative or other support personnel have direct contact with children.

"Indicated report."

(1) Subject to paragraphs (2) and (3), a report of child abuse made pursuant to this chapter if an investigation by the department or county agency determines that substantial evidence of the alleged abuse by a perpetrator exists based on any of the following:

(i) Available medical evidence.

(ii) The child protective service investigation.

(iii) An admission of the acts of abuse by the perpetrator.

(2) A report may be indicated under paragraph (1)(i) or (ii) for any child who is the victim of child abuse, regardless of the number of alleged perpetrators.

(3) A report may be indicated under paragraph (1)(i) or (ii) listing the perpetrator as "unknown" if substantial evidence of abuse by a perpetrator exists, but the department or county agency is unable to identify the specific perpetrator.

"Institution of higher education." Any of the following:

(1) A community college which is an institution now or hereafter created pursuant to Article XIX-A of the act of March 10, 1949 (P.L. 30, No. 14),6 known as the Public School Code of 1949, or the act of August 24, 1963 (P.L. 1132, No. 484),7 known as the Community College Act of 1963.

(2) An independent institution of higher education which is an institution of higher education located in and incorporated or chartered by the Commonwealth, entitled to confer degrees as set forth in 24 Pa.C.S. § 6505 (relating to power to confer degrees) and entitled to apply to itself the designation "college," "university" or "seminary" as provided for by standards and qualifications prescribed by the State Board of Education under 24 Pa.C.S. Ch. 65.

(3) A State-owned institution.

(4) A State-related institution.

(5) An education enterprise.

"Intentionally." The term shall have the same meaning as provided in 18 Pa.C.S. § 302 (relating to general requirements of culpability).

"Knowingly." The term shall have the same meaning as provided in 18 Pa.C.S. § 302 (relating to general requirements of culpability).

"Law enforcement official." The term includes the following:

(1) The Attorney General.

(2) A Pennsylvania district attorney.

(3) A Pennsylvania State Police officer.

(4) A municipal police officer.

"Mandated reporter." A person who is required by this chapter to make a report of suspected child abuse.

"Matriculated student." A student who is enrolled in an institution of higher education and pursuing a program of study that results in a postsecondary credential, such as a certificate, diploma or degree.

"Near fatality." A child's serious or critical condition, as certified by a physician, where that child is a subject of the report of child abuse.

"Newborn." As defined in section 6502 (relating to definitions).

"Parent." A biological parent, adoptive parent or legal guardian.

"Perpetrator." A person who has committed child abuse as defined in this section. The following shall apply:

(1) The term includes only the following:

(i) A parent of the child.

(ii) A spouse or former spouse of the child's parent.

(iii) A paramour or former paramour of the child's parent.

(iv) A person 14 years of age or older and responsible for the child's welfare or having direct contact with children as an employee of child-care services, a school or through a program, activity or service.

(v) An individual 14 years of age or older who resides in the same home as the child.

(vi) An individual 18 years of age or older who does not reside in the same home as the child but is related within the third degree of consanguinity or affinity by birth or adoption to the child.

(vii) An individual 18 years of age or older who engages a child in severe forms of trafficking in persons or sex trafficking, as those terms are defined under section 103 of the Trafficking Victims Protection Act of 2000 (114 Stat. 1466, 22 U.S.C. § 7102).

(2) Only the following may be considered a perpetrator for failing to act, as provided in this section:

(i) A parent of the child.

(ii) A spouse or former spouse of the child's parent.

(iii) A paramour or former paramour of the child's parent.

(iv) A person 18 years of age or older and responsible for the child's welfare.

(v) A person 18 years of age or older who resides in the same home as the child.

"Person affiliated with." A person that directly or indirectly, through one or more intermediaries, controls, is controlled by or is under common control with a specified person.

"Person responsible for the child's welfare." A person who provides permanent or temporary care, supervision, mental health diagnosis or treatment, training or control of a child in lieu of parental care, supervision and control.

"Police department." A public agency of a political subdivision having general police powers and charged with making arrests in connection with the enforcement of criminal or traffic laws.

"Police officer." A full-time or part-time employee assigned to criminal or traffic law enforcement duties of a police department of a county, city, borough, town or township. The term also includes a member of the State Police Force.

"Police station." The station or headquarters of a police department or a Pennsylvania State Police station or headquarters.

"Private agency." A children and youth social service agency subject to the requirements of 55 Pa. Code Ch. 3680 (relating to administration and operation of a children and youth social service agency).

"Program, activity or service." Any of the following in which children participate and which is sponsored by a school or a public or private organization:

(1) A youth camp or program.

(2) A recreational camp or program.

(3) A sports or athletic program.

(4) A community or social outreach program.

(5) An enrichment or educational program.

(6) A troop, club or similar organization.

"Protective services." Those services and activities provided by the department and each county agency for children who are abused or are alleged to be in need of protection under this chapter.

"Recent act." Any act committed within two years of the date of the report to the department or county agency.

"Recent act or failure to act." Any act or failure to act committed within two years of the date of the report to the department or county agency.

"Recklessly." The term shall have the same meaning as provided in 18 Pa.C.S. § 302 (relating to general requirements of culpability).

"Resource family." A family which provides temporary foster or kinship care for children who need out-of-home placement and may eventually provide permanency for those children, including an adoptive family.

"Risk assessment." A Commonwealth-approved systematic process that assesses a child's need for protection or services based on the risk of harm to the child.

"Routine interaction." Regular and repeated contact that is integral to a person's employment or volunteer responsibilities.

"Safety assessment." A Commonwealth-approved systematic process that assesses a child's need for protection or services, based on the threat to the safety of the child.

"School." A facility providing elementary, secondary or postsecondary educational services. The term includes the following:

(1) Any school of a school district.

(2) An area vocational-technical school.8

(3) A joint school.

(4) An intermediate unit.

(5) A charter school or regional charter school.

(6) A cyber charter school.

(7) A private school licensed under the act of January 28, 1988 (P.L. 24, No. 11),9 known as the Private Academic Schools Act.

(8) A private school accredited by an accrediting association approved by the State Board of Education.

(9) A nonpublic school.

(10) An institution of higher education.

(11) to (13) Deleted by 2015, July 1, P.L. 94, No. 15, § 1, imd. effective.

(14) A private school licensed under the act of December 15, 1986 (P.L. 1585, No. 174),10 known as the Private Licensed Schools Act.

(15) The Hiram G. Andrews Center.

(16) A private residential rehabilitative institution as defined in section 914.1-A(c) of the Public School Code of 1949.11

"School employee." An individual who is employed by a school or who provides a program, activity or service sponsored by a school. The term does not apply to administrative or other support personnel unless the administrative or other support personnel have direct contact with children.

"Secretary." The Secretary of Human Services of the Commonwealth.

"Serious bodily injury." Bodily injury which creates a substantial risk of death or which causes serious permanent disfigurement or protracted loss or impairment of function of any bodily member or organ.

"Serious mental injury." A psychological condition, as diagnosed by a physician or licensed psychologist, including the refusal of appropriate treatment, that:

(1) renders a child chronically and severely anxious, agitated, depressed, socially withdrawn, psychotic or in reasonable fear that the child's life or safety is threatened; or

(2) seriously interferes with a child's ability to accomplish age-appropriate developmental and social tasks.

"Serious physical neglect." Any of the following when committed by a perpetrator that endangers a child's life or health, threatens a child's well-being, causes bodily injury or impairs a child's health, development or functioning:

(1) A repeated, prolonged or egregious failure to supervise a child in a manner that is appropriate considering the child's developmental age and abilities.

(2) The failure to provide a child with adequate essentials of life, including food, shelter or medical care.

"Sexual abuse or exploitation." Any of the following:

(1) The employment, use, persuasion, inducement, enticement or coercion of a child to engage in or assist another individual to engage in sexually explicit conduct, which includes, but is not limited to, the following:

(i) Looking at the sexual or other intimate parts of a child or another individual for the purpose of arousing or gratifying sexual desire in any individual.

(ii) Participating in sexually explicit conversation either in person, by telephone, by computer or by a computer-aided device for the purpose of sexual stimulation or gratification of any individual.

(iii) Actual or simulated sexual activity or nudity for the purpose of sexual stimulation or gratification of any individual.

(iv) Actual or simulated sexual activity for the purpose of producing visual depiction, including photographing, videotaping, computer depicting or filming.

This paragraph does not include consensual activities between a child who is 14 years of age or older and another person who is 14 years of age or older and whose age is within four years of the child's age.

(2) Any of the following offenses committed against a child:

(i) Rape as defined in 18 Pa.C.S. § 3121 (relating to rape).

(ii) Statutory sexual assault as defined in 18 Pa.C.S. § 3122.1 (relating to statutory sexual assault).

(iii) Involuntary deviate sexual intercourse as defined in 18 Pa.C.S. § 3123 (relating to involuntary deviate sexual intercourse).

(iv) Sexual assault as defined in 18 Pa.C.S. § 3124.1 (relating to sexual assault).

(v) Institutional sexual assault as defined in 18 Pa.C.S. § 3124.2 (relating to institutional sexual assault).

(vi) Aggravated indecent assault as defined in 18 Pa.C.S. § 3125 (relating to aggravated indecent assault).

(vii) Indecent assault as defined in 18 Pa.C.S. § 3126 (relating to indecent assault).

(viii) Indecent exposure as defined in 18 Pa.C.S. § 3127 (relating to indecent exposure).

(ix) Incest as defined in 18 Pa.C.S. § 4302 (relating to incest).

(x) Prostitution as defined in 18 Pa.C.S. § 5902 (relating to prostitution and related offenses).

(xi) Sexual abuse as defined in 18 Pa.C.S. § 6312 (relating to sexual abuse of children).

(xii) Unlawful contact with a minor as defined in 18 Pa.C.S. § 6318 (relating to unlawful contact with minor).

(xiii) Sexual exploitation as defined in 18 Pa.C.S. § 6320 (relating to sexual exploitation of children).

"Student." An individual enrolled in a public or private school, intermediate unit or area vocational-technical school who is under 18 years of age.

"Subject of the report." Any child, parent, guardian or other person responsible for the welfare of a child or any alleged or actual perpetrator in a report made to the department or a county agency under this chapter.

"Substantial evidence." Evidence which outweighs inconsistent evidence and which a reasonable person would accept as adequate to support a conclusion.

"Substantiated child abuse." Child abuse as to which there is an indicated report or founded report.

"Under investigation." A child abuse report pursuant to this chapter which is being investigated to determine whether it is "founded," "indicated" or "unfounded."

"Unfounded report." Any report made pursuant to this chapter unless the report is a "founded report" or an "indicated report."

(b) Deleted by 2013, Dec. 18, P.L. 1170, No. 108, § 1, effective Dec. 31, 2014.

(b.1) Child abuse.--The term **"child abuse"** shall mean intentionally, knowingly or recklessly doing any of the following:

(1) Causing bodily injury to a child through any recent act or failure to act.

(2) Fabricating, feigning or intentionally exaggerating or inducing a medical symptom or disease which results in a potentially harmful medical evaluation or treatment to the child through any recent act.

(3) Causing or substantially contributing to serious mental injury to a child through any act or failure to act or a series of such acts or failures to act.

(4) Causing sexual abuse or exploitation of a child through any act or failure to act.

(5) Creating a reasonable likelihood of bodily injury to a child through any recent act or failure to act.

(6) Creating a likelihood of sexual abuse or exploitation of a child through any recent act or failure to act.

(7) Causing serious physical neglect of a child.

(8) Engaging in any of the following recent acts:

(i) Kicking, biting, throwing, burning, stabbing or cutting a child in a manner that endangers the child.

(ii) Unreasonably restraining or confining a child, based on consideration of the method, location or the duration of the restraint or confinement.

(iii) Forcefully shaking a child under one year of age.

(iv) Forcefully slapping or otherwise striking a child under one year of age.

(v) Interfering with the breathing of a child.

(vi) Causing a child to be present at a location while a violation of 18 Pa.C.S. § 7508.2 (relating to operation of methamphetamine laboratory) is occurring, provided that the violation is being investigated by law enforcement.

(vii) Leaving a child unsupervised with an individual, other than the child's parent, who the actor knows or reasonably should have known:

(A) Is required to register as a Tier II or Tier III sexual offender under 42 Pa.C.S. Ch. 97 Subch. H (relating to registration of sexual offenders),12 where the victim of the sexual offense was under 18 years of age when the crime was committed.

(B) Has been determined to be a sexually violent predator under 42 Pa.C.S. § 9799.24 (relating to assessments) or any of its predecessors.

(C) Has been determined to be a sexually violent delinquent child as defined in 42 Pa.C.S. § 9799.12 (relating to definitions).

(D) Has been determined to be a sexually violent predator under 42 Pa.C.S. § 9799.58 (relating to assessments) or has to register for life under 42 Pa.C.S. § 9799.55(b) (relating to registration).

(9) Causing the death of the child through any act or failure to act.

(10) Engaging a child in a severe form of trafficking in persons or sex trafficking, as those terms are defined under section 103 of the Trafficking Victims Protection Act of 2000 (114 Stat. 1466).

SUBCHAPTER B

PROVISIONS AND RESPONSIBILITIES FOR REPORTING SUSPECTED CHILD ABUSE

Sec.

6311. Persons required to report suspected child abuse.

6311.1. Privileged communications.

6312. Persons encouraged to report suspected child abuse.

6313. Reporting procedure.

6314. Photographs, medical tests and X-rays of child subject to report.

6315. Taking child into protective custody.

6316. Admission to private and public hospitals.

6317. Mandatory reporting and postmortem investigation of deaths.

6318. Immunity from liability.

6319. Penalties.

6320. Protection from employment discrimination.

Effective: July 1, 2015

23 Pa.C.S.A. § 6311

§ 6311. Persons required to report suspected child abuse

(a) Mandated reporters.--The following adults shall make a report of suspected child abuse, subject to subsection (b), if the person has reasonable cause to suspect that a child is a victim of child abuse:

(1) A person licensed or certified to practice in any health-related field under the jurisdiction of the Department of State.

(2) A medical examiner, coroner or funeral director.

(3) An employee of a health care facility or provider licensed by the Department of Health, who is engaged in the admission, examination, care or treatment of individuals.

(4) A school employee.

(5) An employee of a child-care service who has direct contact with children in the course of employment.

(6) A clergyman, priest, rabbi, minister, Christian Science practitioner, religious healer or spiritual leader of any regularly established church or other religious organization.

(7) An individual paid or unpaid, who, on the basis of the individual's role as an integral part of a regularly scheduled program, activity or service, is a person responsible for the child's welfare or has direct contact with children.

(8) An employee of a social services agency who has direct contact with children in the course of employment.

(9) A peace officer or law enforcement official.

(10) An emergency medical services provider certified by the Department of Health.

(11) An employee of a public library who has direct contact with children in the course of employment.

(12) An individual supervised or managed by a person listed under paragraphs (1), (2), (3), (4), (5), (6), (7), (8), (9), (10), (11) and (13), who has direct contact with children in the course of employment.

(13) An independent contractor.

(14) An attorney affiliated with an agency, institution, organization or other entity, including a school or regularly established religious organization that is responsible for the care, supervision, guidance or control of children.

(15) A foster parent.

(16) An adult family member who is a person responsible for the child's welfare and provides services to a child in a family living home, community home for individuals with an intellectual disability or host home for children which are subject to supervision or licensure by the department under Articles IX and X of the act of June 13, 1967 (P.L. 31, No. 21),1 known as the Public Welfare Code.

(b) Basis to report.--

(1) A mandated reporter enumerated in subsection (a) shall make a report of suspected child abuse in accordance with section 6313 (relating to reporting procedure), if the mandated reporter has reasonable cause to suspect that a child is a victim of child abuse under any of the following circumstances:

(i) The mandated reporter comes into contact with the child in the course of employment, occupation and practice of a profession or through a regularly scheduled program, activity or service.

(ii) The mandated reporter is directly responsible for the care, supervision, guidance or training of the child, or is affiliated with an agency, institution, organization, school, regularly established church or religious organization or other entity that is directly responsible for the care, supervision, guidance or training of the child.

(iii) A person makes a specific disclosure to the mandated reporter that an identifiable child is the victim of child abuse.

(iv) An individual 14 years of age or older makes a specific disclosure to the mandated reporter that the individual has committed child abuse.

(2) Nothing in this section shall require a child to come before the mandated reporter in order for the mandated reporter to make a report of suspected child abuse.

(3) Nothing in this section shall require the mandated reporter to identify the person responsible for the child abuse to make a report of suspected child abuse.

(c) Staff members of institutions, etc.--Whenever a person is required to report under subsection (b) in the capacity as a member of the staff of a medical or other public or private institution, school, facility or agency, that person shall report immediately in accordance with section 6313 and shall immediately thereafter notify the person in charge of the institution, school, facility or agency or the designated agent of the person in charge. Upon notification, the person in charge or the designated agent, if any, shall facilitate the cooperation of the institution, school, facility or agency with the investigation of the report. Any intimidation, retaliation or obstruction in the investigation of the report is subject to the provisions of 18 Pa.C.S. § 4958 (relating to intimidation, retaliation or obstruction in child abuse cases). This chapter does not require more than one report from any such institution, school, facility or agency.

§ 6311.1. Privileged communications.

(a) General rule.--Subject to subsection (b), the privileged communications between a mandated reporter and a patient or client of the mandated reporter shall not:

(1) Apply to a situation involving child abuse.

(2) Relieve the mandated reporter of the duty to make a report of suspected child abuse.

(b) Confidential communications.--The following protections shall apply:

(1) Confidential communications made to a member of the clergy are protected under 42 Pa.C.S. § 5943 (relating to confidential communications to clergymen).

(2) Confidential communications made to an attorney are protected so long as they are within the scope of 42 Pa.C.S. §§ 5916 (relating to confidential communications to attorney) and 5928 (relating to confidential communications to attorney), the attorney work product doctrine or the rules of professional conduct for attorneys.

§ 6312. Persons encouraged to report suspected child abuse.

Any person may make an oral or written report of suspected child abuse, which may be submitted electronically, or cause a report of suspected child abuse to be made to the department, county agency or law enforcement, if that person has reasonable cause to suspect that a child is a victim of child abuse.

§ 6313. Reporting procedure.

(a) Report by mandated reporter.--

(1) A mandated reporter shall immediately make an oral report of suspected child abuse to the department via the Statewide toll-free telephone number under section 6332 (relating to establishment of Statewide toll-free telephone number) or a written report using electronic technologies under section 6305 (relating to electronic reporting).

(2) A mandated reporter making an oral report under paragraph (1) of suspected child abuse shall also make a written report, which may be submitted electronically, within 48 hours to the department or county agency assigned to the case in a manner and format prescribed by the department.

(3) The failure of the mandated reporter to file the report under paragraph (2) shall not relieve the county agency from any duty under this chapter, and the county agency shall proceed as though the mandated reporter complied with paragraph (2).

(b) **Contents of report.**--A written report of suspected child abuse, which may be submitted electronically, shall include the following information, if known:

(1) The names and addresses of the child, the child's parents and any other person responsible for the child's welfare.

(2) Where the suspected abuse occurred.

(3) The age and sex of each subject of the report.

(4) The nature and extent of the suspected child abuse, including any evidence of prior abuse to the child or any sibling of the child.

(5) The name and relationship of each individual responsible for causing the suspected abuse and any evidence of prior abuse by each individual.

(6) Family composition.

(7) The source of the report.

(8) The name, telephone number and e-mail address of the person making the report.

(9) The actions taken by the person making the report, including those actions taken under section 6314 (relating to photographs, medical tests and X-rays of child subject to report), 6315 (relating to taking child into protective custody), 6316 (relating to admission to private and public hospitals) or 6317 (relating to mandatory reporting and postmortem investigation of deaths).

(10) Any other information required by Federal law or regulation.

(11) Any other information that the department requires by regulation.

(c), (d) Repealed by 2014, April 15, P.L. 417, No. 33, § 2, effective Dec. 31, 2014.

(e) **Applicability of Mental Health Procedures Act.**--Notwithstanding any other provision of law, a mandated reporter enumerated under section 6311 (relating to persons required to report suspected child abuse) who makes a report of suspected child abuse pursuant to this section or who makes a report of a crime against a child to law enforcement officials shall not be in violation of the act of July 9, 1976 (P.L. 817, No. 143),1 known as the Mental Health Procedures Act, by releasing information necessary to complete the report.

§ 6314. Photographs, medical tests and X-rays of child subject to report.

A person or official required to report cases of suspected child abuse may take or cause to be taken photographs of the child who is subject to a report and, if clinically indicated, cause to be performed a radiological examination and other medical tests on the child. Medical summaries or reports of the photographs, X-rays and relevant medical tests taken shall be sent to the county agency at the time the written report is sent or within 48 hours after a report is made by electronic technologies or as soon thereafter as possible. The county agency shall have access to actual photographs or duplicates and X-rays and may obtain them or duplicates of them upon request. Medical summaries or reports of the photographs, X-rays and relevant medical tests shall be made available to law enforcement officials in the course of investigating cases pursuant to section 6340(a)(9) or (10) (relating to release of information in confidential reports).

§ 6315. Taking child into protective custody.

(a) General rule.--A child may be taken into protective custody:

(1) As provided by 42 Pa.C.S. § 6324 (relating to taking into custody).

(2) By a physician examining or treating the child or by the director, or a person specifically designated in writing by the director, of any hospital or other medical institution where the child is being treated if protective custody is immediately necessary to protect the child under this chapter.

(3) By a physician or the director, or a person specifically designated by the director, of a hospital pursuant to Chapter 65 (relating to newborn protection) if the child is a newborn.

(4) Subject to this section and after receipt of a court order, the county agency shall take a child into protective custody for protection from abuse. No county agency worker may take custody of the child without judicial authorization based on the merits of the situation.

(5) By a police officer at a police station under Chapter 65.

(6) By an emergency services provider on the grounds of an entity that employs or otherwise provides access to the emergency services provider under Chapter 65.

(b) Duration of custody.--No child may be held in protective custody for more than 24 hours unless the appropriate county agency is immediately notified that the child has been taken into custody and the county agency obtains an order from a court of competent jurisdiction permitting the child to be held in custody for a longer period. Each court shall insure that a judge is available 24 hours a day, 365 days a year to accept and decide the actions brought by a county agency under this subsection within the 24-hour period.

(c) Notice of custody.--

(1) Except as provided in paragraph (2), an individual taking a child into protective custody under this chapter shall immediately, and within 24 hours in writing, notify the parent, guardian or other custodian of the child of the whereabouts of the child, unless prohibited by court order, and the reasons for the need to take the child into protective custody and shall immediately notify the appropriate county agency in order that proceedings under 42 Pa.C.S. Ch. 63 (relating to juvenile matters) may be initiated, if appropriate.

(2) In the case of a newborn taken into protective custody pursuant to subsection (a)(3), the county agency shall within 24 hours make diligent efforts to notify a parent, guardian, custodian or other family member of the whereabouts of the newborn, unless prohibited by court order, and the reasons for the need to take the newborn into protective custody.

(d) Informal hearing.--In no case shall protective custody under this chapter be maintained longer than 72 hours without an informal hearing under 42 Pa.C.S. § 6332 (relating to informal hearing). If, at the hearing, it is determined that protective custody shall be continued and the child is alleged to be without proper parental care or control or is alleged to be a dependent child under 42 Pa.C.S. § 6302 (relating to definitions), the county agency shall within 48 hours file a petition with the court under 42 Pa.C.S. Ch. 63 alleging that the child is a dependent child.

(e) Place of detention.--No child taken into protective custody under this chapter may be detained during the protective custody except in an appropriate medical facility, foster home or other appropriate facility approved by the department for this purpose.

(f) Conference with parent or other custodian.--A conference between the parent, guardian or other custodian of the child taken into temporary protective custody pursuant to this section and the employee designated by the county agency to be responsible for the child shall be held within 48 hours of the time that the child is taken into custody for the purpose of:

(1) Explaining to the parent, guardian or other custodian the reasons for the temporary detention of the child and the whereabouts of the child, unless prohibited by court order.

(2) Expediting, wherever possible, the return of the child to the custody of the parent, guardian or other custodian where custody is no longer necessary.

(3) Explaining to the parent, guardian or other custodian the rights provided for under 42 Pa.C.S. §§ 6337 (relating to right to counsel) and 6338 (relating to other basic rights).

§ 6316. Admission to private and public hospitals.

(a) General rule.--Children appearing to suffer any physical or mental condition which may constitute child abuse shall be admitted to, treated and maintained in facilities of private and public hospitals on the basis of medical need and shall not be refused or deprived in any way of proper medical treatment and care.

(a.1) Newborns.--A newborn taken into protective custody pursuant to section 6315(a)(3) or (5) (relating to taking child into protective custody) shall be admitted to, treated and maintained in facilities of public and private hospitals on the basis of medical need and shall not be refused or deprived in any way of proper medical treatment and care. Once a newborn is taken into protective custody pursuant to section 6315(a) (3) or (5), the newborn shall be considered immediately eligible for Medicaid for payment of medical services provided. Until otherwise provided by court order, the county agency shall assume the responsibility for making decisions regarding the newborn's medical care.

(b) Failure of hospital to admit child or newborn.--The failure of a hospital to admit and properly treat and care for a child pursuant to subsection (a) or (a.1) shall be cause for the department to order immediate admittance, treatment and care by the hospital which shall be enforceable, if necessary, by the prompt institution of a civil action by the department. The child, through an attorney, shall also have the additional and independent right to seek immediate injunctive relief and institute an appropriate civil action for damages against the hospital.

§ 6317. Mandatory reporting and postmortem investigation of deaths.

A person or official required to report cases of suspected child abuse, including employees of a county agency, who has reasonable cause to suspect that a child died as a result of child abuse shall report that suspicion to the appropriate coroner or medical examiner. The coroner or medical examiner shall accept the report for investigation and shall report his finding to the police, the district attorney, the appropriate county agency and, if the report is made by a hospital, the hospital.

§ 6318. Immunity from liability.

(a) General rule.--A person, hospital, institution, school, facility, agency or agency employee acting in good faith shall have immunity from civil and criminal liability that might otherwise result from any of the following:

(1) Making a report of suspected child abuse or making a referral for general protective services, regardless of whether the report is required to be made under this chapter.

(2) Cooperating or consulting with an investigation under this chapter, including providing information to a child fatality or near-fatality review team.

(3) Testifying in a proceeding arising out of an instance of suspected child abuse or general protective services.

(4) Engaging in any action authorized under section 6314 (relating to photographs, medical tests and X-rays of child subject to report), 6315 (relating to taking child into protective custody), 6316 (relating to

admission to private and public hospitals) or 6317 (relating to mandatory reporting and postmortem investigation of deaths).

(b) Departmental and county agency immunity.--An official or employee of the department or county agency who refers a report of suspected child abuse for general protective services to law enforcement authorities or provides services as authorized by this chapter shall have immunity from civil and criminal liability that might otherwise result from the action.

(c) Presumption of good faith.--For the purpose of any civil or criminal proceeding, the good faith of a person required to report pursuant to section 6311 (relating to persons required to report suspected child abuse) and of any person required to make a referral to law enforcement officers under this chapter shall be presumed.

§ 6319. Penalties.

(a) Failure to report or refer.--
(1) A person or official required by this chapter to report a case of suspected child abuse or to make a referral to the appropriate authorities commits an offense if the person or official willfully fails to do so.
(2) An offense under this section is a felony of the third degree if:
(i) the person or official willfully fails to report;
(ii) the child abuse constitutes a felony of the first degree or higher; and
(iii) the person or official has direct knowledge of the nature of the abuse.
(3) An offense not otherwise specified in paragraph (2) is a misdemeanor of the second degree.
(4) A report of suspected child abuse to law enforcement or the appropriate county agency by a mandated reporter, made in lieu of a report to the department, shall not constitute an offense under this subsection, provided that the report was made in a good faith effort to comply with the requirements of this chapter.
(b) Continuing course of action.--If a person's willful failure under this section to report an individual suspected of child abuse continues while the person knows or has reasonable cause to suspect a child is being subjected to child abuse by the same individual, or while the person knows or has reasonable cause to suspect that the same individual continues to have direct contact with children through the individual's employment, program, activity or service, the person commits a felony of the third degree, except that if the child abuse constitutes a felony of the first degree or higher, the person commits a felony of the second degree.
(c) Multiple offenses.--A person who, at the time of sentencing for an offense under this section, has been convicted of a prior offense under this section commits a felony of the third degree, except that if the child abuse constitutes a felony of the first degree or higher, the penalty for the second or subsequent offenses is a felony of the second degree.
(d) Statute of limitations.--The statute of limitations for an offense under this section shall be either the statute of limitations for the crime committed against the minor child or five years, whichever is greater.

§ 6320. Protection from employment discrimination.

(a) Basis for relief.--A person may commence an action for appropriate relief if all of the following apply:

(1) The person is required to report under section 6311 (relating to persons required to report suspected child abuse) or encouraged to report under section 6312 (relating to persons encouraged to report suspected child abuse).

(2) The person acted in good faith in making or causing the report of suspected child abuse to be made.

(3) As a result of making the report of suspected child abuse, the person is discharged from employment or is discriminated against with respect to compensation, hire, tenure, terms, conditions or privileges of employment.

(b) Applicability.--This section does not apply to an individual making a report of suspected child abuse who is found to be a perpetrator because of the report or to any individual who fails to make a report of suspected child abuse as required under section 6311 and is subject to conviction under section 6319 (relating to penalties) for failure to report or to refer.

(c) Location.--An action under this section must be filed in the court of common pleas of the county in which the alleged unlawful discharge or discrimination occurred.

(d) Relief.--Upon a finding in favor of the plaintiff, the court may grant appropriate relief, which may include reinstatement of the plaintiff with back pay.

(e) Departmental intervention.--The department may intervene in an action commenced under this section.

Questions for Discussion:

1. Are mediators mandated reporters under the Pennsylvania statute? Does it make a difference what the mediator's "primary profession" is? In other words, does a licensed psychologist mediator have a different duty from that of an attorney-mediator?

2. What provision under §6311 (b) requires a report to be made based on second-hand knowledge?

3. Does an attorney mediator violate confidentiality under §6311.1 if a report is made?

Rule 1.6 of the ABA Model Rules of Professional Conduct for attorneys provides:

Client-Lawyer Relationship

(a) A lawyer shall not reveal information relating to the representation of a client unless the client gives informed consent, the disclosure is impliedly authorized in order to carry out the representation or the disclosure is permitted by paragraph (b).

(b) A lawyer may reveal information relating to the representation of a client to the extent the lawyer reasonably believes necessary:

(1) to prevent reasonably certain death or substantial bodily harm;

(2) to prevent the client from committing a crime or fraud that is reasonably certain to result in substantial injury to the financial interests or property of another and in furtherance of which the client has used or is using the lawyer's services;

(3) to prevent, mitigate or rectify substantial injury to the financial interests or property of another that is reasonably certain to result or has resulted from the client's commission of a crime or fraud in furtherance of which the client has used the lawyer's services;

(4) to secure legal advice about the lawyer's compliance with these Rules;

(5) to establish a claim or defense on behalf of the lawyer in a controversy between the lawyer and the client, to establish a defense to a criminal charge or civil claim against the lawyer based upon conduct in which the client was involved, or to respond to allegations in any proceeding concerning the lawyer's representation of the client;

(6) to comply with other law or a court order; or

(7) to detect and resolve conflicts of interest arising from the lawyer's change of employment or from changes in the composition or ownership of a firm, but only if the revealed information would not compromise the attorney-client privilege or otherwise prejudice the client.

(c) A lawyer shall make reasonable efforts to prevent the inadvertent or unauthorized disclosure of, or unauthorized access to, information relating to the representation of a client.

A Final Note on Child Abuse Reporting

Every state[121] as well as the District of Columbia, Guam, Puerto Rico and the Virgin Islands has child abuse reporting laws similar to the examples given, although they vary greatly in style and content. The penalty for failure to report includes criminal sanctions. Immunity is given to the reporter for ramifications of making the report in good faith, such as protection in employment and immunity from liability for a false report. Most statutes enumerate, inexhaustively, mandated reporters. Only five states, Kansas,[122] Louisiana,[123] Nebraska,[124] Virginia,[125] and Wisconsin[126] include "mediator" among the enumerated reporters. Oregon[127] and Wisconsin[128] state that a mediator does not violate confidentiality by reporting child abuse. Other states simply state that anyone who becomes aware of child abuse has a duty to report it, with some exceptions. New Jersey,[129] North Carolina,[130] Rhode Island[131], Tennessee[132], Utah,[133] and Wyoming[134] are among this group. Florida,[135] New Mexico,[136] South Carolina[137] Tennessee,[138] and West Virginia[139] include judges among their mandated reporters. Most states require religious healing practitioners to report abuse or the withholding of medical care,[140] while some states specifically exempt them.[141] Time required within which to report abuse varies from immediately,[142] promptly,[143] at the first opportunity but no longer than 48 hours,[144] and most statutes prescribe a minimum period within which the investigation must commence most commonly 48 hours. In some states,[145] an attorney is a mandated

---

[121] 50 State Statutory Survey, Westlaw, 2007
[122] K.S.A. 38-2223.
[123] LSA-Ch. C. Art. 603.
[124] Nebraska, Neb.Rev.St. § 43-2939.
[125] Virginia Ann. Code 63.2-1509.
[126] WIST 48.98 1 (Also protects unborn children at risk).
[127] O.R.S. §36.222 permits mediator to report if mediator is listed as a person required to report under ORS 419 B.010.
[128] W.S.A. 904-085.
[129] NJ ST 9:6-8.10.
[130] N.C.G.S.A. § 7B-301.
[131] Gen Laws 1956 §40-11-3.
[132] T.C.A. §37-1-403.
[133] U.C.A. 1953 §62A-4a-403.
[134] W.S. 1977 §14-3 205.
[135] West's F.S.A. §39.201.
[136] N.M.S.A. 1978 §32A-4-3.
[137] S.C. Ann Code §63-7-310.
[138] Tenn. Ann Code §37-1-403.
[139] W.Va. Code §49-2-803(c).
[140] e.g., Arizona. A.R.S. 13-3620, Arkansas A.C.A. 12-18-402, Colorado C.R.S.A. 19-3-304, New Hampshire N.H. Rev. Stat. § 169-C: 29, South Carolina Code 1976 § 63-7-310.
[141] Alaska. AS 47-17-020 (In pertinent part: "This section does not require a religious healing practitioner to report as neglect of a child the failure to provide medical attention to the child if the child is provided treatment solely by spiritual means through prayer in accordance with the tenets and practices of a recognized church or religious denomination by an accredited practitioner of the church or denomination."), Idaho (report made by confession) I.C. 16-1605.
[142] Mississippi, Miss. Code Ann. § 43-21-353.
[143] Montana, MCA 41-3-201.
[144] Washington, West's RWCA 26.44.030.
[145] Nevada, N.R.S. 432B.225, Ohio, R.C. § 2151.421.

reporter if the report doesn't violate attorney-client privilege. In Oklahoma, "No privilege or contract shall relieve any person from the requirement of **reporting** pursuant to this section."[146]

III. SELECTED LEGISLATION ESTABLISHING COURT-CONNECTED MEDIATION PROGRAMS

PENNSYLVANIA PA. R.C.P. 1940.1-1940.9

Editors' Notes
EXPLANATORY COMMENT--1999

Introduction

In recent years, the use of mediation as a means for alternative dispute resolution of custody and visitation cases has received widespread attention from legislators, judges, attorneys and mental health professionals. As two noted mediation experts observed: "[c]ourts are ill-equipped to mandate particular visitation schedules and custodial arrangements, the wisdom of which depend on the situations of the parents and children rather than on legal rules." Nancy G. Rogers & Craig A. McEwen, Mediation Law Policy Practice 230 (1989). Many share this frustration with the adversarial system and a growing body of research suggests that mediation may be the more satisfactory and desirable means of conflict resolution in these cases. Mediation offers more flexibility both in terms of the subject matter that may be discussed during mediation and the range of solutions available to the parties. Effective mediation also assists the parties in shaping their own framework for future discussion and resolution of conflicts that arise following separation and divorce.

In 1996, the Pennsylvania legislature amended the Divorce Code, Act No. 20-1996, § 2, codified at 23 Pa.C.S. §§ 3901-3904, to encourage local courts to establish voluntary mediation programs for divorce and custody cases. The following Rules of Civil Procedure are intended to govern custody cases only. They set forth the procedures for referring cases to mediation, minimum mediator qualifications, the duties of the mediator, the procedures for terminating mediation as well as sanctions for noncompliance with these rules. These are all areas in which statewide uniformity of practice and procedure is essential to successful mediation in Pennsylvania. These rules are flexibly designed to encourage the establishment of mediation programs.

---

[146] 10A Okl.St.Ann. § 1-2-101.

Pursuant to 23 Pa.C.S. § 3903, the Supreme Court is directed to monitor and evaluate the overall effectiveness of mediation programs statewide. At present, the Domestic Relations Procedural Rules Committee is working on the development of uniform statewide reporting requirements and evaluation forms. Reporting is necessary to assess the overall effectiveness of mediation as an alternative to litigation and it will eventually be required. The current lack of reporting requirements, however, should not be a cause for delay in the establishment of mediation programs or the implementation of statewide mediation rules.

These rules do not address confidentiality and privilege in the context of mediation. Those issues are governed by 42 Pa.C.S. § 5949, and the Committee concluded that to address them further in the rules would confuse rather than clarify any legal issues arising from the statutory language.

Rule 1940.1. Applicability of Rules to Mediation

The rules in this chapter shall apply to all court-established custody mediation programs and to any court-ordered mediation of individual custody cases.

Credits

Adopted Oct. 28, 1999, imd. effective.

Editors' Notes
EXPLANATORY COMMENT--1999

23 Pa.C.S. § 3901 authorizes a court to establish a mediation program for both divorce and custody cases. At the present time, these rules apply only to court-connected mediation of custody cases because most, if not all, court-connected mediation programs that have been established for domestic relations, are limited to mediation of custody disputes. If, in the future, these programs expand to include mediation of divorce issues, these rules will be revised accordingly.

These rules do not apply to private mediation, which may be agreed to by the parties and conducted independent of the custody proceeding. They do apply, however, whenever the court refers a custody case for mediation, regardless of whether the referral is made to a formal program established and operated by the court or to a less formal arrangement between courts and mediators such as a court-approved list of mediators or, in the absence of such a list, to individual mediators appointed by the court to mediate particular cases.

(2014)

Rule 1940.2. Definitions

As used in this Chapter, the following terms shall have the following meanings:

"Mediation" is the confidential process by which a neutral mediator assists the parties in attempting to reach a mutually acceptable agreement on issues arising in a custody action. The role of the mediator is to assist the parties in identifying the issues, reducing misunderstanding, clarifying priorities, exploring areas of compromise and finding points of agreement. An agreement reached by the parties must be based on the voluntary decisions of the parties and not the decision of the mediator. The agreement may resolve all or only some of the disputed issues. Parties are required to mediate in good faith, but are not compelled to reach an agreement. While mediation is an alternative means of conflict resolution, it is not a substitute for the benefit of legal advice.

"Memorandum of Understanding" is the written document prepared by a mediator which contains and summarizes the resolution reached by the parties during mediation. A Memorandum of Understanding is primarily for the benefit of the parties and is not legally binding on either party.

"Orientation Session" is the initial process of educating the parties on the mediation process so that they can make an informed choice about continued participation in mediation. This process may be mandated by the court and may be structured to include either group or individual sessions. An orientation session may also include an educational program for parents and children on the process of divorce and separation and the benefits of mediation in resolving custody disputes.

Credits

Adopted Oct. 28, 1999, imd. effective.

Editors' Notes
EXPLANATORY COMMENT--1999

The definitions of "orientation session" and "mediation" follow the legislative distinction between the initial orientation session, which the court may order the parties to attend, and actual mediation of the issues in dispute by the parties, which may be ordered only upon the parties' agreement. See 23 Pa.C.S. § 3901(b). The purpose of the orientation session is to educate the parties on the availability of mediation, the advantages and disadvantages of mediation, and the process of mediation so that the parties can make an informed decision about whether they wish to proceed further with mediation.

The definition of mediation set forth in this rule is not intended to restrict, expand or otherwise modify the statutory definition of mediation in 42 Pa.C.S. § 5949(c) relating to confidentiality. The statutory provision defines mediation for the purpose of determining when confidentiality and privilege attach to communications made or documents submitted during a mediation session.

Rule 1940.3. Order for Orientation Session and Mediation. Selection of Mediator

(a) Except as provided in (b), the court may order the parties to attend an orientation session at any time upon motion by a party, stipulation of the parties, or the court's own initiative.

(b) The court may not order an orientation session if a party or a child of either party is or has been the subject of domestic violence or child abuse either during the pendency of the action or within 24 months preceding the filing of the action.

Note: See also **Rule 1940.6(a) (4)** requiring termination of mediation when the mediator finds that the proceeding is "inappropriate" for mediation. The mediator has a continuing ethical obligation, consistent with **Rule 1940.4(b)**, during the mediation to screen for abuse and to terminate the mediation in the event he or she determines that the abuse renders the case unsuitable for mediation.

(c) Following the orientation session and with the consent of the parties, the court may refer the parties to mediation. The mediation may address any issues agreed to by the parties unless limited by court order.

Credits

Adopted Oct. 28, 1999, imd. effective.

Editors' Notes

EXPLANATORY COMMENT--1999

Rule 1940.3 describes the circumstances under which a case may be referred to mediation. Consistent with 23 Pa.C.S. § 3901(c)(2), it prohibits the referral of any case involving past or present domestic violence or abuse because of the substantial imbalance of negotiating power that exists between the parties. The parties themselves, however, may always agree to mediation. Although each court may devise its own procedures for screening these cases, screening must occur prior to referral of a case to the orientation session.

Rule 1940.4. Minimum Qualifications of the Mediator

(a) A mediator must have at least the following qualifications:

(1) a bachelor's degree and practical experience in law, psychiatry, psychology, counseling, family therapy or any comparable behavioral or social science field;

(2) successful completion of basic training in domestic and family violence or child abuse and a divorce and custody mediation program approved by the Association for Conflict Resolution, American Bar Association, American Academy of Matrimonial Lawyers, or Administrative Office of Pennsylvania Courts;

(3) mediation professional liability insurance; and

(4) additional mediation training consisting of a minimum of 4 mediated cases totaling 10 hours under the supervision of a mediator who has complied with subdivisions (1) through (3) above and is approved by the court to supervise other mediators.

(b) The mediator shall comply with the ethical standards of the mediator profession as well as those of his or her primary profession and complete at least 20 hours of continuing education every two years in topics related to family mediation.

(c) A post-graduate student enrolled in a state or federally accredited educational institution in the disciplines of law, psychiatry, psychology, counseling, family therapy or any comparable behavioral or social science field may mediate with direct and actual supervision by a qualified mediator.

Credits

Adopted Oct. 28, 1999, imd. effective. Amended July 21, 2004, imd. effective.

Editors' Notes
EXPLANATORY COMMENT--1999

Mediator qualifications are a key component of any successful mediation program. This rule sets forth the minimum qualifications that a mediator must have in order to participate in court-connected mediation. Local courts may impose additional, more stringent qualifications.

In addition to a bachelor's degree and practical experience, a mediator must have basic training in a program approved by one of the organizations listed in subdivision (a) (2). While these are the organizations which have been recommended by mediators and other trained professionals, the Domestic Relations Procedural Rules Committee and the Administrative Office of Pennsylvania Courts may, from time to time, propose to the Court that additional organizations be added to this list. Subdivision (a) (3) of the rule requires the mediator to have his or her own professional liability insurance. Prior to mediating independently, subdivision (a) (4) of the rule requires that the mediator co-mediate at least four cases under the supervision of a court-connected mediator.

Rule 1940.5. Duties of the Mediator

(a) As part of the orientation session, the mediator must inform the parties in writing of the following:

(1) the costs of mediation;

Note: **Rule 240** sets forth the procedures for obtaining leave to proceed in forma pauperis when the parties do not have the financial resources to pay the costs of litigation. This rule applies to court-connected mediation services as well, so that parties without sufficient resources may file a petition seeking a waiver or reduction of the costs of mediation.

(2) the process of mediation;

(3) that the mediator does not represent either or both of the parties;

(4) the nature and extent of any relationships with the parties and any personal, financial, or other interests that could result in a bias or conflict of interest;

(5) that mediation is not a substitute for the benefit of independent legal advice; and

(6) that the parties should obtain legal assistance for drafting any agreement or for reviewing any agreement drafted by the other party.

(b) When mediating a custody dispute, the mediator shall ensure that the parties consider fully the best interests of the child or children.

(c) With the consent of the parties, the mediator may meet with the parties' children or invite other persons to participate in the mediation.

Credits

Adopted Oct. 28, 1999, imd. effective.

Editors' Notes
EXPLANATORY COMMENT--1999

Rule 1940.5 sets forth the mediator's responsibilities to the parties. Subdivision (c) permits the participation of third persons with the consent of both parties. Such persons would include attorneys, other family members, mental health professionals or any other person who may be of assistance in resolving the disputed issues.

Rule 1940.6. Termination of Mediation

(a) Mediation shall terminate upon the earliest of the following circumstances to occur:

(1) a determination by the mediator that the parties are unable to reach a resolution regarding all of the issues subject to mediation;

(2) a determination by the mediator that the parties have reached a resolution regarding all of the issues subject to mediation;

(3) a determination by the mediator that the parties have reached a partial resolution and that further mediation will not resolve the remaining issues subject to mediation; or

(4) a determination by the mediator that the proceedings are inappropriate for mediation.

(b) If the parties reach a complete or partial resolution, the mediator shall, within 14 days, prepare and transmit to the parties a Memorandum of Understanding. At the request of a party, the mediator shall also transmit a copy of the Memorandum of Understanding to the party's counsel.

(c) If no resolution is reached during mediation, the mediator shall, within 14 days, report this in writing to the court, without further explanation.

Credits
Adopted Oct. 28, 1999, imd. effective.

Editors' Notes
EXPLANATORY COMMENT--1999

This rule sets forth the circumstances for termination of mediation. Subdivision (a)(4) reflects the mediator's continuing ethical obligation, consistent with **Rule 1940.4(b)**, to screen for domestic violence, substance abuse and any other factors, which make the case unsuitable for mediation.

Subdivision (b) requires the mediator to prepare a Memorandum of Understanding, as that term is defined in Rule 1940.2.

Reducing the parties' resolution to a binding and enforceable agreement is accomplished either by the parties' attorneys or, if not represented, the parties themselves, but in no event is the mediator responsible for drafting the parties' agreement. Court approval of the final agreement is not necessary for the purpose of enforcing it to the same extent as a court order.

Rule 1940.7. Mediator Compensation

Mediators shall be compensated for their services at a rate to be established by each court.

Credits

Adopted Oct. 28, 1999, imd. effective.

Editors' Notes
EXPLANATORY COMMENT--1999

Mediator compensation is necessary to establish and maintain a quality mediation program. Presently, however, the absence of a statewide office for alternative dispute resolution means that each court must develop and secure its own funds for the mediation program. Because the availability of such funds varies significantly from court to court, each court may establish its own rate and method of compensation at this time, provided that the fees are structured so that all parties are assured equal access to mediation services. As Pennsylvania moves in the direction of a unified judicial system, a statewide fee schedule setting forth uniform fee standards may eventually be established for mediation compensation.

Rule 1940.8. Sanctions

On its own motion or a party's motion, the court may impose sanctions against any party or attorney who fails to comply or causes a party not to comply with these mediation rules. Sanctions may include an award of mediation costs and attorney fees, including those reasonably incurred in pursuing the sanctions.

Note: To the extent court orders are employed to direct parties regarding mediation, contempt proceedings may also be instituted to enforce these orders.

Credits

Adopted Oct. 28, 1999, imd. effective.

Rule 1940.9. Changes or Amendments to any Existing Programs

These rules shall not affect any existing mediation program established in any judicial district pursuant to local rule prior to October 29, 1999. However, any changes or amendments to any existing program shall be consistent with these rules.

Credits

Adopted Oct. 27, 2000, imd. effective.

Editors' Notes

EXPLANATORY COMMENT--2000

This new rule is consistent with 23 Pa. C.S. § 3904.

FLORIDA

F.S.A. Mediator Rule 10.100

Rule 10.100. Certification Requirements

(a) General. For certification as a county court, family, circuit court, dependency, or appellate mediator, a mediator must be at least 21 years of age and be of good moral character. For certification as a county court, family, circuit court or dependency mediator, one must have the required number of points for the type of certification sought as specifically required in rule 10.105.

(b) County Court Mediators. For initial certification as a mediator of county court matters, an applicant must have at least a high school diploma or a General Equivalency Diploma (GED) and 100 points, which shall include:

(1) 30 points for successful completion of a Florida Supreme Court certified county court mediation training program;

(2) 10 points for education; and

(3) 60 points for mentorship.

(c) Family Mediators. For initial certification as a mediator of family and dissolution of marriage issues, an applicant must have at least a bachelor's degree and 100 points, which shall include, at a minimum:

(1) 30 points for successful completion of a Florida Supreme Court certified family mediation training program;

(2) 25 points for education/mediation experience; and

(3) 30 points for mentorship.

Additional points above the minimum requirements may be awarded for completion of additional education/mediation experience, mentorship, and miscellaneous activities.

(d) Circuit Court Mediators. For initial certification as a mediator of circuit court matters, other than family matters, an applicant must have at least a bachelor's degree and 100 points, which shall include, at a minimum:

(1) 30 points for successful completion of a Florida Supreme Court certified circuit mediation training program;

(2) 25 points for education/mediation experience; and

(3) 30 points for mentorship.

Additional points above the minimum requirements may be awarded for completion of additional education/mediation experience, mentorship, and miscellaneous activities.

(e) Dependency Mediators. For initial certification as a mediator of dependency matters, as defined in Florida Rule of Juvenile Procedure 8.290, an applicant must have at least a bachelor's degree and 100 points, which shall include, at a minimum:

(1) 30 points for successful completion of a Florida Supreme Court certified dependency mediation training program;

(2) 25 points for education/mediation experience; and

(3) 40 points for mentorship.

Additional points above the minimum requirements may be awarded for completion of additional education/mediation experience, mentorship, and miscellaneous activities.

(f) Appellate Mediators. For initial certification as a mediator of appellate matters, an applicant must be a Florida Supreme Court certified circuit, family or dependency mediator and successfully complete a Florida Supreme Court certified appellate mediation training program.

(g) Senior Judges Serving as Mediators. A senior judge may serve as a mediator in a court-ordered mediation in a circuit in which the senior judge is presiding over criminal cases or in a circuit in which the senior judge is not presiding as a judge, or in both, only if certified by the Florida Supreme Court as a mediator for that type of mediation.

(h) Referral for Discipline. If the certification or licensure necessary for any person to be certified as a family or circuit mediator is suspended or revoked, or if the mediator holding such certification or licensure is in any other manner disciplined, such matter shall be referred to the Mediator Qualifications Board for appropriate action pursuant to rule 10.800.

(i) Special Conditions. Mediators who are certified prior to August 1, 2006, shall not be subject to the point requirements for any category of certification in relation to which continuing certification is maintained.

Rule 10.105. Point System Categories

(a) Education. Points shall be awarded in accordance with the following schedule (points are only awarded for the highest level of education completed and honorary degrees are not included):

High School Diploma/GED	10 points
Associate's Degree	15 points
Bachelor's Degree	20 points
Master's Degree	25 points
Master's Degree in Conflict Resolution	30 points
Doctorate (e.g., Ph.D., J.D., M.D., E.D., LL.M.)	30 points
Ph.D. from Accredited Conflict Resolution Program	40 points

An additional five points will be awarded for completion of a graduate level conflict resolution certificate program in an institution which has been accredited by Middle States Association of Colleges and Schools, the New England Association of Schools and Colleges, the North Central Association of Colleges and Schools, the Northwest Association of Schools and Colleges, the Southern Association of Colleges and

Schools, the Western Association of Schools and Colleges, the American Bar Association, or an entity of equal status.

(b) Mediation Experience. One point per year will be awarded to a Florida Supreme Court certified mediator for each year that mediator has mediated at least 15 cases of any type. In the alternative, a maximum of five points will be awarded to any mediator, regardless of Florida Supreme Court certification, who has conducted a minimum of 100 mediations over a consecutive five-year period.

(c) Mentorship. Ten points will be awarded for each supervised mediation completed of the type for which certification is sought and five points will be awarded for each mediation session of the type for which certification is sought which is observed.

(d) Miscellaneous Points.

1. Five points shall be awarded to applicants currently licensed or certified in any United States jurisdiction in psychology, accounting, social work, mental health, health care, education or the practice of law or mediation. Such award shall not exceed a total of five points regardless of the number of licenses or certifications obtained.

2. Five points shall be awarded for possessing conversational ability in a foreign language as demonstrated by certification by the American Council on the Teaching of Foreign Languages (ACTFL) Oral Proficiency Test, qualification as a court interpreter, accreditation by the American Translators Association, or approval as a sign language interpreter by the Registry of Interpreters for the Deaf. Such award shall not exceed a total of five points regardless of the number of languages in which the applicant is proficient.

3. Five points shall be awarded for the successful completion of a mediation training program (minimum 30 hours in length) which is certified or approved by a jurisdiction other than Florida and which may not be the required Florida Supreme Court certified mediation training program. Such award shall not exceed five points regardless of the number of training programs completed.

4. Five points shall be awarded for certification as a mediator by the Florida Supreme Court. Such award shall not exceed five points per category regardless of the number of training programs completed or certifications obtained.

Credits

Added Nov. 15, 2007 (969 So.2d 1003).

Editors' Notes
COMMITTEE NOTES

The following table is intended to illustrate the point system established in this rule. Any discrepancy between the table and the written certification requirements shall be resolved in favor of the latter.

Points Needed Per Area of Certification		Minimum Points Required in Each Area
County	100	30 certified county mediation training; 10 education (minimum HS Diploma/GED); 60 mentorship
Family	100	30 certified family mediation training; 25 education/ mediation experience (minimum Bachelor's Degree); 30 mentorship [and requires 15 additional points]
Dependency	100	30 certified dependency mediation training; 25 education/mediation experience (minimum Bachelor's Degree); 40 mentorship [and requires 5 additional points]
Circuit	100	30 certified circuit mediation training, 25 education/mediation experience (minimum Bachelor's Degree); 30 mentorship; [and requires 15 additional points]
Education/Mediation Experience (points awarded for highest level of education received)		

HS Diploma/GED	10 points	Master's Degree in Conflict Resolution	30
Associate's Degree	15 points	Doctorate (e.g., J.D., M.D., Ph.D., Ed.D., LL.M.)	30
Bachelor's Degree	20 points	Ph.D. from accredited CR Program	40
Master's Degree	25 points	Graduate Certificate CR Program	+5

Florida certified mediator: 1 point per year in which mediated at least 15 mediations (any type) OR any mediator: - 5 points for minimum of 100 mediations (any type) over a 5 year period

Mentorship- must work with at least 2 different certified mediators and must be completed for the type of certification sought

Observation	5 points each session
Supervised Mediation	10 points each complete mediation

Miscellaneous Points

Licensed to practice law, psychology, accounting, social work, mental health, health care, education or mediation in any US jurisdiction	5 points (total)
Florida Certified Mediator	5 points (total)
Foreign Language Conversational Ability as demonstrated by certification by ACTFL Oral Proficiency Test; qualified as a court interpreter; or accredited by the American Translators Association; Sign Language Interpreter as demonstrated by approval by the Registry of Interpreters for the Deaf	5 points (total)
Completion of additional mediation training program (minimum 30 hours in length) certified/approved by a state or court other than Florida	5 points (total)

Rule 10.110. Good Moral Character

(a) General Requirement. No person shall be certified by this Court as a mediator unless such person first produces satisfactory evidence of good moral character as required by rule 10.100.

(b) Purpose. The primary purpose of the requirement of good moral character is to ensure protection of the participants in mediation and the public, as well as to safeguard the justice system. A mediator shall have, as a prerequisite to certification and as a requirement for continuing certification, the good moral character sufficient to meet all of the Mediator Standards of Professional Conduct set out in rules 10.200-10.690.

(c) Certification. The following shall apply in relation to determining the good moral character required for initial and continuing mediator certification:

(1) The applicant's or mediator's good moral character may be subject to inquiry when the applicant's or mediator's conduct is relevant to the qualifications of a mediator.

(2) An applicant for initial certification who has been convicted of a felony shall not be eligible for certification until such person has received a restoration of civil rights.

(3) An applicant for initial certification who is serving a sentence of felony probation shall not be eligible for certification until termination of the period of probation.

(4) In assessing whether the applicant's or mediator's conduct demonstrates a present lack of good moral character the following factors shall be relevant:

(A) the extent to which the conduct would interfere with a mediator's duties and responsibilities;

(B) the area of mediation in which certification is sought or held;

(C) the factors underlying the conduct;

(D) the applicant's or mediator's age at the time of the conduct;

(E) the recency of the conduct;

(F) the reliability of the information concerning the conduct;

(G) the seriousness of the conduct as it relates to mediator qualifications;

(H) the cumulative effect of the conduct or information;

(I) any evidence of rehabilitation;

(J) the applicant's or mediator's candor; and

(K) denial of application, disbarment, or suspension from any profession.

(d) Decertification. A certified mediator shall be subject to decertification for any knowing and willful incorrect material information contained in any mediator application. There is a presumption of knowing and willful violation if the application is completed, signed, and notarized.

Credits

Added effective April 1, 2000 (762 So.2d 441). Amended May 11, 2006, effective August 1, 2006 (931 So.2d 877).

A Final Note about Court-Connected Mediation

For mediators in a court-connected mediation program, the program's rules and requirements become part of the mediator's professional responsibility. For instance, in the Pennsylvania rule at 1940.4 (b), a mediator is required to comply with the "ethical standards of the mediator profession as well as those of his or her primary profession…." This section applies to mediators who also practice another profession such as law, social work, or counseling. Such professionals must abide by the rules and standards of both professions. Increasingly, mediators consider mediation to be their primary profession, while perhaps maintaining another professional license. *Query* whether attorney standards, for example, should apply to the mediator-client relationship where an attorney-client relationship does not exist?

Ideally, a court-connected program will address the following considerations:

- Mandatory or compulsory nature of the mediation
- Qualifications of the mediator
- How the service is provided, i.e., by the court or private contract
- How the mediator is paid.

Many jurisdictions throughout the U.S. claim to have court-connected custody mediation programs when, in truth, they provide a form of dispute resolution that more closely resembles conciliation or negotiation, not mediation. Some courts provide a list of mediators parties may choose from, making mediation optional. Other programs use existing court personnel to act as mediators without qualified, accredited mediation training. Differences exist among jurisdictions concerning the mandatory vs. voluntary nature of court-connected mediation. Many jurisdictions make the process voluntary. Others require it upon the request of either party or in the discretion of the court. A few jurisdictions require it legislatively and by court rule, with a domestic violence exception, giving no discretion to individual judges. In actual practice, a court-connected mediation program cannot be effective unless it is mandatory because the average divorce or custody party does not know enough about mediation and, justifiably, believes that if the court does not require it, it must not be that important. When courts require mediation, parties rarely, if ever, complain. I find they tend to be grateful for the opportunity to jump off of the roller-coaster of litigation. Mandatory mediation has advanced the profession by giving the process exposure and credibility. Mandatory mediation has resulted in more private, contractual mediation.

In addition to being compulsory, an effective court-connected mediation program uses trained mediators who meet minimum training and professional requirements. Those requirements are, ideally, set forth in the rule or law creating the program. Finally, the court's involvement in engaging the mediator is of ultimate importance. If clients have to contract privately with a mediator whose name appears on a list, there can be less satisfaction with the process because of inconvenience and cost. Courts that provide mediators onsite (as independent contractors, and not court employees lacking the appearance of impartiality) at a reasonable cost, or, ideally, paid for in whole or part by the court, tend to have successful programs.

CONCLUSION

Mediation ethics derive from various sources including model standards and comments, as well as state laws and rules and the rules applicable to particular mediation programs. Attention is given, as well, to one's "primary profession" if applicable, albeit confusing, since such divided loyalty could create conflict between opposing codes of ethics. The Ethics Quiz on the following pages focuses on real world mediation ethics. In some cases, there may be more than one correct answer. Be prepared to provide one or more answers, your reasons for your answers, and to identify the Standard or Standards applicable to each scenario. Correct answers are set forth at the end of the Quiz.

MEDIATION ETHICS QUIZ

1. Although lawsuits against mediators are rare, ethics complaints most likely to be brought against mediators involve:

    a. Breach of confidentiality

    b. Breach of neutrality

    c. Both of the above

    d. False Advertising

2. Parties know Mediator is a licensed attorney. They ask Mediator to file divorce complaint because they are using mediation for the primary purpose of avoiding attorneys. Mediator should:

a. Recommend that both parties employ separate attorneys.

b. File the divorce complaint, affidavits of consent and other papers to obtain a decree in divorce after a negotiated agreement has been reached in mediation.

c. Recommend that at least one of the parties employ counsel.

d. End the mediation and refuse to work with the parties.

3. At the first session during custody mediation, Mother tells Mediator in caucus that she was hospitalized 13 months ago for a fractured spine from being pushed by Father. The incident occurred in front of their six-year-old son. Mediator should:

a. Explore Mother's ability to negotiate with Father.

b. End the mediation due to domestic violence.

c. Give Miranda warnings to Father.

d. Explore the possibility of bringing the child into mediation.

4. Both parties in complex divorce mediation are represented by counsel. After three (3) sessions, they have mediated an Interim Agreement for support pending resolution of all economic issues. Relieved, the parties come to their fourth session with the agreement drafted and reviewed by counsel. They have both been directed by their attorneys to sign the agreement. They do so in the mediation session and ask Mediator to sign where it says "Witness" next to both names. Mediator should:

a. Sign the agreement as a witness.

b. Decline to sign as a witness.

c. Sign the agreement but only if a Notary is present.

d. Have the office secretary sign as a witness.

5. During mediated negotiations regarding amount and duration of alimony, Husband states that his attorney believes Wife would get no alimony if a judge decided the case, and Wife states that her attorney says she would get alimony for 5-10 years. Parties want the mediator to give a neutral opinion. Mediator should:

   a. Give a neutral opinion and explain that it is only an opinion.

   b. Call a caucus to alleviate the tension.

   c. Request a 5-minute break to think about what to do.

   d. Decline to give an answer because the question relates to a gray area.

6. Prior to beginning the session, Mediator is making small talk with the parties in a custody case. Father states he works for Bartko Industries. Mediator knows that Frank Bartko, President of Bartko Industries lives somewhere on mediator's street. Mediator states, "Frank Bartko lives on my street. He seems like a really good guy." Father states, "Really? Yeah, he's a nice guy. He's been my boss for 9 years. I'm lucky to work for such great company." Mediator's statement was:

a. Fine because it's just small talk before a session.

b. Fine because it puts Father at ease.

c. Both of the above.

d. Risky because it could make Father feel uncomfortable.

7. During caucus, Mediator learns that Wife, who insists she is entitled to 60% in equitable distribution, has been told by her attorney that it is a 50/50 case. Wife asks Mediator not to tell Husband she will settle for less than 60% because she wants to see how far she can push him. Mediator should:

   a. Tell Wife that Mediator is ethically bound to share the information with Husband.

   b. Keep Wife's secret and refrain from sharing the information with Husband without Wife's permission.

   c. Tell both parties that this is clearly a 50/50 case and invite Wife's attorney to come to mediation to defend her viewpoint.

   d. None of the above

8. The parties to an equitable distribution, support, and alimony case have grown children. They have been married 38 years. Wife feels completely in the dark about Husband's income and assets which are derived from multiple businesses he started and ran during the marriage. Wife wants Mediator to meet privately with Wife and her attorney in order for Wife to better understand what is being

said to her about Husband's complicated business dealings by both her attorney and Mediator. In order for Mediator to meet privately with Wife and her attorney, Mediator needs:

a. Husband's permission.

b. Husband's attorney's permission only.

c. Wife's permission only.

d. Wife's attorney's permission only.

9. Prior to meeting the parties, Mediator speaks to Husband on the phone to make the first appointment. Husband states that he feels confident in the Mediator because she was referred to them by several independent sources. He also states that his sister (a therapist) knows Mediator but asks Mediator not to mention it to his Wife. Mediator does not know his sister but has heard of her and believes she may have seen her at professional gatherings. Mediator should:

a. Tell Husband he must disclose this relationship to Wife.

b. Call the sister and make sure she does not say anything to Wife either.

c. Tell Husband she is required to disclose the relationship to Wife.

d. Tell Husband okay, she will not tell Wife she knows his sister.

10. Mediator is called in to settle a dispute between landlord and tenant. Mediator did not call in ahead of time to check on the parties' names. The day of the mediation, Mediator recognizes the landlord as his optometrist whom he has been seeing regularly for annual check-ups and eyeglasses for five years. Mediator should:

a. Disclose the relationship to all parties.

b. Recuse himself from the mediation.

c. Not do anything; the relationship is not close or personal.

d. Make his next eye appointment prior to beginning the session.

11. Attorney Alex refers divorce cases for litigation to Attorney Barry. Attorney Barry pays 30% of all fees on these cases to Attorney Alex as a referral fee. Attorney Alex has recently become a divorce mediator. At the conclusion of his mediations, clients often ask Attorney (now Mediator) Alex to refer them to attorneys. Attorney Alex routinely refers at least one of the parties to Attorney Barry, getting his usual referral fee. This is:

   a. Ethical because attorneys are allowed to share fees.

   b. Unethical because mediators are not allowed to share fees.

   c. Unethical because it creates an attorney-client relationship between Mediator and one of the mediation clients.

   d. Unethical because it leaves the other client out of the loop.

12. Divorce Mediator is not an attorney. He is, however, often asked to refer clients to attorneys both in and out of mediation. Mediator is familiar with many attorneys in the divorce field and is aware that attorneys share fees from referrals. Mediator decides to establish a professional relationship with Attorney Uriah whereby he receives 25% of fees on all clients he refers, none of whom are in mediation with him. This is:

a. Ethical because Divorce Mediator is only referring clients who are not in mediation with Divorce Mediator.

b. Ethical because the clients consent.

c. Unethical because Attorney Uriah is not a mediator.

d. Unethical because Divorce Mediator is not an attorney.

13. Mediator finds herself disliking and judging Wife in divorce mediation because Wife is domineering, selfish, manipulative, spoiled, and cruel towards Husband. Husband is just learning to stand up to Wife and is working hard in therapy and in mediation to deal with the guilt he feels whenever he asserts himself. Mediator needs to:

    a. Deal with her feelings towards Wife and refrain from acting on her feelings.

    b. Not judge Wife.

    c. Both of the above.

    d. Stop working with Husband against Wife.

14. In high-conflict divorce mediation, the clients are still living under the same roof because neither is willing to separate until they have a written shared custody order. They come into every session with bottled-up emotion and must spend at least an hour arguing before they get any constructive negotiating done. The mediator should:

    a. Tell them to leave their emotions at the door.

b. Talk to them about the arguing.

c. Caucus immediately.

d. Set rules to control the arguing.

15. Confidentiality of mediation sessions typically means:

a. The Mediator cannot discuss the mediation with anyone except the parties.

b. The parties cannot discuss the mediation with anyone except each other or the Mediator.

c. The parties may discuss the mediation with their closest friends or relatives but no one else.

d. Neither the parties nor the Mediator may discuss the mediation with any outside person.

16. The parties in a contentious divorce/property distribution ask the mediator to help them negotiate a mediated settlement. They want the mediator to act as arbitrator if they are not able to reach agreement after a certain point. The Mediator should:

a. Accept the challenge and follow the Mediator/Arbitrator model.

b. Agree to the proposal but only with consent of both attorneys.

c. Decline to act as Arbitrator and stick to Mediation.

d. Decline to act as Mediator and stick to Arbitration.

17. Mediator has taken voluminous notes during a complex divorce mediation resulting in settlement of economic issues. Mediator drafted the Memorandum of Understanding. The attorneys do not agree on the wording of the paragraph regarding sale of the marital residence and division of proceeds. They want to look at the Mediator's notes. Mediator should:

    a. Open his file to the attorneys and the clients.

    b. Make notes available only to the clients by mailing them each a copy.

    c. Make notes available only to the clients in session.

    d. Destroy the notes.

18. During court-connected custody mediation, the parties disclose they use corporal punishment when necessary to discipline their children and that their son was treated for an infection on his back resulting from open wounds inflicted by Father's belt. Mediator should:

    a. Make a "child-line" report.

    b. Keep the information confidential.

    c. Tell only the attorneys.

    d. Inform the court.

19. In an advertising brochure, Mediator lists qualifications, memberships in professional associations, mediation trainings attended, and "60% settlement rate. The advertising is unethical because:

    a. Mediators are not allowed to advertise.

    b. Mediators may only list professional associations if they are for Mediators.

    c. Mediators are not permitted to advertise a settlement rate.

    d. Only attorneys may list their trainings.

20. In joint session in divorce negotiations, Mediator learns that Wife's attorney apparently is not aware of new court rules that would lengthen the period of time during which Wife could receive alimony. Mediator should:

    a. Ask the parties if they would consent to Mediator speaking to the attorneys about the new rules.

    b. Tell the parties about the new rule and how it might affect their case.

    c. Both of the above.

    d. Neither of the above. Mediator should leave all legal issues to the attorneys and not discuss contested legal issues.

21. During divorce mediation, parties exchange bank statements and other financial information. After three sessions, they reach an impasse and terminate mediation. During discovery, Husband notices that Wife has failed to disclose a bank account containing $30,000 for her massage therapy

business. Wife's attorney states that this information is privileged because it was revealed during mediation. The court should:

    a.   Rule that the material is privileged.

    b.   Rule that the material is confidential

    c.   Rule that the material is otherwise discoverable and must be produced.

    d.   Rule that the statute of limitations bars discovery of records more than two years old.

22.   Parties reached an impasse and both parties hired attorneys to litigate their divorce and economic issues. Mediator destroyed all notes taken during mediation sessions. Destruction of notes is:

    a.   Unethical unless parties were first given the opportunity to receive copies.

    b.   Ethical because it is standard practice.

    c.   Unethical because the parties paid the mediator to take those notes.

    d.   Ethical only if the parties were advised in the Agreement to Mediate that notes would be destroyed.

23.   A court has ordered parties into mediation regarding custody issues. Wife tells the mediator her attorney has advised her to keep silent and that she has nothing else today and will not speak any further during mediation. Husband is willing to speak and to cooperate with mediation. The mediation ends in impasse because Wife will not participate. Husband's attorney has filed a Petition for Contempt and sent mediator a subpoena to testify regarding Wife's silence. Mediator should:

a. Obey the subpoena but only agree to speak on the condition she receives payment from Wife, who has not paid the mediator.

b. Obey the subpoena but only speak about Wife's silence, Wife's statement, and nothing else.

c. Resist the subpoena.

d. Notify the parties of the subpoena and advise them that she intends to obey it unless one or both of them obtains an order quashing the subpoena.

24. A new client contacts attorney mediator for purpose of retaining representation in a divorce action. Attorney (mediator) listens to details of client's case and suggests mediation instead of litigation, using attorney (mediator) as the mediator. Ethically, attorney (mediator) is:

    a. Skating on thin ice due to conflict of interest.

    b. Engaging in illegal bait and switch tactics.

    c. Properly responding to the client's needs.

    d. Lacking boundaries.

25. Between sessions, parties email mediator, copying each other on the messages. In one of the messages, an agreement is reached to change the custody schedule adding a new overnight to Father's time and modifying the support agreement to include a provision that Mother alone will pay the cost of their oldest daughter's SAT Prep class. Father's attorney prepares a modified

agreement, but Mother will not sign it. Father subpoenas Mediator to a hearing to authenticate the email exchanges. Mediator should:

a. Resist the subpoena with a Motion to Quash since the Agreement to Mediate stated parties would not subpoena Mediator.

b. Comply with the subpoena because it does not apply to email messages.

c. Sue the attorney for abuse of process since mediation communications are privileged.

d. Comply with the subpoena but assert the privilege at the hearing and refuse to testify.

ANSWERS TO MEDIATION ETHICS QUIZ

1. Ethics complaints most likely to be brought against mediators involve:

    a. Breach of confidentiality

    b. Breach of neutrality

    c. Both of the above

    d. False advertising

ANSWER: (Standards IV and VII) The answer to No. 1 is **c.** Unintentional breaches of confidentiality occur when the mediator mistakenly shares information obtained in caucus, improperly reports conduct or information from the mediation, or speaks to attorneys without both parties' permission. Neutrality can be broken unintentionally by using language that creates the appearance of bias, failing to disclose a conflict of interest, or trying to impose a mediator-selected outcome.

2. Parties know Mediator is a licensed attorney. They ask Mediator to file divorce complaint because they are using mediation for the primary purpose of avoiding attorneys. Mediator should:

    a. **Recommend that both parties employ separate attorneys.**

    b. File the divorce complaint, affidavits of consent and other papers to obtain a decree in divorce after a negotiated agreement has been reached in mediation.

    c. Recommend that at least one of the parties employ counsel.

    d. End the mediation and refuse to work with the parties.

ANSWER: (Standards VI and IV) The answer to No. 2 is **a**. To protect the integrity of the mediation process both parties should have independent counsel and the mediator should promote that model. The legal profession's most legitimate criticism of mediation is that the mediator is engaging in the unauthorized practice of law, or, if the mediator is an attorney, engaging in unethical representation due to conflict of interest and/or causing an unrepresented party to be prejudiced. When a mediator does not promote the use of separate attorneys, the mediator is encouraging such criticism of the mediation process. Granted, **c** is, practically speaking, a potential answer, although not the best answer. The reality is that couples using mediation to save money often have the attitude that attorneys are only needed to formalize the agreement; therefore, only one is needed. These clients apparently genuinely believe they do not need legal advice because they understand everything they are doing (which may or may not be true.) These clients are unwitting followers of O.J. Coogler's Do-It-Yourself movement. The mediator's duty when clients make this choice is to advise them of the need for independent advice from separate attorneys.

3. At the first session during custody mediation, Mother tells Mediator in caucus that she was hospitalized 13 months ago for a fractured spine from being pushed by Father. The incident occurred in front of their six-year old son. Mediator should:

a. **Explore Mother's ability to negotiate with Father.**

b. End the mediation due to domestic violence.

c. Give Miranda warnings to Father.

d. Explore the possibility of bringing the child into mediation.

ANSWER: (Standards III, X, and XI) The answer to No. 3 is **a** because the issue presented is mother's perceived lack of power. An exploration of that issue could lead to the choice of **b**.

4. Both parties in complex divorce mediation are represented by counsel. After three (3) sessions, they have mediated an Interim Agreement for support pending resolution of all economic issues. Relieved, the parties come to their fourth session with the agreement that has been drafted and reviewed by counsel. They have both been directed by their attorneys to sign the agreement. They do so in the mediation session and ask Mediator to sign where it says "Witness" next to both names. Mediator should:

   a. Sign the agreement as a witness.

   b. **Decline to sign as a witness.**

   c. Sign the agreement but only if a Notary is present.

   d. Have the office secretary sign as a witness.

ANSWER: (Standard IV) The best answer to No. 4 is **b**. Although signing as witness could be completely harmless, there is a potential that adoption of the role as "witness" could conflict with the role of mediator. If the signatures were ever to be challenged, mediator would find himself in another role for which he did not sign up. Mediator's office personnel are an extension of mediator and the same conditions would apply to them.

5. During mediated negotiations regarding amount and duration of alimony, Husband states that his attorney believes Wife would get no alimony if a judge decided the case and Wife states that her attorney says she would get alimony for 5-10 years. The parties want the mediator to give a neutral opinion. Mediator should:

   a. Give a neutral opinion and explain that it is only an opinion.

   b. Call a caucus to alleviate the tension.

   c. Request a 5-minute break to think about what to do.

   d. Decline to give an answer because the question relates to a gray area.

ANSWER: (Standard IV) The answer to No. 5 is **d** because giving an opinion on a dispositive issue that is subjective legal advice (a "gray area") cannot possibly be a helpful intervention for a mediator. The mediator role would be compromised. The mediator would become a third expert rendering an opinion, instead of a mediator. Some mediators find it helpful to be directive and to offer a neutral opinion to "help" the parties. In theory, this might be a good idea; however, in actual practice the parties typically value the mediator's opinion as fact, which is misguided. Worse, if the parties, or one of them, does not like the opinion, it could alienate the party and create the appearance of bias. The risk of losing trust and blurring the mediator/client boundary is not worth any potential benefit to the parties of hearing a mere opinion that purports to be (and likely is) "neutral." This does not mean a mediator can never express an opinion. It is perfectly acceptable for a mediator to express an opinion on whether or not the parties appear to be candidates for mediation; whether or not the mediator agrees with certain laws and policies, etc. The test is whether or not the opinion will blur boundaries and/or create bias or the appearance of bias.

6. Prior to beginning the session, Mediator is making small talk with the parties in a custody case. Father states he works for Bartko Industries. Mediator knows that Frank Bartko, President of Bartko Industries lives on mediator's street. Mediator states, "Frank Bartko lives on my street. He seems like a really good guy." Father states, "Really? Yeah, he's a nice guy, he's been my boss for 9 years. I am very lucky to work for such great company." Mediator's statement was:

   a. Fine because it's just small talk before a session.

   b. Fine because it puts Father at ease.

   c. Both of the above.

   d. Risky because it could make Father feel uncomfortable.

ANSWER: (Standards IV [Comment I] and XI) The answer to No. 6 is **d**, risky because it could make Father feel uncomfortable. This question often invites differences of opinion. Many students choose **a** because they see nothing wrong with the mediator being friendly and making small talk. The key, however, is to put oneself in the place of the client. The mediator has no information about the client's true feelings towards his boss. Many people have resentments or ambiguous feelings toward their bosses. The mediator has no idea how the client feels about his job, and whether or not he even has job security. By referring to the client's boss in a setting where the client was only expecting to be talking about confidential, sensitive matters involving his family at the very least detracts from the purpose of the mediation, and, at worst, could be deeply disturbing and frightening to the client, who may feel uncomfortable, knowing there is a connection between his boss and this new person to whom he is now expected to reveal his deepest feelings and thoughts or even secrets about his family. If indeed Frank Bartko is someone living on the same street as the mediator, this fact, arguably, does not create a conflict of interest because it is not necessarily relevant. Living on the same street does not automatically imply a relationship. Obviously, if there is a relationship, then the mediator would have to disclose the relationship and possibly recuse himself. This is a case where, even if the clients consented, the mediator's recusal should override the clients' desire to continue with this mediator because of potential discomfort and distractions that could result from the relationship.

7. During caucus, Mediator learns that Wife, who insists she is entitled to 60% in equitable distribution, has been told by her attorney that it is a 50/50 case. Wife asks Mediator not to tell Husband she will settle for less than 60% because she wants to see how far she can push him. Mediator should:

a. Tell Wife that Mediator is ethically bound to share the information with Husband.

b. Keep Wife's secret and refrain from sharing the information with Husband without Wife's permission.

d. Tell both parties that this is clearly a 50/50 case and invite Wife's attorney to come to mediation to defend her viewpoint.

d. None of the above

ANSWER: (Standard VII) The answer to No. 7 is **b** because mediator has a duty of confidentiality regardless of whether statements are made in joint session or caucus.

8. The parties to an equitable distribution, support, and alimony case have grown children. They have been married 38 years. Wife feels completely in the dark about Husband's income and assets which are derived from multiple businesses he started and ran during the marriage. Wife wants Mediator to meet privately with Wife and her attorney in order for Wife to better understand what is being said to her about Husband's complicated business dealings by both her attorney and Mediator. In order for Mediator to meet privately with Wife and her attorney, Mediator needs:

   a. Husband's permission.

   b. Husband's attorney's permission only.

   c. Wife's permission only.

   d. Wife's attorney's permission only.

ANSWER: (Standard VII) The answer to No. 8 is **a** because mediator must have both parties' permission to speak to anyone about the mediation, even the attorney for one of the parties.

9. Prior to meeting the parties, Mediator speaks to Husband on the phone to make the first appointment. Husband states that he feels confident in the Mediator because she was referred to them by several independent sources. He also states that his sister (a therapist) knows Mediator, but asks Mediator not to mention it to his Wife. Mediator does not know his sister but has heard of her and believes she may have seen her at professional gatherings. Mediator should:

   a. Tell Husband he must disclose this relationship to Wife.

   b. Call the sister and make sure she does not say anything to Wife either.

   c. Tell Husband she is required to disclose the relationship to Wife.

   d. Tell Husband okay, she will not tell Wife she knows his sister.

ANSWER: (Standards IV and VII) The answer to No. 9 is **c**. The mediator might hesitate to recognize her awareness of the existence of Husband's sister as an issue (they are just barely acquainted as the question suggests) but Husband has made an issue out of the relationship, presumably because he believes this gives him an advantage or some sense of advantage; therefore the "relationship" must be disclosed. Standard VII's requirement of confidentiality in caucus (mediator's caucus with husband when he revealed his sister's identity and his request that mediator not tell wife) does not necessarily apply because this information is independently obtainable.

10. Mediator is called in to settle a dispute between landlord and tenant. Mediator did not call in ahead of time to check on the parties' names. The day of the mediation, Mediator recognizes the landlord as his optometrist whom he has been seeing regularly for annual check-ups and eyeglasses for five years. Mediator should:

   a. Disclose the relationship to all parties.

b. **Recuse himself from the mediation.**

c. Not do anything; the relationship is not close or personal.

d. Make his next eye appointment prior to beginning the session.

ANSWER: (Standard IV) The answer to No. 10 is **b** because the mediator's relationship with his eye doctor, although not personal, is a professional relationship that tends to be long-standing. It is also not a relationship of equals because doctors have a confidential relationship with patients and, perceivably, superior authority in the relationship. At minimum, to continue the mediation, even with consent of the parties, would create the appearance of impropriety.

11. Attorney Alex refers divorce cases for litigation to Attorney Barry. Attorney Barry pays 30% of all fees on these cases to Attorney Alex as a referral fee. Attorney Alex has recently become a divorce mediator. At the conclusion of his mediations, clients often ask Attorney (now Mediator) Alex to refer them to attorneys. Attorney Alex routinely refers at least one of the parties to Attorney Barry, getting his usual referral fee. This is:

a. Ethical because attorneys are allowed to share fees.

b. **Unethical because mediators are not allowed to share fees.**

c. Unethical because it creates an attorney-client relationship between Mediator and one of the mediation clients.

d. Unethical because it leaves the other client out of the loop.

ANSWER: (Standard V [Comment D]) The answer to No. 11 is **b** because mediators are not permitted to share fees, period. Nevertheless, keep in mind co-mediators may and do share the fee because they are both providing mediation services.

12. Divorce Mediator is not an attorney. He is, however, often asked to refer clients to attorneys both in and out of mediation. Mediator is familiar with many attorneys in the divorce field and is aware that attorneys share fees from referrals. Mediator decides to establish a professional relationship with Attorney Uriah whereby he receives 25% of fees on all clients he refers, none of whom are in mediation with him. This is:

   a. Ethical because Divorce Mediator is only referring clients who are not in mediation with Divorce Mediator.

   b. Ethical because the clients consent.

   c. Unethical because Attorney Uriah is not a mediator.

   d. Unethical because Divorce Mediator is not an attorney.

ANSWER: (Standard 5 [Comment D]) The answer to No. 12 is **d** because mediators are not permitted to share fees.

13. Mediator finds herself disliking and judging Wife in divorce mediation because the Wife is domineering, selfish, manipulative, spoiled, and cruel towards Husband. Husband is just learning to stand up to Wife and is working hard in therapy as well as in mediation to deal with the guilt he feels whenever he asserts himself. Mediator needs to:

   a. Deal with her feelings towards Wife and refrain from acting on her feelings.

   b. Not judge Wife.

c. Both of the above.

d. Stop working with Husband against Wife.

ANSWER: (Standard IV) The answer to No. 13 is **a.** Mediator is not forbidden from having negative feelings about clients, or even judging clients, so long as mediator does not act inappropriately on those feelings and judgments. The mediator should pay attention to her feelings, de-brief (confer) with professional peers, and make an attempt to change her feelings (by changing her thoughts, if possible). In an extreme case where mediator, unfortunately, cannot overcome the natural human tendency to form judgments that are sometimes negative, and is having difficulty controlling her behavior, Comment I to Standard IV would require the mediator to withdraw from the mediation.

14. In high-conflict divorce mediation, the clients are still living under the same roof because neither is willing to separate until they have a written shared custody order. They come into every session with bottled-up emotion and must spend at least an hour arguing before they get any constructive negotiating done. The mediator should:

a. Tell them to leave their emotions at the door.

b. Talk to them about the arguing.

c. Caucus immediately.

d. Set rules to control the arguing.

ANSWER: (Standard III) The best answer to No. 14 is **b** because client behavior that interferes with the process must be addressed. Part of the mediator's duty is to assist participants' understanding of the process and assess their capacity to mediate. By talking to the parties candidly about this issue, the mediator allows clients take responsibility for their participation in the process, while gaining awareness of how their behavior affects the process as a whole. Some students prefer answer **d**; however, rules are risky in mediation. It is possible with cooperative clients to set rules that are effective. With uncooperative clients (who are the ones this example refers to and the parties who are likely to need rules in the first place) setting rules will simply create more opportunities for (otherwise unnecessary) conflict by tempting the clients to break the rules. Then the conflict becomes one between the clients and the mediator, a formula for disaster. Set rules at your own risk.

15. Confidentiality of mediation sessions typically means:

   a. **The Mediator cannot discuss the mediation with anyone except the parties.**

   b. The parties cannot discuss the mediation with anyone except each other or the Mediator.

   c. The parties may discuss the mediation with their closest friends or relatives but no one else.

   d. Neither the parties nor the Mediator may discuss the mediation with any outside person.

ANSWER: (Standard VII) The best answer to No. 15 is **a.** The majority of jurisdictions define confidentiality in this way. The paid professional in the process bears the duty of confidentiality. No duty is imposed upon the participants who are not subject to rules of professional conduct in this process. If parties choose to make their mediation confidential and to undertake the burdens of contractually agreeing to confidentiality, then that choice can be made. The minority rule, legislated in California is the unenlightened view. It imposes upon the general "civilian" population a burdensome, difficult obligation normally only required of paid professionals. Given that mediation may even be legally mandated, with potentially severe legal consequences, this rule seems oppressive and could create an unduly punitive outcome if a party shared details of mediation with a close confidant.

16. The parties in a contentious divorce/property distribution ask the mediator to help them negotiate a mediated settlement. They want the mediator to act as arbitrator if they are not able to reach agreement after a certain point. The Mediator should:

   a. Accept the challenge and follow the Mediator/Arbitrator model.

b. Agree to the proposal but only with consent of both attorneys.

c. **Decline to act as Arbitrator and stick to Mediation.**

d. Decline to act as mediator and stick to arbitration.

ANSWER: (Standards I and IV) The answer to No. 16 is **c**. The Mediation-Arbitration model is in existence, and many respectable mediators follow it. However, it should never be called mediation because it is impossible to mediate as a neutral if the mediator has the power to decide the case. Giving the mediator the power to decide the case disempowers the mediator to perform mediation because it undermines client self-determination, the first standard, and the sine qua non of mediation. This model should simply be called arbitration, with the arbitrator conciliation the case first, as most judges do. Parties who want mediation followed by arbitration may simply choose another individual as the arbitrator. The model can be salvaged by using a different individual to perform the arbitration after mediation is exhausted.

17. Mediator has taken voluminous notes during a complex divorce mediation resulting in settlement of economic issues. Mediator drafted the Memorandum of Understanding. The attorneys do not agree on the wording of the paragraph regarding sale of the marital residence and division of proceeds. They want to look at the Mediator's notes. Mediator should:

a. Open her file to the attorneys and the clients.

b. Make notes available only to the clients by mailing them each a copy.

c. **Make notes available only to the clients in session.**

d. **Destroy the notes.**

ANSWER: The answer to No. 17 is not explicitly set forth in the Standards. The best answer is **d** if the mediator destroys notes (with prior notice to the clients that notes will not be kept) or **c** if the mediator has not destroyed the notes. Producing the mediator's notes, which are intended as a crutch to remember the facts in order to compose the Memorandum of Understanding would compromise the process by introducing information susceptible of misinterpretation, and not intended to be read by parties or attorneys. Notes are work product, and akin to the work product privilege enjoyed in the attorney/client relationship. Destruction of notes is customary in many mediation practices.

18. During a court-connected custody mediation, the parties disclose they use corporal punishment when necessary to discipline their children and that their son was treated for an infection on his back resulting from open wounds inflicted by Father's belt. Mediator should:

   a. **Make a "child-line" report.**

   b. **Keep the information confidential.**

   c. Tell only the attorneys.

   d. Inform the court.

ANSWER: The answer to No. 18 is derived from state mandated reporting laws. If mediators are mandated reporters or otherwise come within the law's purview, the answer is **a.** If mediators are not mandated reporters, then the language of the statute should be carefully analyzed to determine if the mediator falls within the law's intended reporters. Pennsylvania law no longer requires the reporter to come into contact with the child, but includes those who receive a report of abuse. It would seem that attorney-client privilege still applies in Pennsylvania for attorney mediators unless the attorney is affiliated with an agency, institution, or other entity involved in the care, guidance, control, or supervision of children. Pennsylvania law also requires mediators to abide by the ethical rules of their "primary" professions. Therefore, lawyers and psychologists must consider the confidentiality rules of their professions in resolving this dilemma. For attorneys, confidentiality does not permit the revelation of a past crime unless there is danger of imminent bodily harm, damage to financial interests or other exceptions. Therefore, if an attorney mediator reasonably believed the report would prevent future harm, an exception to confidentiality applies. (See 1.6

Model Rules of Professional Conduct). Given the likelihood that most, if not all, mediators are now mandated to call in a report of child abuse, a reasonable practice would be to insert a clause into the Agreement to Mediate (See Chapter 6) clearly disclosing exceptions to confidentiality.

19. In an advertising brochure, Mediator lists qualifications, memberships in professional associations, mediation trainings attended, and "60% settlement rate." The advertising is unethical because:

   a. Mediators are not allowed to advertise.

   b. Mediators may only list professional associations if they are for Mediators.

   c. Mediators are not permitted to advertise a settlement rate.

   d. Only attorneys may list their trainings.

ANSWER: (Standard XII [Comment A]) The answer to No. 19 is **c.** Mediators are prohibited from advertising settlement rates. This is because such conduct would be taking advantage of laymen who may be misled by such advertising.

20. In joint session in divorce negotiations, Mediator learns that Wife's attorney apparently is not aware of new court rules that would lengthen the period of time during which Wife could receive alimony. Mediator should:

   a. Ask the parties if they would consent to Mediator speaking to the attorneys about the new rules.

   b. Tell the parties about the new rule and how it might affect their case.

   c. Both of the above.

d. Neither of the above. Mediator should leave all legal issues to the attorneys and not discuss contested legal issues.

ANSWER: This question relates to the mediator's risk of engaging in the unauthorized practice of law. The best answer is **c.** The new rule is not a secret. It is appropriately a public law that everyone should be aware of. By transparently treating the information as something the parties can handle (with the help of their attorneys), the mediator is serving the clients' interests and is not practicing law.

21. During divorce mediation, parties exchange bank statements and other financial information. After three sessions, they reach an impasse and terminate mediation. During discovery, Husband notices that Wife has failed to disclose a bank account containing $30,000 for her massage therapy business. Wife's attorney states that this information is privileged because it was revealed during mediation. The court should:

    a. Rule that the material is privileged.

    b. Rule that the material is confidential

    c. Rule that the material is otherwise discoverable and must be produced.

    d. Rule that the statute of limitations bars discovery of records more than two years old.

ANSWER: The answer to No. 21 is **c** because privilege only goes so far.

22. Parties reached an impasse and both parties hired attorneys to litigate their divorce and economic issues. Mediator destroyed all notes taken during mediation sessions. Destruction of notes is:

    a. Unethical unless parties were first given the opportunity to receive copies.

b. Ethical because it is standard practice.

c. Unethical because the parties paid the mediator to take those notes.

d. **Ethical only if the parties were advised in the Agreement to Mediate that notes would be destroyed.**

ANSWER: The answer to No. 22 is **d**; however **b** could also be an acceptable answer if the notes are considered work product and, therefore, privileged.

23. A court has ordered parties into mediation regarding custody issues. Wife tells the mediator her attorney has advised her to keep silent and that she has nothing else to say and will not speak any further during mediation. Husband is willing to speak and to cooperate with mediation. The mediation ends in impasse because Wife will not participate. Husband's attorney has filed a Petition for Contempt and sent mediator a subpoena to testify regarding Wife's silence. Mediator should:

   a. Obey the subpoena but only agree to speak on the condition she received payment from Wife, who has not paid the mediator.

   b. Obey the subpoena but only speak about Wife's silence, Wife's statement, and nothing else.

   c. **Resist the subpoena.**

   d. **Notify the parties of the subpoena and advise them that she intends to obey it unless it is quashed.**

ANSWER: The answer to No 23 is **d**, although **c** is also acceptable if the mediator wants to incur the expense.

24. A new client contacts attorney mediator for purpose of retaining representation in a divorce action. Attorney (mediator) listens to a few details about client's case and suggests mediation instead of litigation, using attorney (mediator) as the mediator. Ethically, attorney mediator) is:

    a. Skating on thin ice due to conflict of interest.

    b. Engaging in illegal bait and switch tactics.

    c. Properly responding to the client's needs.

    d. Lacking boundaries.

ANSWER: The answer to No. 24 is **c.** It is acceptable for an attorney to evaluate a client's needs and recommend the role of mediator rather than advocate for the client. Caution needs to be taken during intake and the initial interview that the advocate role is not undertaken so strongly that the mediator's ability to be impartial is threatened.

25. Between sessions, parties email mediator, copying each other on the messages. In one of the messages, an agreement is reached to change the custody schedule adding a new overnight to Father's time and modifying the support agreement to include a provision that Mother alone will pay the cost of their oldest daughter's SAT Prep class. Father's attorney prepares a modified agreement, but Mother will not sign it. Despite a clause in the Agreement to Mediate stating parties will not subpoena Mediator, Father subpoenas Mediator to a hearing to authenticate the email exchanges. Mediator should:

    a. **Resist the subpoena with a Motion to Quash since the Agreement to Mediate stated parties would not subpoena Mediator.**

    b. Comply with the subpoena because it does not apply to email messages.

c. Sue the attorney for abuse of process since mediation communications are privileged.

d. Comply with the subpoena but assert the privilege at the hearing and refuse to testify.

ANSWER: The answer to No. 25 is **a** because the parties have signed the Agreement to Mediate, which expressly sets forth the parties' agreement not to subpoena the mediator. If possible, the mediator should seek sanctions.

Chapter Five

"People are generally more persuaded by the reasons which they have themselves discovered than by those which have come into the mind of others." –Blaise Pascal

The Art of Mediation: How Does a Mediator Inspire Change?

Change

Mediators know that a failure to reach settlement is not necessarily the mark of a "failed" mediation because the process can have profound effects on the conflict and can impact future attempts to come to resolution. Therefore, the true goal of mediation can only be to bring about change. Any change is the mark of a successful mediation. Change does not have to be visible; it can be internal or unseen. Change does not have to occur on the part of all parties; one party's change is capable of changing an entire conflict. It is often true, but certainly not always true, that "everyone must give up something." There exist those intractable conflicts where only one party needs to budge. At the outset, it is rarely known who must change and how, despite the myth that conflict can be "diagnosed."[147] Even the best conflict diagnosis cannot predict the exact change that will ultimately resolve a conflict because so much of what drives conflict is internal and hidden, not subject to analysis by any tool. Therefore, the mediator's objective is to catalyze change in order to move parties from frozen positions to, at minimum, a willingness to question the status quo. The process begins with the mediator whose approach to conflict is to "befriend" it.[148] "To be most effective in bridging conflict we need our whole selves interacting with others' whole selves in genuine inquiry."[149] By modeling curiosity and openness to conflict, including its negative aspects, the mediator is creating the possibility for participants to see their conflict in a way they've never viewed it before.

Conflict and Power

Being mediators means changing the way we think about conflict. A mediator must learn to be comfortable with conflict by addressing it in three ways: Appreciate it, respond to it, and manage it. If this sounds like a tall order, it is.

---

[147] Coltri, 2010.
[148] LeBaron, M. (2003), p. 169
[149] Id.

Appreciating Conflict

Appreciating conflict means recognizing its positive aspect. A cliché among mediation trainers is the Chinese symbol for conflict, made up of the symbols for Danger and Opportunity, demonstrating the true nature of conflict as recognized in Eastern cultures as having a positive side. In Western culture, conflict has a negative connotation with little positive meaning. Conflict is not appreciated; rather, it is maligned. Subtly, however, our culture does acknowledge a love for conflict. News reporters who want to attract attention know that stories about conflict receive the most interest. Conflict is at the center of every popular movie and book. Without conflict, nothing is attractive. Children learn in elementary school to write a book report by identifying the conflict in the story. Any story worth its salt has some kind of conflict, external or internal, personal or interpersonal. Fictional conflict fascinates while conflict in real life is something we wisely prefer to avoid. We think of conflict almost solely in terms of its dangerous aspect and almost never in terms of its opportunity. The opportunity offered by conflict is the opportunity to grow and change.

Every conflict, even an inner conflict, creates growth. Without conflict, there would be no personal growth and no progress as a society. This is the model nature provides. In nature, conflict is inherent—eat or be eaten—as seen in the animal kingdom. Clearly, conflict is dangerous because it can lead to destruction, but its benefits should not be overlooked. It's the "friction" M. Scott Peck refers to in A *Road Less Traveled*[150] wherein he makes the case for marriage, however painful and difficult it may be. In marriage, the friction created by conflict creates spiritual growth similar to how sand polishes a stone. Conflict as a resource is not optional. It is the only path to a satisfying life. It creates satisfying relationships, sound mental health, happy families, better workplaces, and a better world.[151] An understanding of conflict, therefore, involves an appreciation of its positive aspect and its benefits to mankind, individually and collectively.

There are many definitions of conflict. In law, conflict of interest and conflict of laws refer to incompatibilities. In international affairs, conflict can mean war, genocide, or conquest. In interpersonal relations, conflict is defined as "an expressed struggle between at least two interdependent parties who perceive incompatible goals, scarce resources, and interference from others in achieving their goals."[152] It's interesting that conflict only requires a *perception* of incompatible goals, not necessarily an actual incompatibility. Recognizing that conflict can be an illusion helps the mediator bring about change in the conflict merely by illuminating it.

In appreciating conflict, the mediator behaves counter-intuitively because people nearly always (wisely) avoid conflict. The typical initial reaction to conflict is negative. Putting a positive spin on the

---

[150] Peck, M. Scott. (1978). *The road less traveled: A new psychology of love, traditional values and spiritual growth*. New York: Simon and Schuster.
[151] Wilmot, W., Hocker, J. (2001). *Interpersonal conflict* (6th ed). New York: McGraw Hill, 5-7.
[152] Id., 41.

concept takes time, study, and practice. Once a mediator begins to appreciate conflict, it becomes obvious that conflict is never resolved, and with good reason. It is the lifeblood. Conflict is not "resolved" until we are in the grave, and, perhaps, not even then. It seems that as long as we walk the earth, conflict will continue to polish and refine our characters by forcing us to grow.

Responding to Conflict

Responding to conflict is the second responsibility of the mediator. An effective mediator response to conflict is to allow it. Allowing conflict is not avoiding or ignoring it. It is not resisting or denying it. It is not judging it. These are the typical intuitive reactions humans have to conflict because of their thought that conflict is to be avoided as dangerous, which, in certain cases, is perfectly appropriate. Allowing conflict is to accept it in the moment when it appears. Mediators who allow conflict are empowered because they have not placed themselves in a defensive position against the conflict and have no urge to retaliate, defend, or prohibit the conflict. This is not the same as remaining passive in the presence of destructive behavior requiring immediate, defensive action. Conflict is merely an incompatibility between two perspectives, and, as noted above, a "perception" not always real. Too often, mediators and mediation participants respond to mere conflict in the same way they would respond to inappropriate behavior. Conflict alone (the perception) is to be allowed if it is ever to be addressed.

Managing Conflict

Managing conflict is the third responsibility of the mediator. In order to manage conflict the mediator must be present as a third party who recognizes that they are not part of the conflict. The mediator is an observer, an interpreter, a guide and support, a leader and follower, but never a party to the conflict. In order to manage conflict, the mediator must know the boundary in the process.

The Mediator-Client Boundary

The boundary between the mediator and the parties is the essence of mediation. Every profession defines itself by the boundary between the professional and the client. Because mediation is a therapeutic process, it is helpful to compare mediation to psychotherapy in understanding the boundary. Mediation can seem similar to psychotherapy, but it is a discrete profession that is decidedly separate from psychotherapy and law practice, its not-so-distant cousins. The mediator must listen, understand, synthesize, and empathize— all therapeutic interventions in that they provide comfort and meaning-making for the client by promoting introspection. In psychotherapy, the therapist enters the client's inner world with the client. In mediation, the client must enter his or her own inner world, and the mediator does not accompany the client as a matter of course. There is a boundary between the client's psyche and the mediator in mediation. The psychotherapeutic relationship is much more intimate than the mediator-client relationship. The boundary between the mediator and client is more distinct. There are certainly times when mediation and therapy appear to overlap, such as when parties express strong emotions and invite the mediator's empathy. However, the mediator, by definition, is not working for only one party (as the therapist is in one-on-one therapy) but exists to support all parties in managing their conflict. The mediator role is to manage the conflict, not to help one party manage life. I believe we are all born mediators and that the techniques can be practiced by anyone with mediation training, not limited to mental health professionals.

In many ways, the two processes are similar. The interventions—refraining from judgment, understanding, listening, synthesizing, and empathizing—are similar. They are all therapeutic practices. They evoke change in similar ways—by inspiring internal change that leads to external change. The boundaries, and, therefore, the methods, are different. In mediation, all participants, including the mediator, go inside themselves-- into their own inner worlds-- to process and seek comfort with emotions, as well as to reconcile thoughts with those emotions. Every participant in mediation is responsible for their own behavior, feelings, and perspectives. There is no dependency as there can be (permissibly) in a psychotherapist-client relationship. Every person in mediation, including the mediator, is engaging in introspection, in order for there to be an effective mediation.

The fundamental quality of the mediator-client boundary is personal responsibility for the conflict. Part of that responsibility is to allow client self-determination by maintaining neutrality, defined by Bush & Folger as "a commitment to use influence only for the sake of keeping the ultimate decision on outcome in the parties' hands."[153] When a mediator trespasses the boundary and extends the helper role to join in ownership of the conflict with the parties, the mediator does a disservice to clients and to the process. Mediators are caring, helping professionals, and the temptation to break the boundary and try to fix the problem for the parties is strong. One simple indication that a mediator has stepped over the line is use of the pronoun "we," as in, "Last session we agreed that Billy would see his dad on weekends," or "Now, we've already agreed that your daughter Lucy will not be around when you are dating." Psychotherapists are accustomed to using "we" with clients because their relationship is so intimate and the therapist truly is partnered with the client in solving the client's problems. The mediator, however, cannot take ownership of clients' problems because that dilutes the clients' personal responsibility and autonomy that are necessary to fuel the parties' needed efforts to resolve the conflict, forming the essence of the boundary.

Parties notice the subtle use of "we." Often, they react in a not-so-subtle, largely unconscious, way. When they hear "we," parties immediately feel a burden lifted from them, sensing that the mediator is willing to take on responsibility for their problem. And, in many cases, this naïve mediator is so "helpful" that she really believes it is her role to take on the clients' problems. The result can be disastrous leading the parties to withdraw their ownership of the problem and relax efforts to work on a resolution. It is a sure killer of a healthy, robust mediation where introspection promotes personal responsibility to solve the problem. By joining with the parties simply with language, the mediator has taken on a disproportionate responsibility for the parties' problem. When my students use "we" in role plays, as in, "Okay, so, how are we going to arrange the schedule so that Dad can have Jacob overnight even when he works late?" I might interrupt and ask with my tongue in cheek, "Does the mediator also plan to go home with Dad this evening and tuck Jacob in at bedtime? Maybe read him a story first?" The word "we" is, of course, appropriately

---

[153] Bush and Folger, 1994, 105.

used when it involves the mediator's work within the boundary, such as, "We should schedule your next appointment now." When used appropriately, "we" reinforces the boundary. When used inappropriately to join with the parties in ownership of their problem, "we" weakens the boundary and disempowers the parties by depriving them of resources to solve the problem because the best resources to solve the problem come from the parties.

Establishing the Boundary

The mediator's job is a role. The mediation room is a stage. The mediation performance is an art. A mediator's medium is primarily words, and, secondarily, body language. What does it mean when a mediator sneezes or coughs? Probably nothing, but how about when a mediator yawns or stretches? Laughs, looks surprised, or smiles? Mediators are human and, even though the mediator's behavior in session with clients is a role (similar to an actor playing a part), there is no script and the mediator's personality inevitably becomes part of the role.

The mediator is a participant, but the clients own the problem. The mediator establishes the boundary with "I" statements. "We" statements sound helpful on the surface, but they are boundary-destroyers. When the boundary is destroyed, the door of disrespect is opened. To create a "we" is dangerous. Clients often present themselves in a vulnerable and raw state. When they don't detect an appropriate boundary, they are liable to attack the mediator out of fear, resentment or disrespect. The lack of the boundary not only leads to disrespect for the mediator, but makes clients feel violated and disrespected. It is the mediator's responsibility to maintain the boundary, not the clients'. "I" statements give the mediator power. "I" statements by the mediator are anchoring, informing and reassuring clients that they are secure, and that an appropriate boundary is being observed. There is nothing more powerful in a mediation session than a mediator observing and expressing the boundary with effective, genuine "I" statements.

What Are "I" Statements?

True "I" statements don't transgress an individual's boundary by attempting to describe the other with use of the word "I." For example, "I feel that you are being mean," is not a pure "I" statement because it is a description of the other. In addition to being accurate, an "I" statement should be genuine and truthful. In mediation, clients often describe difficult situations and overwhelming emotions. When a mediator responds with "I understand," in response to an expression of grief, this "I" statement could feel presumptuous to the client who believes no one who hasn't experienced the same grief could possibly understand. This mediator seems patronizing or insincere by suggesting that they actually understands a party's singular, profound experience. Such grief is special and unique. It is safer for the mediator to say, "I can imagine," or, if the grief is profound, "I can only imagine."

When parties express negative emotions, a normal human response may be to reject the negative feelings. A mediator who accepts feelings and says, genuinely and truthfully, "I hear what you are saying," or "I hear what you are saying and I am okay with it," establishes the mediator's distinct role and boundary, not enmeshed with the clients and experiencing their emotions with them, and not judging them, but accepting them. Such a boundary creates respect for the mediator. Parties don't want a mediator who claims to feel their pain because they find it dishonest. Parties also don't want a mediator who acts like a therapist and says, "Tell me how that feels." This can feel intrusive in mediation. Psychotherapists who become mediators must overcome their tendency to go right into their clients' inner worlds and ask intimate, intrusive questions that expose emotions participants don't want to expose in a session with an ex. Similarly, attorneys who become mediators need to be mindful that not every fact is available to them, as is customary in the attorney-client relationship. Attorneys have a license to pry into their clients' private lives. Mediators do not. In a mediation training session, five successive attorneys (and law students) spontaneously asked mediation clients who stated they were "separated' but still living together in the marital residence, "Are you sleeping in separate beds?" To an attorney, this fact has legal significance because it directly relates to the establishment of a "date of separation," an important fact in divorce law.[154] To a mediator, it does not because the mediator is interested in what the parties are expressing at the moment, not in creating legal positions for the parties.

Appropriate "I" statements relate to anything in the process for which the mediator has ownership. The mediator has rights in the process, just as the parties do, and the mediator's use of "I" statements to assert rights is appropriate. "I need to stop you," "I need to do my job," "I will tell you….," "I'd like to check in with you," or "I am wondering if this is helpful, or if you would like some feedback, or if you would like to discuss a, b, or c….," "Help me understand," "I sense that…," "I feel like…." are all powerful "I" statements that clients can easily understand and accept. They are not an attempt to patronize or to intrude on the client's inner world.

Mediators who understand their role and act within their boundary know that mediation works by promoting internal change within the parties. Internal change leads to external change. The parties go inside themselves privately to process emotions and thoughts evoked in the mediation session. Their internal process brings about change in themselves individually, leading to changes in their interactions and relationship. For this reason, time is also a factor in bringing about changes in perceptions because clients process emotions, which often requires time and sleep. It is very common in mediation for clients to process positive change within themselves between sessions, coming back to easily resolve an issue that seemed impossible at first.

Meanwhile, the mediator also goes inside self to become comfortable with their own emotions. All individuals in the process are responsible for their own emotions. The mediator's emotions are rarely of interest to the clients. For instance, when mediators find themselves judging clients or feeling negative reactions, the mediator's professional responsibility is to attend to those feelings. On the other hand, at times the mediator's feelings are of interest to clients. Sometimes a mediator's feeling will be of value to the process. The test of relevance of the mediator's feeling is, does it relate to what the clients are doing or

---

[154] See Chapter 8, infra.

saying in the session? Whether it should be shared with the clients is determined by whether or not it is helpful to the clients and does not step over their boundary. An example is a mediator who truly does not understand what clients are saying. It is perfectly fine, and helpful, for the mediator to say, "I am having trouble understanding what you mean. Help me understand." (A highly effective "I" statement.) On the other hand, it would not be helpful for the mediator to say, "I am confused." This could step on the boundary by disguising a "you" statement as an "I" statement. It can be heard by clients as, "You are confusing." Another context in which to think about boundaries and appropriate "I" statements is the context of mediator and client rights.

MEDIATOR'S RIGHTS

The mediator has the right to feel comfortable, to have feelings, to express feelings, to have boundaries, to be safe, to be paid. The mediator does not have the right to intrude on clients' privacy and inner world, to initiate conflict with clients, or to express feelings or thoughts without regard to the clients' rights to feel safe and respected. The mediator has a duty to be respectful of every client's boundary. Most mediations that fail are the result of the mediator not respecting boundaries. This alienates the parties, erodes their trust in the mediator, and disempowers the process.

CLIENTS' RIGHTS

Clients have the right to feel comfortable, to have feelings, to have a neutral mediator, to have a mediator free of ego, to be safe, to make mistakes, to speak freely, to have the process explained to them, to get value for their money (i.e., a skilled mediator), and to have a mediator who respects boundaries. Parties know that a mediator is not a lawyer or a therapist, and when the mediator exhibits these professional qualities too much, parties sense that the process is off-course.

Maintaining the Boundary

The mediator is responsible for maintaining the mediator-client boundary throughout the process. This is done using visualization, impartiality, and language. Visualization is literally visualizing a physical line of demarcation between the mediator and the clients. For most of us who are visual learners, this technique serves as a reminder of the importance of tending to the boundary at every possible opportunity throughout the process. For example, if a party provokes the mediator by challenging the mediator's neutrality, the mediator may be tempted to take defensive action that could result in conflict between the mediator and the party. Engaging in conflict with a party is not a mediator's right. Therefore, focusing on the imaginary boundary line helps the mediator to refrain from engaging in conflict with a party. If a party questions the mediator's neutrality, the mediator should respond without defensiveness. The mediator's gut may be goading her to defend herself. However, by focusing on the boundary line, the mediator is reminded that she must use this opportunity to reinforce the boundary by defining her role. Such an exchange could go like this:

Client: (interrupting while Mother airs her perspective) *I get it. The female is always right. Your job is to side with the mother to make sure she gets what she wants. That's the way it goes in this state. The father gets nothing. I thought you said you were impartial. But that's not really how it is.*

Mediator: *Let me see if I can explain. I am impartial between the 2 of you, but I am not really impartial because I <u>am</u> on the side of your kids. In here, I want to make sure both of you have the same chance to express yourselves. If that isn't happening, I have to get involved to make sure it does. But my main concern is for the kids' well-being. Now, I would like to listen to what Mom was saying, and then I want to hear your response, okay? This isn't about either parent having an advantage, only about presenting all sides and giving the kids the best possible arrangement that the 2 of you can live with.*

Client: *Sure*

Mother completes her thoughts, and Mediator turns to Father.

Mediator: *Phillip, now I'd like to hear your perspective to listen so that both of you have the same chance to say what you want to say and then respond to each other.*

    The key to this kind of dialog is to place the importance of the mediator-client boundary above the mediator's ego's need to defend. By not acting defensively, the mediator will disarm Phillip because he is expecting to engage in conflict with the mediator. By focusing on non-defensive body language and tone of voice, the mediator reassures Phillip that the commitment to impartiality is more important than the mediator's ego. When Phillip sees and believes this, he will gain trust in the mediator. Reinforcing the boundary creates this trust.

    The second way to maintain the boundary is with impartiality. In the above dialog, Phillip apparently began to see the mediator as partial to the other party merely because the mediator was listening attentively to the other party's perspective. The mediator might have avoided this perception by paying closer attention to Phillip while the mother was speaking. By using body language, eye contact, and hand motions, the mediator can maintain contact with both parties while only one party is speaking, sometimes when necessary even interrupting to tell the other party, "Please hold on because I do want to hear your perspective." The skill of attending to two parties while listening attentively to one party speak is a skill that is tricky at first, but does become second nature to a mediator over time.

    A third way to maintain the mediator-client boundary is with language. Using the parties' names to address them directly reinforces the party's importance as an individual. In my many observations of mediators, I see them address parties without using a party's name. Worse, I notice the mediator referring to the other party as "her" when she is sitting right there. The simple practice of using party's names (the sweetest sound in any language[155]) is a golden opportunity to personalize the process and create a bond of

---

[155] Carnegie, D. (1936). How to win friends and influence people. New York: Simon & Schuster.

trust and good will between the mediator and the parties. Generous use of the terms "I" and "you" reinforce the boundary to remind everyone in the room that there is a line of demarcation that separates responsibility for solving the problem. The parties' problem will never be my problem, and I will never try to make it my problem.

The Case of Jennifer and Patrick
Case Study in Boundaries

Jennifer and Patrick are married professional adults. They have two children, Jordan, a daughter age 5 and Eric, age 3. They are in mandatory mediation because Jennifer filed a complaint for custody.

About five months ago, Patrick informed Jennifer he had a girlfriend named Nina. Nina was pregnant, and he was leaving Jennifer to go live with Nina.

Patrick was filled with guilt. When he finally brought himself to tell Jennifer about Nina, Jennifer was able to capitalize on Patrick's guilt and convince him to visit a renowned "divorce therapist" thought to be one of the best "co-parenting counselors" in the city, Dr. Bill. For the past five months, Jennifer, Patrick, and their two children have been attending regular therapy sessions with Dr. Bill.

Jennifer tells the mediator that after Patrick moved out, on the advice of Dr. Bill, they did not tell the children that Mommy and Daddy were separating or that Daddy was moving out. Instead, Daddy picked up the children from school every week day, took them home to the marital residence, ate dinner with the children and Jennifer, and left after the children went to bed, to go home to Nina. This went on until two and a half weeks ago, when, on the advice of Dr. Bill, Jennifer and Patrick told the children that Daddy is now living in an apartment and that Mommy and Daddy do not live together anymore. The children took the news badly and cried a lot. Jordan, especially, was very disturbed by the news and is having problems accepting that Mommy and Daddy are no longer going to be together.

On the advice of Dr. Bill, Patrick is continuing the same schedule of visiting the children and Jennifer will not consent to Patrick having any other time with the children. She especially does not want Patrick to take the children to his apartment where he lives with Nina and their new baby.

Patrick has told Dr. Bill that he is willing to work things out in co-parenting counseling because he thinks involving the court could be traumatic to the family, but he has stated that he will only do so if he sees progress towards his ultimate goal of introducing the children to Nina (whom he wants to marry when he and Jennifer are divorced), and their new baby brother, and having them overnight at the apartment like a normal step-family.

Jennifer is resolute against Patrick taking any action that would expose the children to Nina, the baby, or Patrick's home. She does not think that Patrick's home is a good place for her children because

Patrick and Nina have both demonstrated that they have "bad judgment." Jennifer's lawyer has presented a proposed custody order to Patrick that states the parties shall continue seeing Dr. Bill and gradually introduce the children to "Patrick's new reality" over time and that Dr. Bill will be given sole discretion to decide when the time is appropriate. Although Patrick is a lawyer, he does not have a lawyer and will not sign the proposed order because he is not comfortable giving power over his parental rights to a therapist. About a week ago, Dr. Bill deigned that now the children could be introduced to Nina. He suggested a meeting at a local diner where Jennifer, Patrick, Nina, and the two kids met and talked. Nina was presented to the children as Daddy's friend.

Patrick is trying to cooperate because he wants family harmony (for both of his families). He has a nagging feeling that following Dr. Bill's lead may cause problems. He says that every person he respects has told him that this is not normal, and that it is not the right thing to do to lie to your children about still living in your home when you have moved out, then lie to them about your girlfriend, telling the kids she's just a friend, and then to refuse to tell them they have a new baby brother.

Jennifer defends Dr. Bill's approach, saying that he is only trying to appropriately and gradually transition the children, and that it would be too traumatic to introduce all of this new information to them at one time, and that in a few weeks Dr. Bill plans to announce that the children may now be told that Nina is really Daddy's girlfriend. The children have an appointment this weekend with Dr. Bill. The purpose of the appointment is for Dr. Bill to evaluate their progress and see how they reacted to meeting Nina for the first time. Patrick states that this is absurd. Why would the children have any reaction to someone who has been introduced as Daddy's friend?

The mediator is concerned about:

1. Permanent harm to the children that will result when they soon find out the truth about lies their parents are telling them;
2. A therapist who has taken on the role of dictator (or at least the architect of a bizarre family restructuring);
3. Strange and inconsistent ideas about how to handle restructuring of a family;
4. A mother who is (perhaps unintentionally) transferring her anger and heartbreak onto her children;
5. A father who, out of guilt and fear, is failing to do what he thinks is right for his family;
6. A therapist who has no boundaries and has allowed his client (Jennifer) to control him.

Mediator did some very "innocent" reality testing. Mediator said, "I know Dr. Bill is your therapist and I don't want to disagree with his advice because I am not a therapist, but what is being said about the betrayal your children may feel when they do find out they weren't told the truth?"

Both parents acknowledged that this was a concern, but that Dr. Bill thought it was the lesser of two evils to withhold the truth from the children. He thought that giving them complete information would be most harmful.

The parties continued to discuss their perspectives, and it soon became clear that Jennifer was full of rage and was controlling everyone with her intense rage, even Dr. Bill. Her rage came out in a five-second, sudden outburst. She lurched toward Patrick from across the table, looked him in the eye, and in the calm, professional voice she had been using all session, said, "Patrick, you don't understand how HARD this is for me." When she said the word "HARD" her voice became so loud it seemed as if an explosion had hit the building. Her face turned purple and contorted. Large veins popped out of her neck, throbbing. But, then, just as suddenly, within five seconds or less, she reverted to her demure demeanor, her face still beet red and blood vessels in her neck still swollen. It was obvious to mediator Jennifer was very used to getting her way by exhibiting intimidating, nearly debilitating, rageful behavior. It was equally obvious to the mediator that Patrick, who seemed unfazed by Jennifer's outburst, was accustomed to Jennifer's fits of rage. The mediator immediately sensed that it might not be a good idea at all to cross Jennifer. The mediator felt that Patrick should be encouraged to see a lawyer, and suggested to both parties that they seek legal advice and consider trying mediation again after that. The mediator explained that, although Dr. Bill was guiding them from a counseling perspective, he could not guide them legally. Since they were now in the court system, it was important for both of them, not just Jennifer, to have legal advice and counsel.

Power

Conflict goes hand-in-hand with power. In the above example, Jennifer was exerting power over people in her world by manipulating a therapist and her husband to engineer a false reality. Patrick did not really live with her, and their marriage was a sham. It would eventually vaporize, so did Jennifer really have power? In reality, Jennifer was power-less because she had no power to do what she truly wanted to do: get Patrick to come home to her voluntarily. From a mediator's perspective, Jennifer's power created a power imbalance in mediation because Patrick had no defense against her control, except to behave passive-aggressively outside of mediation by acting out against her wishes and establishing a wholly new family. Patrick's choice to avoid confrontation with Jennifer, who used bullying, intimidating behavior to control people (including the family therapist) left him with no ability to negotiate at arm's length (as equals) with Jennifer. Away from Jennifer's presence, he compensated for his weakness by taking drastic actions against her in ways he felt he could safely exercise his own will. In doing so, however, his behavior was self-destructive and destructive to his family. He now found himself in a worse position because he had to appease two women. The mediator's hope for Patrick was that he would hire an attorney to become empowered by an advocate who could see the situation objectively and not in fear of the bully. The mediator's hope for the parties was that they would return to mediation. It is likely that Jennifer had no use for mediation at this point because she had come upon a professional (the mediator) who had her number, and would not be manipulated by her. Jennifer had a much greater advantage in Dr. Bill, whom she could manipulate. By maintaining an appropriate boundary while having compassion and concern for Jennifer, the mediator left the door open for the parties to return to mediation.

Mediators have a duty to assess power and the balance of power in mediation. Some argue that a mediator does not need to balance power because any perceived imbalance of power could simply be the existing power relationship between the parties that has thrived for years, and will continue long after mediation, and it is not the mediator's role to change it. Others insist that the mediator add this task to the mediator's already-full plate of tasks, arguing that a relative balance of power is necessary in order for parties to negotiate effectively.[156] This means the parties need to come to the table as relative equals. Both parties have to possess at least some share of power. It is not necessary for exact balance to exist, and it is not necessary for their power to come from the same source. For example, a husband's power could be economic, and a wife's power could come from her legal rights. Patently unequal power intuitively negates a fair negotiation. This is most evident in an extreme example where one side has all the power, such as in a slave and slave owner or in some employment scenarios where at-will employment allows an employer to dismiss an employee for any reason absent illegal discrimination. It is essential in mediation as in any contract for both parties to have some bargaining power. Otherwise, it is not an arms-length transaction, and coercion or lack of bargaining power can negate a contract, under common law contract principles. Some relative balance of power is necessary for an effective negotiation, and a complete imbalance of power makes mediation impossible. Power is derived from a range of sources, including ability to understand, material resources, and ability to negotiate,[157] just to name a few.

Power is present in all social interactions.[158] Wilmot and Hocker describe power as a product of the interpersonal relationship, not of the individual. This power is neither negative nor positive; it just is. People instinctively try to balance power, either constructively or destructively, depending upon their natures. Everyone is always, mostly unconsciously, assessing every social situation to size up who has power, who has too much power, who has too little power, and "Do I have enough power?" Then they compensate accordingly. This concept is similar to the phenomenon of how an elevator is populated. As soon as one person steps off, the group instinctively shifts to balance the distribution of people. It is a rare person who will not move when someone leaves the elevator.

Power can be apparent power or unseen power. Apparent power is possessed by a bully. The bully appears to have power over others; however, the bully's behavior is born of insecurity and fear, and the bully is in reality powerless, putting on a display of power to overcome insecurity. Apparent power is external. Control, manipulation, aggressiveness, intimidation, invulnerability, and stubbornness are all shields serving as protection to hide behind fear. In *The Power of Now,* Eckhart Tolle states, "Power over

---

[156] Haynes, J. (1988). Power balancing. In Folberg, J., & Milne, A. (Eds.). *Divorce mediation theory and practice.* New York: Guilford Press, 277-296. See also, Wilmot & Hocker, 2001, 115.
[157] Fisher & Ury, 1991, 178-187.
[158] Wilmot & Hocker, 2001, 105.

others is weakness disguised as strength. True power is within…."[159] Some mediators mistake the bully as powerful; whereas, the true analysis is the bully lacks power. A mediator wishing to balance power in such a situation does well to pay attention not only to the bullied, but also to the bully, who is powerless. True power, or unseen power, is internal. It consists of a person's self-esteem, aspirations, and desires. Those who appear powerless, such as prisoners, the oppressed, and pacifists are able to summon power from within and accomplish great things with hunger strikes, unionization, suicide threats, and words. When internal power is accessed, people become resourceful and are able to manifest power seemingly out of thin air. The mediator's task, therefore, is to guide parties to find their internal power. In this manner, the mediator "balances power" by creating more of it, i.e., empowering parties. The mediator's tools for doing this are listening, observing, empathizing, synthesizing, and using non-threatening language to guide parties towards their own power.

The Case of Susan and Joe

Guiding a Disempowered Mom Towards Her Own Power (Empowering Dad in the Process)

Susan and Joe were the never-married parents of a 15 year-old son Corey. When their child was an infant, Joe was an active alcoholic. He essentially abandoned Susan to raise their son on her own. Now Joe is trying to obtain primary custody of his son. Joe has been in recovery from alcoholism for four years and has rebuilt his life to include a loving and close relationship with Corey, a leadership role in a twelve-step program where he sponsors numerous recovering alcoholics, a responsible and well-paying job, and a home he has created for himself as a single father. He has devoted the last three years to making up for lost time with Corey. Father and son have a surprisingly close and loving relationship. Mother has felt extremely resentful of Father for leaving her to fend for herself and their son for twelve difficult years. She seemed full of rage and unresolved anger. Her knee-jerk reaction to any request made by Joe to be with Corey has been, "No." Regardless of what Joe asked, Susan's response was a blanket refusal to everything. She knew she possessed power in the legal system. Her attorney consistently assured her that Joe's past conduct would be so frowned upon by a court that Joe would never rise above his position as part-time parent, and would not be given full legal or physical custody of their child because of his choice to abandon the family and stay away for such a prolonged period of time. Susan's attorney was very confident that Susan would always be favored in the court system and that Joe would have very little say in any custody matter. The attorney told Susan that she could "call the shots," and that Joe would be powerless to do anything about it. Susan seemed to rely on her attorney to assure her that she was doing

---

[159] Tolle, E. (1999). *The power of now*. Novato, CA: New World Library.

the right thing because she had such a superior legal position. Somehow, though, Father and son had managed to work around Susan's refusals and intransigence, and Joe was able to keep his son overnight at his home a fair amount of the time. The two of them were able to find reasons why Dad just "had" to keep him there overnight. The game went into extra innings. The traffic was so bad. It was late. They didn't want to wake up Mom. The one thing Susan could not deny was that Father and son were like two peas in a pod. They had an excellent, very positive relationship, and Corey really seemed to come alive and shine since he came to know his father. Still, in mediation and in meetings with her attorney, Susan was 100% opposed to changing custody. She admitted Corey unequivocally wanted to live with his father. She acknowledged that she and Corey no longer got along, and that their home was a constant battleground with Corey becoming increasingly hostile and hateful towards her. His anger was beginning to worry her a lot. It was unlike typical teenage anger, and seemed to be turning into real hatred towards her. Her honor role, boy-scout son was turning on her. He freely expressed his feelings towards her, and it was getting worse by the day. She did the only thing she knew to do in response: discipline him. This made him resent her more, and life was becoming unbearable for Susan. She told the mediator that to let Corey go to live with his father would mean invalidating all of the work she had done for those twelve years when Joe did nothing. She also feared she was losing her boy, and that to let him go with his father would be his final exit from her life forever. She was clinging to the only power she had.

The mediator empathized with Susan and her situation by reflecting her words back to her, nodding her head, making eye contact, and genuinely feeling concern for Susan's situation. Mediator saw the situation as serious, perhaps more serious than Susan admitted because Susan was using her attorney's confidence and reassurance as a shield from the reality of her deteriorating relationship with her son. The mediator reflected back the pain, observed, and commented on the dilemma, a rock and a hard place, in which Susan found herself. The mediator made it clear to Susan with her body language and eye contact, that Susan had a problem on her hands that needed to be addressed. This simple intervention seemed to empower Susan. She was able to see her situation afresh because it had been presented to her anew by the mediator. She immediately became cognizant that her situation might be worse than she was allowing herself to believe. She seemed to become aware that she needed to take some action because her inaction was making the situation worse. The mediator then asked Susan if she could imagine "letting go" of her son and allowing him to live with his dad as he was requesting. At first, Susan resisted the suggestion and told the mediator she could not imagine it because if she did, it would mean letting Father "win" and letting her son "win" and wasting 15 years of her hard work and discipline. Father, who all along had been observing the conversation between mediator and Mother, and whom mediator had attended to all along with eye contact and body language, chimed in. He was very engrossed in the conversation between mediator and Mother. He supported Susan's good mothering and told her that, if it weren't for all of her hard work and sacrifice while he was AWOL, they would not have the wonderful young man Corey has obviously become today. He gave her credit and praise for her work. Mother was eventually able to imagine letting go of her death grip on her son, and eventually relented and consented to a change in primary custody. As mother continued to consider letting go of her son, her facial expression relaxed, she began to smile and appeared happier.

Questions for Discussion and Analysis:

1. **How did the mediator help Mother gain access to her own power and resolve the conflict within herself? What was the effect of Mediator asking Mother to "imagine" doing what Father and son wanted?**

Answer: The mediator perceived that Mother was actually considering doing this. If Mother did not appear to be entertaining this option at all, or at least to be thinking about it, the mediator would not have taken the risk of making such a suggestion. Prior to making the suggestion, Mediator had already established a bond of trust with mother by truly empathizing with and comprehending her dilemma. Mother appreciated mediator's attention, concern, and grasp of her seemingly impossible situation. Mediator apprehended Mother's pain and Mother sensed that and trusted the mediator. By suggesting that Mother imagine letting go, the mediator was putting it out as an acceptable option without overtly saying so. Mediator could not have done so in a direct way because it would have been too confusing to mother for mediator to suggest something in direct conflict with her attorney, whom she has trusted and relied on for many years. Mediator's suggestion was more of a question than a statement, making it non-threatening to mother. It was put forth as a hypothetical only. The mediator's intent, however, is obvious to everyone, even if only unconsciously. A mediator would never ask a client to imagine doing something dishonest or illegal, or clearly wrong. By merely asking a client to imagine something she seemed to already be considering (very peripherally) the mediator is sending the message that the suggested behavior is an acceptable option. Mother's other advisor, her attorney, would not allow that letting go of Corey was an acceptable option. The attorney was acting appropriately within her legal role. In the end, it was about "face-saving" for Mother, by her own admission. She could not lose face by negating her fifteen years of hard work. She needed to view the situation in a way that supported her past work, validated her role as good mother, and acknowledged the past, while tending to the urgent, present needs of her son. Her motivation for letting go was her realization that a change was needed to counteract the downward spiral of deterioration of her current relationship with her son.

2. **How did the mediator empower Father to come forth and contribute to the process in a constructive way?**

Answer: In attending to Mother, mediator was not ignoring father. Parties sometimes do feel ignored if the mediator engages in a prolonged conversation with the other party. Mediator observed father and noticed that he was involved in the conversation, listening attentively. Mediator attended to him with eye contact and body language. Father's contribution, giving mother acknowledgment and praise, was pivotal to the process. Without it, Mother would not have allowed herself, ultimately, to make the internal change she was able to make because she needed validation. Mediator's conversation with Mother was empowering to Father. He felt supported by the mediator, and gained increasing confidence in himself, as well as appreciation for Mother, because the mediator was implicitly validating his role as father.

Transformative Mediation: Empowerment and Recognition

Although Bush and Folger are credited with the Transformative model of mediation, they were not the first mediators to speak about empowerment. John Haynes regularly stressed the importance of empowerment in mediation. "Intervention that does not empower the clients to take charge of their own lives, to make their own decisions, and to understand enough about the past to be able to avoid replicating the undesirable aspects of it, is, in my opinion, unacceptable intervention."[160] A problem-solving approach to Susan and Joe's situation would have involved the mediator making suggestions, or "generating options" for the parties to solve their problem. The mediator is then in the role of persuader, advocating the mediator's proposed solutions. This approach clearly would have not worked for Susan and Joe. Susan came prepared for such an intervention, but she did not come prepared for a mediator who would try to empower her to make a decision she had been fearfully considering. Susan had shielded herself for years against any challenge to her power as mother, chief decision-maker, superior litigant, and party-in-control. A mediator's overt suggestion that she change her strategy would have met fierce resistance. This approach would have polarized the parties further and would not have helped them to experience a change in perception. What did help them experience a change in their perceptions was "an intervention that empowers the clients" as Haynes advocates. Such an intervention does not push, persuade, overtly suggest, or problem-solve. An empowering intervention is devoid of an attempt to persuade. It is presented in a non-threatening, non-persuasive way, typically as a question. It allows parties to focus on themselves, not on the mediator.

Empowerment

Empowerment in mediation is defined by Bush & Folger as, "the restoration to individuals of a sense of their own value and strength and their own capacity to handle life's problems."[161] Recognition is defined as, "the evocation in individuals of acknowledgment and empathy for the situation and problems of others." Empowerment typically happens to the individual, while recognition is a response individuals experience with each other. Examples of empowerment are self-respect, self-reliance, and self-confidence. Bush & Pope[162] in describing the mediator's participation in transformative mediation, explain, *"Close listening*, combined with observation of what the parties are conveying through body language, is thus a foundational skill that is used continuously throughout the mediation." The transformative mediator avoids the impulse to be directive because directive impulses designed to reduce conflict, avoid unfairness, or impose a mediator-designed solution will not promote self-awareness for the parties and may cause them to focus, instead, on the mediator. Directive impulses will most likely create defensiveness, resentment, or conflict with the mediator. It is not the mediator's right to initiate conflict with the parties. While the mediator is exercising transformative techniques of close listening, empathy, reflection, non-threatening

---

[160] Haynes, 1981, 134.
[161] Bush & Folger, 1994, 2.
[162] Bush & Pope, 2004, 62.

questions, appropriate silence, nods, eye contact and body language, opportunities will present themselves for the parties to experience empowerment. Bush & Folger call these opportunities "signposts."[163] In general, signposts are any point in mediation where the mediator recognizes that something important has arisen that could result in an opportunity for empowerment or recognition for the parties. Examples that routinely occur in nearly every mediation are:

1. Being listened to or listening.

2. Being understood or understanding something for the first time.

3. Being treated with respect or treating with respect, especially when the relationship has lacked respect.

4. Apologizing or taking responsibility.

5. Believing (rather than doubting or accusing) or being believed.

6. Questioning whether or not the mediation process is helpful.

7. Questioning whether or not using a different process (i.e., the legal process) is helpful.

8. Taking time to be thoughtful about decisions instead of jumping to conclusions.

9. Being undecided instead of appeasing or "caving."

10. Realizing something new about oneself.

11. Realizing that a person has changed.

12. Able to accept circumstances beyond one's control instead of resisting or attacking.

13. Saying, "I never realized that," or "I didn't know that," or "I never heard you say that before," or "I have never told you this before," or "I have never told anyone this before."

14. Able to listen instead of shouting and intimidating.

15. Able to laugh at oneself and/or see the humor in the situation.

16. Giving credit to the other or asking for credit from the other.

17. Expressing any emotion, particularly sadness, fear, grief, or anger.

---

[163] Bush & Folger, 1994, 205.

18. Being noticed, noticing, or observing.

The list of ordinary empowering events is nearly endless. All of these "signposts" call for a response from the mediator. An effective mediator regularly praises and thanks the parties. When a party recognizes something good about the other party, the mediator's response of "I heard what you said about Betty's frugality, and I appreciate that. Thank you," will not go unappreciated and will encourage more constructive behavior. Some mediators solicit empowerment by asking a client, "Tell me something good about Betty's parenting." This can seem patronizing to parties. It rarely evokes empowering dialogue. Noticing, praising and thanking clients for unsolicited moments of empowerment and recognition create fertile ground for such moments to take root, grow, and multiply. The mediator's role in the process is surprisingly simple. The mediator is primarily a responder, or, as Bush & Pope describe, a follower of the parties.[164] The process involves many variables and the mediator is not in control of what the parties do, or what happens in the session. Yet, the mediator (as artist) "shapes" the mediation as it evolves, with appropriate responses. As responder and shaper, the mediator has a unique role among professionals. An effective, experienced mediator is aware of what is happening in a mediation session beneath the surface of words and behavior by sensing what parties are experiencing with listening and observing. The mediator responds to seen and unseen events that occur in the session. Because of this phenomenon, some have referred to the "magic" of mediation. This description is used because much of what occurs in mediation is invisible. The invisible part of the process is what's happening inside of the parties, causing them to change. Describing it as magic is merely an appreciation of the mediator's artistry in creating an environment where parties feel comfortable with introspection before a nearly total stranger.

Mediation 101: Reflection and Summarization

The simple transformative techniques of Reflection and Summarization could be called Mediation 101. Reflection is an exact, or near exact, repeating back to a party what the party has said. Although it may sound pedestrian, this intervention is very powerful and useful. It is possible, although not typical, for a mediator to perform an entire mediation quite successfully using only Mediation 101. A party rarely notices that the mediator has just repeated his words back to him. This is true even when the mediator reflects repeatedly, and sounds, to himself, like a broken record. It is not unusual in student role-plays for the role-playing client to learn for the first time during the after-the-role-play debriefing that the mediator was reflecting his words back to him for five minutes. Parties, remarkably, do not find it awkward or unusual, even when the mediator might feel a little silly. An example of reflection is:

Father: *I have a crazy work schedule. I never know from one week to the next which day I will have off—or even if I will have any days off! I need a flexible custody schedule.*

---

[164] Bush & Pope, 2004, 68.

Mediator reflects: *You have a crazy work schedule. You never know from one week to the next which day you will have off, or even if you will have any days off. You need a flexible custody schedule.*

Father: *Well, yeah, but I also need some set times, because the flexible way we have it now isn't working, since every time I ask to see Chelsea, they're busy.*

Mediator reflects: *You also need some set times because the flexible schedule you have now doesn't work since every time you try to see Chelsea, they are busy.*

Father: *Yeah, well I guess it's hard to work with someone like me when no one knows where I'm gonna be, but I am willing to do whatever it takes to get some scheduled time.*

By simply reflecting Father's words, the mediator was able to create an environment for Father to change from somewhat blaming others for his inability to see his daughter to taking responsibility for his part in the problem. The mediator, rather than avoiding conflict, trying to "resolve" conflict, problem solving, or judging the conflict as bad, has used conflict to promote empowerment and recognition so that the parties can find their own resolution.

Another example of reflection is:

Wife: *We've been separated for a really long time—five years—I still don't know why Joe left! I never got an explanation. The last kid graduated from high school and he just packed his bag one day and said he was leaving. The whole family is still waiting for answers. Why he hates me so much I don't know. I never did anything to him except wait on him hand and foot. I think I deserve more than that. So, I'm here to get what I have coming to me and I don't think it is going to be easy to work this out because I don't trust him.*

Mediator reflects: *You've been separated for five years. You don't know why Joe left. You never got an explanation. Your last child graduated from high school and he just packed his bag one day and said he was leaving. The whole family is waiting for answers. You don't know why he hates you so much. You never did anything to him except wait on him hand and foot. You think you deserve more than that. You are here to get what you have coming to you and you don't think this is going to be easy because you don't trust Joe.*

Wife: *Well, he does talk to the kids—we have a grown son and daughter—but they don't like to talk to me about what he says, and yeah, we did have problems, no marriage is perfect, but to just leave like that....I never expected that.*

As can be seen in the examples, reflection brings about changes in perception without any effort on the part of the mediator. Reflection has other benefits, as well.

Benefits of Reflection

1.	Changes a person's perception without persuasion and its accompanying risks of creating conflict between the mediator and parties.

2.	Gives feedback to the client in a non-threatening way. When a party hears his own words for the first time, they sound different to him from the way they sounded during self-talk. Without using any influence, the mediator utters words (the client's own words) and the client hears words that need to be changed, if only slightly.

3.	Effect on the other party. The other party is also hearing the words he has probably heard before anew, because when the mediator says them they sound different to him. This creates the possibility for change in perception of these words in the other party.

4.	Reflection is a neutral, non-threatening way for a mediator to "suggest" a reconsideration of a client's perspective without any judgment. No one needs to defend against this intervention. The client is comfortable because his own words are being used. The mediator is comfortable because the mediator has done nothing to raise any conflict.

5.	Reflection is *presence*. By reflecting, the mediator is being present in the moment with the parties. This is a gift. It does not sympathize or empathize, which could further reinforce a person's pain. Presence reinforces a person's inner essence, the value as a person. It is validating. It's neither more nor less than simply being "in the moment" with another human being. There are not many opportunities in life to have another person's presence. It rarely happens.

6.	Reflection takes the mediator's ego out of the equation, reducing any possibility of conflict between the mediator and the clients.

7.	Reflection is often the most helpful intervention a client can receive because, unlike other interventions, advanced mediator skills, or directive techniques, reflection purely honors the client's autonomy, dignity, and self-determination.

8.	Reflection is defusing, taking the heat out of the moment. If what the client said was heated, reflection will make it more palatable without challenging it. It allows what is to be, even if it is unpleasant, without dismissing, contradicting, or arguing with it.

Reframing

Reflection is not to be confused with other similar interventions such as Reframing, or Active Listening. Reframing is another mediator technique used when the mediator wants to change a person's perspective in a specific way chosen by the mediator. In Reframing, the mediator repeats back part of the client's words, but changes something slightly to twist the meaning to that of the mediator's desired point. Examples of Reframing are:

Party's Statement	Mediator's Reframe
1. It's a disgrace that John does not pay child support. He gets away with murder by lying about his income and being so good at hiding money!	1. You want John to pay support and you think he has income outside of what he is claiming on his tax documents?
2. John's rich grandmother pays all of his legal fees so he can keep dragging me into court.	2. You are saying that John has resources you do not have, and that it is difficult for you to afford a lawyer.
3. We had a good marriage. We were happy until she started to say, "I'm not in love." Becky was only concerned about her own happiness.	3. You didn't choose this divorce and you preferred to stay married to Becky.
4. I don't want my daughter around that sick, needy girlfriend of his who thinks she can make my child call her "Mommy."	4. You want to have some say about who else is present when one of you has Abby.
5. It enrages me that she can make me pay her "spousal support' when she is living with another man—why are the courts so biased against men?	5. A lot of people who have to pay alimony *pendente lite* think it is unfair.
6. Victor wants to have Amanda overnight on Wednesdays instead of dropping her off at 8 o'clock, but that is a school night and she needs to sleep in her own bed on school nights.	6. You agree with Victor having Amanda overnight on weekends and Wednesday evenings after school and for dinner. Your only area of disagreement, is the nine hours of time Wednesday evenings when she is sleeping.
7. Wendy is a slob and the Department of Health came to her apartment to issue a warning. She was almost evicted twice for the mess. What a pig sty you live in.	7. You have concerns about Wendy cleaning her apartment.
8. Our son Jacob definitely wants to live with me. He is always asking me when is the judge going to say I can come live with you, Dad? I don't want to live with mom anymore-- I hate her boyfriend Chet.	8. You are saying Jacob tells you he wants to live with you and, not surprisingly, he is telling you he doesn't like Chet.
9. Robert never makes doctor or dentist appointments for the kids. I make the appointments and tell him when they are—then he never shows up!	9. You make the appointments and you want Robert to come, but then he can't make it?
10. We don't communicate. When he sees my name on the caller ID, he shuts off his phone.	10. Obviously, some method of communication is needed! In here, I like to help you find methods that work for both of you.

In the above examples, the mediator is attempting to take some of the negative charge out of the party's statement and convert it into a more acceptable statement. The mediator is using a shortcut to change the party's statement from one that incites conflict to one that seems reasonable. In some cases, reframing is used to show the client the absurdity of what he is saying, in an indirect and somewhat gentle way, as in Example 3 above. Reframing, clearly, is much different from reflection, and is not considered a "transformative" technique. It is, however, a very useful technique. Reflection is a pure, innocent intervention by the mediator; whereas, reframing is driven by the mediator's agenda to use language to persuade the party to see the statement from the mediator's perspective, seeking agreement that the mediator's view is more enlightened. It is a manipulation not prohibited in mediation. To the contrary, it is an acceptable technique. In order to maintain neutrality, respect for clients and their self-determination, and to promote empowerment and recognition, however, the mediator must be careful with reframing, which is fraught with risks of initiating conflict with the client, and creating the appearance of partiality. Reframing is useful, but more risky than reflection, and should be used with care.

Reframing is also different from Active Listening, a technique used to assist couples with communication, as well as in Parent Effectiveness Training to assist parents in communicating with children.[165] With Active Listening, the listener repeats back to the speaker what the listener heard. The speaker then has the opportunity to correct or change what the listener repeats. This is very different from reflection because the focus is on what the listener hears. Often, a listener will hear a distorted version of what a speaker says because the listener distorts with his own filter. This technique emphasizes accurate communication; whereas reflection emphasizes the speaker. Active listening is also a useful technique to promote accurate communication. In mediation, it can be presented as an exercise to facilitate clear communication.

Summarization is the corollary to reflection. Summarization is what the mediator does after reflecting what each party says. Summarization is simply a reflection of what both sides are saying. "Mary, I hear you saying that the teenagers are too busy to stick to a rigid schedule with Dad, and George, I hear you saying that since you live one hour away, without a rigid schedule, you are afraid you'll never get a chance to see them." The mediator summarizes and juxtaposes what the parties have said. Summarization is often followed by the segue, "Where would you like to go from here?" The effect of summarization and such a question that reinforces the parties' ownership of the conflict (by using the pronoun "you" and not "we") places the problem squarely in the parties' laps. It is a tactful way of reminding parties that the mediator's job is not to solve their problems for them, but to help them manage conflict and promote self-awareness, empowerment and recognition so that they are empowered to solve their own problems. It reinforces the boundary. Summarization is helpful after periods of reflection and moments of empowerment and recognition promoted by the mediator because those moments have the tendency to lull parties into a sense of reliance on the mediator, who has gained trust by reflecting. It is easy for clients to forget that the helpful mediator is not going to take on their problems. The benefits of summarization are:

---

[165] Gordon, T. (1975). *Parent effectiveness training.* New York: New American Library, Inc.

Benefits of Summarization

1. Highlights and re-reflects what both parties have said to reinforce the points they are making.

2. Provides an intermission for the parties and the mediator to think about what has been said and what meaning it has.

3. Places the issues on the table without any blame, judgment, or need to defend.

4. Shifts the focus away from the mediator and onto the parties and the content of their dialog.

5. Tactfully reminds the parties that the problem belongs to them, and the solution must come from them.

6. Goes a step beyond reflection to open up a space for consideration of options.

As a mediation technique, summarization is not new. John Haynes devoted a section of his book *Mediating Divorce* [166] to summarization noting that he used it to achieve "a variety of effects."[167]

The Case of Erin and Luke
A Transformed Relationship in Two Hours or Less

Erin, 24, and Luke, 23, are the unmarried parents of Kiley, age five months. Erin states that she did not attempt to have Luke see Kiley at birth and in early infancy because Erin had moved back into her parents' home "out in the sticks" and that the doctor had told her not to take Kiley out into the cold weather, or in public for about two months, until she had all of her immunizations. Luke filed a custody action seeking partial custody as well as "emergency relief" so that he could see Kiley. Both parties retained attorneys and the attorneys worked out a consent interim order providing for supervised visitation for Luke twice every week, Tuesdays and Fridays, for three hours each time, supervised by Mom at a location agreed upon.

The mediator was struck by the sadness of a young father and daughter beginning life with something as restrictive and disturbing as supervised custody, typically reserved for parents with a "depraved" nature. Mediator asked Erin what her feelings were about Luke having partial custody rights, since that was what Luke was seeking. Erin said, "He drinks and is on drugs. He was in jail. He has three DUI's (driving under influence), no driver's license, and his home is inappropriate for a child. He lives with two girls, and they party and do drugs. I want him to be in Kiley's life, but I won't agree to unsupervised until she is about 2 years old and can fend for herself." The mediator asked Luke to respond

---

[166] Haynes, J. & Haynes, G. (1989). *Mediating divorce*. San Francisco: Jossey-Bass.
[167] Id., 30.

and he said, "I do not drink and do drugs, and I live with my girlfriend Lana who rarely drinks or parties. The other girl was Lana's roommate, and she will be leaving in two months for the Air Force."

The mediator asked the parties if Luke was seeing Kiley according to the interim order they had gotten from the court. Luke nodded his head enthusiastically, and Erin stated that the visits were occurring at a local diner as agreed on, but she did not like that Luke insisted on bringing his girlfriend. She said that Luke rarely holds Kiley but keeps her in her car seat in the booth at the diner and just dangles a toy in front of her. She said that Luke doesn't even know what's going on with Kiley, or what toys she likes. He keeps bringing a lamb stuffed animal, an infant's rattle, and another toy that she does like. She is five months old now and likes to play with her "cool toys." The mediator asked Erin if she would be willing to help Luke find out what Kiley likes and how to become more interactive with her during the visits. Erin said that she tried, but that every time she tells Luke what to do, he takes it as interference and becomes angry with her. As an example, she said that her lawyer said she did not have to provide Luke with bottles to feed Kiley when they are at the diner, and that if Luke wanted to feed Kiley at the diner he should bring his own bottles. Luke showed up with bottles, and Erin asked him if he had sterilized them. Luke told her, yes, they were sterilized. She doubted him and asked, "Well, how did you sterilize them?" Luke said, "It's none of your business." Then an argument ensued. Erin said she was more comfortable when they used to meet without the girlfriend coming along. Luke said that Erin brought her boyfriend one time, so he thought it would be okay for him to bring Lana, and that he and Lana are now engaged, so Lana is the person who will be with him and Kylie when he gets custody rights.

The mediator noticed that the parties seemed to have few co-parenting or communication skills and, perhaps, no awareness of the importance of behaving in a mature, cooperative, and respectful way. The mediator had a hunch that if they had an opportunity to exchange information about themselves, their lives, their situations, their concerns, and their feelings about Kiley, that Mom might feel differently about supervised custody. Mediator asked Luke if he was indeed in prison. Luke said yes, when he was 18 he did something really stupid, a burglary with some people he no longer associates with, and that he had to be in prison for six months, but that was four years ago. He also said that he does not have a drinking problem and rarely drinks now, but when he was younger, he did have a series of DUI's that he is paying for dearly now by having a suspended driver's license. He now has steady employment and believes he may be able to obtain a probationary driver's license soon.

It appeared that the parties had bought into the litigation model as the way to resolve their dispute and that they had not had any meaningful communication since Kiley was born. Erin, especially, seemed to have bonded with her lawyer, and to have half-heartedly decided to take on the role of adversary against Luke. Erin's words sounded at times as if they were exact quotes of what an attorney would say when arguing to a judge, summarizing Luke's worst qualities in sound bites. As the parties described the hostilities that accompanied almost every interaction they had, the mediator turned to Dad and observed, "It seems as if the only obstacle to your having the right to take Kiley yourself, as you would like to do, is Mom, right? I am surprised that you are not trying harder to get along with her." Luke agreed, but seemed to be realizing this simple idea for the first time. Luke said that he does not know how to get along and that he doesn't know what Erin expects him to do with Kiley, since she won't help him. Mediator asked the parties if they attended the mandatory parent education class, and whether they recalled hearing about treating each other with respect? Mediator said, "A lot of people don't realize that whatever they say or do to the other parent they are really doing to Kiley. I can tell you both really love Kiley, and you wouldn't treat her disrespectfully ever." Since the parties appeared to be interested and accepting of what the mediator was saying, the mediator elaborated on the subject and commented on the importance of a child having a childhood where she is allowed to love both parents and have the opportunity to see them being respectful toward each other and getting along. Mediator said that to deny a child this kind of life is to take her childhood away from her because children living in the middle of parents who don't get along automatically feel they have to take care of their parents. Kids really want their parents to be okay. And when you are okay, she will be okay, and will be free to be a child. The parties really seemed to get this, and agree with it. The mediator asked Erin if she would be willing to tell Luke something about Kiley that he may not know. Erin's expression brightened. She obviously loved to speak of her five-month-old baby. Erin proceeded to tell Luke about Kiley's new teeth, her routine at home, her habits, how she comforts her when she cries, and on and on. Luke listened with extreme interest. Erin referred to the recent pediatrician visit (the six-month visit, even though Kiley wasn't quite six months old yet) telling Luke about her height and weight and where she fell on the development charts. Mediator asked Erin if she would consider including Luke in the next pediatrician visit. Both parties wanted to do that. Apparently, neither of their attorneys had made this suggestion.

As the parties continued to talk, the mediator was silent for a while. The mediator noticed that the parties' body language had completely changed. Earlier, they were both sitting far back in their seats; now they were facing each other, leaning forward with their hands folded on the table in front of them, deep in conversation. Luke explained to Erin that he is not the person she remembers and that he has grown up a lot. Erin said that she would be willing to change their visits somewhat if Luke would agree not to bring Lana all the time. She would not bring her boyfriend, and they could change the meeting place to a park or someplace more comfortable. They made a short term plan to gradually move toward partial custody, with the proviso that nothing would be written in stone until Erin saw how things were going. She mentioned that she might require some random testing to be sure that Luke was drug free. The mediator wrote down the terms the parties agreed to. Luke asked the mediator, "How do I know that this is not just something she is saying now, and that as soon as she gets back with her lawyer, it will go back to the way it was?" The mediator said, "Well, if you are able to change the way you talk to each other, with respect instead of exchanging hostilities, then that change will likely lead to more change." Erin said, "Luke, I'm not mad at you anymore. I was mad at you when Kiley was born. I was mad at you for leaving. I was mad at you for fooling around. But I am happy now. I said those things and did those things with my lawyer because I was mad. But now that I am no longer mad, I don't want it to be that way again." Luke said, "So, will you tell me what you want me to do with Kiley? Will you help me take care of her?" Erin said "Yes," and Luke said, "Thank you. I am really glad to hear you say that. I really don't like it when you are mad at me and don't trust me." Erin said, "Well you have been truthful in here and I know that you are capable of taking care of Kiley. I just need to see how things go." The mediator said, "Thank you" to Erin. "I really appreciate your ability to get over your anger, and to tell Luke you are no longer mad at him." Mediator said to Luke, "Thank you for taking all of this in and being willing to change how you and Erin talk to each other for Kiley's sake." Mediator also praised both parties for the obvious passion they have for their daughter whose care and safety included many details that both parents believed were important, such as not letting anyone smoke around her.

The mediator felt that this was a case of two competent, caring, nurturing, and mature young parents who lost their footing as parents and got caught up in the litigation model that encourages parents to act as adversaries even when they are not comfortable in those roles. Just by the parties' body language alone, it was apparent that they felt much more comfortable working together. As soon as they began talking, the communication seemed to flow quickly. Time seemed to speed up and the mediator, who usually asked clients to step out into the waiting area while paperwork was prepared, let the parties stay in the mediation room alone to continue their conversation. The mediator felt good about this case and the way the parties were able to hear the simple truths the mediator spoke about, truths that were likely obscured by attorneys who fueled the dispute. The mediator felt especially good that the parties chose to change their approach and were able to effectuate that change in one mediation session—particularly given that this was a case where a remedy as severe as supervised *custody* had been imposed.

Questions for Discussion:

1.   Are the mediator's statements to the parties about co-parenting children helpful? Are they directive?

Answer: The mediator's statements about the mediator's belief (based on research and years of experience in the field) are not directive in this instance. The mediator is not telling the parties what to do, but is making universal observations. This is almost no different from commenting on the weather. The parties are not threatened or offended by the comments in the slightest. If the parties did show that they were offended the mediator would be creating conflict with the clients and should immediately back off from making uninvited statements that are perceived as controversial. The mediator's motives are purely to help the parties' child, consistent with the parties' goal.

2.   How many instances of empowerment and recognition, or signposts, can be counted in this narrative?

Answer: At least 25.

3. **How did the mediator contribute to the momentum created by mutual empowerment and recognition?**

Answer. The mediator never lectured or suggested any course of action. The mediator asked questions about supervised custody; letting go of supervised custody; whether Erin would help Luke learn to care for Kiley; whether Luke realized that trying harder to get along with Erin might improve his ability to overcome supervision; whether the parties wished to share information about Kiley; and whether the parties wished to share pediatrician visits. These interventions were all in the form of non-threatening questions. The mediator praised the parties when they demonstrated changed perspectives and recognition of each other. Perhaps of most value was the mediator's silence while the parties were deep in conversation about their daughter.

A Final Note about Transformative Mediation

For all of its de-emphasis on settlement as the mediator's goal, and its emphasis on allowing conflict, even welcoming conflict so that it can be used to empower parties, transformative mediation, is, in the end, a powerful way to resolve conflict. Resolutions that are conceived and built by the parties are the most permanent and satisfying solutions. A relationship is transformed, and clients are able to see their way to changing longstanding unhealthy dynamics. The irony of the transformative process, that it does not focus on settlement, yet often produces satisfying solutions seemingly effortlessly, is one of several paradoxes seen in the world of mediation.

Chapter Six

"I thrive in structure; I drown in chaos."—Anna Kendrick

Mediation Procedures

The art of mediation is comprised of skills one masters only in doing. To gain experience, apprentice mediators are advised to observe mediations, to seek co-mediation[168] opportunities and to continue training. Joining professional mediation groups and collaborating with peers are the surest ways to merge with the mediation professional community.

The skilled mediator operates largely on instinct and intuition that are born of knowledge and commitment to theory. A mediator's underlying theory, or belief system about mediation, is also called the mediator's *orientation*. A solid orientation, or theoretical foundation, will serve a mediator well throughout the process, which begins, procedurally, with the initial client contact.

Initial Client Contact

The initial contact typically comes from a prospective party in the form of a telephone call or email. A mediator may be contacted by a party who has already chosen mediation, together with the other party, and simply wants to choose a mediator, or, in the alternative, by a party seeking information about mediation without a decision to use mediation. In either event, parties most often do not have full information on the process and will have questions upon first contacting the mediator. Typical questions at this point are:

1. What is the cost of mediation in terms of both money and time?

2. Do both parties also have to retain lawyers? If so, how is mediation a cost-saving measure? If so, why do lawyers have to be involved if the mediator is also a lawyer?

3. What information do parties need to bring to mediation?

4. Will mediation be a complete process for making legal and economic decisions? Will both parties have the same safeguards that exist in the courtroom

---

[168] Co-mediation is the term for mediators mediating together. Popular combinations for co-mediation are a therapist mediator and attorney mediator, an experienced mediator with an inexperienced mediator, or a mediator with expertise in a substantive area with a mediator with process skills. Co-mediation is acceptable ethically and commercially, but should be exercised with care because of its potential for confusion or conflict if the mediators disagree about how the mediation should be conducted. Compatible co-mediators are rare.

process? How can I choose mediation when all of the lawyers I've spoken with so far say that my case is not appropriate for mediation?

Mediators are almost universally challenged, from the very onset of the process, with the task of not only selling themselves, but by first explaining the process and advancing the cause of mediation. As Robert Benjamin has said, people do not readily know that mediation is "safe and effective."[169] The purpose of the initial client contact is, therefore, to bring the client into the mediator's office to meet in person and further discuss the process. This is because, although it is commendable for a mediator to give free information about mediation over the phone, it is not helpful to anyone unless the parties actually hire the mediator. Therefore, the phone call should be as brief as possible with the primary aim of getting the parties in the door.

The brief initial phone conversation should cover four key topics. Common mistakes mediators make in the first client phone contact are: mediating too soon by agreeing to mediate an issue on the phone with the first contact; trying to sell mediation too hard; providing complicated, confusing explanations of mediation on the phone; or not listening to the party on the other end of the phone. Listening to the client should be a priority, and it is the first of the four key topics to cover.

Listening to the Client

Basic client information should be sought in the initial conversation. The mediator should ask about the parties' current situation: do they live together? (Approximately 50% of voluntary mediation clients do); who referred them to the mediator? Do they have children? What are their names and ages? These questions are important introductory information for the mediator. More important, they put the client at ease knowing that the mediator is interested in details of the parties' lives.

Explaining Mediation

A second key topic is "mediation in a nutshell." It is not necessary or desirable to go into great detail about what mediation is. If an explanation is too elaborate and technical, it will turn people off as too far out of the mainstream. A simple explanation such as, "I sit down with both of you and help you figure out your divorce" will suffice. Clients are already overwhelmed with their situation, puzzled about the process, and bombarded with information from friends, family, lawyers, other mediators, and websites they have visited. A mediator who keeps things simple and clear will be reassuring and inviting. Parties are looking to simplify their lives—not complicate things further. If a more detailed explanation is desired, the mediator might say something like this:

---

[169] Benjamin, 2007

Mediator's Telephone Summary

My job as your mediator is to sit down with both of you in my office. Mediation saves time and money because you communicate and negotiate directly with each other while I assist you instead of hiring attorneys to do the negotiating. That way, you would be paying two attorneys to communicate everything to each other, and then send a letter to you, make a phone call, then get back in touch with the other lawyer, and so on. In Mediation, I use my professional knowledge to make sure all of your concerns and issues and financial information will be discussed. [Or information about your family and child if it is a family mediation involving child custody or other family conflict]. The decisions you make will be reviewed by your attorneys before you sign on the dotted line. The attorneys will also complete the legal paperwork. Most people are able to resolve their issues in a few sessions or less.

This simple explanation satisfies the client's initial **concerns,** which, typically, are:

- Is this a wise move for me economically, or just another "professional" trying to make money from my divorce with endless sessions?

- Is mediation going to be as thorough as the court process or will I be asked to cut corners? Will I get all of the information and attention I need?

- Will I be heard?

- Does this mediator know what the issues are?

- Will this process benefit me?

Acknowledgment of Client Concerns

The third key topic to cover in the initial client contact is acknowledgment of client concerns. By satisfying the initial concerns with a brief explanation of what the mediator does, the mediator has created a comfortable setting for the client to discuss those concerns briefly. If, at this point, the client expresses concerns (anything from the location of the mediator's office to the intractability of the other party), it is a sign that the mediator has correctly completed steps one and two, and the client is considering hiring the mediator. It is important to acknowledge concerns and provide assurance that everything will be addressed thoroughly in joint session, without going into great detail.

To underscore the mediator's impartiality, the mediator should suggest that the other party also call the mediator in order to obtain the same information in a phone call, adding that it is not required. The mediator must take care not to use terms of art with clients. Use of words such as *conflict, transformative, empowerment, recognition, caucus,* and other terms of art used by mediation students, theorists, trainers and scholars are for use with mediators, and not with clients. Mediation theory is not part of their world, and your job will be to step into their world.

Personal Invitation

The fourth key topic to cover in the initial contact is to invite a personal meeting prior to engagement of the mediator, if desired. This often involves either cost to the parties in the form of a nominal consultation fee, or cost to the mediator in terms of donating time free of charge as a "free consultation." Because mediation is an intimate process, it is understandable that clients might want to meet their mediator in person before making a commitment to use him or her as a mediator. As a mediator gains a reputation and credibility by word-of-mouth, this step is increasingly unnecessary.

PHYSICAL SETTING OF THE MEDIATION ROOM

The mediation room will need the following:

Food and Drink

At Least 3 Rooms with Comfortable Seating: Mediation, Break-Out, and Waiting Area

Privacy and Silence

Clock

Easel and Markers

Calendars

Calculators

Kleenex

Writing Paper, Pens, and Writing Surface

Computer and Telephone

Food and drink includes snacks (depending on personal preference) such as wrapped candy, health bars, bottled water and soft drinks. Some mediators provide trail mix or freshly popped popcorn. Clients should be encouraged, if they ask or if they are coming during their lunch hour, to bring their own meal. The purpose of food is threefold: first, the clients' comfort is of utmost importance because the mediation setting can feel uncomfortable for all of the obvious emotional reasons. Second, food can provide the necessary distraction from the intensity of close contact in mediation. Third, parties will be need ready energy to perform higher order thought processes, as explained in Chapter 13 herein. A client feeling confronted, threatened, put on the spot, or mentally exhausted will welcome the convenience of being able to search through a candy bowl or unwrap a piece of bubble gum, while thinking of a response to an uncomfortable question posed by the other party.

Caucus and Break-Out Rooms

Having a separate waiting area and breakout room provides at least two private areas for parties to sit while the mediator holds separate meetings (caucusing) if necessary. Obviously, privacy and soundproof walls are important. It is not unusual, if a separate meeting is expected to take longer than a few minutes, for the mediator to invite the other party to take a walk down the hall, down the block, to a coffee shop, or whatever will make the client feel comfortable. In some cases, an extended caucus can include just one party coming to the mediator's office. Although caucuses are sometimes helpful, caucusing should always be an educated choice. The mediator should know why the caucus is being held, and what the risks and benefits are. Caucusing almost always creates doubt or distrust because parties do not know what is being said. It is safer to do everything in joint session if doubt or distrust seems possible.

An example of a welcomed caucus occurred in a case where the husband was a businessman who knew his corporate structures and relationships well, and had made an offer of settlement to wife that included detailed financial facts and figures. Husband was willing to, and did, provide his own explanation of his offer to wife in joint session. Wife, however, felt the need to go over everything several times because she was not in business and this was new information for her. She wisely wanted to understand the financial facts herself. Wife suggested, and mediator and husband agreed, that wife, wife's attorney, and mediator all meet together in a separate session for purposes of making husband's offer understandable to wife. The parties agreed to share the mediator's fee for the caucus.

Props such as calculators, calendars, writing paper, Kleenex, an easel and markers are helpful in mediation involving economic decisions and/or child custody decisions. Child custody schedules are more easily understood when viewable on a calendar or illustrated on an easel. Divisions of property are understood best by the parties when placed on an easel for the parties to conceptualize visually. Mathematical operations, such as division, percentages of shares to parties, or percentages of income, or court guideline formulas calculating support are best understood when placed on an easel where parties can concretely see the facts in black and white. In addition, the easel provides a "neutral" place to "put" facts that parties sometimes find disturbing. For example, parties sometimes find some aspects of divorce distribution or support payments offensive. A party who finds that he may be looking at an equitable distribution that provides for more than 50% of the marital estate going to the other party (in states that provide for equitable distribution) is less likely to negatively associate the idea with the mediator when the proposal is placed on an easel as a hypothetical in black and white, where other possible distributions can also be placed side by side for comparison. Similarly, guideline formulas for child support can sometimes come as a shock, both for the payor and the payee. Although many people find the support guidelines for their state to be appropriate, some might find the guideline amount to be too much to pay, or too little to live on. Allowing the parties to see the numbers in black and white on a board figuratively de-personalizes the information, taking it away from the mediator and moving it onto a neutral location, the easel. Although parties learn and process data in a variety of ways, most people include visual processing as an important way of taking in information.

Introductory Session and Mediator's Opening Statement

The introductory session includes the mediator's opening statement. Bush & Folger consider this procedure so important they proclaim that, "The opening statement says it all," in their list of the ten hallmarks of Transformative Mediation.[170] The opening statement is a singular opportunity for the mediator because it is the only point in the process when the mediator has undivided attention to initiate clients into the strange, new world they are about to enter. Particularly where clients have inhabited the world of legal processes, the air of the mediation room will feel unfamiliar, even shocking, as if they have jumped into a pool of cold water on a hot day. Typically, this is a relief. The opportunity to introduce parties to the process is the opportunity to introduce them to a world where they will no longer be expected to go into their separate corners preparing for battle, but will be taught to work together and adopt adult, businesslike, *responsible* roles themselves. The opening statement is also important in establishing the unique role of mediator, and the mediator/client boundary.

Opening Statement

In the opening statement, the mediator must cover several key points, the first being an explanation of the mediator role. Parties must understand that the mediator (even an attorney) does not give legal advice, but may share legal information, as well as guidance through the process. The mediator lets the clients know that she possesses knowledge about the law and procedure and that expertise will ensure a thorough agreement; however, it will not include individual coaching or legal advice. In other words, the mediator will not help one side strategize against the other. The parties may meet with their attorneys as often as they like during the process in order to consult with attorneys. Although the procedure varies from state to state, in most states, attorneys do not typically attend mediation sessions with clients in family mediation, although they sometimes do. This is the clients' choice, and is usually dictated by available funds to pay attorneys' fees.

Legal Advice vs. Legal Information

It is important for parties to understand the difference between legal advice and legal information. The mediator should never give legal advice, which would include advice and opinions, such as telling clients what the amount of support should be or what a fair division of property would be. In custody, it would be telling them what a court would do in their fact situation. Legal information, on the other hand can be given by the mediator. This distinction involves information that does not come with advice or opinion. For example, the support guidelines can be referred to, and simple formulas can be applied; however, support guidelines rarely have simple formulas that cannot be manipulated by attorneys. Tax withholding, net income calculations, including or excluding certain types of income, defining "income" are issues that affect support calculations in a way that go beyond "legal information." Therefore, the

---

[170] Folger & Bush, 1996.

mediator who provides support guidelines as legal information for the parties to negotiate support should do so with the assistance and cooperation of the parties' attorneys. The use of support software can also be helpful, so long as the parties can take the results to their attorneys for review. Several types of software are available at a reasonable cost. Because clients struggle with understanding the murky distinction between legal advice and legal information, it is important to encourage them to ask any questions they have, and caution them not to withhold questions for fear of violating the mediators' boundary of not providing legal advice. The mediator can manage that boundary for them.

Parties should be permitted to ask any question without fear of feeling ashamed of asking the "wrong" question. If a client's question involves the giving of legal advice or opinion, the mediator can take the opportunity to explain the difference again. For instance, suppose a client asks a mediator, "What do you think we should do about alimony? My attorney says I can get three years. John's attorney says I can get two years? What do you think?" In this instance, the mediator has an excellent opportunity to illustrate the mediator role as impartial, yet engaged in assisting the parties through the process. The mediator can say, "I am glad you were able to at least get a range of possibilities from your attorneys. This is good because it will help you to find a period of time that works for both of you. I would suggest that you spend time in here looking at the practical aspects of how long you need alimony, how much you need, how long John can afford to pay it, and how much he can afford to pay. I cannot give you an opinion because it is a gray area and no one, even an attorney, knows exactly what a court would do." This information, of course, applies in states where there is no set formula for alimony.

It is not unusual for parties to ask strategy questions, particularly on the telephone or by email, in passing, when they are making a change to an appointment, for example. Clearly, strategizing against the other party is something a party appropriately does with their attorney. The mediator must not repel the question because it is a legitimate question and highly relevant to the process. The mediator should transparently and candidly discuss the issue without getting involved in strategy. As an example, Krista, the wife of a business owner, had consulted with at least three attorneys in her thorough effort to become informed about her rights. Her husband had two businesses that brought in significant cash flow, while also being heavily leveraged, and, according to her husband, on the verge of insolvency due to extreme indebtedness during bad economic times when banks were no longer lending money, particularly to him. During an unexpected rescheduling phone call, the mediator was faced with Krista's questions about advice given to her by attorneys, "Every attorney I have talked to said I should ignore his insistence that he 'has no money,' and tell him that a court will just order him to sell his assets to pay me." A mediator who refuses to respond to a question that solicits advice would not be doing their job. The appropriate mediator response is to be willing to discuss the issue, either in joint session or in caucus. The mediator can explore the options offered by Krista's attorneys without giving legal advice to Krista and without cooperating in the strategy against her husband, as well as without defending Krista's husband, which would also be inappropriate, because the mediator would then be taking the husband's side. The mediator's response could be, "Well, the attorneys are right that you do have that option. I think you know that the choice is yours, and exploring that option and what results would come from forcing a sale of the business is something I suggest you look at thoroughly in mediation before you make a decision. I would be happy to look at that question from every angle possible with you, and, if you are ready, it might be helpful to do that at your next joint session."

Ground Rules

If the mediator believes that certain ground rules help parties to feel comfortable and safe or that they help the mediator to manage conflict, ground rules can be discussed during the opening statement or later. My personal approach to ground rules is that they can be risky and should only be imposed if the risks are calculated. The mere mention of ground rules has implications for the mediator-client relationship and affects the mediator-client boundary. At a minimum, it implies that the mediator believes at least one party holds the potential for unruliness and needs to be reined in. Many mediators are fine with this implication; I am not. I prefer to give clients the benefit of the doubt first. Ground rules can always be added later, as needed. Once they are imposed at the very outset, before the mediator knows much about the parties, the die is cast and the message, "You need ground rules" and its implications cannot be retracted.

I find it more effective to model respectful behavior by behaving with an abundance of respect towards my clients. If I show even the slightest disrespect (or do something like set ground rules that could be perceived as prejudging the parties), I miss the opportunity to command respect by modeling respect. The risks of setting ground rules at the outset are the implied disrespect that is conveyed as well as the potential for initiating conflict with the parties. In the beginning the mediator doesn't know the parties. There are parties who love to test boundaries and, given a rule, will always break it just to see what the consequence is. These are the parties who will always "push the envelope," and the mediation environment is filled with them. Setting ground rules with this client can cause more trouble than it's worth by initiating conflict with the client, which is not one of the mediator's "rights." When the need for a rule arises, there is always an opportunity to address it. For example, instead of saying "No yelling" at the outset of a mediation before anyone has yelled, and possibly in a case where no one intends to yell, I will assume that parties know that yelling is a behavior to avoid in a professional setting. Then, if yelling erupts, I will get involved immediately by saying something along these lines, "Hold on. Stop. I need to tell you now that this is a professional setting. There are others in the building who need to do their work too. I need you to lower your voice." If a stronger statement is needed, I will say that the mediation has to stop if yelling continues.

Explaining Confidentiality

The opening statement also includes defining confidentiality and informing clients of their right to confidentiality and any exceptions. There are legal and ethical exceptions such as child abuse reporting laws (Scc Chapter 4) and the legal obligation to report a threat of harm. There can also be exceptions to confidentiality provided contractually based on the needs of the mediator. For example, in the United States Postal Service REDRESS mediation program, mediators are obligated to report information on a crime committed on postal service property. So long as all parties are aware and agree to the rules of confidentiality, those rules may properly be expanded beyond those provided by law.

In addition, parties should be made aware of confidentiality surrounding private caucusing, if it occurs. Information shared privately in caucus should not be shared if the caucusing party does not want it to be shared with the other party or parties. Parties are also informed that the mediator cannot be subpoenaed to testify or become a witness in any court case, should the parties not resolve their case in mediation. Issues such as fees, length of sessions, any written agreement that will be produced, destruction of notes after the process is ended, termination of mediation, exceptions to confidentiality, and alternatives should an agreement not be reached, have to be addressed. Mediators typically use an Agreement to Mediate (required by Standard 5) in addition to orally explaining all of these details to clients in the opening statement. The written agreement to mediate should be signed by the parties and mediator at the first session. The agreement does not bind the parties to commit to mediation; they are free to end the process. It does outline the mediator's role and provides for payment of fees. A sample Agreement to Mediate follows.

Lynn E. MacBeth
Mediator
1805 Law & Finance Building
429 Fourth Avenue
Pittsburgh PA 15219

AGREEMENT TO MEDIATE

In consideration of services rendered and payment by clients, it is agreed and understood as follows:

1. Mediator will not give legal advice to either party. Both parties are advised to seek separate legal counsel during the mediation process and before signing any final agreement. Mediator may give legal information to both parties in order for them to make informed decisions.

2. The mediation process is confidential, and the mediator will not discuss the case with anyone unless authorized by clients. Exceptions to confidentiality exist such as reporting certain crimes or threats where there is possibility of future harm; child or elder abuse or neglect; or use of mediation to further such ends.

3. The fee for mediation services is $400 per hour. Sessions will normally last two hours, unless otherwise discussed and agreed upon by parties and mediator. Any representation by mediator stating how many sessions the case will take are only estimates, as it is impossible to predict how long a case will take to mediate, or whether or not a case will end in resolution. Fees are to be paid at the time of the session.

4. Mediator has discretion to declare an impasse or that a case is inappropriate for mediation.

5. Mediator will prepare a Memorandum of Understanding (which is not a legally binding contract) at the request of the parties at the conclusion of the sessions, and the fee for preparation of same shall be paid in advance, based on the mediator's projection of how much time it will take to prepare said memorandum.

6. Parties agree not to request Mediator to testify in court or to produce notes, records, files, or the like relating to the case. Client files will be destroyed 90 days after the last mediation session. Mediation communications are privileged and cannot be used as evidence in court, including but not limited to emails, phone calls, and correspondence between sessions. If, for any reason, mediator is called to testify or provide any evidence whatsoever on behalf of a party or parties hereto, the party or parties causing same will pay all of mediator's costs, hourly fee, and expenses.

_____   _____
Date   Party

_____   _____
Mediator   Party

The original purpose of an Agreement to Mediate was to define the process and protect confidentiality and privilege. The mediator role had no official, legal definition and there were no laws providing for confidentiality and privilege. Although the original purpose of the agreement is less applicable now, mediators continue to use it because it has benefits to clients and the mediator and because it is required by the standards of conduct. The benefits to the parties are that the duty of the mediator to maintain confidentiality is clearly defined, whereas some statutes set forth unclear definitions and confuse confidentiality with privilege. The benefits to the mediator are that the agreement sets forth a fee agreement (Standard 5B-this is also a benefit to clients) and delineates the mediator's role as a neutral, and not as an attorney or other professional, which could be a mediator's "primary profession," eliminating confusion. The mediator is protected from possible misunderstandings by providing a disclaimer regarding number of sessions needed, the keeping of client records, and the mediator's duty to prepare a written memorandum or testify in court.

The Agreement to Mediate should, if possible, fit on one page. Clients should not be burdened with having to read a long, complicated agreement to mediate that, inevitably, benefits the mediator more than the clients, who, for the most part, are protected by laws.

Sample Opening Statement

Hello, my name is Lynn MacBeth. You can call me "Lynn," and you are Justin and Marie, right? My role as your mediator is to help you discuss the issues in your case and come to decisions so that you have a complete agreement. When you are ready to have it all put in writing, I can prepare a document (called a memorandum of understanding) that you can take to your attorneys to have your agreement formalized with the divorce. The attorneys finish your case at that point, drawing up deeds, dividing assets, and getting the decree. I am no longer involved at that point unless you need more mediation to agree on an issue. Mediation is designed to save time and money, and clients typically save a large amount of money on attorneys' fees by limiting the lawyers' roles to reviewing the agreement and making everything legal. You are encouraged to consult with your attorneys when you have legal questions that need to be addressed independently. We do discuss some of the legalities in here- the difference is that I don't represent one of you and I do not give legal advice to one of you against the other. I don't direct your actions, as in telling you what to do. I rarely give legal opinions because legal opinions are not all that helpful since they are just opinions. If you want a legal opinion, the best place to get that is from your attorney. We often will discuss your attorneys' legal opinions in here so that both of you can hear each other's perspectives and make your own decisions about what you think makes sense. I will give you legal information. An example of legal information would be what issues need to be addressed for you to have a complete agreement. I actually have a checklist that we go through to make sure nothing has been omitted. Even though I have just said I don't give legal advice, you shouldn't be afraid to ask a question. If you have a question, please ask it and I will decide how to respond. Occasionally, but certainly not always, I will have separate meetings with you if that becomes necessary [Standard III-6]. An example of how that could be needed would be if one of you was having trouble getting clear on something that you wanted me to help you talk through without the other person listening in. I do believe, though, that you get the best value in mediation by working in joint session because that's where all of the negotiation and bargaining happens, and you learn each other's perspectives. It's important to me that each of you, individually, has a clear understanding of what you want for yourself because in a divorce situation, the decisions are going to impact you the rest of your life! Sometimes you might want to seek advice from a financial professional, a child expert, a tax preparer, or some other professional [Standard III-5]. My philosophy is, the more information you have, the better. Most people want to know how many sessions this process requires, mainly because you are investing money in each session. I understand your need to receive value for your money and I can tell you that I am committed to working hard in each session and making maximum use of our time. Probably by the end of today's session you are going to have a good idea of the pace you are making and how long it will take to finish. Here is my Agreement to Mediate. Every mediator has one of these. Mine is the best because it is all on one page. (Explain Confidentiality and details of Agreement). Okay, if there are no further questions, we should start. Would it be okay if I first just ask you some routine questions about you and your family? This will be helpful to me when I prepare your agreement—everything I need will already be here.

Often, after the intake, I will kick-off the mediation by asking: Have you had an opportunity to discuss things? This is one way to neutrally get the discussion started.

Intake Questions

The mediator then takes a short history, including names, addresses, date and place of birth, date and place of marriage, names and birthdates of children, employment history, education, salary history (brief), assets, debts, income, health issues, and legal activity. Attorneys appreciate mediators who have already gathered this information in a comprehensive document. Social security numbers, account numbers, and names of financial institutions (or actual statements) are also helpful to attorneys. Information on children such as residence, schedule, school, activities, health issues, caregivers is also taken. The mediator should not routinely ask parties why they are getting divorced. This is something that is often done, particularly mediators with a mental health background. There is nothing to be gained by the mediator in doing this, and everything to lose. The mediator will know the whole story by the end of the mediation, or at least as much of it as the mediator needs to know. The clients will, at minimum, give strong clues, and, typically, will reveal the entire story soon enough. To ask this question directly is offensive. It implies that there is a simple answer to something that is so complex, it takes years for the parties themselves to sort it out. It implies blame and responsibility, which is also complex, and shared. It implies judgment as if someone had to do something wrong in order for this to have happened, as if divorce is out of the ordinary, which it is not. It implies that the mediator has the right to intrude into the parties' privacy. When clients share this information voluntarily, it is welcomed information. The mediator seldom needs to understand the psychological aspects of the clients' marriage. If a psychological reason is relevant to the legal issues in the divorce, such as compulsive gambling that resulted in "dissipation" of the marital estate, for example, this fact would certainly be explored by the mediator by asking an appropriate factual question, such as, "What happened to that account?"

Memorandum of Understanding

After the parties have reached an agreement, the mediator, for an additional fee, prepares what is euphemistically referred to as the Memorandum of Understanding. The mediation world is filled with euphemisms because of the powerful and sometimes harsh effect of words on people's sensibilities. Mediation theory is full of euphemisms, and this word is used to distinguish the parties' agreement from a legally enforceable, final agreement parties reach with attorneys. There is nothing wrong with using the word agreement, so long as parties understand that in the mediation world, an agreement, despite its ordinary definition, is not final until it is reviewed by attorneys and signed by the parties.

Writing the memorandum of understanding can be done at the very end or in increments. For instance, if parties want to memorialize the agreements entered into in a single session before the next session, the mediator can provide them with a writing to reflect agreements or potential agreements to date, or even a summary of discussions. Sometimes a temporary, "interim" agreement is needed pending a final agreement on issues such as custody, separation, or support. In that case the mediator can prepare an initial memorandum of understanding if the clients want to incur this expense.

The procedure is for the mediator to prepare a writing that sets forth in detail the parties' agreement without purporting to be a legally binding document. The memorandum expresses the parties' agreement neutrally without consideration of only one party's needs. Attorneys typically draft agreements as advocates. One party's attorney provides a draft that is reviewed and, ordinarily, revised by the other attorney. Drafting is part of advocacy. When both attorneys feel that the language of the agreement protects their clients individually, the agreement is ready to be signed by the parties. However, the mediator's writing records the terms only, and is not a work of advocacy on behalf of either party.

In single issue family cases, such as custody, or a single issue family dispute (i.e., In which nursing home should Grandmother reside?) the task of drafting the memorandum is not as taxing for the mediator as it is in complex divorce cases involving financial matters. In such cases, the mediator and the clients benefit from the mediator's legal education and experience. In mediating the case, and in drafting the memorandum, the mediator must think like a lawyer. Lawyers are taught to think of the following questions in every transaction:

• What will happen if someone files for bankruptcy?

• What will happen if someone dies?

- What will happen if someone violates the agreement?

- What safeguards should there be to avoid problems in the future?

- What are the tax consequences?

Therefore, few mediators who are not attorneys are willing to act as mediators in complex legal cases without an attorney co-mediator. Even though there is typically not a requirement that a mediator be an attorney, mediators are required by ethical standards to be competent (Standard 2). There are mediators who are not attorneys who do an excellent job mediating financial issues in divorce. Although they did not obtain a law degree, they did study divorce laws, tax laws, finance, accounting, and the many disciplines necessary in order to effectively mediate economic claims in a divorce.

After the Memorandum of Understanding is delivered to the parties, the parties have an opportunity to review it and, if necessary, request stylistic or substantive changes they both agree upon, to the mediator. When the memorandum is completed, the parties take it to their attorneys for review to convert its terms into the legal language of a binding agreement to be signed by the parties and filed with the court. The attorneys will then execute the terms of the agreement by preparing deeds, court orders to transfer retirement assets, obtaining the decree, and, in some cases, changing the parties' wills and estate plans. The mediator's job of mediating and reducing to writing a divorce and economic settlement is complete. If, however, during this phase another dispute arises, the parties should return to mediation to resolve the disputed issue or issues.

The Memorandum of Understanding does not have to be drafted in legal language or have "boilerplate" clauses that lawyers typically place in an agreement. The parties' attorneys can take a memorandum containing only the terms the parties have agreed upon and add boilerplate clauses and legal language. However, boilerplate clauses and legal language are often part of the agreement the parties want to discuss in mediation. For instance, parties are often concerned about enforceability of an agreement, particularly where a party has the potential for insolvency. For this reason, an attorney mediator may want to include some legal language and boilerplate provisions in the memorandum. At a minimum, the mediator drafting the memorandum should address the following items.

Divorce and Custody Memorandum Checklist

Custody

- Parenting Agreement (Custody Schedule)
- Regular Schedule during School Year and Summer
- Holiday Schedule (supersedes regular schedule)
- Vacations
- Transportation Sharing
- Legal Labels: Legal Custody (Right to make decisions, access to records, etc.)
- Physical Custody (Who has physical control of child, and when)
- Birthdays (Child's and Parents')
- Alternate caregiver arrangements (if in dispute)
- (Should other parent be given right of first refusal for long absence?)
- Other agreements (Prior orders, pre- or post-nuptial agreements)
- Vacation custody and information (address, itinerary, phone, etc.)
- Parents' Responsibilities
- Telephone, Webcam Contact

Child Support

- Modifiability
- Tax Exemptions
- Monthly amount
- Day Care Expenses
- Health, Dental, Optical, Psychological, Orthodontic Coverage

- Unreimbursed Medical Costs

- Extraordinary Expenses (Field Trips, Lessons, Activities, Sports)

- Bonuses, Lump Sums, Extraordinary Income

- Disability Insurance

Alimony

- Amount

- Duration

- Deductibility/Taxability (eliminated by Trump tax reforms but could be part of an agreement prior to those reforms).

- Termination upon Death or Remarriage

- Life Insurance

- Disability, Long-term Care Insurance

- Modifiability

Counsel Fees

Property Division

- List of all Property/Debts

Assets

- Retirement assets- defined benefit and defined contribution plans, IRAs

- Who pays for QDRO? Who pays for a refinance of a mortgage?

- Mutual fund accounts

- Stocks

- Savings, Cash
- Checking, Cash
- Stock Options
- Medical Savings Accounts
- Stock Purchase Plans
- Annuities
- Business Interests
- Real Estate
- Mortgages
- Contracts
- Time Shares
- College savings (Who receives if child dies or does not attend college?)
- Children's custodial accounts
- Household Goods, Furniture, Tools, Jewelry, Personal Items
- Pets
- Professional Licenses, Practices
- Automobiles, Boats
- Any non-marital property that could have a marital component
- Timing of Division-Change of Value Issues
(What to do if asset appreciates or depreciates before distribution?)
- Children's Property
- Inheritances
- Real Estate; how to be titled?
- If any property remains in joint names:

- When to be transferred/sold?
- Party responsible for maintenance, expenses
- Party Reimbursed
- What happens on death, remarriage, insolvency
- Who is entitled to rents?
- Mortgages refinanced
- If Real Estate Sold, Expenses of Sale

Debts

- Liability for Debts
- Indemnification/Security

Taxes

- Who receives deductions?
- Who received exemptions?
- Who receives refund?
- Do parties file jointly?
- Liability for past years' deficiencies?
- Sharing of refund from past years?
- Indemnification for past deficiencies?
- Capital Gains Reporting on Sales of Assets

Life Insurance

- Ongoing beneficiary designations

- Enforceability (Direct communication between insured and company)
- Premiums Paid By
- Long-Term Care

Filing of Divorce

- Is Divorce Intended? If not, what are the legal implications of remaining married while separated?
- Parties obligated to consent and cooperate
- Timing
- Who is Plaintiff?
- Attorneys' and Mediator's fees
- Delay decree for any reason?
- Health Insurance Continuation

Educational Expenses

- College (children)
- College (spouse)
- Private school
- Tuition, books, room & board, incidentals

Enforceability

- Security provisions
- Mortgage, Life Insurance, Indemnification
- Desired Boilerplate Provisions
- Waivers

- Changes to Wills, Estate Plans

- Superseding of Prior Agreements

A Final Note about Property and Economic Issues in Divorce

Clearly, a comprehensive financial settlement involving a marriage of any duration is much more complicated than sitting down at the kitchen table and making a list. There are many legal considerations with lifelong consequences. The decisions parties make in divorce can have grave financial penalties if not carefully examined and should not be undertaken without an expert mediator, attorney, and possibly other professionals, such as a qualified financial adviser.

SAMPLE MEMORANDA OF UNDERSTANDING WITH COMMENTARY

Sample #1

Lynn E. MacBeth
Mediator
1301 Grant Building
310 Grant Street

MEMORANDUM OF UNDERSTANDING

This Memorandum has been prepared following mediation between CHARLOTTE DOE (hereinafter "CHARLOTTE" or "Wife" or "Mother") and JOHN DOE (hereinafter "JOHN" or "Husband" or "Father"). ALTHOUGH THIS MEMORANDUM IS DRAFTED IN A FORM RESEMBLING AN AGREEMENT, AND MAY BE REFERRED TO AS "THE AGREEMENT," IT IS NOT INTENDED TO BE SIGNED, OR TO BE INTERPRETED AS A BINDING AGREEMENT BETWEEN THE PARTIES UNTIL REVIEWED BY LEGAL COUNSEL. Mediation occurred April 7, 2022and April 26, 2022 and April 30, 2022 with Lynn E. MacBeth, Mediator.

I. PREMISES

WHEREAS, the parties were married March 17, 2012 in Washington County, PA; and

WHEREAS, the parties have decided to separate and divorce; and

WHEREAS, the parties are the parents of one child, David Doe, born March 14, 2015; and

WHEREAS, the parties acquired income, assets, savings, and debt during the marriage, and

WHEREAS, the parties wish to enter into an Agreement settling all of the property and economic rights and responsibilities arising out of their relationship. It is the intention of the parties to enter into a final Agreement settling all economic matters including but not limited to equitable distribution, alimony, support, alimony *pendente lite*, counsel fees, costs, expenses, equitable relief, and all other possible claims, known and unknown; and

WHEREAS, the parties intend that their Agreement shall be incorporated but not merged into any Decree in Divorce to be entered in this matter.

II. TERMS AND CONDITIONS

The parties agree as follows:

Description of Marital and Non-Marital Property

1. The property the parties intend to divide and/or set apart to each of them is set forth below:

    a. **Joint Savings**

XYZ Bank Account consisting of three (3) accounts including a Certificate of Deposit with an approximate balance as of March 31, 2022 of $5,348.22. Total value of three accounts including C.D.: $20,029 as of March 31, 2022.

    b. **Real Estate**

Marital residence located at 1000 McGillicutty Lane, Anytown, Washington County, Pennsylvania. Parties agree that current fair market value of property is $360,000 and the mortgage balance on December 1, 2021 (the date chosen by the parties as date of separation for purposes of valuing equity in the house) was $89,150. The equity in the residence for equitable distribution is, therefore, agreed to be $270,850.

    c. **Household Goods and Furnishings**

The parties have estimated the fair market value of their household goods and furnishings and have divided and distributed them so that Charlotte has received furniture worth $15,800 and John has received furniture worth $1,615. These items have been divided in kind and no further division of personal property is necessary.

d. **Automobiles/Vehicles**

Charlotte owns a 2019 Honda Accord with no loan balance and John owns a 2017 Honda Accord with a loan balance of approximately $3,760.

e. **Retirement Accounts**

i. Charlotte's XYZ Bank Roth IRA Rollover account with a balance of approximately $100,400 as of January 2022.

ii. Charlotte's ABC Bank 401(k) account with her current employer with a balance of approximately $42,000 as of January 2022.

iii. John's XYZ Bank IRA Rollover, Life Insurance, and Mutual Funds accounts with a total balance of approximately $239,000 as of January 2022.

Plan of Distribution

2. The parties agree to distribute all of the above property and debt as follows:

a. To Charlotte: Charlotte shall receive her entire XYZ Bank Roth IRA Rollover account and her ABC Bank 401(k) account and John waives all right, title and interest therein. Charlotte shall also receive her automobile and the household goods and furnishings set aside to her as stated above. The parties shall divide equally the balance of their Joint XYZ Bank account immediately, provided, however, that the Certificate of Deposit shall not be divided until it matures in September 2022, at which time they shall divide the account equally. Charlotte shall retain the marital residence and shall have sole and exclusive possession thereof. John shall, prior to the entry of a decree in divorce, transfer all of his right, title and interest in the marital residence to Charlotte by Quitclaim Special Warranty Deed. Charlotte shall hereafter be responsible to pay the mortgage, including principal and interest, and all taxes, insurance and any other expenses associated with the former marital residence and shall indemnify and hold

John harmless thereon. Within six (6) months from the date of this agreement, Charlotte shall refinance the current mortgage on the marital residence in order to remove John's name therefrom. The terms of the refinancing are addressed below.

        b.   <u>To John:</u>   John shall receive his entire XYZ Bank account (rollover from 123 Company) and life insurance and mutual fund accounts and Charlotte waives all right, title and interest therein except as otherwise set forth herein. John shall also retain his automobile and the household goods and furnishings set aside to him as stated above. John shall be responsible for the loan on his automobile and shall indemnify and hold Charlotte harmless thereon. John shall also receive half of the parties' joint savings in XYZ Bank as described above. In addition, John shall receive the sum of $_____ from Charlotte in order to effectuate a roughly equal distribution of assets. The parties stipulate that said sum is the amount they have agreed to. This sum shall be paid to John within six (6) months of the date of this agreement. Costs (including up to 2 points) of refinancing the current mortgage balance shall be split equally

     3.   All of the above distributions shall be characterized as equitable distribution and not as alimony or support.

Alimony, Alimony Pendente Lite, Support

     4.   Charlotte shall pay John alimony (which shall be considered spousal support prior to the entry of the decree in divorce) in the amount of $500 per month for a period of one year beginning in May 2022 and ending June 30, 2023. Payment shall be by direct deposit and shall be due in full on the first day of every month. Payment of alimony shall terminate upon the death of either party and upon remarriage or cohabitation with an unrelated person of the opposite sex by John. This provision shall not be modified by any court without the written consent of both parties.

     5.   John shall pay Charlotte child support in the amount of $800 (eight hundred dollars) per month beginning May 2022, in two equal installments every month on the 15th and the 30th. John shall arrange for automatic deposits from his account into Charlotte's checking

account for these payments. Charlotte shall provide health insurance coverage for David for so long as it is available to her at her current employment. All unreimbursed medical, dental, orthodontic, and optical expenses incurred on behalf of David shall be divided between the parties with John being responsible for 37% and Charlotte for 63% after payment by Charlotte of the first $250 per year. In addition, the parties shall divide all day care expenses 37% payable by John and 63% payable by Charlotte. The parties' net monthly incomes on which the current child support agreement is based are: Charlotte, $6,056.48 and John: $3,492.73.

6. Charlotte and John shall be responsible for their own health insurance coverage and both waive any right to claim a contribution from the other.

Life Insurance

7. The parties agree to maintain each other as primary beneficiary of all life insurance currently in force, including Charlotte's policy through her employment and John's policy with DOT as well as through employment. After the parties are divorced, they shall both continue to be obligated to name the other as primary beneficiary of life insurance policies in the amount of $100,000 each until David reaches age 18. Accordingly, the parties shall execute authorizations in each other's favor, permitting access to all information relating to the policies and premium payments from their respective life insurance companies.

College Fund

8. John shall pay $114 per month into the 529 College Fund he has already established with a current balance of approximately $1,078. Charlotte shall be custodian of said funds for David's benefit. The amount that has already been accumulated by John for this purpose shall also be part of this account. In addition, Charlotte shall be custodian of the existing Audubon account established by John for David's benefit with a current balance of approximately $2,000.

Custody

9. The parties shall have joint and shared legal custody of their son David. It is their desire to cooperate in the best interests of David to jointly provide for the nurturing, development, health, education and welfare of their son. The parties agree to discuss and jointly decide all major decisions and to communicate when possible about day-to-day decisions. David shall reside primarily with Charlotte and shall be with John every week as follows.

Week 1: Thursday night after school through Saturday at lunch time. Week 2: Saturday at 4:00 p.m. through Monday morning. Weeks 1 and 2 shall then repeat continuously. Holidays shall be divided as evenly as possible by mutual agreement. Thanksgiving shall be with John either in Metropolis or out of town. Christmas shall be spent with both parents, but primarily with Charlotte. David shall sleep in Charlotte's house Christmas Eve and remain with her through most of Christmas Day. Both parties shall have the right to take David on vacation for two (2) non-consecutive vacations every year, during his summer vacation. While on vacation, the parties shall provide each other with information relating to their location and contact information.

Miscellaneous

10. The parties shall execute their agreement as soon as practicable and file Affidavits of Consent and Waivers of Notice so that a divorce decree may be entered as soon as possible.

11. The parties are not aware of any unpaid debts incurred during their marriage. If any debt exists, it shall be the responsibility of the party for whose benefit it was incurred and shall be assumed and paid by such party, who shall indemnify and hold the other harmless thereon.

12. The parties agree that they have had full disclosure from each other of all of their assets, income, liabilities, expectancies, and the values of the same. They further stipulate that they have had the opportunity to have each and every asset appraised, and, in some cases, with full knowledge and understanding of their legal rights, have waived the right to do so. In the case of the marital residence, they are aware of an appraisal that states a higher value, but both parties stipulate and agree that the appraisal is wrong. Both parties are fully knowledgeable of the values of all assets, and agree that full disclosure of all assets and their values, with documentation thereof, has been given to each by the other. The parties agree that they know of no other marital property, or marital component of non-marital property, or marital debt, except as set forth above. Both parties waive any further division of such assets as they have engaged in extensive disclosure and valuation thereof.

13. Both parties waive all claims of alimony, alimony *pendente lite,* support, equitable distribution, costs, expenses, counsel fees, equitable relief, or other claims that may be brought in connection with a divorce, except as set forth in this agreement. This provision shall not be modifiable by any court. The parties have agreed to this provision with full knowledge of all relevant facts, and the law regarding their respective rights and responsibilities, and, with such knowledge, waive any right they have to said claims.

14. John and Charlotte shall both consult with separate legal counsel of their choice, for the purpose of reviewing their agreement and receiving advice on the relevant facts and law.

15. Each of the parties hereto covenants and agrees that, except as otherwise set forth herein, he or she has not and will not at any time in the future incur or contract any debt, charge, contract or liability whatsoever for which the other party, his or her legal representatives or property or estate may become liable; and both parties further covenant and agree at all times to keep the other free, harmless and indemnified from all debts, charges and liabilities hereafter contracted by them. The parties and their heirs and assigns shall be bound by this agreement.

16. If either party defaults in the due performance of any of the terms, conditions, and covenants of this Agreement on his or her part to be performed, the non-defaulting party shall have the right to sue for specific performance or damages for breach of the Agreement, and the defaulting party shall pay all costs and the reasonable legal fees and other professional fees for any services rendered by the non-defaulting party's attorney in any action or proceeding to compel the defaulting party's due performance. Both parties agree to execute any document necessary to effectuate the terms of their agreement.

17. Except as otherwise expressly provided herein, each party hereby releases and discharges completely and forever the other from any and all rights of past, present, or future support, division of property, right to receive proceeds as a beneficiary on any life insurance policy or policies insuring the life of the other party, right of dower and curtesy, right to act as administrator or executor in the estate of the other, right of distributive share in the other's estate, right of exemption in the estate of the other, or any other property rights, benefits or privileges accruing to either party by virtue of said marriage relationship, or otherwise, and whether the same are conferred by the statutory law or by the common law of the Commonwealth of Pennsylvania, of any other state, or of the common law of the United States of America. It is the understanding between the parties that their agreement, except as otherwise provided for herein, forever and completely adjusts, settles and disposes of, and completely terminates, any and all rights, claims, privileges and benefits that each now has, against the other arising out of the marriage relationship or otherwise and whether the same are conferred by the laws of the Commonwealth of Pennsylvania, or of any other state, or of the United States of America, and which are now or which may hereafter be in force and effect.

18. All matters affecting the interpretation of this Agreement and the rights of the parties hereto shall be governed by the laws of the Commonwealth of Pennsylvania.

_____

Sample #2

MEMORANDUM OF UNDERSTANDING

This Memorandum has been prepared following mediation between HUSBAND (hereinafter "Husband" or "Father") and WIFE (hereinafter "Wife" or "Mother"). ALTHOUGH THIS MEMORANDUM IS DRAFTED IN A FORM RESEMBLING AN AGREEMENT, AND MAY BE REFERRED TO AS "THE AGREEMENT," IT IS NOT INTENDED TO BE SIGNED, OR TO BE INTERPRETED AS A BINDING AGREEMENT BETWEEN THE PARTIES UNTIL REVIEWED BY LEGAL COUNSEL. Mediation occurred January 28, 2015 and February 11, 2015 with Lynn E. MacBeth, Mediator.

I. PREMISES

WHEREAS, the parties hereto were married July 24, 1999 in Fairfax County, GA; and

WHEREAS, the parties have decided to separate and divorce; and

WHEREAS, the parties are the parents of one child, Child born January 20, 2009; and

WHEREAS, the parties acquired income, assets, savings, and debt during the marriage, and

WHEREAS, the parties wish to enter into an Agreement settling all of the property and economic rights and responsibilities arising out of their relationship. It is the intention of the parties to enter into a final Agreement settling all economic matters including but not limited to equitable distribution, alimony, support, alimony *pendente lite*, counsel fees, costs, expenses, equitable relief, and all other possible claims, known and unknown; and

WHEREAS, the parties intend that their Agreement shall be incorporated but not merged into any Decree in Divorce to be entered in this matter.

II. TERMS AND CONDITIONS

The parties agree as follows:

Description of Marital and Non-Marital Property

1. The property the parties intend to divide and distribute is set forth below:

a. Retirement Investment Accounts (values as of 12/31/14)

    i. ABC Company 401(k) Husband   45,347.25

    ii. Husband's IRA   35,042.48

    iii. Wife's Tax-Deferred Annuity
(from employment at XX Employer)   14,080.59

b. Other Investment Accounts

See Attached Exhibit A for a complete list of the parties' investment accounts owned jointly and/or individually.

c. Separate Funds Deemed Non-Marital

    i. Husband's XYZ stock
as of 9/10/14   1,578.98

    ii. Husband's ABC stock
as of 12/16/14   1,005.79

These funds were owned by Husband before the marriage; although they may have increased in value during the marriage, the parties have elected to treat them as Husband's separate property for purposes of their agreement.

    d.   **Real Estate**

        i.   Location, Location, Location, County, PA
Fair market value approx. $81,000
Mortgage balance appx. $47,900
Net equity= $33,100

        ii.   New residence possibly to be purchased by Husband- parties agree Husband will purchase with his share of the settlement agreed to herein and it will not be considered a marital asset.

    e.   **Household Goods/Furnishings/Jewelry**
To be divided in kind $36,543
Total value- see attached inventory

    f.   **Automobiles/Vehicles**
2008 Ford Taurus $4,500.00
Jointly titled, Paid in full

    g.   **Debts**
        i.   Citibank account- $60 balance (Husband)
        ii.   Bank of America VISA- $30 balance (Wife)

Plan of Distribution

2.   The parties agree to distribute all of the above property and debt as follows:

a. To Wife: Wife will receive the marital residence and Husband shall execute a Quitclaim (Special Warranty) Deed conveying all of his right, title, and interest to her prior to the entry of a Decree in Divorce. Husband shall move out of the marital residence immediately. It is the parties' intention for Husband to move out as soon as possible and practicable. Prior to the date on which Husband moves, he shall be responsible for all expenses associated with the marital residence. After Husband moves out and begins paying support, Wife shall assume and be responsible for payment of the mortgage, principal and interest, taxes and insurance and all expenses associated with the house. She shall make timely payments and indemnify and hold Husband harmless thereon.

In addition, Wife shall receive her tax-deferred Annuity (rollover from XYZ employer); her ABCDEF Annuities (2); and her individual E-Trade account ($1,977.46 as of 12/31/14). In addition, Wife shall receive all of the stocks and/or investments and/or accounts listed on Exhibit A as property distributed to her. In addition, Husband will pay Wife $2,250 in consideration of Husband keeping the Ford Taurus automobile. Wife will purchase a vehicle, which shall not be considered part of the marital estate. Wife shall receive her automobile.

b. To Husband: Husband shall receive his ABC Annuity; his IRA; his Comptrol Corp. 401(k). In addition, Husband shall receive all of the stocks and/or investments and/or accounts listed on Exhibit A as property distributed to him. In addition, Husband shall retain his XXXXX and XXXXXX stock and Wife waives all right, title, and interest therein. Husband shall receive the Ford Taurus automobile.

c. Waivers: Both parties waive all interest in each other's retirement accounts and in all assets distributed to the other pursuant to Exhibit A.

d. Household goods and furnishings: The parties have agreed to a relatively equal in-kind division of household goods, furnishings, tools, appliances and personal property and there is no need for further division thereof.

e. **Unpaid Visa, Citibank account:** The parties have a small balance on these accounts which they shall pay off in equal amounts forthwith.

f. **After-acquired property:** In the event that Husband purchases a new residence for himself, if necessary, Wife shall sign any paper required to waive her interest therein.

g. **Proration of real estate taxes on marital residence:** Real estate taxes for 2014 regarding the marital residence shall be pro-rated so that Husband pays the portion attributable to January through March 1, 2014 and Wife pays the portion attributable to the rest of the year. Husband shall reimburse Wife for his portion if necessary.

3. All of the above distributions shall be characterized as equitable distribution and not as alimony or support.

Alimony, Alimony Pendente Lite, Support

4. Both parties waive alimony, alimony pendente lite and spousal support from each other except as set forth herein. This provision shall not be modified by any court without the written consent of both parties.

5. Husband shall pay Wife spousal support and child support in the amount of $1,179 ("basic support") per month beginning March 1, 2014. This amount shall be paid in two (2) equal monthly installments on the 5th and 20th day of every month. The parties shall make arrangements for direct deposit into an account designated by Wife. This shall be an unallocated order for spousal and child support and be deductible from income of Husband and includible in income of Wife. The spousal support portion shall be deemed alimony and continue after the parties are divorced for total payments for a period of 4.5 years through August 30, 2019. Payments shall terminate upon death of either party. Alimony shall terminate in the event of the remarriage or cohabitation with an unrelated member of the opposite sex by Wife. Payments are modifiable based on substantial, material change in circumstances. Payments are based on guideline of $4,375 gross income of Husband and $700 net income

(assigned earning capacity) of Wife. In addition, a portion of Husband's bonuses, when paid, shall be paid to Wife as follows: Wife shall receive a percentage of Husband's net (after actual income taxes) bonus within 30 days from the date said bonus is paid equal to the percentage of basic support Husband is paying for the applicable period over his net income. For example, the current percentage of support over Husband's net income is 1,179 (numerator) over 3,202 (denominator) or 36.8% which is the current rate for payment of his net bonus. In the case of any modification of the basic support amount, the Pa. guidelines formula shall control for spousal (or alimony portion) and child support. After alimony terminates as stated herein, there shall be no further right by Wife to claim alimony.

6. The parties agree to exchange income information every quarter (on the first day of each quarter for the previous quarter) in the form of pay stubs, tax returns and any other accounting applicable to income received by either of them. For example, on January 1 they shall exchange information for the previous quarter October-December. Within 30 days from the date they exchange such information, either party shall have the right to request an adjustment upward or downward in child support and/or spousal support and/or alimony and the adjustment shall be made retroactively to the beginning of the previous quarter. After 30 days, provided that full disclosure was made, the parties waive any right to request modification retroactively if the request was not made within the 30 day period. The Pa. guidelines formula shall apply to any modification.

7. In addition to the above payments, Husband shall also be responsible for health and medical insurance for Child (but credit shall be given to him per the guideline formula.) The parties shall split the following expenses (but only if they mutually agree upon the need for them) in proportion to their net incomes: car insurance for Child; field trips, camp costs. Unreimbursed medical expenses, dental and vision shall also be split in proportion to their net incomes (82% by Husband/18% by Wife) after Wife pays the first $250 per year.

8. Husband shall continue to provide health insurance coverage for Wife until the parties are divorced. When they are divorced, Wife shall be eligible for COBRA coverage and shall be provided with all appropriate notices from Husband and his employer. Wife may elect

such coverage or other coverage if she wishes and shall be responsible for her own premiums and unreimbursed expenses.

Life Insurance

9.	To the extent that either or both parties has life insurance provided through employment at no cost or at nominal cost, both are obligated to provide the other with information regarding the policy(ies) and shall name each other as sole beneficiary thereof until Child reaches age 18.

Custody

10.	The parties shall have joint and shared physical and legal custody of their son Child. Child currently resides with Wife and shall continue to do so but shall also spend substantial time in the home of his Father Husband, at least 26 weekends per year. If Child desires to change his residence and live with Husband, the parties agree to allow him to do this so long as Husband resides in the same school district. In the event of a custody change, child support shall change accordingly using guidelines. Both parties shall share the transportation and responsibilities regarding Child's activities.

Miscellaneous

11.	The parties shall execute their agreement as soon as practicable and file 3301(c) Affidavits of Consent and Waivers of Notice so that a divorce decree may be entered as soon as possible.

12.	The parties are not aware of any unpaid debts incurred during their marriage, except as stated above. If any debt exists, it shall be the responsibility of the party for whose benefit it was incurred and shall be assumed and paid by such party, who shall indemnify and hold the other harmless thereon.

13. The parties agree that they have had full disclosure from each other of all of their assets, income, liabilities, expectancies, and the values of the same. They further stipulate that they have had the opportunity to have each and every asset appraised, and, in some cases, with full knowledge and understanding of their legal rights, have waived the right to do so. Both parties are fully knowledgeable of the values of all assets, and agree that full disclosure of all assets and their values, with documentation thereof, has been given to each by the other. The parties agree that they know of no other marital property, or marital component of non-marital property, or marital debt, except as set forth above. Both parties waive any further division of such assets as they have engaged in extensive disclosure and valuation thereof.

14. Both parties waive all claims of alimony, alimony *pendente lite,* support, equitable distribution, costs, expenses, counsel fees, equitable relief, or other claims that may be brought in connection with a divorce, except as set forth in this agreement. This provision shall not be modifiable by any court. The parties have agreed to this provision with full knowledge of all relevant facts, and the law regarding their respective rights and responsibilities, and, with such knowledge, waive any right they have to said claims.

15. Wife and Husband shall both consult with separate legal counsel of their choice, for the purpose of reviewing their agreement and receiving advice on the relevant facts and law. If any provision of this agreement is unenforceable, then, to the extent possible, counsel shall draft the agreement in such a way as to give the provision full force and effect.

16. Each of the parties hereto covenants and agrees that, except as otherwise set forth herein, he or she has not and will not at any time in the future incur or contract any debt, charge, contract or liability whatsoever for which the other party, his or her legal representatives or property or estate may become liable; and both parties further covenant and agree at all times to keep the other free, harmless and indemnified from all debts, charges and liabilities hereafter contracted by them. The parties and their heirs and assigns shall be bound by this agreement.

17. If either party defaults in the due performance of any of the terms, conditions, and covenants of this Agreement on his or her part to be performed, the non-defaulting party shall have the right to sue for specific performance or damages for breach of the Agreement, and the defaulting party shall pay all costs and the reasonable legal fees and other professional fees for any services rendered by the non-defaulting party's attorney in any action or proceeding to compel the defaulting party's due performance. Both parties agree to execute any document necessary to effectuate the terms of their agreement.

18. Except as otherwise expressly provided herein, each party hereby releases and discharges completely and forever the other from any and all rights of past, present, or future support, division of property, right to receive proceeds as a beneficiary on any life insurance policy or policies insuring the life of the other party, right of dower and curtesy, right to act as administrator or executor in the estate of the other, right of distributive share in the other's estate, right of exemption in the estate of the other, or any other property rights, benefits or privileges accruing to either party by virtue of said marriage relationship, or otherwise, and whether the same are conferred by the statutory law or by the common law of the Commonwealth of Pennsylvania, of any other state, or of the common law of the United States of America. It is the understanding between the parties that their agreement, except as otherwise provided for herein, forever and completely adjusts, settles and disposes of, and completely terminates, any and all rights, claims, privileges and benefits that each now has, against the other arising out of the marriage relationship or otherwise and whether the same are conferred by the laws of the Commonwealth of Pennsylvania, or of any other state, or of the United States of America, and which are now or which may hereafter be in force and effect.

19. All matters affecting the interpretation of this Agreement and the rights of the parties hereto shall be governed by the laws of the Commonwealth of Pennsylvania.

_____

Explanatory Comments on Memorandum of Understanding

Premises

The premises section of the Memorandum is included because this is helpful information for the attorneys preparing the final documents for the parties' divorce. For purposes of providing anonymous examples the terms "Husband" and "Wife" are used in these memoranda; however, divorcing parties are not always fond of such terminology. It may be best to use first names or "Mother" and "Father" if appropriate.

List of All Assets and Liabilities

The entire marital estate (even items that could be "hybrid" or partially marital, such as items with an increase in value that would be considered marital property in some states) are listed here, with all liabilities. The primary legal reason for this is that in order for the parties to have a fair mediation and a fair, enforceable agreement, "full disclosure" must be made. By including this list in the agreement, there can be no doubt that the parties disclosed all information. The requirement of "full disclosure" underlies more than mere fairness, but is legally necessary for enforceability of an agreement as well. Signed (and, sometimes, unsigned) property settlement agreements are enforceable in most states; however, an agreement entered into as a result of fraud is voidable. Therefore, in order to prevent any allegation of fraud, both parties must make full and fair disclosure in writing. If a material asset is missing from the list, it could be grounds to void the agreement. In order for parties to receive value for their money, the mediator must urge full and fair disclosure. It is not unusual for clients to want to omit items from this list. When they express this desire, they should be advised that such an omission could result in problems enforcing their agreement.

Division of Assets/Liabilities

The sections that divide and distribute the assets typically state who receives the item, and, often, as in the case of retirement assets, that the other party "waives" his or her share. This is because a spouse typically has an interest by law in the other party's qualified retirement benefits. This right must be waived in order for an asset to be effectively distributed to one party. In the case of retirement accounts which can only be titled in one party's name, they should be distributed to the party in whose name the account is titled, where possible, to avoid the need for transfers which typically require a court order (A Qualified Domestic Relations Order under the Retirement Equity Act of 1984) or other paperwork performed by the attorneys. When real estate is transferred between spouses, it is typically done by Quitclaim deed rather than a General Warranty Deed, which is usually the way real estate is transferred in an arm's length transaction. The reason for this is that the spouse is relinquishing his or her interest in the real estate (such as it is) to the other spouse without making warranties respecting title. I have found that the legal language in a deed transferring ownership between spouses varies widely from state to state.

When payment of a lump sum of money is to be made, the mediator should include language in the memorandum stating when payment is due. When joint real estate is transferred to one spouse, the agreement typically requires refinancing of the joint mortgage so that the transferring spouse has his or her name removed from the mortgage obligation. This is typically done within a set timeframe, sometimes up to several years, depending upon the party's ability to refinance and the other party's desire to remove their name.

Alimony, Spousal Maintenance, Support, and Child Support

These items must be stated with specificity, particularly amount due, timing of payments, timing of termination of payments, and deductibility or taxability of payments with respect to payments to a spouse. Occasionally, an agreement will "allocate" support to distinguish between the portion of support that is not taxable as income (and not deductible) child support from spousal support, which is taxable as income and deductible, pursuant to state law.

Questions for Discussion

1. **Why is Husband's new residence listed even though it was purchased shortly after separation?**

2. **What does the second agreement say about the parties' responsibilities and rights while they are still residing in the marital residence together? Why would the parties do this?**

3. **Why do the parties agree to continue to provide each other with life insurance after they are divorced? Why would a non-custodial parent paying child support be interested in being named as beneficiary of life insurance in the event of the death of the custodial parent?**

Some agreements and Memoranda relate solely to custody. Following are samples of agreements relating to custody and/or support only, without divorce provisions. There are many types of custody arrangements and provisions. While many parents choose to keep their written custody provisions flexible and general, others prefer specific dates, times, and details in writing. Several examples of custody agreements as well as portions of custody provisions taken from memoranda follow.

Sample Custody and Support Memorandum #1

MEMORANDUM OF UNDERSTANDING REGARDING CUSTODY AND SUPPORT

(DRAFT CONSENT ORDER)

AND NOW this _____ day of _____, 2023, pursuant to the agreement of the parties, it is hereby ORDERED, ADJUDGED and DECREED as follows:

1. The custody hearing scheduled for January 13 and January 14, 2023 before Honorable John H. Smith and the parties' support hearing, which was continued pending the results of the custody hearing have been cancelled due to the parties' settlement of their pending claims as set forth herein.

2. The Plaintiff Dorothy Anne Mother ("Mother") shall have custody of the parties' minor children James (D.O.B. X-XX-XX) and Carpenter (D.O.B. X-X-XX) as follows: Every Thursday at 3:00 pm. through Sunday at 3:00 p.m. except for the third week of every month. On the third week of every month, Mother shall have the children from 5:00 p.m. Wednesday until 5:00 p.m. on Friday. Mother shall also have the children every remaining Wednesday from 5:00 p.m. until 7:00 p.m. The Defendant Chester J. Father ("Father") shall have them at all other times except as otherwise stated herein.

3. Holidays shall be shared as follows:

Father will have the children from 8:00 p.m. Thanksgiving Day until 10:00 a.m. on the Saturday after Thanksgiving. Mother will have the children overnight Mother's Day. On Memorial Day weekend, Mother will have James from 3:00 p.m. Friday until 3:00 p.m. Monday and Father will have Carpenter during those times. On Labor Day weekend, Mother will have

Carpenter from 3:00 p.m. Friday until 3:00 p.m. Monday and Father will have James during those times. For Easter, in odd years, Mother shall have the children from Saturday evening at 5:00 p.m. until Sunday at noon. In even years, Father has them from Saturday evening at 5:00 p.m. through Sunday morning and Mother has them from noon until 7:00 p.m. Mother shall have the children on Christmas Eve in even-numbered years from 8:00 p.m. until Christmas Day until noon and Father shall have them in even-numbered years from noon Christmas Day until December 26 at 8:00 p.m. In odd years, the parties shall reverse the 2 Christmas segments. Holidays shall supersede the regular schedule.

4. Father shall pay Mother child support in the amount of $825 per month beginning January 1, 2023. Father shall claim James as an exemption on his tax return and Mother shall claim Carpenter from 2023 on. When James is no longer eligible, the parties shall alternate taking Carpenter as an exemption.

5. Father shall pay $160 to Dr. Smith within 30 days.

6. Both parties shall have access to the children on their birthdays. Both parties shall allow the parties to speak on the phone to the other parent during their custody time.

_____

Sample Custody Language #2

CUSTODY AGREEMENT

1. The parties shall have joint and shared physical and legal custody of their son Jordan. Jordan shall continue in Sacred Heart kindergarten for school year 2022/23. For first grade, he shall be enrolled in Public school district. Beginning on the date when Mother moves into her new town home, Mother shall have custody every Monday and Tuesday and Father shall have custody every Wednesday and Thursday. Weekends (Friday through Sunday) shall be alternated with Father receiving the first weekend. Because both parents have a very close and nurturing relationship with Jordan, the parties intend to have daily contact with him when the other parent has custody and to have frequent telephone contact, attendance at all activities, and school events. It is the parties' intention to share all parenting responsibilities and decisions as much as possible. All holidays shall be shared and both parties shall have the right to take Jordan on vacation. The parties do not desire to set forth specific times and limitations regarding holidays and vacations because they have a good working relationship and believe they will be able to work out all of these times by mutual agreement. In the event either parent requires child care for the child overnight or for an entire day or longer, both parties shall give the other reasonable notice and right of first refusal to care for the child before a third party is used.

Sample Custody Language #3

CUSTODY AGREEMENT

Child Custody

1. The parties shall have joint and shared physical and legal custody of their children, equating as closely as possible to 50/50 sharing of physical custody time. The regular schedule shall be as follows:

The children shall spend the first part of every week beginning Saturday night (or sometimes Sunday mornings as the parties agree) through Wednesday at 7:00 p.m. with Mother. They shall spend the second part of the week beginning Wednesday at 7:00 p.m. through Saturday night or Sunday morning with Father. During summer children shall follow same schedule, but they shall spend days when Father is working with Mother at her residence.

Vacations:

Parents shall each be allowed one or two (as parties agree) weeks per summer for vacation with the children.

Separate Times:

Both parties shall plan and cooperate so that each parent has time alone occasionally with each child.

Activities:

Both parents will take the children to their regularly scheduled activities during their custody time, including but not limited to Church, School, and Cub Scouts. In addition, the parties will consult with one another about other activities.

Holidays:

Parties shall celebrate holidays with the children so that both parents have time with the children every holiday. To the extent possible, they shall celebrate holidays together as a family.

In the event the parties need a written holiday schedule, they understand they can do this in mediation.

The parties intend to share all parenting responsibilities and decisions as much as possible. The parties do not desire to set forth specific times and limitations regarding holidays and vacations because they have a good working relationship and believe they will be able to work out all of these times by mutual agreement. In the event either parent requires child care for the children overnight or for an entire day or longer, both parties shall give the other reasonable notice and right of first refusal to care for the children before a third party is used.

Sample Custody and Support Language #4

CUSTODY AGREEMENT

Child Support and Child Custody

1. The parties have had joint physical and legal custody of their son Johnny and it is their desire to continue their current schedule, or some modification thereof as mutually agreed, as long as possible. Childcare costs for Johnny have been divided equally and the parties have cooperated with sharing major expenses and living expenses associated with Johnny. It is their desire at this time to continue those financial arrangements, *provided however,* that with respect to health insurance and any unreimbursed health care costs including dental, optical, medical, and other necessary health care costs for Johnny, the parties shall divide the costs in proportion to their net incomes. Health insurance shall be provided by the parent who is able to obtain coverage at the lowest cost. Both parties acknowledge that Debra plans to move to Los Angeles, California to continue her education and Chet plans to move there also so the parties can co-parent Johnny. In California it is their intention to continue joint and shared custody. The parties also agree that wherever they live in the future, if one of them lives in the St. Louis, Missouri area, that parent shall be given preference for physical custody of Johnny if the other party does not live in the St. Louis area. Otherwise, their preference is shared and joint custody to the extent

possible. Holidays shall be shared as follow: In odd numbered years, Mother shall have custody every Easter and Thanksgiving and Father shall have custody every Christmas. In even numbered years, Father shall have Easter and Thanksgiving and Mother shall have Christmas.

Sample Custody Language #5

CUSTODY AGREEMENT

A.   During School Year: Shared custody- Father's time shall be every Tuesday and Thursday after school until the following morning when Father takes Kristi to school and every other weekend from Thursday after school until Monday morning when Father takes Kristi to school.

B.   Summers: Alternating weeks exchanging Kristi every Sunday evening.

C.   Holidays: 2022 and all even-numbered years Father shall have Kristi on Easter and Mother shall have her on Thanksgiving. In 2023 and all odd-numbered years thereafter, Mother shall have Kristi on Easter and Father shall have her on Thanksgiving. Christmas Eve from 10:00 a.m. to 10:00 p.m. and Christmas Day from 10:00 p.m. Christmas Eve through Christmas Day shall be alternated so that Mother has Kristi Christmas Day in even years and Father has Christmas Day odd years.

D.   Summer vacations shall be taken during the parties' own custodial time with reasonable additional time given if either party plans a vacation that lasts more than a week.

E.   Parties may mutually agree to adjust the schedule and both parties shall provide each other with at least 30 days' notice of their chosen vacation schedule. Parties shall give each other contact information (address and phone number) regarding the location of the vacation.

F.   Parties shall have shared legal and physical custody of Kristi.

Sample Custody Language #6

CUSTODY AGREEMENT

1. The parties shall share legal custody of their son Zach. Kathryn shall have primary physical custody and Luke shall have partial physical custody of Zach. Luke's partial custody schedule shall be: every Wednesday to Thursday and every other weekend from Friday through Sunday and any other times the parties shall agree to. Advance notice will be given of any times not set forth herein. Luke shall maintain possession of a garage door opener to the home on Mercyhurst Drive so that he may have emergency access to the home for Zach's protection. Each party shall have up to nine (9) consecutive days in the summer for vacation with Zach.

6. Holidays: Until March 2023 parties agree all holidays shall be shared unless otherwise agreed. Every Mother's Day shall be spent with Mother and every Father's Day with Father. When both parents are available, they will share time with Zach on: Thanksgiving, Christmas Eve/Christmas, New Year's, Zach's birthday, Easter, Memorial Day, Fourth of July, Labor Day and Halloween. For Thanksgiving, Christmas Eve/Christmas and Easter, either parent may go out of town with Zach, but for no more than one of these holidays per calendar year with reasonable prior notice. In the event one parent goes out of town for a holiday, that parent will not go out of town for the same holiday the following year. The parties agree to continue living within five (5) miles of each other until Zach graduates from high school unless otherwise agreed.

Explanatory Comments on Custody Memorandum

Schedule

The children's basic schedule, summer and school year, and holiday and vacation schedules should be set forth with as much specificity as possible to avoid problems with enforcement. Parties sometimes resist restrictive time frames because it makes them feel hemmed in. This personal preference should prevail if the parties and the mediator are confident that they are capable of forming mutual agreements as occasions arise. If one or both parties believe specific times are necessary, then they should be negotiated and set forth. Parties should be reminded that having specific times gives them something to "fall back on" if there is a problem. Also, a court can't enforce an order or agreement that is vague. When in doubt, it does not hurt to include specificity with a catchall stating that times can be changed by mutual agreement.

Legal Labels

Although mediators, the children, and even the parties rarely care what legal labels (i.e., primary physical custody, shared physical custody, etc.) apply to their brand of parenting, the attorneys, and sometimes judges, may require it.

Order of Court vs. Agreement

The mediator should be aware of the rules of a particular jurisdiction with regard to enforceability of a custody order vs. a signed custody agreement. Some courts will not enforce an agreement unless it is reduced to a court order.

A Final Note on Mediation Procedures

The purpose of this chapter is to provide a sense of what really happens in a mediation session. Reference was made to the mediator rarely giving an opinion. This means that the mediator's opinion in a gray area (such as duration or amount of alimony, appropriate property division, other legal questions) would not be helpful to the parties. The mediator would be acting as a judge or arbitrator in offering such an opinion, which, to the parties, would likely have the force of a decision. It would handicap the parties in making their own decisions, and it compromises the mediator's neutrality. There are situations, however, when the mediator can and should ethically make a suggestion with appropriate safeguards. The following account is from a mediator who did just that in a session headed towards impasse.

One Mediator's Suggested Settlement

As an experienced transformative mediator, I rarely give my opinion of how a couple should decide financial issues in divorce. My practice is to acquaint them with the issues, encourage them to get legal advice from independent attorneys, and then go through each issue, discussing the laws and facts, and facilitate a discussion. This usually results in a spirited dialogue that leads to a productive, if sometimes heated, negotiation. My job is usually to help the parties when they seem to lose control, get discouraged, frustrated, misunderstand each other, or have questions that I am qualified to answer.

Recently I had a case where it occurred to me that I wanted to share an idea for settlement. The idea came to me during a heated exchange with a husband and wife during their third mediation session. The parties had decided that Wife would keep one of their residences and her new car, would receive alimony for four years, child support for their two children, $50,000 as a furniture and moving allowance, would be a homemaker and not work outside of the home unless she wanted to, and would receive $400,000 as a lump sum from Husband. Husband would receive his struggling business (started before the marriage), their other residence, his two cars, his premarital rental property, and his $125,000 Individual Retirement Account (IRA). The issue that seemed irresolvable was how the husband would pay the lump sum to the wife. He was trying to expand his business and had taken out mortgages on all but the residence Wife was to receive. He was offering to pay Wife in installments over ten years. Wife was unwilling to receive "her money" in "dribbles" and felt she needed something in a lump sum to compensate her for having given up her career to raise children and for agreeing to waive any right to Husband's business. Although Husband had a cash flow from the business, it had always fluctuated with the economy. His accountant had told him that to pay $400,000, even if over ten years' time, would create "the perfect storm" that would bankrupt him. Emotions were high. The parties' anxieties heightened the more they discussed this final issue. I listened intently as I heard them argue about how Husband's business was the cause of the divorce, and Wife's "pessimism and negativity" were the problem in the marriage. They had both solicited opinions from their attorneys about how to resolve this question. Wife's attorney told her that in court they could easily get the money in a lump sum, but it would require a liquidation of assets. Husband's attorney suggested that Husband do nothing, and wear Wife down with litigation, so that there would not be any money left for a lump sum.

As I listened for what seemed like hours to the parties' repartee, the idea that occurred to me was a simple one that I did not expect the parties to welcome with open arms, but I decided to share it. I said, "Hold on. Okay. It's my turn. I have a suggestion to make. I have been listening to you and I want you to consider this suggestion. You do not have to like it or accept it. You can use it however you want. Perhaps you can tweak it and improve upon it. Here it is. Melissa gets $100,000 in a lump sum from your IRA to an IRA in her name. You pay the remaining $300,000 over ten years [with appropriate security and life insurance]. Melissa gets the car, the furniture allowance, the alimony, the house. Tom, you get your cars, the big house, your business, your rental property, and the balance of the IRA. The room transformed. Both parties obviously felt comfortable with this idea! They began talking about this plan with an entirely different tone. The anxiety level went down. Husband apologized to me for getting so upset. The wife wanted to know whom I could refer her to for investment advice for her "nest egg." After review by Husband's accountant and both attorneys, the agreement was finalized.

Was the mediator giving an improper opinion? Clearly, what the mediator offered as a suggestion was an opinion and influenced the outcome in a directive way. If the mediator did not believe the suggestion was a good one, the mediator would not have offered it. The mediator was seemingly at the end of her rope. She had listened to the parties' dialogue for hours. She knew the case inside and out. She had before her a puzzle to be solved that the parties' attorneys were not helping to piece together. The mediator was uniquely situated to offer a possible solution, which, in reality, was an opinion. The mediator's idea was the result of inspiration that came from listening intently to parties whose needs and interests were thoroughly laid out. The mediator made it clear that her suggestion was not to be taken as gospel. This is an example of a suggestion that was given in an impartial way, with no agenda by the mediator. If the parties rejected this suggestion, the mediator would simply have moved on to the next step in the process, which could have been impasse.

Chapter Seven

"When my parents got divorced, there was a custody fight over me...and no one showed up." --Rodney Dangerfield

Child Custody

Best Interests of the Child

Mediators work in the shadow of the law. This popular phrase recognizes the law's influence on the mediation process—its presence is pervasive, yet its effect is only that of a "shadow." Ever mindful of the law, mediation participants are not constrained by it. Parties are not required to follow solutions crafted by legislators and courts. Nevertheless, they examine those solutions in order to make decisions with "informed consent." Mediation participants are not limited to legal precedent and are free to agree to any terms they want, regardless of whether or not a court would order the same terms. There are no "support" police checking to see if parties are living by the support guidelines, nor are there "custody" police watching custody agreements. Courts do, however, have discretion over what consent orders (signed by both parties) will be signed off on by the court. A court will refuse to sign a custody consent order if it does not appear to be in the best interests of a child. Examples of agreements a court might reject are orders that switch custody of a child every six months, change a child's school enrollment with disruptive frequency, split up siblings,[171] or have children make prison visits, although all of these examples are readily observable as working custody arrangements and/or adjudications in the real world. Courts are not fond of signing orders that give a child the ability to choose, such as, "David will spend summers with Father, unless David does not want to," because such an agreement is considered vague, unenforceable, and, worse, places David in an unconscionable position. Giving a child power that belongs to parents and/or judges places the child at undue risk by expecting him to make decisions he may be ill equipped to make and giving him the illusion of inappropriate control. Such a child is essentially being asked to make adult decisions because the adults have not met their responsibility to make those decisions. The child is being placed in the unfair position of having to parent himself and the catch-22 of inevitably disappointing one of the two most important people in his life. Every child deserves to have his welfare looked after by adults; delegating adult decisions to him deprives him of his right to a carefree childhood. This question, as well as other questions about what is proper and appropriate for a child, cannot always be answered by legislation. Typically, courts are called upon to deliberate over questions of what is in the best interests of a child on a case-by-case basis. Case law has addressed numerous parenting questions ranging from relocating out of state, agreement to raise a child in a particular religion, rights of non-parents, and choice of school, among many other issues.

---

[171] However, this practice, by necessity, is becoming more widely accepted as step-families increase and more and more siblings are half- or step-siblings.

This chapter examines the evolution of the law of child custody to familiarize the family mediator with the legal standards that have developed. In the U.S., where one has the choice of more than fifty jurisdictions in which to reside, laws vary significantly from state to state and territory. This is true even though all states have adopted at least portions of uniform custody laws.

Legal History of the Family

In the modern Western world, it is taken for granted that children should receive education and nurturing from their parents and community. They are not expected to work until they are at least in their later teens, and, even then, under limited, protected conditions. Their innocence is guarded by laws that prohibit their admission to explicit movies and their access to alcohol, tobacco, and explicit video games and music. Truancy laws require them to go to school. Laws against statutory rape, pornography, and the free movement of sexual predators are intended to further protect children. Juvenile courts give them special legal status in the criminal justice system, limiting criminal punishment, protecting confidentiality and sealing juvenile court records. The doctrine of *parens patriae,* first reported in 1838,[172] created a duty on the part of the state to protect and care for children when their parents failed to. There was, however, a time in relatively recent history when children were considered small adults, not innocent, and scarcely separate from adults.[173]

Prior to the sixteenth century, children were generally not considered to be in a special class. Their value to the family derived from their ability to work, and they were judged according to their competencies. There was little recognition of their innocence, and children who disobeyed their parents could be subject to capital punishment.[174] In colonial times, orphaned children could be rounded up from the streets of England and shipped to America as indentured servants.[175] According to historian Mary Ann Mason, "One-half of all persons who came to the colonies south of New England were indentured servants and most of them less than nineteen years old," and by the end of the eighteenth century, fully one-fifth of all children in America were slaves. Until the nineteenth century, children were considered the property of their fathers, and, in a custody dispute, would be awarded to their fathers. Their value as property derived from their status as laborers, apprentices, and indentured servants. There was no legal attention given to their "best interests." Economic considerations were paramount. The father alone was responsible for the family, and had complete control over each member. A married woman could not own property, enter into contracts, or make a will without her husband's consent. Divorce was rare. Children born to unmarried women slaves or indentured servants were treated not as property (since it was unknown who their legal father was) but stigmatized as problems. These children inherited the status of their mother, and slave fathers were legally

---

[172] Horowitz, R.M. & Davidson, H.A. (Eds.). (1984). *Legal rights of children.* New York: McGraw Hill.
[173] Hart, Stuart N. (1991). From property to person status: Historical perspective on children's rights. *American Psychologist,* 46 (1). 53-59.
[174] Horowitz & Davidson, 1984.
[175] Mason, M.A. (1994). *From father's property to children's rights: The history of child custody in the United States.* Columbia University Press.

irrelevant. The person who had control over these children was the white male head of household who owned the slaves.[176] Slavery was abolished in the late nineteenth century, and industrialization brought men to the factory and workplace and away from home. Women became homemakers, resulting in the development of the tender years' doctrine.[177] Society began to view children, especially those of a young age, or "tender years" as belonging with their mothers. The idealized role of mother led to a recognition of the importance of nurturing and the idea of the best interests of the child.[178]

Gradually, children's status transitioned to a special class and their parents were expected to maintain and protect them, as schools became the norm. The shift to protection of children was due, in part, to philosopher John Locke's introduction of *tabula rasa,* or blank slate: the idea that the human mind is born without good or evil, and that the environment formed a person's character. In the nineteenth and twentieth centuries, forces external to the family began to influence the care of children. Sigmund Freud was the first modern theorist to divide periods of human development into stages, suggesting that nearly all of personality is formed in the early years of life. His sixth and youngest child, Anna Freud, continued his work in psychoanalytic theory principally working with children and popularizing the phrase "best interests of the child" in a book she co-authored in 1973 *Beyond the Best Interests of the Child.* The second half of the twentieth century emphasized children's best interests as the standard for determination of custody disputes. Legally, children began to receive due process rights and "person" status, including, among other things, the right to refuse mental health treatment and the right to obtain an abortion without parental consent.

Reportedly, the female employment rate in 2021 was 53.2 percent,[179] while the employment rate of men was 63.9 percent.[180] Fathers' groups have lobbied for equal rights, and joint custody is increasingly the norm. A determination of a child's best interests today entails consideration of numerous factors, many of which were never before part of the picture, i.e., rights of step-parents, biological parents, grandparents or other non-parents, and relocation decisions, among the numerous fact situations that arise in an increasingly mobile and diverse society.

Custody Laws

Webster[181] defines custody as--at best--"ownership," and, at worst, "confinement, imprisonment." The term seems offensive when used in connection with parenting, and the mediation community almost always attempts to avoid it, using, instead, the term "parenting." Legislatively, instead of the term

---

[176] Id.
[177] Id.
[178] Id.
[179] Statista. (2022). Employment rate of women in the United States. Retrieved from • Employment rate - women in the U.S. 2021 | Statista
[180] Id. Retrieved from • Employment rate of men in the U.S. 2021 | Statista
[181] *Webster's encyclopedic unabridged dictionary of the English language.* (1996). New York: Gramercy Books.

"custody," a minority of states use other terms—"access," "rights and responsibilities,"[182] "parenting plan,"[183] or "parenting."[184] Mediators try to use "parenting"; however, for the most part, the term custody endures, left over from the days when children literally were thought of as possessions. In general, a short glossary of legal terms used today in custody law is as follows.

Physical Custody- The actual physical possession and control of the child.[185]

Legal Custody- The legal right to make major decisions affecting the best interest of a minor child, including, but not limited to, medical, religious, and education decisions.

Partial Physical Custody- The right to assume physical custody of a child for less than a majority of the time.

Shared Physical Custody- The right of more than one individual to assume physical custody of the child, each having significant periods of physical custodial time with the child.

Supervised Physical Custody- Custodial time during which an agency or an adult designated by the court or agreed upon by the parties monitors the interaction between the child and the individual with those rights. [This term replaced the term *visitation* which was eliminated from the Pennsylvania custody statute in 2011. Prior to 2011, *visitation* meant, "the right to visit a child. The term does not include the right to remove a child from the custodial parent's control." In California, however, visitation has the popular meaning-- that of the right to spend time with the child-- not necessarily supervised.[186] In addition, many jurisdictions also use the term "joint custody" to refer to shared custody.]

Legal Custody

Legal custody affects parties' rights to make major decisions affecting the child as well as the right to obtain records or speak to professionals (i.e., teachers, physicians) about the child. A more child friendly

---

[182] Vermont Family Proceedings Rule 4
[183] West's RCWA 26.09.050 (Washington).
[184] 23 Pa.C.S.A. § 5331
[185] Definitions are from 23 Pa. C.S.A. §5322 unless otherwise noted.
[186] CA Family Code 3100.

term has also popped up in the legislation, "decision-making." The typical arrangement is for parents to share legal custody or decision making, regardless of the schedule for physical custody. Parties sharing legal custody both have access to medical and school records. Ideally, it shouldn't be necessary to order one parent to share all information with the other parent if the other parent has an equal ability to contact the school and obtain the information on his or her own. However, there are always instances where sharing is needed, as in when a singular item is delivered to the home via the child, such as a fundraiser packet, raffle tickets, or Flat Stanley project.[187]

The school and teachers should be discouraged from becoming overly involved in the drama of divorce and treating a child differently because he lives in two homes. Teachers who tell a child to "make two Valentines- one for your dad and one for your mom," are not helping their young student by treating him differently. The child who lives with Mom and Dad in the same home also has two parents who will need to find a way to share the Valentine.

Shared legal custody places the burden upon parents of keeping each other informed about details relating to events in the child's life. Even when the school is communicating with both parents, some items will only go home to one house; therefore, parents must be responsible to relay materials between houses, when important. Shared legal custody is the norm, even where parents live far away from each other.[188] The child should have the benefit of both parents' involvement in major decisions, barring extreme circumstances.

Joint or Shared Physical Custody

Historically, courts followed the "rule of one," believing that custody should be awarded to only one parent.[189] The trend today is toward joint or shared physical custody, meaning equal or close to equal time for both parties. Custody statutes often set forth the "policy of this state" at the beginning of the custody statute, declaring that children should have "frequent and continuing contact" with both parents.[190] States have gone so far as to create a rebuttable presumption in favor of joint physical custody,[191] although the majority of states do not formally have the presumption. Informally, many jurisdictions approach cases with a presumption of shared custody, at least informally. Several states set out in the statute that a court should favor the parent who is "more likely to encourage, permit, and allow frequent and continuing contact and physical access between the noncustodial parent and the child."[192] Such a provision contains insight

---

[187] e.g., See http://equator.eftours.com/the-ef-passport/traveling-with-flat-stanley
[188] *Bernard v. Green*, 412 Pa. Super 201, 602 A.2d 1380 (1990).
[189] DiFonzo, J.H. (2014). From the rule of one to shared parenting: Custody presumptions in law and policy. *Family Court Review*, 53, 213.
[190] Texas Family Code §153.001.
[191] U.C.A. 1953 § 30-3-10 (Utah), West's Ann.Cal.Fam.Code § 3040
[192] 23 Pa. C.S.A. §5328, *see also* NEV REV STAT ANN 125.480.

into the best interests of children by encouraging parents to promote shared custody and sidestepping the Solomonic, all-or-nothing task of deciding between two true parents.

In mediation, attention should be given to a parent who wants to exclude the other parent from the child's life. With intervention, the parent can be guided to see the other parent from the child's perspective. It is rarely out of love and appreciation for the child's best interests that a parent would choose to try to erase the other parent, although, at times, there may be one parent who creates unnecessary mischief in the child's life. Such a situation also offers an opportunity in mediation to bring about understanding and appreciation of the need to improve that parent-child relationship. In this way, mediation can be a healing, therapeutic process for the family.

Sole Custody

Sole custody is the award of legal and physical custody to one parent, excluding the other parent. Occasionally, a mandatory mediation party presents this request, at least initially. This is rarely, if ever, granted by a court.[193] Where one parent murdered the other parent, a Pennsylvania court excluded the convicted murderer from exercising custody rights, based on "severe moral or mental deficiencies" in the parent.[194] When a parent is a prisoner, visitation has been allowed,[195] the court finding that because of the constitutionally protected liberty interest[196] parents have the rights to visitation with their children, and parental visitation would not be denied or limited unless visitation with the parent posed a grave threat to the child. The grave threat standard could, obviously, clash with the supposed gold standard of best interests of the child. In this case, parents' liberty interests arguably trumped the child's best interests due to the "grave threat" requirement to defeat the parent's rights.

Increasingly, all state custody statutes address the effect of domestic violence on the court's custody decision. Some states have a rebuttable presumption that the perpetrator of domestic violence be denied sole or joint custody of a child.[197]

Rights of Non-Parents

Since parents have a prima facie right to uninterrupted custody of their children, non-parents must have standing in order to interfere with those rights. "Standing" refers to the right of a party to seek relief in court. Generally, non-parents may seek custody only if they have a statutorily defined right, or if they

---

[193] *Pamela J.K. v. Roger D.J.*, 277 Pa. Super 579, 419 A.2d 1301, 1309 (1980).
[194] *Green v. Sneeringer*, 431 Pa. Super 66, 635 A.2d 1074 (1993).
[195] In re CJ, 729 A.2d 89, 1999 Pa. Super. 94 (1999).
[196] *See also Winston by Winston v. CYS of Del. County*, 748 F. Supp. 1128 (E.D. Pa. 1990), cert. denied.
[197] Delaware Code Title 13. Domestic Relations § 705A. The majority of states, like Pennsylvania, include domestic violence as a factor to consider, including its effect on the child. 23 Pa.C.S.A 5328(2). Pennsylvania also directs the court to provide "safety conditions" if any type of custody is awarded to a party who committed abuse. 23 Pa. C.S.A. §5323(e).

stand in loco parentis. In other words, not just any third party can ask a court for custody of a child. The term in loco parentis means "in the place of a parent." A person with whom a child lives and who provides care for the child, even though not a parent or not even related to the child, and without a formal court order, can have standing to assert custody rights.[198] Grandparents have traditionally had to establish standing before seeking custody; therefore, grandparent's visitation acts were enacted in the 1980's and 90's to establish custody rights for grandparents who sought contact with grandchildren whose parents were divorced or deceased. The decline of the family unit due to divorce, out-of-wedlock births, and a more mobile society led to increased child custody rights for grandparents who could seek custody in the event of death, divorce or separation of parents, or if the child lived with the grandparent. In 2011 Pennsylvania revised its custody statute consolidating grandparents' rights into the principal custody statute, allowing the following individuals to file a custody action[199]:

(1) A parent of the child.

(2) A person who stands in loco parentis to the child.

(3) A grandparent of the child who is not in loco parentis to the child:

(i) whose relationship with the child began either with the consent of a parent of the child or under a court order;

(ii) who assumes or is willing to assume responsibility for the child; and

(iii) when one of the following conditions is met:

(A) the child has been determined to be a dependent child under 42 Pa.C.S. Ch. 63 (relating to juvenile matters);

(B) the child is substantially at risk due to parental abuse, neglect, drug or alcohol abuse or incapacity; or

(C) the child has, for a period of at least 12 consecutive months, resided with the grandparent, excluding brief temporary absences of the child from the home, and is removed from the home by the parents, in which case the action must be filed within six months after the removal of the child from the home.

---

[198] *Gradwell v. Strausser,* 416 Pa. Super 118, 610 A.2d 999 (1992).
[199] Pa. C.S.A. §5324

Although grandparents have greater standing than other third parties, their rights are still limited and subject to certain conditions including some degree of parental consent. Although grandparent contact is typically welcome, helpful, nurturing, and important, there are also cases where grandparents cause havoc in a family, and their favored status brings on trouble. To lawyers and family mediators, such "family revenge" scenarios occur where vindictive grandparents use their enhanced standing as a weapon against their own children, threatening to use the courts to take the grandchildren away from the parent. When mediators and lawyers see this multi-generational conflict that began with the grandparents (at least presumably), it is obvious that the very people who created the original problem (the grandparents) may likely repeat their poor parenting practices if given custody of their grandchildren. Grandparents are not always the stereotype they have been assigned by society; abusive parents whose children are now adults do, in the course of time, become grandparents, a status that does not erase abusiveness. Despite the benevolent image of grandparents that lawmakers might imagine, some grandparents are responsible for generational abuse. Given the right to interfere with child custody of their grandchildren, they will attempt to harm their own children, with the backing of the law, their attorneys, and sometimes the misguided support of courts. In these situations, the right of children to be raised by their own parents should take precedence.

Other states have similarly promoted grandparent interference in families. Up until 2916, in Alabama, a grandparent could petition for rights if the parents in an intact family have "used their parental authority to prohibit a relationship between the child and the grandparent,"[200] although this statute was found to be unconstitutional by an Alabama appeals court.[201] Such a law would give courts the deciding vote over parents who have, typically, forbidden the relationship for a reason a court can scarcely know or understand. Worse, in Connecticut, any third party can petition for visitation rights of any minor child, subject to a showing that a parent-like relationship exists.[202] Although these statutes recite the best interests of the child standard, it is difficult to imagine how it can be in a child's best interests for any person, without limitation, to initiate a court action to interfere with parental rights and the privacy of a family.

Parenting Arrangements

The appropriate parenting schedule, usually called "the regular schedule" to distinguish it from superseding arrangements such as holidays, vacations, and birthdays, involves consideration of the parents' concerns, the child's lifestyle, the parents' lifestyles, the parents' work schedules, and other factors. The mediator's task of listening to parents' work schedules and children's activities is undeniably tedious, but necessary. One of the many benefits of mediation to families is avoidance of cookie-cutter schedules that

---

[200] Ala. Code 1975-§30-3-4.1
[201] *L.T. v. J.D.*, 109 So. 3d. 652. (2012)
[202] C.G.S.A. 46b-59.

may be imposed in emergency court proceedings, or by courts that lack the time and resources to hear lengthy, boring details. A detail-oriented personality and patient disposition are obligatory traits for custody mediators.

Parties seeking shared physical custody may choose among several popular schedules. The alternating weeks schedule, where each parent takes a week at a time, has the benefit of allowing parents to plan well in advance for adult-only activities, work obligations, as well as for family vacations and activities. Parents become a tag-team, learning to assume parenting responsibilities exclusively for one week, while enjoying a week off knowing the children are being cared for by the only other person in the world who loves them in the same parental way. Many adults adjust well to this schedule, recognizing the benefits it has for them. Children adjust to living in two homes in the same way they "adjust" from birth to having two parents. Even when the two homes vary in rules, bedtimes, mealtimes, etc., children adapt. This phenomenon seems to be similar to their ability to adapt to different rules in different classrooms, to different teachers, or at school as opposed to at home, or at church, for instance. Children can adjust positively to joint custody arrangements due to the obvious advantages of having ongoing contact with both parents.[203] Detractors concerned with the trouble involved with going back and forth from one house to another would do well to consider the quality of the households over the mere act of switching households periodically. As concluded by Joan Kelly, "….many of the psychological symptoms seen in children of divorce can be accounted for in the years before divorce…. While children of divorced parents as a group have more adjustment problems than do children of never-divorced parents, the view that divorce per se is the major cause of these symptoms must be reconsidered in light of…research documenting the negative effects of troubled marriages on children."[204]

The alternating week schedule accommodates children's needs by reducing the frequency of transition. Parents choose the day of the week on which to switch based on their schedules, usually Friday or Sunday. Rather than a "Ping-Pong ball," a child who moves from one parent to another should be viewed as a child who is being loved and properly cared for by two parents (nature's model). Parents have the obligation to alleviate inconvenience to the child by taking measures to make parenting in two houses as seamless as possible. There are undeniable losses to children, most notably loss of continuity with friendships in each neighborhood.[205] Parents should be encouraged to impose organization on the system by living within reasonable proximity of each other, keeping lists and checklists of items needing to be transferred, and purchasing duplicates of video game systems, computers, favorite toys, and other conveniences. Children do not have to bear the brunt of cooperative parenting after divorce when parents work to relieve logistical problems. To clients who complain, a suggested mediator refrain is, "Welcome

---

[203] Warshak, R. A. (2014). Social science and parenting plans for young children: A consensus report. *Psychology, Public Policy, And Law*, 20(1), 46-67. See also Bauserman, R. (2002). Child adjustment in joint-custody versus sole-custody arrangements: A meta-analytic review. *Journal of Family Psychology*, 16 (1), 91-102.
[204] Kelly, J.B. (2000). Children's adjustment in conflicted marriage and divorce: A decade review of research. *Journal of the American Academy of Child & Adolescent Psychiatry*, 39 (8), 963-973.
[205] Dunn, J., Davies, L., O'Connor, T., Sturgess, W. (2001). Family lives and friendships: The perspectives of children in step-, single-parent, and non-step families. *Journal of Family Psychology*, 15(2), 272-287.

to parenthood!" Even children from intact families forget their backpacks occasionally, and parenting in one home is never seamless. When asked whether they would prefer to experience the occasional forgotten backpack or lost homework over being completely deprived of living with one of their parents, children are clear. "Young adults, who have lived through their parents' divorces and have gone on to college, do not think equal time with parents is necessarily unworkable, and, in fact, they believe with remarkable consensus that it is the best arrangement...."[206]

The alternating week schedule's drawback is the absence of the other parent for a solid week. Parents compensate for this drawback by assisting each other with transportation to and from activities as a way of spending time with their children, attending games, performances, and activities, occasional meals out mid-week, and limiting this schedule for use with children over the age of five. Flexibility is key for children to feel comfortable with this schedule. Children who feel that parents' rigidity forbids any deviation from the schedule are made to feel responsible if their desires conflict with the schedule. For example, a child who wants to attend an event for Dad's family on Mom's time will tend to feel the pressure of one parent's discontent if the parents cannot amicably resolve flexibility issues. For younger children, parents sometimes opt for a shared schedule that lessens time away from the other parent, the 5/2/2/5 schedule being one model. This schedule treats Friday through Sunday as the weekend. Weekends are alternated between parents. Of the four remaining weekdays, each parent takes two consecutive days as consistent days for that parent. The classic 5/2/2/5 schedule looks like this:

Sunday	Monday	Tuesday	Wednesday	Thursday	Friday	Saturday
MOM	DAD	DAD	MOM	MOM	DAD	DAD
DAD	DAD	DAD	MOM	MOM	MOM	MOM
MOM	DAD	DAD	MOM	MOM	DAD	DAD
DAD	DAD	DAD	MOM	MOM	MOM	MOM

This schedule has an appealing stability in the consistency of weekdays. Even young children develop a consistent routine knowing that they are always with Dad every Monday and Tuesday and with Mom every Wednesday and Thursday. Planning is easier for everyone. The drawback of the 5/2/2/5 schedule is that up to three transitions are needed every week. This is typically not a problem for infants, but increases in

---

[206] Fabricius, W.V. & Hall, J.A. (2000). Young adults' perspectives on divorce living arrangements. *Family and Conciliation Courts Review, 38(4),* 446-461.

difficulty as children grow[207] and establish connections to their environments. Some children will complain about transitions. This phenomenon is more often than not related to their desire to continue doing whatever it is they are doing at the moment of change, and not necessarily related to "not wanting to go to Dad's." Parents too willing to interpret their child's recalcitrance at changing homes as a sign of unhappiness with the other parent, or even abuse, should be encouraged to explore other reasons behind the complaint. In older children, the complaint may be that the transitions are too frequent, or that time with one parent is not significant enough to establish a strong connection with that parent's environment.

Some parents find that alternating weeks and 5/2/2/5 require too much time away from one parent. An alternative shared custody arrangement can usually be found that will meet their needs. Potential deviations are to alternate Friday or to not treat Friday as the weekend, but to add Friday to the schedule of the parent who has Wednesday and Thursday. This is a shared custody arrangement that does not equate to exactly 50/50 percent, but is nevertheless deemed to be close enough to equality to be called shared. Another alternative to the classic 5/2/2/5 is the 2/2/3 below:

Sunday	Monday	Tuesday	Wednesday	Thursday	Friday	Saturday
MOM	DAD	DAD	MOM	MOM	DAD	DAD
DAD	MOM	MOM	DAD	DAD	MOM	MOM
MOM	DAD	DAD	MOM	MOM	DAD	DAD

Alternatively, I have seen parents of infants and very young children successfully alternate 1, 2, or 3 day intervals. This schedule is clearly not permanent and not as easily illustrated on a weekly calendar but can be planned out on an annual basis.

Some parents believe their child is not a candidate for shared custody because children should have a "home base" or should have "consistency" by living with one parent, particularly Monday through Friday. Occasionally, this is true. By asking questions of both parents about the child and the parents' abilities to

---

[207] Kline, M., Tschann, J., Johnston, J., Wallerstein, J. (1989). Children's adjustment in joint and sole physical custody families. *Developmental Psychology, 25 (3)*, 430-438.

accommodate a shared arrangement, the answer usually surfaces. If a party works out of town Monday through Friday and plans to use a nanny to watch the children during the school week, shared physical custody during the school week is likely not the best alternative in that child's best interests.

Siblings

There has been a strong preference in the law in favor of keeping siblings, and half-siblings, together.[208] However, this preference can be overcome in cases where there is not a strong bond between siblings, or where it is otherwise not in the best interests of the child. In today's world, the prevalence of multiple step-families has diluted this preference.

School

There can be a preference for keeping a child in a situation in which the child has thrived, such as a particular school, along the lines of, *"If it ain't broke, don't fix it."* The failure of parents to agree on choice of school is often seen in mediation. When parents cannot agree, a court will look at the circumstances of the case, taking into consideration relevant facts such as the quality of the schools, the convenience of parents, availability of transportation or other services, schedules, and the child's needs. Continuity of school will not control a case where there are other, more important factors militating in favor of a parent who advocates a change of school.[209] I have mediated many school choice disputes to a successful conclusion. When a settlement is reached, I have noticed that, most often, there is one parent who, in the end, did not hold school choice as his or her #1 priority, and eventually revealed willingness to compromise in exchange for concessions on other matters. The key to getting there was to keep the conversation between them going without judgment and with a spirit of inquiry[210] by the mediator.

Relocation

Increasingly, parents want to move away from a jurisdiction with their children, making it difficult for the other parent to have a shared custody schedule. This can be brought on by a job transfer, a desire to be near extended family, a remarriage, or a desire to leave a city that was only inhabited for a short time. Courts require parents who want to leave to request relocation, and will order parents to return if they leave with the children in violation of a court order, or without the other parent's consent. There is a myth that relocation cases cannot be mediated; this myth probably developed because of the "all or nothing" perceived solution to the problem. Often, however, these cases are resolved in mediation with solutions that are not "all or nothing." Parents occasionally will agree to relocation. The benefits to a parent who has not been able to enjoy shared custody are that in relocation cases, that parent is likely to be awarded large periods of partial custody time to offset the relocating parents' advantage of having primary custody. The relocating

---

[208] *Karner v. McMahon*, 433 Pa. Super 290, 640 A.2d 926 (1994).
[209] *Swope v. Swope*, 455 Pa. Super 587, 689 A.2d 264 (1997).
[210] LeBaron, p. 246.

parent is often advised that he or she will most likely be expected to agree to summers and school breaks with the other parent. When relocation is not agreed to, the relocating parent will sometimes relent and choose not to take the children away from the other parent. In other cases, a parent will choose to follow a relocating parent. This option should always be considered and parents should be encouraged to see the logic behind following their children, when career and other considerations do not present insurmountable obstacles. Mediation participants will, at first, bristle at this idea, but thought through, the idea of following the other spouse to be near one's children is not unreasonable. The relocated city probably has jobs; in the grand scheme of things, being near one's children has a bigger impact on the lives of parents and children than what job Dad had. A mediator who gently and compassionately explores this option with the parties does them a great service.

Pennsylvania law on child relocation, 23 Pa.C.S.A. §5337, prevents a party from relocating with a child unless all parties agree or the court approves the relocation. A party intending to relocate must give notice, subject to objection by the other party or parties. In deciding the parties' relocation dispute, the court lists the following factors.

(h) Relocation factors.--In determining whether to grant a proposed relocation, the court shall consider the following factors, giving weighted consideration to those factors which affect the safety of the child:

(1) The nature, quality, extent of involvement and duration of the child's relationship with the party proposing to relocate and with the nonrelocating party, siblings and other significant persons in the child's life.

(2) The age, developmental stage, needs of the child and the likely impact the relocation will have on the child's physical, educational and emotional development, taking into consideration any special needs of the child.

(3) The feasibility of preserving the relationship between the nonrelocating party and the child through suitable custody arrangements, considering the logistics and financial circumstances of the parties.

(4) The child's preference, taking into consideration the age and maturity of the child.

(5) Whether there is an established pattern of conduct of either party to promote or thwart the relationship of the child and the other party.

(6) Whether the relocation will enhance the general quality of life for the party seeking the relocation, including, but not limited to, financial or emotional benefit or educational opportunity.

(7) Whether the relocation will enhance the general quality of life for the child, including, but not limited to, financial or emotional benefit or educational opportunity.

(8) The reasons and motivation of each party for seeking or opposing the relocation.

(9) The present and past abuse committed by a party or member of the party's household and whether there is a continued risk of harm to the child or an abused party.

(10) Any other factor affecting the best interest of the child.

(i) Burden of proof.--
(1) The party proposing the relocation has the burden of establishing that the relocation will serve the best interest of the child as shown under the factors set forth in subsection (h).

(2) Each party has the burden of establishing the integrity of that party's motives in either seeking the relocation or seeking to prevent the relocation.

(j) Failure to provide reasonable notice.--The court may consider a failure to provide reasonable notice of a proposed relocation as:

(1) a factor in making a determination regarding the relocation;
(2) a factor in determining whether custody rights should be modified;
(3) a basis for ordering the return of the child to the nonrelocating party if the relocation has occurred without reasonable notice;

(4) sufficient cause to order the party proposing the relocation to pay reasonable expenses and counsel fees incurred by the party objecting to the relocation; and

(5) a ground for contempt and the imposition of sanctions against the party proposing the relocation.

(k) Mitigation.--Any consideration of a failure to provide reasonable notice under subsection (i) shall be subject to mitigation if the court determines that such failure was caused in whole, or in part, by abuse.

(l) Effect of relocation prior to hearing.--If a party relocates with the child prior to a full expedited hearing, the court shall not confer any presumption in favor of the relocation.

Religion

Courts are loathe to make religious decisions concerning children unless it is shown that actual harm can result from the religious practice. A court can place restrictions upon a parent's right to inculcate religious beliefs if there is competent evidence that the actions present a substantial threat of present or future physical or emotional harm.[211] In *Shepp v. Shepp*[212] the Pennsylvania Superior Court ruled that Father's advocacy of polygamy to his daughter posed a substantial threat of harm. In *Wireman v. Perkins*,[213] a Kentucky Court of Appeals ruled that even though Father had the contractual right to "determine the child's upbringing," which included religious training, Father did not have the right to dictate that Mother

---

[211] *Zummo v. Zummo*, 394 Pa. Super 30, 574 A.2d 1130, 1137 (1990).
[212] *Shepp v. Shepp*, 821 A.2d 635, 2003 Pa Super 140. (2003)
[213] *Wireman v. Perkins*, 229 S.W. 3d 919 (Court of Appeals of Kentucky, 2007).

take the child to church during her custodial time. This, the court, ruled, infringed on Mother's right to express her religion or lack of religion and to be meaningfully involved in her child's upbringing. In *Zummo v. Zummo*, a Pennsylvania case often cited by other states, the parties shared legal custody, while Mother, who was Jewish, had primary physical custody and Father, a Roman Catholic, had partial physical custody. The parties had an agreement that Father was not to take the children to religious services contrary to the Jewish faith. The court held that such an agreement could not be enforced without infringing upon Father's religious liberty, stating that it could not inquire into exactly what practices would be "contrary" to Judaism without impermissibly evaluating religious doctrine, nor would it inhibit the religious freedom of individuals to change their religious views as they progress through life, rather than being bound by an agreement signed during a past religious phase. A court will not interfere with the religious preference of either parent.[214] Although courts may not render value judgments on merits of a particular religious view or belief, they may properly examine the effect that views or beliefs have on development of the child involved in the custody dispute.[215] In custody disputes where parents cannot agree on one religion for their children, courts will order the teaching of two religions. "For children of divorce, exposure to parents' conflicting values, lifestyles, and religious beliefs may indeed cause doubts and stress. Stress, however, is not always harmful nor is it always to be avoided and protected against. Restrictions must be imposed sparingly.[216]"

In 2010, the case of *Reyes v. Reyes*[217] out of Cook County, Illinois made national headlines when Judge Renee Goldfarb initially denied Joseph Reyes the right to take his daughter Ela to church, upholding the parties' agreement that Ela be raised in her mother's Jewish faith. Days later, after much media attention, the judge reversed her decision, finding no harm in Father taking his daughter to church during his visitation. Interestingly, one of Father's arguments to gain the right to take his daughter to Catholic Church despite the divorce agreement that she be raised in the Jewish faith was that Catholicism is a radicalized form of Judaism. The court did not cite this rationale as part of its decision, however.

Child's Preference

Many states are required by statute to consider the child's preference.[218] This is typically based on the child's "reasoned preference" and maturity. Factually, the information is elicited either in an in camera interview of the child (when the judge speaks to the child in chambers, or the judge's office) or via a guardian ad litem. Consideration of the child's preference is an enlightened view of children's rights, although the opposing view has some merit. Children who are placed in a position of having to state a

---

[214] *Tripathi v. Tripathi*, , 787 A.2d 436, 2001 Pa. Super 322.
[215] *Morris v. Morris*, 271 Pa. Super. 19, 412 A.2d 139 (1979). (Parent restricted from taking child with him during door-to-door proselytizing.)
[216] *Frank v. Frank*, 2003 Pa. Super 355, 833 A.2d 194.
[217] No. 2008D004072 Cook County Municipal Court, 4/13/2010.
[218] e.g., AS §25.24.150(c)(3)(Alaska), DC ST §16-914(a)(3), 23 Pa. C.S. § 5328 (a)(7). In Georgia, a child over the age of 14 has the right to choose which parent to live with unless the parent is unfit. GA CODE ANN §19-9-3(a)(5).

choice of parent can be indecisive. Courts and lawyers have found such children to be less than reliable as witnesses. Depending upon the child's age and priorities, some children truly do not care where they live, so long as their needs are met and they have access to both parents. Other children, sadly, have priorities that go far beyond their own welfare. These are the children who have learned from an early age that they can be instruments of peace between their parents. They have taken on the role of placating both parents by telling each parent what he or she wants to hear. This child witness has psychological and survival concerns that compromise the ability to be truthful. For these reasons, some believe children should never be consulted. Giving the child such a choice places an undue burden on the child, who should be living a carefree childhood, knowing his welfare is being looked after for him by responsible adults. Giving a child this choice conveys an exaggerated sense of his own power. Children are not often equipped to handle an excess of power.

Modification

States differ in the standard used to determine whether modification may be requested. Some states allow modification of custody to be requested any time if the modification will be in the best interests of the child.[219] This is a child-friendly standard because it places the child's best interests over judicial economy or procedure. Parents may request modification any time so long as it is alleged the modification is in the child's best interests. A party dissatisfied with a custody order resulting from a lengthy trial can, at least theoretically, return to court immediately for another hearing, alleging that a modification would be in the child's best interests. Such an approach could even substitute for an appeal of the unpopular order. This view can and does burden courts, although it might relieve the burden on appellate courts because appeal is less likely if the order can be revisited at the trial court level. This standard's downside from the child's point of view is that it enables the wealthier parent to constantly force the other parent into court, using the legal system as a weapon of harassment and financial drain. Surprisingly, this type of behavior is relatively rare and has not resulted in any drive to change the law. Unfortunately, this child-friendly standard is the minority view.[220] Other states distinguish between modification of an adjudication (where, presumably a trial has occurred) and a consent decree.[221] There, modification based on a best interest standard applies to the consent decree, and the adjudication can be modified only based on a material change in circumstances. Other states distinguish between modification of a shared physical custody arrangement and some other arrangement.[222] In those states, modification of shared custody requires the stricter standard of changed circumstances. This could have a chilling impact on the ease with which shared custody arrangements are entered into or ordered by a court.

---

[219] *McMillen v. McMillen*, 529 Pa. 198, 602 A.2d 845 (1992)
[220] Most states, and the Uniform Marriage & Divorce Act, Sec. 409, advocate the majority standard requiring changed circumstances for a modification of custody, regardless of the child's best interests, "stability" being the goal.
[221] *R.L.H. v. J.A.B.*, 642 So. 2d 482 (Ala. Civ. App. 1994)
[222] *Alberswerth v. Alberswerth*, 184 S.W.3d 81 (Mo. Ct. App. W.D. 2006)

Contempt

Disobedience of a custody order triggers the possibility of a contempt petition brought by the disgruntled parent. When all is said and done, most contempt actions are the result of misunderstandings or one-time disruptions in parties' lives or schedules. Occasionally, a parent will be in true contempt. Contempt of court is the willful violation, without justification, of a court order for custody. It is punishable by a modest fine, (i.e., $500[223]) imprisonment or probation, (i.e., six months[224]) or suspension of driver's license privileges. The statute does not list any other sanction, such as awarding make-up time.

When a parent is found to be in contempt, the court is faced with a dilemma because punishing the parent can directly result in punishment of the child. Fining a parent may mean the child is deprived financially. Courts have reduced child support as a punishment for contempt. This is clearly not intended by the statute, and is an improper sanction.[225] Courts have jailed the custodial parent. This is permitted by statute, but could result in unintended harm to the child. Undoubtedly, limiting a parent's driving ability would impact a child in many families, yet it is permitted by the statute. Sometimes a request for more time with the child (make-up time) will be made by the parent seeking a remedy for contempt. Courts give in to this suggestion because it seems non-punitive and satisfies the complaining party's need for justice. Even this result may not be appropriate if such a variation in the child's schedule is not beneficial to the child.[226] Moreover, "more time with the child" is not one of the sanctions advanced in the Pennsylvania Domestic Relations Code; however, in other jurisdictions this remedy is provided by statute.[227] Punishing the custodial parent seems counter-productive when there are adverse effects on the child. Statutes that provide for giving additional time to the petitioning parent as a sanction seem to view the child as a "reward" for winning a lawsuit. In the majority of contempt cases, some justification exists for the violation of the court order. If the deviation from the court order was reasonable and justified, then a finding of contempt will not be made. In resolving any custody matter, care must be taken not to punish the child or use time with the child as a punishment or reward. The focus of these proceedings is still on the best interests of the child. This is not to say that there are not true cases of deliberate, willful contempt of custody orders. True contempt of a court order for custody can be devastating to children; however, many, if not most, contempt actions appear to be motivated by parents who do not seem capable of viewing the effects of their litigious actions upon their children. One such example is evident in the decision of Pennsylvania state court judge[228] David Wecht in the case of *Mossburger v. Eiler*.[229]

---

[223] 23 Pa. C.S.A. §5323(g).
[224] Id.
[225] In some jurisdictions, such a sanction is specifically prohibited by statute, e.g., V.A.M.S. 452.365 (Vermont).
[226] Lambert v. Lambert, 409 Pa. Super 552, 598 A.2d 561 (1991).
[227] E.g., West's RCWA 26.09.160(2)(b)(i) (Washington) and I.C.A. §598.23 (2)(b) (Iowa).
[228] Now Pennsylvania Supreme Court Justice
[229] 157 PLJ 318 (2009).

Mossburger v. Eiler

Pa. Common Pleas, 2009

Wecht, A.J., May 1, 2009—Here lies yet another sad tale of a broken family whose contentious, long-distance custody dispute has been aggravated and intensified by our essentially unregulated, unaccountable, and uncaring airline industry. It is not the first such episode. Sadly, there is every reason to suspect that it will not be the last.

Pursuant to an Order of Court dated July 25, 2008, Defendant Kevin A. Eiler ["Father"] exercises primary custody of the parties' eight-year-old child, Lita [d.o.b. 2/12/01], in Allegheny County, Pennsylvania, while Plaintiff Christina M. Mossburger ["Mother"] exercises partial custody in Fairbanks, Alaska. In compliance with that Order, Father purchased airline tickets to travel with Lita from Pittsburgh to Fairbanks (via Chicago and Anchorage) on December 23, 2008. The reason for Father's traveling with the child was that the child was too young to travel unaccompanied.

On December 23, 2008, Father and Lita arrived at the Pittsburgh Airport at 12:30 p.m. or 1:00 p.m. for a 3:45 p.m. flight. American Airlines rewarded them for their diligence in arriving early by consigning them to wait until approximately 7 p.m.

Because of Father's and Lita's delayed departure from Pittsburgh, they arrived too late in Chicago to catch their connecting flight to Anchorage on American Airlines' "partner" Alaska Airlines.

When Father and child left Pittsburgh, the airline must (or should) have known that there was no way Father and Lita could make their connecting Chicago to Anchorage flight, and that the "weather" in Chicago (Chicago weather being a new discovery for the airline) would not allow for any other flights that evening. Had any airline employee advised Father of these facts before he left Pittsburgh, Father could have stayed in Pittsburgh, tried to make other arrangements immediately, and avoided the rest of the expense, delay, stress and inconvenience he and the then seven-year-old Lita encountered.

When Father and Lita arrived in Chicago on the night of December 23, they were met by enormous milling crowds in the airport terminal. While there was an airline employee waiting near the gate, that employee merely directed the passengers to a line of several hundred people waiting to speak with a ticketing agent. Father faithfully waited in line for two to three hours with his seven-year-old child to gain information about how and when he could connect to Fairbanks via Anchorage. After finally reaching the counter, Father displayed this Court's Order to the airline clerk because Father knew that he was required to deliver Lita to Mother. The clerk told Father that he could try to stand-by for a flight on December 26, but that his chances of actually getting on that flight were not good, and that Father could elect to wait for the privilege of purchasing new tickets for seats on flights scheduled for December 28.

Faced with the prospect of staying in Chicago, with all the attendant expenses, for several days, at Christmas, with a seven-year-old child, or returning home and trying again, Father reasonably decided to try to return to Pittsburgh. Father then was forced to overnight with the child in Chicago at a cost of $90.00 for the hotel room (not including meals and other expenses; the airline could only spring for a portion of the room), and then catch a flight to Philadelphia the next morning (Christmas Eve) (Pittsburgh being unavailable for some unknown reason) with the intention to return to Pittsburgh the same day.

Father was met in Philadelphia with yet another "weather" delay. He and Lita then were forced to spend Christmas Eve in Philadelphia and return to Pittsburgh on Christmas Day. While the airline did pay for the hotel in Philadelphia, Father was forced to incur expenses for meals. More importantly, Lita was forced to incur a Christmas Eve spent in an airport hotel. A casual observer might wonder how this situation would have played out if the child had been a year or two older and had been traveling alone in this wintry ordeal. Would the airline have let a minor wait in the Chicago airport for four or five days until the next available flight? Does the airline even care?

Upon his eventual return to Pittsburgh on Christmas Day, Father (who is a cook, not a lawyer) was compelled to spend hours of the family's remaining holiday time making several telephone calls to the airline trying to get the child and himself to Alaska on a different flight. After many calls, Father finally was able to book December 28 travel. During these telephone calls, Father initially was put on hold for hours, and initially was told that he would have to buy an entirely separate ticket for an additional $2,000.00 [footnote omitted] for the Pittsburgh to Chicago and Chicago to Pittsburgh portions of his original tickets that he and the child had used [footnote omitted].

Mother presented a Petition for Contempt, alleging that Father had willfully failed to comply with the Order's requirement that the child travel on the first flight available after school recesses for winter break pursuant to the July 25, 2008 Order. Father opposed the Petition and this Court scheduled a hearing.

At the hearing, there was no proof that Father had willfully failed to comply. To the contrary, Father diligently had attempted to comply. He had been thwarted by the airlines' misfeasance, incompetence, and utter callousness.

Because Father was not in contempt, the Court did not hold him in contempt. The Court will order that Mother obtain two extra days on both end of the summer this year. Currently, Mother obtains custody of the child the seventh day after school recesses for the summer, and returns custody the seventh day before school begins. This coming summer, she will obtain custody the fifth day after school ends, and return custody the fifth day before school begins. The Court is aware that Father may already have purchased tickets for the child and that this may, unfortunately, cause additional expense for changing the tickets. In such case, we once again see proof that, regardless of responsibility for causing a problem, the airline always profits in the end.

Parental Alienation

The phenomenon of Parental Alienation was first popularized by Richard A. Gardner, M.D. in 1988[230]. It has been further developed by Douglas Darnell, Ph.D. of Youngstown Ohio. Darnell works with parents and mediators, describing the "syndrome" in his book *Divorce Casualties: Protecting Your Children from Parental Alienation.*[231]

Although proposed,[232] Parental Alienation Syndrome (PAS) is not currently an official medical or mental health diagnosis and does not appear in the Diagnostic and Statistical Manual of Mental Disorders[233] used to diagnose disorders. PAS is not universally accepted by courts as a recognized condition and has its share of opponents, particularly parents and advocates who believe that children choose to cut themselves off from a parent for a good reason, typically sexual, physical, or emotional abuse. Nevertheless, it is widely

---

[230] Gardner's initial statements that the syndrome mostly originated with mothers' alienation were later modified to state that the syndrome manifests equally among mothers and fathers who alienate. Weller, C. (2014). *Newsweek*. Retrieved from http://www.newsweek.com/2014/07/18/parental-alienation-syndrome-isnt-dsm-yet-its-plenty-arguments-258079.html

[231] Darnell, D. (1998) *Divorce casualties: protecting your children from parental alienation.* Lanham, MD: Taylor Trade Publishing.

[232] Widiger, T. A. (2013). A postmortem and future look at the personality disorders in DSM-5. *Personality Disorders: Theory, Research, and Treatment*, 4(4), 382-387. doi:10.1037/per0000030

[233] American Psychiatric Association.

accepted and reported in the literature of family law and psychology,[234] and is assessed by experts such as Darnell, who defines the syndrome as follows.[235]

Parental Alienation Definition: A parent's purposeful campaign of vilification characterized by anger, resistant and inconsistent compliance with court orders, conscious or unconscious denigration of the child's other parent, and interference with the other's parent/child relationship.

The Alienated Child: One who expresses freely and persistently, unreasonable negative feelings and beliefs (such as anger, hatred, rejection, and/or fear) towards a parent that are significantly disproportionate to the child's actual experience with that parent.

Parental Alienation Syndrome: Arises primarily in the context of child-custody disputes…is the child's campaign of denigration against a parent, a campaign that has no justification. It is the result from a combination of a programming (brainwashing), parent's indoctrination and the child's own contribution to the vilification of the targeted parent.

Rarely, a mediator or lawyer will encounter true PAS. More often it is accused or perceived PAS, much like the case of Vince and Julie where a weak parent blames other people for his or her lack of interest in parenting, and subsequent lack of involvement with a child. Real PAS, according to Darnell, is absurd. It is totally black and white (the alienated parent has no good qualities) and there is no room for any gray area, forgiveness, excuse, or mercy toward the alienated parent. It is a campaign with no ambivalence on the part of the child. The child is defensive and is heard to say, "I'm an independent thinker." The child's language is reflexive and indicates an unwavering support of the alienating parent. The alienating parent is seen as a saint. The alienating parent's entire extended family uniformly shares the animosity. The child's language echoes the alienating parent's. "We have to put up with him." The child demonstrates no remorse. The child's hatred is generalized to others associated with the alienated parent (his friends, family, and associates). The alienated child is not intimidated by the court and demonstrates no forgiveness. The alienated child's beliefs are not based on personal experience or actual experience. His language parrots that of the alienating parent, "He won't pay us support, but he can afford to pay three thousand dollars to

---

[234] Kelly, J.B., Johnston, J.R. (2005). The alienated child: a reformulation of parental alienation syndrome. *Family Court Review*, 39, 3, 249-266.
[235] Darnell, Douglas. Workshop on Parental Alienation: Its Impact on Children and Managing High Conflict Families, Rivers Club, Pittsburgh, PA (2003).

fly to Europe." According to Darnell, PAS may be brought on by, or is associated with the following events or circumstances:

- A new boyfriend or girlfriend

- Feeling of being out of control (by the alienating parent)

- Very controlling or intrusive personality

- Threats of abduction by the alienating parent.

- Suggestions of physical or sexual abuse (often fabricated by the alienating parent)

- Severe mental or substance disorder

- Child refusing to visit alienated parent

- Child having too much power.

Darnell reports that after the child reaches age 12, some alienated parents decide to give up. If a parent makes this choice, Darnell says it is important:

- for the parent to make sure the child always knows how to reach him or her, and that it is okay to do so;

- for the alienated parent to assure the child that the parent is not angry;

- for the parent to refrain from discussing the alienation with the child and not to push the child to see the alienated child's point of view;

- for the parent to continue to acknowledge birthdays and holidays; and

- to look for a crisis, which is sometimes a catalyst for change.

Logically, the alienated child's behavior makes sense. The child behaves the way anyone would when forced to live in a war zone. In such a situation, the child's decision to choose a side may be a rational coping mechanism allowing the child to salvage some kind of childhood and avoid involvement in the conflict.

A Final Note on Custody Laws

This overview gives a mere flavor of the world of custody litigation and mediation—a world inhabited, some might say, by only the most courageous and compassionate of professionals. The mediator knows that the law is in the background during custody mediation, not in the foreground. The parties' discussions will focus on the details of their lives, tedious as they may be, and on their children. The mediator will attempt to use her knowledge of the law, customary practices, typical situations, child development and welfare, and common sense to assist the parties with creating a parenting plan.

Chapter Eight

"My husband and I have never considered divorce... murder sometimes, but never divorce." — Dr. Joyce Brothers

Divorce Primer

The Economic Issues of Divorce

The Standards of Conduct for family mediators require a mediator to have knowledge of family law.

Standard II (With Comment, emphasis supplied)

A family mediator shall be qualified by education and training to undertake the mediation.

A. To perform the family mediator's role, a mediator should:

1. have knowledge of family law;

2. have knowledge of and training in the impact of family conflict on parents, children and other participants, including knowledge of child development, domestic abuse and child abuse and neglect;

3. have education and training specific to the process of mediation;

4. be able to recognize the impact of culture and diversity.

B. Family mediators should provide information to the participants about the mediator's relevant training, education and expertise.

This standard serves as a warning to those brave enough to navigate the choppy waters of divorce economic issues mediation. Marriage and divorce can have grave financial and personal consequences. Unknowing parties who sign divorce agreements on the dotted line without (and sometimes with) legal advice can find themselves paying non-modifiable lifetime alimony or being prohibited from seeing their children, to name only two potential landmines. A mediator must have a sophisticated level of subject-matter expertise when mediating divorce and its economic consequences. Although there are those rare individuals not formally trained in the law who also understand legal issues attendant to divorce, a law degree coupled with family law concentration gives one a measure of authority that is difficult to match. Few mediators wish to tackle the daunting task of mediating a complex financial divorce without family law expertise, which includes knowledge of tax, real estate, probate and estate planning, and other areas of substantive law besides familiarity with divorce laws. A sizable portion of family mediators who are not attorneys, or who are attorneys inexperienced in economic issues in divorce, limit their family mediation practice to custody cases. Even those familiar with family law often choose to bring in expert consultants to inform mediation. There are several reasons why family law expertise or consultation is ideal for a mediator of economic issues in divorce:

1. ***Clients' Comfort-*** Parties need a strong mediator in order to feel safe and trust that the process will address all of their concerns. At the first sign that the mediator does not understand family law, clients feel insecure and distrustful.

2. ***Efficiency-*** Parties need a mediator with understanding of divorce law in order to receive value for money invested in the process. A mediator who does not understand the interplay between income, assets, tax, and financial issues will not be able to guide parties to a comprehensive agreement that deals with all of the issues. A particular settlement might look good to the parties and to an unschooled mediator, while a lawyer's view finds it lacking consideration of tax, real estate, or estate planning issues, or simply unenforceable.

3. ***Other Experts-*** Parties to mediation of economic issues in divorce require counsel to be involved throughout the process, and to speak to the mediator when needed; therefore, the mediator needs to converse in depth with other experts familiar with the legal and financial issues.

4. ***Information Gathering-*** Parties with (or without) high income and/or net worth often do not understand their own finances and will need a mediator to interface with lawyers, accountants, and

appraisers for a variety of reasons, including information gathering. A mediator who gathers information from other experts needs to know what he or she is gathering.

5. **Generating Options**- A mediator with subject matter expertise can generate options,[236] i.e., make suggestions or offer creative ideas for settlement that the parties and/or their attorneys have not thought of.

6. **Time Savings**-A mediator with subject matter expertise can perform a more efficient mediation because less time is needed to educate the mediator.[237]

7. **Explore Interests**- One of the mediator's fundamental tasks is to explore the parties' interests. Without familiarity with parties' legal options, a mediator is not equipped to help parties explore their interests.

According to authors of the popular legal website Nolo, the average cost of a mediated divorce is $3000-$8000, split between the parties.[238] This is a substantial cost saving when compared with the estimated average cost of a litigated divorce per party of $11,300.[239] To me, this seems conservative, as I am aware of countless recent clients whose litigated divorces easily reach six figures, even for clients of very modest means, who tend to go into debt in an effort to get off of the roller coaster of litigation in one piece. The mediated divorce is quite possibly one of the world's most underrated bargains.[240] After deciding upon a parenting plan, parties in divorce mediation generally address the remaining issues in divorce in the following order, when applicable:

---

[236] Expert offers advice on how to pick the right mediator for your case. (April 3, 2000). *Journal of Commerce*, p. 10. Retrieved September 9, 2009, from ABI/INFORM Global. (Document ID: 52162676).

[237] Id.

[238] Gjelten, E.A. (2022). How much will my divorce cost? How Much Will My Divorce Cost? | Cost of Divorce | Nolo

[239] Id.

[240] Jessani, A.D. (2009). Dealing with objections to mediation along the continuum of case complexity. *American Journal of Family Law*, 23 (2), 85-89.

Agenda of Economic Issues in Divorce

- Temporary, also called "interim" issues

- Child Support

- Spousal Support and Maintenance

- Health Insurance

- Tax Exemptions

- Taxability of Support Payments

- Property division

- Life Insurance

- Additional Tax Issues- Exemptions, Filing Status, Capital Gains, et al.

- Support and/or Education of Adult Children

Child and Spousal Support and Maintenance

Child support is typically modifiable, but only upon a showing of a material change in circumstances; therefore, it is an important, precedent-setting decision when parties agree upon an amount of child support. Parents have a legal obligation to support their children, and state laws provide guidelines or formulas to calculate the amount payable uniformly across families. Prior to the 1970's when guidelines were first formulated, courts ordered support on a case-by-case basis, and parties of similar incomes could be found paying widely divergent amounts of support per child. The implementation of guidelines moved away from arbitrariness towards uniformity. Guidelines were based on "income shares" (majority) or percent of income (minority) models[241] that follow standardized assumptions about what intact families spend to raise children.

In addition to children, spouses have an obligation to support each other. Therefore, the higher income earner may have a duty to provide spousal support and maintenance to the other party pending, and/or after a final decree in divorce. The first step in consideration of support is a determination of both parties' incomes. What constitutes income for purposes of support differs from state to state. Income includes, generally: earnings, wages, interest income, dividends, rents, profits, royalties, lottery and gambling winnings, bonuses, capital gains, social security and unemployment benefits, SSI (welfare cash assistance), and some unrealized capital gains, among other receipts. In order to arrive at the amount of income available for support (net income), actual taxes (as opposed to withheld taxes) are deducted. Parties' pay stubs are generally unreliable for this purpose because taxpayers' withholdings are determined by a W-9 form provided to the Internal Revenue Service (IRS) by the employee; therefore, withholdings can be increased by simply claiming more dependents than one has. The IRS does not seem to mind withholding more money for income taxes than is due, and then issuing a refund at the end of the tax year.

Fortunately, software is available for purposes of calculating estimated income taxes for the parties. In the alternative, the parties may use their tax returns, if the information is still current, i.e., incomes and taxes have not changed, to determine actual gross income minus actual taxes to arrive at net income. Parties also have the option of using their accountant to provide this information for the mediation, or performing their own calculations based on tax tables. An excellent resource for calculating income taxes is Jim Lange's Tax Planning Card.[242] Software for calculating child and spousal support obligations based on state law for all U.S. states is available at www.supportcalc.com, BradleySoftware.com and other websites. There is nothing wrong with the mediator using the income numbers the parties have arrived at to search the guideline grids to locate the amount of support prescribed by the guidelines, with the caveat

---

[241] American Bar Association. 41 FAM. L. Q. 711 (2008).
[242] 2020-2021 Lange's Tax Card (paytaxeslater.com)

that the mediator is never the "expert" providing information about appropriate support amounts. Exploring all issues, which includes the guidelines' prescription, is part of the mediation process.

In mediation, parties explore and negotiate support by examining the legal perspective (guidelines) as well as by testing any proposals against a "need and ability to pay" assessment. This involves preparation of budgets by both parties in order to measure the impact of any decision on their personal and household finances. If needed, budgets are discussed in mediation, particularly if the parties are having difficulty agreeing upon support.

Courts determine income by examining parties' pay stubs and income tax documents. Statutes typically catalog, inexhaustively, items considered to be "income."[243] In addition, courts "impute" income to parties who are unemployed, underemployed, or concealing income. In such a case, a court will assign an "earning capacity."[244] Consideration of a person's skills, employability, age, and health enter into a determination of earning capacity.[245] Where a person cares for a young child, earning capacity takes into account the child's needs for the caretaker to stay at home in some jurisdictions.[246] In general, deductions for non-mandatory pension and/or retirement plan contributions will be added back in determining net income, and premiums deducted from a paycheck to provide health insurance will either be deducted, or credited as part of the guideline formula.[247]

Additional Support Issues

After the amounts of basic child and spousal support are discussed the parties proceed to addressing extraneous support matters such as health insurance, payment of co-pays, deductibles, and other unreimbursed medical, dental, optical, orthodontic, psychological, and other possible expenses. Extraordinary, also referred to as extracurricular, costs such as day care, private lessons, sports, camps, and other activities must also be addressed, as they may not be included in basic child support. Parties must also determine who is the best able to provide for health insurance, usually determined by its availability through employment or other means. Co-pays, unreimbursed medical expenses, childcare (while a parent is working) and extraordinary expenses are typically shared in some division proportional to the parties' incomes.

Spousal support, maintenance, and alimony used to be taxed as income and deductible from the payor's income under federal law, but Section 11051 of the Tax Cuts and Jobs Act of 2017 amended the Internal Revenue Code by repealing the alimony deduction -- the amount of spousal support,

---

[243] West's F.S.A. §61.30 (2)(a) (Florida), 23 Pa. C.S.A. §4302 (Pennsylvania)
[244] *Dulaney v. Dulaney*, 547 S. 2d 1185 (Ala. Civ. App. 1989), *Kent v. Kent*, 16 A.3d 1158, (Pa. Super, 2010), Pa. R.C.P. 1910.16-2(d)(4)
[245] *Gentile v. Carneiro*, 107 Conn. App. 630, 946 A.2d 871 (2008), *Portugal v. Portugal*, 798 A.2d 246 (Pa. Super, 2002)
[246]*Settle v. Settle*, 635 So. 2d 456 (La. App. 2 Cir. 1994). *See also* West's F.S.A. §61.30 (2)(b)(Florida), "However, the court may refuse to impute income to a parent if the court finds it necessary for that parent to stay home with the child who is the subject of a child support calculation or as set forth below."
[247] Pa.R.C.P. No. 1910.16-4

alimony *pendente lite*, and alimony paid or received -- from the payor's gross income and the alimony inclusion into the payee's gross income. Therefore, beginning with 2018, alimony is no longer deducted or includible on parties' federal income tax returns, although alimony ordered prior to 2018 may still be. Child support is not taxable or deductible under federal tax laws.

The right to claim a child as a dependent for purposes of filing status and exemptions is determined by the Internal Revenue Code[248] and code regulations. Filing status and availability of exemptions can provide valuable tax savings to both parties; therefore, these items are part of any negotiation. In general, a child is the dependent of the parent with whom the child lives for over one-half of the tax year. In particular, the details become quite intricate, as seen in the code section itself below. When two parties can claim the dependent, the party with whom the child resides for the longest period of time during the taxable year can claim the child or, if the child lives with both parties for the same amount of time, the party whose adjusted gross income is the highest may claim the exemption for the child. Parties may agree upon which taxpayer has the right to claim the dependency exemption and may release that right by signing IRS Form 8332. In mediation, parties can negotiate this right if they have multiple children, or even if they have only one child by alternating years.

Alimony

Even with no-fault divorce laws, alimony typically entails a small consideration of fault[249] including marital misconduct such as spousal abuse and adultery, although proposed legislation could eventually change this trend. No-fault divorce laws provide for alimony (also called maintenance) for the dependent spouse based on enumerated factors intended to guide the court towards fairness and justice, considering multiple facts that include the payor's ability to pay, the payee's needs, and the parties' respective financial circumstances. Some states allow alimony of any duration, even permanent alimony, while others limit alimony to situations with extreme need or limit its duration. The trend appears to be away from providing generous alimony for the dependent spouse. Parties everywhere are free to enter into contractual alimony, enforceable by courts. In addition to amounts and duration of support and alimony payments, parties in mediation should negotiate any income tax issues, including, but not limited to, potential liability for past jointly filed tax returns and future entitlement to any refunds issued thereon.

Parties typically address custody, child support, and alimony, although alimony and property division go hand-in-hand. This is because property division will sometimes provide a spouse with income-producing assets, and will affect whether or not alimony is appropriate, as well as what amount is appropriate.

---

[248] 26 U.S.C.A. §152 (2017).
[249] e.g., Fla Stat Ann 61.08, 23 Pa. C.S.A. §3701(b)(14)

Property Division

With no-fault divorce, property division changed from being based on title to the concept of marital property or (in a minority of states) community property.[250] These terms refer to all property and debt acquired during the marriage by either party regardless of how property is formally or informally titled, with certain exceptions such as, among other things, gifts and inheritances. The distribution of property in divorce is set forth in no-fault laws, requiring the marital estate to be distributed either 50/50 (as in community property states) or "equitably" which, as case law developed, became a case-by-case determination based on enumerated factors (in most states) describing what a court should consider in determining what was equitable. Some states, such as Indiana, have a rebuttable presumption of 50/50 property division.[251] Where property is distributed "equitably," factors a court considers in determining what is equitable include, among other things, length of marriage, existence and extent of separate property, future earnings or earning capacity, custody of children, sources of income, and contributions to the marital estate, including contribution as a homemaker.[252] Conspicuously absent from equitable considerations is who initiated the separation and divorce and who, if anyone, committed marital misconduct or "indignities" such as adultery or spousal abuse. Distribution of property in no fault is blind to "marital misconduct." In a majority of states, however, it is not blind to financial misconduct, also known as dissipation of the marital estate, a factor in many no-fault equitable distribution statutes.

Marital property (or community property) is all property acquired by either party during the marriage. In order to assist the parties with negotiating a property division, the mediator must first take steps to identify all marital property. The mediator gathers this information from the parties by eliciting facts, gathering documents, and, in some cases, speaking to the parties' attorneys, accountants, and financial advisers. In a complicated case involving complex business or financial interests, an accountant may be used to compose the list of marital assets. Marital property consists of all real estate, pensions and retirement accounts, cash, investments, business interests, securities, contracts, receivables, deferred compensation, proceeds from personal injury or other types of lawsuits, automobiles, household goods and furnishings, and the like. Even where parties choose not to treat property as marital, it should be identified and listed in mediation (and in the Memorandum of Understanding) for purposes of the viability of their agreement as one entered into with "full disclosure," a requirement for valid property settlement agreements. Marital property is divided "equitably," while community property is divided equally.

Marital property is identified as of the date of "classification." In most cases, this is the date of final separation of the parties. After that date, the parties no longer accumulate marital property and the marital estate is determined as of a fixed date. Since value of an asset can fluctuate with the passage of time, valuation is not necessarily fixed as of the same date, but more often established on or close to the

---

[250] Arizona, California, Idaho, Louisiana, Nevada, New Mexico, Texas, Washington, and Wisconsin.
[251] Indiana Code 31-15-7
[252] 23 Pa. C.S. §3502

date of distribution. If an asset is wholly marital, increases in value due to appreciation or interest will become part of the value of the item on the date of distribution. For instance, a 401(k) account will presumably gain or lose value from the date of separation to the date of distribution. If it loses value, the lower value on date of distribution is obviously the value of the asset. Parties who choose to divide such an asset by percentage will need to isolate the marital portion if the owner of the account continued to contribute to the account after separation. Parties are cautioned not to divide such an asset by a set amount (rather than percentage) if there is a possibility it can lose value because this ould result in a windfall to the spouse who received a sum certain. If Husband's 401(k) is worth $35,000 and the parties agree Wife will receive $17,500 from that account, and on the date of distribution the account is only worth $28,000, Wife has received an unintended windfall. Similarly, if the parties decided to split the account equally and Husband made contributions of $3,500 after separation, the parties will need to deduct Husband's contributions (taking into account any gain or loss thereon) in order to divide only the marital portion of the account.

Not all property acquired during the marriage becomes marital property because legislation provides exceptions. Generally, property owned before the marriage and property exchanged for property owned before the marriage, property inherited, and property received by gift during the marriage is excluded. Interspousal gifts are marital property in some states[253] and separate property in others.[254] Engagement rings are treated differently among states. An engagement ring is a conditional gift that should be returned if the marriage does not take place, regardless of whose fault caused the broken engagement.[255] After the marriage, the ring is premarital property and belongs to the donee.[256] States are divided on whether increases in value of non-marital property are included as marital property. In some states, passive appreciation in value is not marital because it is not a result of a person's labor.[257] Non-passive appreciation resulting from interest or "income" attributable to an asset is considered marital.[258] The majority view, however, is consistent with the Uniform Marriage and Divorce Act, eliminating a dual classification altogether and counting all increases in value, however accomplished, as marital. Such increases result in hybrid, or "mixed" property consisting of a non-marital asset with a "marital property component." An example of such property is pre-owned real estate titled in one party's name. Appreciation in value of the real estate could be considered "marital," as well as repayment of the debt on the property during the marriage.[259] This theory of marital property—that it can be mixed—is the majority rule. A small minority supports a unitary theory of marital property holding that property has to be either marital or non-marital,

---

[253] e.g. Murray v. Murray, 636 So. 2d 536 (Fla. Dist. Ct. App. 1st Dist. 1994)
[254] In re: Balanson, 25 P.3d 28 (Colo. 2001), Binder v. Thorne-Binder, 186 S.W. 3d 864 (Mo. Ct. App. W.D. 2006).
[255] Carroll v. Curry, 912 N.E. 2d 272, 2009 WL 2004038 (Ill. App. 2d Dist. 2009), Cooper v. Smith, 155 Ohio App.3d 218, 800 N.E. 2d 372 (Ohio App. 4 Dist., 2003).
[256] NK v. MK, 17 Misc. 3d 1123 (A), 851 N.Y.S. 2d 71 (N.Y. Supp 2007).
[257] Moore v. Moore, 189 S.W. 3d 627 (Mo. App. W.D. 2006).
[258] In re Marriage of Box, 968 S.W. 2d 161 (Mo. Ct. App. S.D. 1998).
[259] Calhoun v. Calhoun, 331 S.C. 157, 501 S.E. 2d 735 (Ct. App 1998), aff'd in part, rev'd in part on other grounds, 339 S.C. 96, 529 S.E. 2d 14 (2000).

and there can be no hybrid property. This theory has little support except with respect to the marital home.[260] When non-marital property is commingled with marital property, it becomes marital property with few exceptions.[261] The theory of "transmutation" of non-marital property to marital property is based on the difficulty of sorting out the two portions as well as an imputed intention on the part of the commingling spouse to donate the non-marital property to the marital estate. Examples of this type of transmutation occur when a spouse places an individual inheritance into a joint account or places solely owned real estate into joint names.

Once the marital property is identified, it must be divided. With community property, a 50/50 division is mandated.[262] In equitable distribution states, marital property is divided "equitably," often with equal division as the starting point.[263] This means that the court makes a case-by-case analysis to determine what is equitable, or fair. Statutes enumerate factors the courts must consider.[264] Typically, the factors relate to length of the marriage, incomes and earning capacities of the parties, parties' health and age, whether or not a parent will be serving as primary custodian of minor children, and parties' separate estates, if any, among other factors. A parties' "dissipation" of the marital estate is considered to reduce that party's distribution. Losing money by gambling or criminal activity or spending money on a mistress is considered dissipation for a potentially non-marital purpose.[265] Amassing excessive debt for living expenses is not generally considered dissipation.[266] Debts incurred by either party during the marriage are considered a marital obligation regardless of which party incurred them. Such debts can be presumed to be marital[267] regardless of purpose. A majority of states follow a less extreme view, considering the purpose of the debt, acknowledging that even debts benefitting only one party may still be considered to have a marital purpose, such as having clothing.[268]

The example chart on the following page illustrates how parties divided their marital estate. As illustrated, a chart is a helpful way to characterize the marital estate for the parties. It helps the mediator to de-personalize the "facts" of the marital estate. Where distribution of some assets causes pain or disappointment, the mediator should deliver the news in the form of an external chart or table, together with another table of proposed distribution.

---

[260] *Duncan v. Duncan*, 915 So. 2d 1124 (Miss. 2005).
[261] *Stewart v. Stewart*, 864 So. 2d 934 (Miss. 2003).
[262] Cal. Fam. Code §2550.
[263] 120 A.C.A. §9-12-315 (Arkansas).
[264] 23 Pa.C.S.A. §3502.
[265] *Turner v. Turner*, 147 Md. App. 350, 809 A.2d 18 (2002), Rabath v. Farid, 4 So. 3d, 778 (Dist. Ct. of Appeal, Fla, 2009)
[266] *Karimi v. Karimi*, 867 So. 2d 471, 475 (Fla. Dist. Ct. App. 5th Dist. 2004).
[267] *In re Marriage of Jorgenson*, 143 P.3d 1169, 1172 (Colo. Ct. App. 2006).
[268] *In re Marriage of Coyle*, 671 N. E. 2d 938 (Ind. Ct. App. 1996).

Mediation of Property Division

Description of Asset or Debt	Title/Possession	Value of Asset	Notes
House located at 615 Fawn Road	Joint	$212,000	Fair Market Value is $450,000 subject to mortgage with current principal balance of $193,000 and projected costs of sale of $45,000
Husband's 401(k) with current employer	Husband	327,000	Value as of current date. Since date of separation of 4/3/10, Husband has made contributions of $8,000 which have been subtracted to arrive at value.
Husband's IRA from former employer	Husband	94,000	Asset is all marital; therefore increases will continue to be marital. No post separation contributions will be made.
Wife's IRA from former employer	Wife	10,000	Current value of IRA is $25,000. Parties have deducted value on date of marriage of $15,000.
Savings Account- Niagara Bank	Joint	$132,000	
Automobile- 2009 Camry	Wife	2,000	Fair Market value of car is $32,000 less loan balance of $30,000.
Automobile- 2010 Ford Explorer	Husband	1,000	Fair Market Value of car is $34,000 less loan balance of $33,000.
Household furnishings	Joint	45,000	
Jewelry	Wife	10,000	
Total		**833,000**	

In addition to the marital assets, the parties have a Capital One VISA card with a balance of $5,268. Initially, the parties will have thought about what to do with their largest asset, the marital residence. One or both of the parties will want to live in the marital home, particularly if they have children and do not want to uproot them. If they have not decided that one party will keep the residence and live in it, then they are likely disputing the right to possession or considering selling it because neither party can afford it alone. This issue is often mediated early in the property division negotiations. If the parties reach an impasse on this issue, the mediator should explore the available options hypothetically, illustrating each scenario with the parties. In the above example, the Wife is going to remain in the residence and the parties have decided on a 50/50 division. Parties do not always agree on 50/50 division, especially if the factors set forth in the applicable divorce laws weigh in favor of a party receiving more than a 50% distribution. Nevertheless, it is often helpful to demonstrate a 50/50 division as a "starting point" just for sake of illustration. That way, a party who agrees to a different distribution will have awareness of what he or she is giving up or getting by receiving more or less than half. It is also helpful for parties who are stuck negotiating over 10% to see exactly what that ten percent is. Percentages are, after all, positions. Actual numbers, on the other hand, address the parties' interests in receiving concrete amounts of money in their pockets.

To illustrate a 50/50 division, the mediator will have another list that appears as follows:

Sharon		**Steve**	
House	212,000	401(k)	327,000
IRA	10,000	IRA	94,000
Savings	100,000	Savings	32,000
Camry	2,000	Explorer	1,000
Household Goods	45,000		
Jewelry	10,000		
Sub-Total	**379,000**		**454,000**
Payment of VISA	(2,634)	Payment of VISA	(2,634)
From Steve	37,500	To Sharon	(37,500)
Total	**413,866**		**413,866**

By assigning the assets to the party already in possession, or to the party agreed to gain possession (as in the marital residence) the mediator has distilled the case to one the parties can understand and manage. The cash payment needed to effectuate an equal distribution of $37,500 will be the subject of further negotiation. In this case, the parties divided their cash in unequal portions, likely because Husband has a higher income and Wife wanted to have a cushion of savings in the event she needed it for emergency repairs to the marital residence, or other financial security. Here, Steve will probably elect to pay Sharon from his IRA or his 401(k). Either account can be used to transfer this amount to Sharon under federal tax laws that allow transfer of otherwise nontransferable funds under the Retirement Equity Act of 1984 which provides for a special type of court order called a Qualified Domestic Relations Act, or QDRO, transferring money from qualified retirement accounts from one spouse to another as part of a decree in divorce. The transfer is exempt from tax and penalties so long as it is a direct rollover into an individual retirement account or other qualified account in the name of the transferee spouse. Because a court order is required for qualified accounts (i.e., the 401(k)) and not for an Individual Retirement Account or IRA, Steve will likely prefer to use funds in the IRA which can be done directly with the custodian of the fund in which the account is invested with a copy of the divorce agreement, saving attorneys' fees by not needing a QDRO.

Frequently, parties will reach a tentative agreement for equal division that involves a transfer of value from one party to the other, but be unable to agree on the actual payment, due to lack of liquidity or some other reason. The mediator may explore other options, such as installment payments, alimony, or an in-kind (unliquidated asset) transfer. Additionally, parties sometimes have defined benefit pensions, which are different from a 401(k) or other retirement savings account. A 401(k) can be quantified in the same way as a savings account (with the caveat that it is pre-tax money); a defined benefit, on the other hand, is a right to receive a certain amount of money at retirement age, typically at age 65, but sometimes earlier. Valuing such a benefit requires an expert calculation by an actuary. The present value will be comparable to the cost of an annuity contract with terms similar to those of the defined benefit pension plan. A present value calculation is only necessary if the parties choose to value the asset as part of the marital estate and do not want to divide it on a deferred basis. A deferred distribution of such an asset would entail splitting it when it is actually received. This is accomplished with a QDRO that is entered on or before the time of the divorce decree and secures the parties' rights so that a subsequent spouse's rights do not attach to the pension to defeat the former spouse's rights. It must be done before a divorce decree is entered because if the spouse owning the pension dies unmarried, the former spouse's rights can be lost without a QDRO. If the parties do not opt for a deferred distribution of a defined benefit pension plan, then the lump sum "present value" is assigned to the marital value and the pension is distributed accordingly, most often to the party who owns the pension. Retirement assets are owned individually by the employee/retiree and are not eligible for joint ownership under IRS rules.

It is not unusual for parties in mediation to resolve their divorce by going outside of the law for solutions. Typical examples of forgoing legal solutions are the parties' choice not to value household items, not to "touch" each other's retirement accounts, to agree upon college support for their children even when it is not required by law, to set support at amounts higher or lower than guidelines, to delay their divorce decree for purposes of maintaining health insurance coverage or extending the duration of the marriage to ten years in order to receive social security retirement benefits as a spouse, among other possibilities.

Mediation of Alimony Issue

Parties will leave their first economic mediation session with their heads full of numbers, figures, and strange new ideas. It is usually not wise for final decisions to be made until they have had time to synthesize this new information after the first session. The alimony decision involves consideration of the factors set forth in relevant legislation, the parties' sense of fairness and entitlement to alimony, as well as the parties' budgetary needs reflecting need for alimony and ability to pay alimony. Alimony typically ends upon death, remarriage or cohabitation with a partner. Alimony is ordered for temporary periods or, in cases where it is necessary and practicable, long-term. Rehabilitative alimony is maintenance for a spouse who has been out of the job market and needs temporary assistance to obtain new skills and/or education. Alimony is generally considered a "secondary remedy,"[269] which means that it is not automatic, but only granted when shown to be necessary and appropriate. At the outset of a case, when parties are newly separated, support or maintenance is somewhat automatic where income disparity exists, and is thought to put the parties on equal footing to sort out (litigate or mediate) the legal issues. Depending upon the law of the individual state, the parties may or may not include a recipient's alimony income as income available for child support, should either party request a modification of child support in the future. When alimony is intended to provide general income and not specifically earmarked for a particular purpose, it is typically included in the party's income for purposes of child support. It is a wise mediator who can foresee such potential areas of disagreement in the future, and assist the parties in considering them before they become disputes.

Counsel Fees

Payment of counsel fees by the party in a financially superior position, or from marital assets, can be provided for by statute.[270] However, in mediation this is rarely an issue because the counsel fees are minimal. After mediation, the parties will have to pay attorneys' fees for legal advice, pleadings, drafting the final agreement and decree, steps to obtain the divorce decree, and actions necessary to execute the provisions of the agreement such as deeds to transfer real estate and QDROs to transfer retirement account funds. Parties generally share mediator fees by paying them jointly from their household budget if they are still residing together. If they are separated, they typically pay them in proportion to their incomes. If support is being paid during separation, the division is typically 50/50. *Caveat,* the mediator should not mediate the issue of how the parties pay the mediator unless the mediator is prepaid.

---

[269] *Nemoto v. Nemoto,* 423 Pa. Super 269, 620 A.2d 1216, 1219 (1993).
[270] 23 Pa. C.S.A. §3702.

After the major issues have been decided, the parties should have a "tying up loose ends" session to decide upon life insurance, division of personal property, moving issues, and any other extraneous issues not decided that appear on the Divorce Checklist on pages 233 *et seq*. Life insurance, if the parties can afford it, is a typical consideration for parties who are parents of minor children, college-age children, or if there are outstanding joint debts, or a continuing financial obligation by one party towards the other. Since alimony terminates on death, life insurance provides a measure of security. Some parents prefer not to name the other party as beneficiary on life insurance. If they realize that they depend on the other's labor for purposes of raising children, and are able to see child rearing in economic terms, they often find it easier to name the other party as beneficiary of an appropriate sum of life insurance benefits rather than establishing a trust or naming the minor children as beneficiaries, which would require a trust or a guardian of the children's estates. These alternatives are available and somewhat popular, but lack the simplicity of outright benefits to the surviving parent. Even a parent who does not receive child support payments (but pays them) and receives the services of the other parent may want life insurance to cover that person's life and the value of those services.

A Final Note on Knowledge of Divorce Law

The mediator's fundamental task (yet another one) of ensuring that parties have "sufficient information and knowledge" to make decisions is met by having awareness and familiarity with regard to substantive family law as well as court procedures. This task is required by Standard 6:

STANDARD VI: A family mediator shall structure the mediation process so that the participants make decisions based on sufficient information and knowledge.

Not only are parties served by being guided globally to resolve their issues, but the mediation process itself is enabled by a mediator who is able to enter the clients' world and make them feel safe and comfortable with a body of knowledge and resources relevant to this unique time in their lives.

Chapter Nine

"I am here because I lose control of myself sometimes. I need to get a better grip." I always correct him: "Your problem is not that you lose control of yourself, it's that you take control of your partner. In order to change, you don't need to gain control over yourself, you need to let go of control of her." – Lundy Bancroft

High Conflict

High conflict parties range from relationships where domestic violence has occurred to average families with challenging issues. In every situation, the mediator's task is to maintain a safe and comfortable environment while managing the process to ensure parties' informed consent on all issues, maintain order, promote introspection and awareness, and listen to and respond to concerns. The mediator knows that high conflict, accompanied by high emotion, is not always as it initially appears. Important information lies beneath emotional behavior and words. Intervention, such as caucusing, that simply attends to the behavior, and not to the cause, is of little help in addressing the actual issues, and of little lasting help to the mediator who seeks to change the nature of the conflict.

Domestic Violence or Intimate Partner Violence (IPV)

It's estimated that over half of all female homicide victims are killed by intimate partners.[271] In the United States more than 10 million adults experience domestic violence annually.[272] Domestic violence is thought to be on the rise as it is known to have increased by 42 percent from 2016 to 2018.[273] In 70 to 80 percent of intimate partner homicides, the man physically abused the woman before the murder. Approximately 30 to 60 percent of children whose mothers are being abused are themselves likely to be abused.[274]

The divorce mediator is positioned to encounter some of these very couples. Many established family mediators have the unenviable privilege of having been one of the last people to see one or both members of a violent couple alive. Some have known families where a child or children were victimized or killed during an exchange between parents. Unlike medical practitioners, who also want to identify

---

[271] Domonoske, C. (2017). CDC: Half of all female homicide victims are killed by intimate partners. CDC: Half Of All Female Homicide Victims Are Killed By Intimate Partners : The Two-Way : NPR
[272] National Coalition Against Domestic Violence. (2019). National statistics. domestic_violence-2020080709350855.pdf (speakcdn.com)
[273] Id.
[274] United States Department of Justice, http://www.ojp.usdoj.gov/nij/topics/crime/violence-against-women/selected-results.htm

domestic violence, but from a healthcare perspective, mediators have an active role in the conflict of the couple. As host to a process in which the parties are asked to participate together, the mediator bears the responsibility to not only identify, but also to attend to abuse. There is little a mere mediator can do when a violent partner is intent on harming an estranged wife or partner. Yet, given the mediator's unique position, it is the consensus of professionals that the mediator has a duty to "screen" couples for potential violence. By looking for intimate partner violence, the mediator can assess the parties' capacity to mediate as well as possibly identify violence, address it, and perhaps prevent it. Proponents of screening believe that domestic violence affects the parties' capacity to mediate, and that the mediator has an ethical obligation under the Standards of Conduct to ensure that a party or parties to mediation are not likely to use violence to exert power in the process.

> **STANDARD III**: A family mediator shall facilitate the participants' understanding of what mediation is and assess their **capacity to mediate** before the participants reach an agreement to mediate.

Capacity to mediate requires a relative balance of power and a degree of equality, free from physical intimidation. Few would disagree that the mediation environment should feel safe and comfortable if parties are to discuss issues and make decisions free from coercion.[275] Feminists and battered women's advocates have raised numerous objections to the use of mediation where domestic abuse is present. Among their arguments are that mediation encourages domestic violence where there is a history of abuse by bringing the parties together instead of separating them, reinforcing patterns of domination.[276] Another concern is that mediation "…decriminalizes domestic abuse and encourages a conciliatory approach that does not hold the abuser accountable for his behavior…[and]…that mediation undermines the great strides that the women's movement has made in defining domestic abuse and treating it in the justice system."[277] By inviting the abuser to negotiate, mediation is seen as giving the "bully" credibility and not taking abuse seriously.[278] Victims of domestic violence are seen as unlikely to assert themselves in mediation when sitting opposite their abuser, having been conditioned to serve the needs of their abuser.[279] An unfortunate myth about mediation and domestic violence is that "an abuser is more likely to use mediation as an opportunity to continue to control and manipulate the victim than to reach a mutual agreement…."[280] The implication is that lawyers and judges will hold the abuser accountable while a mediator will not. This myth is propagated by those who perceive a weak mediator and a process devoid of appropriate boundaries and

---

[275] Pearson, J. (1997) Mediating when domestic violence is a factor: Policies and practices in court-based divorce mediation programs. *Mediation Quarterly, 14* (4), 319-335.
[276] Rifkin, J. (1984) Mediation from a feminist perspective: Promise and problems. *Law and Inequality, 21*, 330-342.
[277] Pearson, 1997, 320.
[278] Clemants, E., Gross, A. (2007). "Why aren't we screening?" A survey examining domestic violence screening procedures and training protocol in community mediation centers. *Conflict Resolution Quarterly, 24*(4), 413-431.
[279] Rimelspach, R. (2001). Mediating family disputes in a world with domestic violence: How to devise a safe and effective court-connected mediation program. Retrieved from http://www.mediate.com/articles/rimelspach.cfm
[280] Illinois Coalition Against Domestic Violence, *Mediation and Domestic Violence,* http://www.ilcadv.org/legal/mediation_n_DV.htm

assessment and intervention for client readiness. As described in Chapter 5, an effective mediator is neither weak nor tolerant of inappropriate behavior. An effective mediator demands boundaries in a mediation and will make it clear to every party that part of the mediator's role is to assess for readiness and ensure each party's readiness which includes a relative balance of power, full disclosure, and informed consent. In many ways, a party attempting to exert force in mediation will do worse in mediation than in court where force is tolerated in the form of clever lawyers protecting information and assets, abusing their opponent with harassment and excessive and irrelevant discovery demands, deliberate delays, deliberate factual misrepresentations, mischaracterizing the facts, and inflicting trauma with the legal system.[281]

The mediation profession has fought against this perception from the beginning of the mediation movement. In addition to Standard 3, the standards address domestic abuse directly in Standards 9 and 10.

STANDARD IX: A family mediator shall recognize a family situation involving child abuse or neglect and take appropriate steps to shape the mediation process accordingly.

STANDARD X: A family mediator shall recognize a family situation involving domestic abuse and take appropriate steps to shape the mediation process accordingly.

The myth that a weak mediator will simply allow an abuser to control the process buys into the perceived power and domination of the abuser and fails to recognize the heavy ethical burden placed on the mediator to maintain a process free from coercion and power imbalances. Believers of the myth perceive the abuser as "all powerful" and fail to notice that the mediator stands with judges, lawyers, and feminists against abuse.

If screening detects domestic violence, that is not necessarily the end of the story. Mediation may still be possible. Proponents of mediation where domestic violence is or was present argue that there is a place for mediation in domestic abuse cases. They point to the "violence" that courts do when the legal process encourages parties to take extreme, polarized positions and vilify each other in order to win their cases.[282] Mediation, some say, provides a possible tool for addressing violence.[283] Additionally, the continuum of abuse needs to be considered; abuse and intimidation are not an "all or nothing" proposition. A case where violence has occurred in an isolated instance is different from a case where battering has been a pattern.[284]

---

[281] *See* Huffer, K. (1995). *Overcoming the Devastation of Legal Abuse Syndrome*. Retrieved from http://www.legalabusesyndrome.org.
[282] Pearson, 1997, 321.
[283] Rimelspach, R. (2001).
[284] Id.

SCREENING

Screening is the mediation community's answer to blanket objections to using mediation. It is universally accepted that court-connected or mandatory mediation programs must have some sort of domestic screening device. Unfortunately, for various reasons, screening measures are either not present in some programs, or are not used effectively in programs where they are present.[285] Current U.S. Health and Human Services guidelines require health insurance coverage of preventive services for women that include domestic violence screening by physicians. This has raised a concern, however, that doctor/patient confidentiality may be affected by state mandated reporting laws that require physicians to report abuse.[286]

Numerous screening tools and models have been proposed, typically questionnaires designed to tease out the truth. For mediators, directly asking spouses if they fear each other, or if they are aware of reasons to feel unsafe, or unable to negotiate with each other are not always effective questions because domestic violence is a subject cloaked in fear that people do not automatically reveal when questioned. Most commonly treated as a secret to be ashamed of, domestic violence is more likely to be revealed when approached indirectly, as in the question, "How have you and your spouse made decisions in your marriage when you disagreed on an important issue?" Unfortunately, such a question too often invites an exaggerated confession of abuse when, during the conflictual stage of post-separation divorce negotiations, a spouse may tend to exaggerate every negative behavior of the other spouse. "It was always his way or the highway," is not a reliable indicator of abuse.

Abuse can arise after separation where it was not present during a relationship,[287] as a need for control by the abuser, rather than an anger response.[288] In either case, the screening mediator must identify and respond to the violence and decide if mediation is possible and/or recommended. Ellis and Stuckless identify 19 predictors of abuse, among them calling police, previous separations, drinking, outbursts of anger, poor communication and social skills, extreme possessiveness and jealousy, emotional dependence, male partner control, mental health problems, and sexual violence and general control.[289] Their questionnaire, called "DOVE" used these predictors to screen for abuse. However, many of the predictors mentioned could easily exist in a non-violent relationship. Numerous screening tools exist for mediators who choose to use a standardized method for screening. Some popular questionnaires or "tools" include the Tolman Screening Model developed by Richard Tolman at the University of Illinois; Screening Questionnaire used in the study conducted by Newmark, Harrell and Salem; the Ellis Screening Model used in the Maine Domestic Abuse and Mediation Project; and the Conflict Assessment Protocol (CAP)

---

[285] Clemants & Gross (2007).
[286] Office on Women's Health, U.S. Dept. of Health and Human Services. (2014). http://www.womenshealth.gov/publications/our-publications/fact-sheet/screening-counseling-fact-sheet.html
[287] Ellis, D., Stuckless, N. (2006). Separation, domestic violence, and divorce mediation. *Conflict Resolution Quarterly*, 23(4), 461-485.
[288] Id., 463.
[289] Id., 476.

developed by Linda Girdner.[290] A tool known as Domestic Violence Screening Instrument-Revised (DVSI-R) exists for detecting the probability of recidivism where abuse occurred in the past.[291] Regardless of the tool used, the screening mediator will be called upon to ask the parties questions, in separate caucuses, such as, "Has your spouse ever hit you or used any other type of physical force towards you?"[292] and "Are you currently afraid that your spouse will physically harm you?"[293] Not surprisingly, abuse may be over-reported in cases presented for divorce and separation mediation which have been found to report abuse in 50% to 60% of cases.[294] Nevertheless, the screening mediators were found to determine the existence of domestic violence in only 50% of the cases where it was reported in a questionnaire.[295]

Screening questions, asked in a court-connected or mandatory mediation program, may be asked by a mediator or in a separate pre-mediation screening session, or by a non-mediator screener. They typically do not threaten the existence of a public mediation program because they are mandated by law and parties expect red tape in a public program. Nevertheless, there is some hesitance among mediation programs to uniformly offer formal screening. One study of community mediation centers found that only 69 percent of the centers conducted screening, and fewer than half of them used a formal screening process.[296] Informal screening was seen as "looking for" abuse without use of a standardized procedure or questionnaire. Informal screening is an indirect approach where the mediator solicits information and draws conclusions based on the mediator's instincts and reasoning about the parties. Clemants & Gross imply that lack of screening could be related to lack of exposure to domestic violence issues by the personnel charged with screening; however, another study found no such correlation, "An unanticipated finding was the discovery of no relationship between exposure to *domestic violence* content during social work education and either perceptions of barriers to *screening* or *screening behavior.*"[297] Mediators are not the only recalcitrant professionals; the medical profession also struggles with pro-active intimate partner violence screening. Another study found that, despite guidelines encouraging screening, medical professionals are "missing opportunities" to identify abuse because "… [p]atient attitudes, lack of institutional support, and other environmental factors may hinder efforts to address intimate partner abuse in clinical settings. In addition, physicians' feelings of discomfort and powerlessness may also contribute to

---

[290] Vestal, A. (2007). Domestic violence and mediation: Concerns and recommendations. Retrieved from http://www.mediate.com/articles/vestalA3.cfm
[291] Williams, K.R. (2012). Family violence risk assessment: A predictive cross-validation study of the Domestic Violence Screening Instrument-Revised (DVSI-R). *Law and Human Behavior, 36*(2), 120-129.
[292] Tolman Screening Model mandated by court rule in York County, Pennsylvania, Pa. Bulletin, Doc. No. 00-1156 (July 7, 2000).
[293] Id.
[294] Ballard, R.H., Holtzworth-Munroe, A., Applegate, A.G., & Beck, C.J.A. (2011). Detecting intimate partner violence in family and divorce mediation: A randomized trial of intimate partner violence screening. *Psychology, Public Policy, and Law, 17*(2), 241-263.
[295] Id.
[296] Clemants & Gross, 2007, 422.
[297] Tower, L.E. (2003). Domestic violence screening: Education and institutional support correlates. *Journal of Social Work Education, 39* (3), 479-494.

this low level of inquiry."[298] Another study concluded that fear of offending the patient by asking about abuse, among other deterrents, is a barrier to screening.[299] Some have proposed computer-assisted screening to avoid these difficulties. Using a flow diagram and assigning values to certain predictors of domestic violence, questionnaire responses are evaluated by a computer program, eliminating the need for human judgment in assessing the presence of violence.[300] Nevertheless, even where screening is formalized, violence goes undetected because it is difficult to discern, or the parties actively hide it.[301]

If formal screening is deficient in public mediation sessions, it is all but nonexistent in private mediation. Private mediators who independently contract with parties to provide a professional service generally do not see themselves in a position to filter out a large share of the work that comes their way. There is little incentive for private mediators to pursue a robust screening process that will eliminate parties from mediation. Of even more concern to the private mediator is that the screening process, successfully eliminating the remotest possibility that Mr. and Mrs. Smith engaged in domestic violence, will scare the Smiths away and mark the mediator as paranoid, negative, suspicious, fearful and scary. One commentator, observing the mediator's difficult position, proposed that the mediator should not be put in the position of determining competency, and that the standards do not require "screening" so much as they intend to encourage the mediator to promote competency by "facilitating the participants' mediation competencies."[302] The article suggests, and I agree, that private mediation parties can be presumed competent until they are proven to be otherwise. Just as the law presumes that all adults are competent and only a judge, applying the strictest standards, can deny one's competency, so the mediator should not presume to determine competency or capacity, a role that lies outside the scope of mediation. To presume that a party must pass an initial test can frustrate the purpose of mediation to "transform" individuals. Or, as the authors (Crawford, et al., 2003) state:

> …This implies that either a party has the capacity to mediate or not. The term *capacity* may mislead mediators and make a complex individual unidimensional. It centers solely on the party, not the mediator's abilities, the relationship between the mediator and the parties, or the interrelationship of the parties. Discussion about capacity in mediation usually focuses only on disempowered individuals, thereby keeping them forever captive by the terms used to describe their incapacity. Focusing on individual capacity has other implications. It creates an oversimplification

---

[298] Rodriguez, M., Bauer, H., McLoughlin, E., Grumbach, K. (1999). Screening and intervention for intimate partner abuse. *Journal of the American Medical Association, 282*(5), 468-474.
[299] Terebelo, S. (2006). Practical approaches to screening for domestic violence. *Journal of the American Academy of Physician Assistants, 19* (9), 30-35.
[300] Ahmad, F., Hogg-Johnson, S., Stewart, D., Skinner, H., Glazier, R., Levinson, W. (2009). Computer-assisted screening for intimate partner violence and control. *Annals of Internal Medicine, 151* (2), 93-115.
[301] Ver Steegh, N., Dalton, C. (2008). Report from the Wingspread Conference on Domestic Violence and Family Courts. http://www.mediate.com/pdf/Report%20from%20the%20Wingspread%20Conference%20on%20Domestic%20Violence%20and%20Family%20Courts.pdf
[302] Crawford, S., Dabney, L., Filner, J., Maida, P. (2003). From determining capacity to facilitating competencies: A new mediation framework. *Conflict Resolution Quarterly, 20* (4), 385-401. (The article touches on domestic violence screening, but primarily addresses client competency in general.)

not only of the individual but also the relationship between the party and the mediator. An individual's capacity in mediation is interactive; that is, the capacity of an individual is often intertwined with the relationships the individual has with others in the mediation. Optimally, mediation practice acknowledges and incorporates multiple competencies, individual and group, as well as procedural or dynamic processes. The role of the mediator is to facilitate these multiple competencies. Focusing on whether a party has capacity limits the mediator in assisting the parties to exercise self -determination, autonomy, and collaboration…A determination that a party has impaired or diminished capacity may create bias, threaten mediator impartiality, and undermine party self-determination. In addition, mediators have an obligation under the ADA not to discriminate on the basis of disability…A high probability exists that mediators will rely on misinformation, bias, and stereotypes to determine capacity significantly increasing the potential for unlawful discrimination.[303]

This observation argues against the myth that the mediator is too weak or imperceptive to confront abuse. In addition to frustrating the mediator's goal of working with parties despite apparent obstacles, formal screening is also perceived by some as the responsibility of others involved in the process, for instance, the referring attorney, or court.[304] Regardless of who conducts the screening, it seems inevitable that a micro focus on domestic violence screening by a family mediator will engender some fear and suspicion, especially where domestic violence is not present. In my view, the mediator's duty to assess parties' capacity to mediate and to assess for the possibility of domestic violence are non-negotiable obligations, but the method for doing so should not dominate the process and overshadow the positive benefits of mediation for nearly every couple. Moreover, most parties who report the existence of abuse nevertheless do not want to be excluded from the opportunity to mediate.[305]

The Wingspread Conference on Domestic Violence and its subsequent report attempted to bring some consensus on the wide range of beliefs about domestic violence. On the issue of screening, the consensus was that a variety of screening tools should be used, "…each developed for a specific purpose and for potential use at different stages of the proceeding. For example, while the initial focus of screening might concern lethality and safety, that initial inquiry might trigger a mental health or substance abuse assessment, or a further screening to assess the appropriateness of participation in …mediation."[306] The study found that most screening instruments do not take into account cultural and socioeconomic differences, or other nuances that an objective survey cannot detect, concluding that most instruments are not tested or validated.[307] Of interest to mediators is the study's observation that, "If the focus of the analysis is on the identification of a serious incident or recurring incidents of physical violence, for example, a

---

[303] Id., 386.
[304] Gerencser, A. (1995). Family mediation: Screening for domestic abuse. *Florida State University Law Review*, Retrieved from http://www.law.fsu.edu/Journals/lawreview/issues/231/gerencse.html#FNT2
[305] Id.
[306] Ver Steegh & Dalton, 2008.
[307] The study favored the DOVE instrument for the sophistication of its types and levels of predictors and validation by a two-year study.

historic pattern of coercive control may be overlooked, and the ongoing risk to family members may not be addressed." To avoid such a circumstance, the authors recommend, a "multi-method, multi-informant approach to family assessment featuring increasingly intense inquiry as higher levels of conflict and abuse are uncovered." This conclusion implies that the objective detection of domestic abuse with questionnaires and "instruments" may well be beyond the function of a mere divorce mediator.

The report also points out the "nuances" of testing, implying that human judgment (i.e., informal screening) is always part of the equation. Although it is axiomatic that a mediator should never ignore domestic abuse, and should do everything possible to protect the integrity of the mediation process so that it is not used or perceived as a way for an abuser to take advantage of a victim, neither should a private divorce mediator be expected to spend vast amounts of time and attention to administering complicated "instruments" upon a population of clients privately contracting for services, the vast majority of whom are non-violent. As the field of assessment and screening for domestic violence (and perhaps other capacity issues) develops,[308] the trend could be in the direction of separate assessment measures apart from the mediation process, relieving the mediator from the burden, at least initially, of taking on a difficult, and often, intrusive role of screening. The mediator, as the professional working intimately with the parties, will always, so long as the standards require it, have the responsibility for assessing the parties' ongoing capacities to mediate and for detecting any problematic power imbalance.

After Screening

Once the mediator has assessed capacity and screened for abuse, the decision must be made by the mediator and the parties whether mediation is appropriate. It is not unusual for a perceived power imbalance caused by a single incident of violence to shift in favor of the *victim* who may have become empowered as a result of the incident. Therefore, both parties should be assessed for ability to negotiate. An example of the mediator's words in such a conversation could be, "Nancy, you informed me that Peter assaulted you and you filed a petition with the court to have him removed from your home. In mediation, this information raises a concern that violence could erupt again, or that fear or intimidation could prevent the two of you from being able to negotiate on equal footing. I am going to need to speak to both of you separately to try to find out if the impact of that incident has an effect on your ability to mediate." After the caucus, in this case, the parties both decided that their situations had stabilized and that, with the assistance of attorneys, counselors, friends and family, they were able to put the isolated incident behind them and move forward. They did not want to be screened out of mediation and miss out on the economic and personal benefits it offered. If either party had expressed a concern about continuing violence, control, or abuse by the other, the mediator would have been obligated to question the appropriateness of mediation for this family.

---

[308] Ellis, D. (2008). Divorce and the family court: What can be done about domestic violence? *Family Court Review*, 46(3), 531-536.

The mediator walks a thin line in making judgments about whether or not a case is appropriate for mediation based on the existence of, or potential for, violence. Scientific approaches have been studied and developed because of the unreliability of mere judgment in making the assessment. The thin line is the borderline between the "typical" angry and embittered divorcing couple who present in a confrontational mode (as expected), versus the truly dangerous case where someone is a ticking time bomb preparing to commit a deadly act. Whether a mediator conducts formal or informal screening, exploration of abuse issues should happen in caucus, either in person or on the telephone before the initial meeting. In some cases, however, the imminence of violence is concealed, and the mediator is left forever wondering if anything could have been done differently to prevent a tragedy.

The Case of Ron and Natalie
Case Study in Hidden Domestic Violence

Ron and Natalie appeared on Thursday in the mediator's office for a brief initial consultation for private divorce mediation. The mediator had spoken on the phone to Natalie, who made the appointment on Tuesday. Natalie said she was interviewing mediators on a list provided by a local mediation professional organization. She explained that she and Ron had been married for ten years and had two children, a son, age 9 and daughter, age 7. Natalie was a graduate professor at a large university with a doctorate in nursing. Ron owned a car repair garage and worked as a mechanic. They also owned several apartment units that Ron supervised and maintained. Natalie explained that she wanted a divorce because she no longer loved Ron. She told the mediator that Ron did not want a divorce and that he would not agree to leave or cooperate with shared custody so that she could leave, and that he would not agree to go to counseling or even discuss divorce with her. She had retained a lawyer, and her lawyer first suggested that they file a complaint in divorce to send the message to Ron that she was seriously pursuing divorce. When that didn't work, the lawyer suggested she try to get Ron to visit a divorce mediator. She was hoping that a mediator could help Ron open up and they could have a conversation about her dissatisfaction with their marriage. She hoped the combination of having already initiated a divorce action in court, and beginning to speak with a mediator would convince Ron that the expense of a litigated divorce would cost them too much money. She said that one thing Ron did understand was money, and saving money would motivate him to come to an appointment.

When Ron and Natalie appeared for their appointment, Natalie was dressed in nursing garb, having come directly from class, and Ron was dressed in his mechanic's gear, complete with grease-covered hands. The mediator began the meeting by introducing herself and telling the parties that the purpose of the initial consultation was to explain to them what a mediator does to enable the parties to decide whether or not mediation could help them. The mediator explained that the process was designed to save time and money typically spent on lawyers in the traditional courtroom divorce process. The mediator explained that the process only works when both parties agree to discuss their issues in the mediation session and want to resolve them amicably, rather than using the legal system. The parties listened and agreed that they were interested in mediation. The mediator asked the parties what their concerns were about negotiating together, and informed them that, as part of the process, the mediator would speak to them separately in order to determine if there were reasons mediation might not be appropriate for them because in some cases the parties cannot fairly negotiate as equals because of their history as a couple. The mediator stated that she had spoken to Natalie separately on the phone and asked Ron if he would be willing to call the mediator to have a similar separate conversation, so that there would be balance in the mediator's separate contacts with each party. Ron agreed that he would try to call the mediator, if he had time, but that he was very busy with work, and didn't really see a need to speak with the mediator separately, and that he did not mind that Natalie had spoken with the mediator separately on the phone.

As part of the consultation, the mediator asked each party what their concerns were. Natalie answered first that she was concerned that Ron was so "shut down" and that his refusal to talk worried her. She said that she knew Ron did not want her to leave, but that she had made up her mind, and that she really needed him to talk to her, for the benefit of their kids and making divorce as smooth as possible for them. Ron sat in his chair and looked down at the floor, making little, if any, eye contact with the mediator. The mediator noticed that Ron was wringing his hands repeatedly with his head drooping. The mediator asked Ron what his concerns were. Ron answered, making only the slightest eye contact, that he was mostly concerned with his father. The mediator asked him to explain what he meant. Ron answered that his father is just not going to be able to accept this, that his father won't understand a divorce. The mediator reassured Ron that, in mediation, all of the parties' concerns are addressed, and that it was her hope that Ron's concerns about his father could also be addressed. The parties decided that they wanted to try mediation and made an appointment for the following Tuesday.

That weekend, the mediator was home with her family leisurely reading the Sunday paper with her husband as their children played. Scanning the headlines under local news briefs, the mediator gasped at reading, "Man Kills Wife, Self" and finding the names of Ron and Natalie within the short text reporting that Ron had strangled his wife while she slept in their bed, then driven to his father's garage and asphyxiated himself in the running car. The parties were survived by two young children who were being cared for by relatives.

Questions for Discussion and Analysis

1.   **Besides the mediator, what other professionals might have had a duty to "screen" the case for domestic violence?**

2.   **What else could the mediator have done to prevent this tragedy?**

3.   **Were the mediator's actions reasonable?**

4.   If you were the mediator, what would you do differently in the future?

5.   **Class Assignment: Find a screening tool and compare the various tools found by members of the class. Determine what aspects of the various tools are most effective and user-friendly. Screening tools are plentiful online and within journal articles. Numerous tools have been created by scientists, researchers, domestic violence shelters, courts, alternative dispute resolution organization, mediation organizations, bar associations, state legislatures, and women's rights groups.**

In light of Ron and Natalie's situation, a mediator should explore any "weird" behavior reported by a party, and look for what a party feels worried about. In retrospect, we know that Ron was, perhaps unconsciously, signaling his thoughts of killing his wife when he continually squeezed and wrung his dirtied hands (the murder weapon), refusing to make contact. Clients who hint at fear of potential violence should be warned, in general terms, about what happened to Natalie and advised to seek protection and to take safety measures. The image of a vital, optimistic Natalie, full of hope for her future away from Ron, serves as a reminder of the reality of domestic terror. Unfortunately, in Natalie's case, no clear warning signal was present and no report of domestic violence had ever been made.

Remedies for Intimate Partner Violence

When abuse is detected and the mediator decides to terminate mediation, the mediator's duty is to provide a safe exit from the process. The mediator's safety and the safety of all parties are of paramount concern. An excuse other than the real reason usually must be fabricated if the victim will suffer as a result of the abuser's knowing she reported the abuse. This can be something as innocuous as, "My assessment of your issues led me to believe that I cannot help you," or blaming the problem on the content of their disputes rather than the conduct of the disputants. If the parties came together, or if, in leaving, they face the threat of confrontation, the mediator should take steps to arrange separate, safe exit from the building and follow-up resources including domestic abuse hotline information, women's shelter information, and legal advice on abuse, usually available through legal aid. The mediator should consider alerting law enforcement, if appropriate. The mediator should also be aware of legal remedies that exist for victims of domestic abuse.

Legislation protecting victims of domestic abuse arose in the 1970's with the women's movement. Protection from Abuse statutes, also called restraining orders or temporary restraining orders (TROs), exist in every state. Common features of the legislation consist of a procedure for granting exclusive, emergency, possession of a common residence, evicting the alleged abuser, without notice, for a temporary period (i.e., ten days[309]) pending a hearing to determine whether or not a permanent eviction will be granted. Temporary

---

[309] 23 Pa.C.S.A. §6108 (2020).

relief is granted based on a showing of "immediate and present danger" to the petitioner. Factors listed in the statute, if present, allow the court to order relinquishment of firearms *ex parte* (without notice to the defendant who has no opportunity to be present at the emergency hearing). Factors include threats of suicide, stalking, killing or threatening pets, drug use, sexual violence, or escalation of violence. Statutes provide for support and custody provisions to be made immediately, on a temporary basis, as well as payment for medical costs and therapy, permanent relinquishment of firearms after hearing, payment of fees, arrest for violation, and a no-contact order for up to three years.

Pennsylvania Statute.

Title 23 Chapter 61 Abuse of Family

§ 6108. Relief.

(a) General Rule.--Subject to subsection (a.1), the court may grant any protection order or approve any consent agreement to bring about a cessation of abuse of the plaintiff or minor children. The order or agreement may include:

(1) Directing the defendant to refrain from abusing the plaintiff or minor children.

(2) Granting possession to the plaintiff of the residence or household to the exclusion of the defendant by evicting the defendant or restoring possession to the plaintiff if the residence or household is jointly owned or leased by the parties, is owned or leased by the entireties or is owned or leased solely by the plaintiff.

(3) If the defendant has a duty to support the plaintiff or minor children living in the residence or household and the defendant is the sole owner or lessee, granting possession to the plaintiff of the residence or household to the exclusion of the defendant by evicting the defendant or restoring possession to the plaintiff or, with the consent of the plaintiff, ordering the defendant to provide suitable alternate housing.

(4) Awarding temporary custody of or establishing temporary visitation rights with regard to minor children. In determining whether to award temporary custody or establish temporary visitation rights pursuant to this paragraph, the court shall consider any risk posed by the defendant to the children as well as risk to the plaintiff. The following shall apply:

(i) A defendant shall not be granted custody, partial custody or unsupervised visitation where it is alleged in the petition, and the court finds after a hearing under this chapter, that the defendant:

(A) abused the minor children of the parties or poses a risk of abuse toward the minor children of the parties; or

(B) has been convicted of violating 18 Pa.C.S. § 2904 (relating to interference with custody of children) within two calendar years prior to the filing of the petition for protection order or that the defendant poses a risk of violating 18 Pa.C.S. § 2904.

(ii) Where the court finds after a hearing under this chapter that the defendant has inflicted abuse upon the plaintiff or a child, the court may require supervised custodial access by a third party. The third party must agree to be accountable to the court for supervision and execute an affidavit of accountability.

(iii) Where the court finds after a hearing under this chapter that the defendant has inflicted serious abuse upon the plaintiff or a child or poses a risk of abuse toward the plaintiff or a child, the court may:

(A) award supervised visitation in a secure visitation facility; or

(B) deny the defendant custodial access to a child.

(iv) If a plaintiff petitions for a temporary order under section 6107(b) (relating to hearings) and the defendant has partial, shared or full custody of the minor children of the parties by order of court or written agreement of the parties, the custody shall not be disturbed or changed unless the court finds that the defendant is likely to inflict abuse upon the children or to remove the children from the jurisdiction of the court prior to the hearing under section 6107(a). Where the defendant has forcibly or fraudulently removed any minor child from the care and custody of a plaintiff, the court shall order the return of the child to the plaintiff unless the child would be endangered by restoration to the plaintiff.

(v) Nothing in this paragraph shall bar either party from filing a petition for custody under Chapter 53 (relating to custody) or under the Pennsylvania Rules of Civil Procedure.

(vi) In order to prevent further abuse during periods of access to the plaintiff and child during the exercise of custodial rights, the court shall consider, and may impose on a custody award, conditions necessary to assure the safety of the plaintiff and minor children from abuse.

(5) After a hearing in accordance with section 6107(a), directing the defendant to pay financial support to those persons the defendant has a duty to support, requiring the defendant, under sections 4324 (relating to inclusion of medical support) and 4326 (relating to mandatory inclusion of child medical support), to provide health coverage for the minor child and spouse, directing the defendant to pay all of the unreimbursed medical expenses of a spouse or minor child of the defendant to the provider or to the plaintiff when he or she has paid for the medical treatment, and directing the defendant to make or continue to make rent or mortgage payments on the residence of the plaintiff to the extent that the defendant has a duty to support the plaintiff or other dependent household members. The support order shall be temporary, and any beneficiary of the order must file a complaint for support under the provisions of Chapters 43 (relating to support matters generally) and 45 (relating to reciprocal enforcement of support orders) within two weeks of the date of the issuance of the protection order. If a complaint for support is not filed, that portion of the protection order requiring the defendant to pay support is void. When there is a subsequent ruling on a complaint for support, the portion of the protection order requiring the defendant to pay support expires.

(6) Prohibiting the defendant from having any contact with the plaintiff or minor children, including, but not limited to, restraining the defendant from entering the place of employment or business or school of the plaintiff or minor children and from harassing the plaintiff or plaintiff's relatives or minor children.

(7) Prohibiting the defendant from acquiring or possessing any firearm for the duration of the order, ordering the defendant to temporarily relinquish to the sheriff or the appropriate law enforcement agency any firearms under the defendant's possession or control, and requiring the defendant to relinquish to the sheriff or the appropriate law enforcement agency any firearm license issued under section 6108.3 (relating to relinquishment to third party for safekeeping) or 18 Pa.C.S. § 6106 (relating to firearms not to be carried without a license) or 6109 (relating to licenses) the defendant may possess. The court may also order the defendant to relinquish the defendant's other weapons or ammunition that have been used or been threatened to be used in an incident of abuse against the plaintiff or the minor children. A copy of the court's order shall be transmitted to the chief or head of the appropriate law enforcement agency and to the sheriff of the county of which the defendant is a resident. When relinquishment is ordered, the following shall apply:

(i) (A) The court's order shall require the defendant to relinquish such firearms, other weapons, ammunition and any firearm license pursuant to the provisions of this chapter within 24 hours of service of a temporary order or the entry of a final order or the close of the next business day as necessary by closure of the sheriffs' offices, except for cause shown at the hearing, in which case the court shall specify the time for relinquishment of any or all of the defendant's firearms.

(B) A defendant subject to a temporary order requiring the relinquishment of firearms, other weapons or ammunition shall, in lieu of relinquishing specific firearms, other weapons or ammunition which cannot reasonably be retrieved within the time for relinquishment in clause (A) due to their current location, provide the sheriff or the appropriate law enforcement agency with an affidavit listing the firearms, other weapons or ammunition and their current location. If the defendant, within the time for relinquishment in clause (A), fails to provide the affidavit or fails to relinquish, pursuant to this chapter, any firearms, other weapons or ammunition ordered to be relinquished which are not specified in the affidavit, the sheriff or the appropriate law enforcement agency shall, at a minimum, provide immediate notice to the court, the plaintiff and appropriate law enforcement authorities. The defendant shall not possess any firearms, other weapons or ammunition specifically listed in the affidavit provided to the sheriff or the appropriate law enforcement agency pursuant to this clause for the duration of the temporary order.

(C) As used in this subparagraph, the term "cause" shall be limited to facts relating to the inability of the defendant to retrieve a specific firearm within 24 hours due to the current location of the firearm.

(ii) The court's order shall contain a list of any firearm, other weapon or ammunition ordered relinquished. Upon the entry of a final order, the defendant shall inform the court in what manner the defendant is going to relinquish any firearm, other weapon or ammunition ordered relinquished. Relinquishment may occur pursuant to section 6108.2 (relating to relinquishment for consignment sale, lawful transfer or safekeeping) or 6108.3 or to the sheriff or the appropriate law enforcement agency pursuant to this paragraph. Where the sheriff or the appropriate law enforcement agency is designated, the sheriff or the appropriate law enforcement agency shall secure custody of the defendant's firearms, other weapons or ammunition and any firearm license listed in the court's order for the duration of the order or until otherwise directed by court order. In securing custody of the defendant's relinquished firearms, the sheriff or the appropriate law enforcement agency shall comply with 18 Pa.C.S. § 6105(f)(4) (relating to persons not to possess, use, manufacture, control, sell or transfer firearms). In securing custody of the defendant's other weapons and ammunition, the sheriff or the appropriate law enforcement agency shall provide the defendant with a signed and dated written receipt which shall include a detailed description of the other weapon or ammunition and its condition. The court shall inform the defendant that firearms, other weapons or ammunition shall be deemed abandoned when the conditions under 18 Pa.C.S. § 6128(a) (relating to abandonment of firearms, weapons or ammunition) are satisfied and may then be disposed of in accordance with 18 Pa.C.S. § 6128.

(iii) The sheriff or the appropriate law enforcement agency shall provide the plaintiff with the name of the person to which any firearm, other weapon or ammunition was relinquished.

(iv) Unless the defendant has complied with subparagraph (i)(B) or section 6108.2 or 6108.3, if the defendant fails to relinquish any firearm, other weapon, ammunition or firearm license within 24 hours or upon the close of the next business day due to closure of sheriffs' or appropriate law enforcement agencies' offices or within the time ordered by the court upon cause being shown at the hearing, the sheriff or the appropriate law enforcement agency shall, at a minimum, provide immediate notice to the court, the plaintiff and appropriate law enforcement agencies, as appropriate.

(v) Any portion of any order or any petition or other paper which includes a list of any firearm, other weapon or ammunition ordered relinquished shall be kept in the files of the court as a permanent record thereof and withheld from public inspection except:

(A) upon an order of the court granted upon cause shown;

(B) as necessary, by law enforcement and court personnel; or

(C) after redaction of information listing any firearm, other weapon or ammunition.

(vi) As used in this paragraph, the term "defendant's firearms" shall, if the defendant is a licensed firearms dealer, only include firearms in the defendant's personal firearms collection pursuant to 27 CFR § 478.125a (relating to personal firearms collection).

(7.1) If the defendant is a licensed firearms dealer, ordering the defendant to follow such restrictions as the court may require concerning the conduct of his business, which may include ordering the defendant to relinquish any Federal or State license for the sale, manufacture or importation of firearms as well as firearms in the defendant's business inventory. In restricting the defendant pursuant to this paragraph, the court shall make a reasonable effort to preserve the financial assets of the defendant's business while fulfilling the goals of this chapter.

(8) Directing the defendant to pay the plaintiff for reasonable losses suffered as a result of the abuse, including medical, dental, relocation and moving expenses; counseling; loss of earnings or support; costs of repair or replacement of real or personal property damaged, destroyed or taken by the defendant or at the direction of the defendant; and other out-of-pocket losses for injuries sustained. In addition to out-of-pocket losses, the court may direct the defendant to pay reasonable attorney fees. An award under this chapter shall not constitute a bar to litigation for civil damages for injuries sustained from the acts of abuse giving rise to the award or a finding of contempt under this chapter.

(9) Directing the defendant to refrain from stalking or harassing the plaintiff and other designated persons as defined in 18 Pa.C.S. §§ 2709 (relating to harassment) and 2709.1 (relating to stalking).

(10) Granting any other appropriate relief sought by the plaintiff.

(a.1) Final order or agreement.--The following apply:

(1) Any final order must direct the defendant to refrain from abusing, harassing, stalking, threatening or attempting or threatening to use physical force against the plaintiff or minor children and must order that the defendant is subject to the firearms, other weapons or ammunition and firearms license prohibition relinquishment provisions under subsection (a)(7).

(2) A final agreement may direct the defendant to refrain from abusing, harassing, stalking, threatening or attempting or threatening to use physical force against the plaintiff or minor children and may order that the defendant is subject to the firearms, other weapons or ammunition and firearms license prohibition and relinquishment provisions under subsection (a)(7).

(b) Identifying information.--Any order issued under this section shall, where furnished by either party, specify the Social Security number and date of birth of the defendant.

(c) Mutual orders of protection.--Mutual orders of protection shall not be awarded unless both parties have filed timely written petitions, complied with service requirements under section 6106 (relating to commencement of proceedings) and are eligible for protection under this chapter. The court shall make separate findings and, where issuing orders on behalf of both petitioners, enter separate orders.

(d) Duration and amendment of order or agreement.--A protection order or approved consent agreement shall be for a fixed period of time not to exceed three years. The court may amend its order or agreement at any time upon subsequent petition filed by either party.

(e) Extension of protection orders.--

(1) An extension of a protection order may be granted:

(i) Where the court finds, after a duly filed petition, notice to the defendant and a hearing, in accordance with the procedures set forth in sections 6106 and 6107, that the defendant committed one or more acts of abuse subsequent to the entry of the final order or that the defendant engaged in a pattern or practice that indicates continued risk of harm to the plaintiff or minor child.

(ii) When a contempt petition or charge has been filed with the court or with a hearing officer in Philadelphia County, but the hearing has not occurred before the expiration of the protection order, the order shall be extended, at a minimum, until the disposition of the contempt petition and may be extended for another term beyond the disposition of the contempt petition.

(iii) If the plaintiff files a petition for an extension of the order and the defendant is or was incarcerated and will be released from custody in the next 90 days or has been released from custody within the past

90 days. The plaintiff does not need to show that the defendant committed one or more acts of abuse subsequent to the entry of the order or that the defendant engaged in a pattern or practice that indicates continued risk of harm to the plaintiff or minor children as set forth in subparagraph (i).

(2) Service of an extended order shall be made in accordance with section 6109 (relating to service of orders).

(3) There shall be no limitation on the number of extensions that may be granted.

(f) Support procedure.--The domestic relations section shall enforce any support award in a protection order where the plaintiff files a complaint for support under subsection (a)(5).

(g) Notice.--Notice shall be given to the defendant, in orders issued under this section, stating that violations of an order will subject the defendant to arrest under section 6113 (relating to arrest for violation of order) or contempt of court under section 6114 (relating to contempt for violation of order or agreement). Resumption of co-residency on the part of the plaintiff and defendant shall not nullify the provisions of the court order.

(h) Title to real property unaffected.--No order or agreement under this chapter shall in any manner affect title to any real property.

(i) Third parties and affidavits.--A court requiring relinquishment of firearms under this section shall provide for the hearing of petitions by third parties who request the return of a firearm relinquished by the defendant under subsection (a)(7). The following apply:

(1) A third party claiming to be the lawful owner of a firearm relinquished by the defendant under subsection (a)(7) may request the return of the firearm by providing proof of ownership and a sworn affidavit.

(2) The affidavit under paragraph (1) must affirm all of the following:

(i) The third party who is the lawful owner will not intentionally or knowingly return to the defendant the firearm or allow access to the firearm by the defendant.

(ii) The third party who is the lawful owner understands that violating subparagraph (i) constitutes a misdemeanor of the second degree under 18 Pa.C.S. Ch. 61 (relating to firearms and other dangerous articles).

(iii) If the third party who is the lawful owner is a family or household member of the defendant, any firearm returned under this section must be stored in a gun safe to which the defendant does not have access and will not be permitted to access, or stored in a location outside the third party's home to which the defendant does not have access.

(3) If the court orders the return of a firearm under this section, prior to the return of the firearm, the sheriff shall independently confirm that the person seeking relief under this section is legally eligible to

possess firearms under Federal and State law. The sheriff shall conduct the background check as soon as practicable after the court enters an order under this section.

§ 6115. **Reporting abuse and immunity**

(a) Reporting.--A person having reasonable cause to believe that a person is being abused may report the information to the local police department.

(b) Contents of report.--The report should contain the name and address of the abused person, information regarding the nature and extent of the abuse and information which the reporter believes may be helpful to prevent further abuse.

(c) Immunity.--A person who makes a report shall be immune from a civil or criminal liability on account of the report unless the person acted in bad faith or with malicious purpose.

End of Protection from Abuse portions of Pennsylvania law.

Mediator Interventions in High Conflict Cases

The majority of mediation participants, whether court-mandated, engaged privately, or part of a community mediation program, want to cooperate with each other and please the mediator. For every handful of cooperative clients, a family mediator is statistically destined to receive a "high conflict" case. A minority, estimated informally at 25 percent, of clients present with an array of persistent behaviors that are a challenge to manage. Mediators place these cases under the umbrella of "high conflict." High conflict behavior is oppositional, resistant, and angry. It is the result of unresolved issues, either acute, or of longstanding. High conflict behavior is destructive and involves character assassination, lack of self-control, threats, anger, contempt, hatred, exaggerated blame, and unrelenting attack. Long-term high conflict involves intractable disagreement where a solution ostensibly cannot be reached.

The mediator's response to high conflict is a triage approach where maintaining order and safety overshadow the mediator's usually sophisticated interventions aimed at the magical moments of empowerment and recognition. This is not to say that such moments do not occur in high conflict cases. They do, and when they do, they are that much more magical. In maintaining order and safety, the mediator is attempting to bring some order to chaos. High-conflict parties will resist this attempt, and will continue to re-impose chaos at every opportunity. By fighting back, the mediator sets up a scene for conflict between the mediator and the parties, which does not serve the parties. Therefore, the mediator must be willing to yield, or at least appear to be yielding, to the parties' desire for chaos. The mediator's fundamental task at this point is to find out what is going on beneath the surface.

When conflict appears intractable—a solution has eluded the parties over time—the mediator already has a clue that the answer could be hidden in the emotional world.[310] Retzinger and Scheff "…propose that in seemingly intractable conflict, headway can be made if the mediator is skilled enough to help the parties explore not only the substantive issues but also the emotional and relational side of their conflict."[311] The authors theorize that in impasse, both shame and anger are hidden and that it "…is not the alienation or emotion alone that causes protracted conflict but their denial by the participants. We propose that the denial of emotion and alienation leads to intractable conflict." It is suggested that the mediator approach the parties by speaking openly about the disputed substantive issues as well as about the relationship itself. This transparent approach brings shame and alienation to light, allowing the parties to pierce the alienation by gaining knowledge of each other, while acknowledging emotions that have been hidden and unacknowledged, contributing to the misdirected, sole focus on the disputed "issues." A further intervention of using "narratives" to address the conflict suggests that entrenched conflict is the result of a "narrative" parties tell themselves about the conflict. The narrative is a defense that distorts a party's role in the conflict. For example, an abusive husband tells himself (and believes) that his wife is the culprit and he is the victim. By changing the narrative and offering parties a new "story," the mediator has the opportunity to change the conflict.

---

[310] Retzinger, S., Scheff, T. (2000). Emotion, alienation, and narratives: Resolving intractable conflict. *Mediation Quarterly*, 18(1), 71-85.
[311] Id., 72.

The Case of Bill and Judy
Case Study in Protracted Conflict

Bill and Judy came to a court-connected mediation program specifically for relationship mediation. According to Bill, he heard that mediation—this program in particular—could help with long-term problems between former spouses. He filed a custody complaint seeking modification of an order regarding his three teenage daughters for the expressed purpose of receiving mediation from the court program. He admitted he did not want to change the custody order, but was there as a last ditch effort to do something to help his family. He and Judy were "unable to communicate" and needed help with co-parenting. They reported that family and co-parenting counseling had been attempted but did not work. He felt they were so entrenched in their resentments toward each other that nothing had changed in ten years. Judy agreed that their relationship had deteriorated and that they had nothing but bitterness between them, and that bitterness was "subtly" affecting their daughters who had been in and out of treatment for severe eating disorders and cutting. Judy did not object to Bill's fake custody complaint in order to get them into the court-connected mediation program.

Bill was a formidable public figure—a man with stature in the community, but, apparently, little respect at home. The parties were mostly pleasant and did not display overt anger. Bill complained that he felt alienated and marginalized, and that Judy did nothing but encourage their daughters to disrespect him. He was a prominent professional- always busy, traveling the country, and getting praise from the world at large. His public image was an important source of self-esteem. The mediator suspected that Bill's emphasis on his grandiose public persona was compensation for his failure at home and his feelings of shame around his role as a father, unable to win the respect of his daughters or their mother. Despite his larger-than-life image, he was suffering from a loss of dignity, and the betrayal of those closest to him. The story unfolded that Bill had left Judy over ten years ago for a younger, prettier woman (which Judy once was, he was quick to point out). Bill expressed contempt for Judy for gaining weight and letting herself go. Meanwhile, their daughters' severe emotional problems were getting worse. The mediator detected "stories" the parties were telling themselves and noticed an opportunity to possibly change the stories. The mediator observed that Bill was feeling marginalized and disrespected at home, and seemed to be ashamed of that fact, especially since the opposite was true in his public life. The story Bill had been telling *himself* was that Judy let him down by letting herself go and making him lose interest in her, breaking up their family, and then refusing to better herself, remained "fat" and caused their daughters to disrespect their father and develop their own eating disorders. He bought into the myth of a woman's value deriving solely from her ability to please a man with youth and outward beauty. He believed that Judy was the source of the problem because when he left her, it wounded her so badly that, to get even, she deliberately gained weight and turned their girls against him. The mediator heard none of Bill's part in his story. An alternative story, expressed by the mediator, might help Bill change his story. The mediator pointed out her observations, indicating a pattern she observed in the few minutes she had listened to Bill and Judy. The mediator kept her observations simple and tentative, "Bill, I can't help but notice that you are so revered in the community, yet, from your family, you have only been on the receiving end of disrespect. How ironic and how confusing that must be." Judy gave a big nod and a half-smile. Bill appeared surprised, and the mediator wondered if she had crossed a boundary by challenging the important public figure who sat across from her. After a brief pause, he responded, "They have no respect for me- I only get a phone call when they need something. I'm always there with the checkbook or the airline tickets. I know my girls love me, but Judy beats it into their heads every day what a loser I am as a father- she will never forgive me for what happened in our relationship." Mediator to Judy, "Is that how you see it?" Judy answered, softly scoffing, "Not at all. Bill doesn't understand that I have moved on. I am happy with my life as it is now. He did me a favor by leaving me for Vanessa, who by the way is divorcing him now. It's true, though, that we don't respect him and I do contribute to that. I'm sorry. I am brutally honest with the girls- they see it- their dad is basically a joke in our house." The mediator sensed that both parties were feeling a great deal of shame, which, perhaps they were hiding in the counseling they reported "didn't work." Bill was ashamed of his failures as a husband and father, especially in contrast to his image as a public figure. Judy was ashamed of the way she had allowed herself and her daughters to marginalize Bill, and was beginning to see her part in their family tragedy. The mediator felt an urge to point out to Bill the connection between his measurement of a women's worth and his daughters' apparent obsession with weight, but restrained herself because the parties seemed to be focused on their feelings of shame that had just surfaced, and the mediator did not want to shame him.

The mediator asked the parties a nonjudgmental question, "What do you think could change in the way you relate to each other as a result of what you've heard and said today?" Bill said, "A lot." Judy said, "I'm going to stop encouraging everyone to slam Bill. It isn't helping." Few words were spoken. The parties were quiet, but an air of relief settled into the room. The parties then began to discuss immediate issues such as travel plans Bill had with the girls, psychiatrist appointments with the girls, and other logistical matters. The parties talked with an air of familiarity and congeniality. The mediator asked if there were other issues they wanted to discuss about their children. The session ended and they thanked the mediator for helping them. Bill sent a note to the mediator three weeks later saying that communication between him and Judy had improved and thanking the mediator for helping them resolve their issues.

The mediator was not certain what had happened, but theorized several possibilities. Perhaps Bill's recent divorce action between him and his third wife had opened him to self-examination he had not allowed himself to access prior to this mediation. Perhaps the mediator's observations and re-tooled "story" gave language and labels to the parties' experience, empowering them to see themselves in a new light. In therapy, they may have taken on different roles, and not revealed themselves the way they did to the mediator. In impasse, both shame and anger are hidden. Unexpressed emotions are a burden. A "story" or narrative a party tells themselves adds to the burden when it is incomplete, lacking personal responsibility. Parties are too ashamed to bring their issues to the surface unless they feel extremely safe, ready, and accepted. The parties and this mediator may have simply been in the right place at the right time. The key was unlocking shame (rather than denying it with incomplete "stories"), bringing it out into the open, looking at it, noticing that it is not lethal, then "sitting with" it, or allowing it. Once the mediator fulfilled the fundamental task of bringing the parties to awareness with nonjudgmental observation and even "normalizing" the observations, the mediator's task was finished.

Questions for Discussion and Analysis:

1. **How was "narrative" used by the mediator?**

2. **Was this a high conflict case? Why or why not?**

3. **How does a mediator detect and respond to shame?**

4. **How was the mediator "transparent?"**

Transparency and Trust

In mediation, transparency is the mediator's unedited expression of what he observes or is experiencing. The mediator is innocent, candid, and nonjudgmental. The transparent mediator is vulnerable, risking attack for laying all of his cards on the table, defenseless. Dictionary definitions are "free from guile," "forthright," "candid or open."[312] The risks inherent with transparency can be worth the corresponding rewards because true transparency yields trust. The transparent mediator earns the trust of the parties, but only if that trust is not eradicated by distrust. As observed by Morton Deutsch,[313] "...trust and distrust are *functionally interrelated*... 'He who distrusts most should be trusted least.'" The acquisition of trust is complex, because it can just as easily be lost as acquired. The choice to trust is equally as complicated and can be based on a foundation as flimsy as hope or fantasy or on the firmer foundation of confidence.[314] In other words, people trust for a variety of reasons. A person who indiscriminately trusts everyone based on the misplaced belief that everyone can be trusted, does so out of desperation; whereas, the person who trusts out of confidence does so out of courage, placing desire over fear. How parties react to a mediator, with trust or distrust, is critical to the mediation process because some trust in the mediator is necessary in order for parties to fully participate. Mediation participants may be naturally distrustful of a mediator because of unfamiliarity with the process and its lack of a proven track record. The mediator most often has to earn trust. When a mediator risks transparency, distrust can be created. Parties may reasonably

---

[312] Oliver, R.E. (2004). *What is transparency?* NY: McGraw Hill, 3.
[313] Deutsch, M. (1973). *The resolution of conflict.* New Haven: Yale University Press, 143.
[314] Id., 148.

distrust a mediator who shares her feelings too openly, creating the impression that the mediator's feelings are more important than the parties' feelings.

The parties may not be as tolerant of negative emotions (i.e., discomfort) in a mediator as the mediator, who is paid to be tolerant of parties' emotions, should be. A mediator risking transparency must be certain of her motives. If the motive is to manipulate the parties by putting on a show of feelings, this may be a perfectly acceptable mediator technique, but it is not transparency, which is innocent and free from ulterior motive. True transparency in mediation is motivated by a sincere desire by the mediator to bring parties to awareness of reality the mediator believes the parties are ready to accept. The best way for the mediator to know if such transparency is sincere is to check her own "gut" for feelings of fear or guilt. Fear or guilt indicates that the mediator senses the parties could feel threatened by the mediator's desired statement. Fear may very well be what prevented Bill and Judy's mediator from going further with her transparency and connecting Bill's judgments about Judy's weight to his daughters' eating disorders. With such statements, the mediator's motives would have been to judge and even chastise Bill, and not merely to observe him. Transparency, when sincerely offered, moves the parties to powerfully trust the mediator, a reward for the process. When improvidently offered, transparency can damage the process. It is a risk few mediators take because of its potentially damaging effects. The more experienced the mediator, the less risky transparency becomes. In cases of protracted, intractable conflict, or impasse, transparency can be a powerful intervention.

Emotions and Identity

High conflict is almost always accompanied with high emotion. In *Negotiating Emotions*,[315] Daniel Shapiro argues for using emotions as a tool in negotiation, rather than avoiding getting emotional. He points out that people use emotions to define "identity concerns," which, in turn, are used in making decisions. In other words, when people hear statements, they attach a message to the words based on their emotions. Shapiro argues against exploiting emotions because it can breed distrust if detected or can backfire and have the opposite effect, such as when a car dealer's show of anger at giving into a buyer's price annoys the customer enough to scare him away.[316] Instead, he argues for using emotion as a means of communication where relational identity concerns are involved, particularly one's autonomy, affiliation, role or status. In high conflict where high emotion is present, it is obvious to any mediator that taking advantage of a plentiful resource, emotion, is preferable to suppressing or trying to control emotions. If a mediator can use emotions to help parties resolve conflict, such alchemy is useful especially in a high conflict case.

---

[315] Shapiro, D. (2002). Negotiating emotions. *Conflict Resolution Quarterly*, 20 (1), 67-82.
[316] Id., 70.

The Case of Kim and Rick
Case Study in Emotional Identity Concerns

Kim and Rick are the parents of a nine-month old infant as a result of a very brief relationship while they worked together for approximately three weeks. Rick was married at the time and did not know of Kim's pregnancy until after she quietly gave birth, not knowing what Rick's involvement would be with their child. Rick had two adult children from his first marriage, and his new wife (to whom he was married during his affair with Kim) is currently pregnant. Rick found out through the grapevine about Kim's baby, and Kim eventually filed an action for child support, resulting in a wage attachment for Rick.

Rick has initiated a custody action seeking partial custody of Kim's baby. As a new, first-time mother, Kim is now fearful that Rick, whom she views as a virtual stranger, will try to take away her baby. She also has admittedly exaggerated fears that he could even harm her baby. In mandatory mediation, Rick informs the mediator that Kim refused him any contact with his child; therefore, he filed for interim, "emergency" relief in court and the judge ordered weekly visits supervised by Kim. Rick stated that he knew this judge well because he had to fight for time with his two older children, now adults. He said that Judge Smith, also assigned to this case, stated in open court, that she had no intention of permanently ordering supervised custody, and that if Mom did not make a good faith effort to be reasonable and give him partial custody time, that she would not be happy when they returned. Rick demonstrated an air of confidence in any litigated result based on his history with Judge Smith in his prior custody case and on her purported statements that suggested, in his view, that she would lift the supervision with little deliberation. Kim was relieved that the judge had compassion for her uncertainty about Rick and his parenting. She was fearful of the future, and was not "ready" to agree to unsupervised time for Rick until the child was old enough to tell her what went on during custody visits away from her. (This gave the mediator little confidence there would be a resolution in mediation.) Rick seemed to feed Kim's fears by demanding a rigorous partial custody schedule that included five overnights in a two-week period. Rick also expressed a desire to resolve the case in mediation, stating that he learned from his experiences with his first family that although he knows his way around the court system, he found it damaging to his children to put them through litigation.

The mediator detected the parties' strong emotions and identified the emotions and accompanying "messages" as follows:

Rick came across as feeling very strongly about his *rights* as a father and a belief that his rights were supported by the judge. He felt his rights were being subverted by Kim and her refusal to cooperate. Rick appeared to exhibit a degree of pride in his past abilities to win custody cases in court, his feeling that the judge already recognized him as a fit parent, his competency as a parent stepping up to be a part of this child's life, and his belief in settling custody issues in mediation.

Kim came across as fearful and threatened, yet also resigned to the fact that Rick was going to be given the role of father to her child. She appeared more fearful of Rick's show of power than of any true concern that Rick would harm her child. She wanted the mediator and Rick to understand her need, as a mother, to protect her child, and to know exactly what was happening to her child at all times. By gauging each party's emotional state in the moment and weighing the reasons therefor, the mediator is able to navigate a strategy that addresses their identity concerns.

The mediator began by asking specifically what kind of custody schedule each party wanted. This is essential. As long as the parties are on positions and only discussing custody in the abstract, the mediation will not be successful. Rick's desired schedule was ambitious and contained much more "partial custody" time than Kim was able to accept. Kim wanted to keep things as they were with Rick only having supervised time with the child. They each expressed their concerns and pros and cons of both schedules for over an hour before it became clear to the mediator that they were nearing impasse. The mediator, recalling the emotions described above, said to Rick, "The two of you seem so far apart in what you will accept for a schedule. I don't know about you, but if it were me, I would do everything possible to avoid court. As a parent, I cannot even imagine having a judge tell me when I can or when I can't be with my own child! That just seems unacceptable and almost a violation of a parent's rights and freedom." (The mediator refrained from invoking the Constitution, but the thought did cross her mind.) Apparently, the mediator struck a nerve with Rick, who closely associated with these very feelings in his past court custody experiences. Rick's demeanor changed and he offered a different schedule that represented a compromise of about half of the time he had been demanding. Kim relaxed her guard and immediately agreed to the proffered schedule which also included a transition period for Rick and the baby to get comfortable with each other. Rick changed from being threatening and difficult to very conciliatory. The mediator felt certain that her "...if it were me," and "...as a parent...." statements triggered some emotion in Rick that caused him to back down and offer a more reasonable schedule. A bond of trust and a feeling of safety seemed to have been created. The mediator theorized that Rick felt safe.

Questions for Discussion and Analysis

1. **What emotions were present for Rick? What circumstances were attached to each emotion?**

2. **What emotions were present for Kim? What circumstances were attached to each emotion?**

3.   **How did the mediator use her observations of emotions to guide her words?**

Keith and Suzanne
Case Study in Undifferentiated Couples

Keith and Suzanne, a highly volatile couple, were trying to end a 20-year marriage. They still lived together, and every day they found a new issue to fight about. They had two children, a son 19 in college, and a daughter, 18, a senior in high school, but they rarely thought about or mentioned their children. Keith and Suzanne were fixated on each other. Keith was a maintenance supervisor in a mid-sized company he called a "hedge fund." Five years ago his company transferred stock to every employee as part of a compensation package. Two years ago Keith found out he was a millionaire times fifteen. In the past two years, Keith and Suzanne had spent two million dollars on a new house, furnishings, automobiles, vacation cruises, and divorce attorneys. Six months ago they decided to divorce. Both parties retained the best attorneys money could buy. Suzanne had filed for divorce and was determined to leave Keith. The problem was, she never seemed to get around to leaving. Suzanne's attorney recommended that the parties see a mediator in order to devise a plan of separation. Keith contended that he wanted Suzanne to leave because their marriage had become a "nightmare" for him.

During their first mediation session, both parties tried to monopolize the conversation. The mediator asked them to speak one at a time so she could listen carefully to each party. After two hours, the mediator understood their desire to separate and that the issue they could not agree upon was whether or not Keith would pay Suzanne lifetime alimony. Suzanne was a homemaker but only 45 years old. She had no plans to work because she was "married to a millionaire." Keith expressed frustration that Suzanne just couldn't understand that when this is over she will be a very wealthy woman and will not need alimony. Suzanne, equally frustrated, responded that she would never agree to any deal without permanent alimony from Keith. She maintained that she did not believe in relying on investments because she had seen Keith's stock go up and down, and that the only way she would feel secure would be in knowing she had lifetime alimony from Keith. Keith appeared exasperated and stressed from arguing with Suzanne. He said when they are both home, all they do is fight about this. He thought mediation could help them limit their arguments to the mediator's office so that he could have some peace at home. Suzanne reminded him that he will have no peace until they reach an agreement. When the two-hour session was over, the mediator gave them an appointment for the following week. The next day, the mediator was copied on fifteen emails between Keith and Suzanne. Each email was a long diatribe about what each party's attorney had told them about the legal issues, including alimony and Suzanne's need now for Keith to pay for some plastic surgery she wanted. After the fifth email, the mediator sent a message to the parties asking them to stop copying her on emails, requesting that, instead, if they were important, to bring copies to the next session. Keith then called the mediator, crying. He said he didn't think he could do mediation because the things Suzanne said were so hard for him to hear. The mediator asked him what was hard to hear. "She said I have to pay her alimony. She will ruin me. I will never agree to let her attach my paycheck. I need you to tell her to stop saying that. She said I ruined her life and I will have to pay her forever. I wish I'd never gotten any of this money. We've spent two million, but I can't spend anymore. My company says we're fools if we spend now because this money is going to go through the roof and double in value in the next five years." Keith seemed powerless to defend himself against Suzanne's threats and, to him, her words were fact. The mediator tried to explain to him that Suzanne's statements were simply her feelings, her beliefs, and that he could believe what he wanted to believe and could disagree with her. Keith could not understand or absorb what the mediator was saying, and felt hopeless that he could ever get Suzanne's "constant badgering" out of his head. The parties apparently did not read the mediator's message because the copies kept coming.

At the next session, Suzanne arrived first, informing the mediator that Keith would be about twenty minutes late and asking the mediator if she could speak privately to the mediator about concerns she had. Suzanne sat at the mediation table and began with the words, "I know it may seem to you like we hate each other, but the truth is I love this man more than anything. We began dating in high school...the funny thing is now our sex life is better than ever...." Keith never did show up for the mediation session and the parties did not return to mediation.

Keith and Suzanne are an example of a "couple from Hell."[317] The reference to Hell, however, is not so much where they come from as it is the place they create in the enmeshed world of their relationship. The "undifferentiated couple remain ...emotionally dependent...on each other [and]...often negotiate at length with great intensity, but ...are very unlikely to reach any agreement."[318] Sometimes any negotiation is too painful for them, and even separating is impossible. The emotional dependence between Keith and Suzanne had three essential features. Rather than just one party being emotionally dependent on the other, they were both equally emotionally dependent upon each other, creating a fused bond that neither one could break. The bond they created with each other was likely a re-creation of a fused relationship each had with a parent. The "system" they have created is self-perpetuating; it constantly creates and satisfies a need that neither party believes can be satisfied outside of the relationship. The parties, sadly, are barely able to function as individuals. In Keith and Suzanne's case, the outside influence of money threatened to break their bond rather than enhance it. Suzanne was threatened by Keith's ability to acquire power through money, while Keith saw his money as a windfall (which it was) that merely gave Suzanne greater power to exploit him. He saw himself imprisoned by his newfound wealth, unable to spend it, while he knew on some level that he could lose it as quickly as he had gotten it. In truth, a year later his company went under completely with the "crash" of September 2008. Ironically, the parties' children were extremely

---

[317] Mathis, R. (1998). Couples from Hell: Undifferentiated spouses in divorce mediation. *Mediation Quarterly, 16*(1), 37-49.
[318] Id., 46

independent and rarely interacted with their parents. In some fused families, children become part of the drama as the parents "triangulate" with the children. Suzanne and Keith were so fused that not even their children could weaken their bond. While both parties said they wanted to separate and escape their misery, they seemed to thrive on their conflict and did not appear to see anything unusual about continuing a sexual relationship while a divorce action was pending or to copy the mediator extensively on chronic email arguments. Their focus on each other was so exclusive that they barely noticed the mediator's emails to them asking them to stop copying her.

Interventions suggested by Mathis include maintaining order, improving communication, parent education, promoting autonomy and boundaries, and providing leadership for the "leaderless" family. The mediator "…must be more active with undifferentiated clients than with other types; should take firm control immediately; and should address the systemic condition of poor differentiation first, before attempting to settle any issues under dispute."[319] By assessing the systemic problems, the mediator, using transparency, describes the fusion to the parties, explaining their lack of differentiation to them directly. The family is, indeed, leaderless because their system is cyclical. Their system is one of blame and cause and effect, feeding off each other's constant fueling of the repetitive cycle of attack, blame, and wounding. By identifying their lack of differentiation and urging autonomy, likely with the recommendation for individual (not couples) counseling, the mediator offers the parties a way out of the vicious cycle. The mediator's only choice is to intervene as a strong leader because the parties feel so powerless themselves, anything short of a show of power is perceived by them as weakness that has no ability to rescue them from the irresistible force holding them in their pattern of dysfunction.

Most "couples from Hell" are able to eventually physically separate, and it is hoped that Keith and Suzanne were eventually able to separate, either from their marriage, or, at least, from their fused bond. Once they do separate, however, they typically continue to play out their conflict, fighting over money, children, or any other issue available. In working with such couples, the mediator's primary goal must always be to view the parties as individuals and demand individual accountability from each party, ignoring their perceived need of each other. The court system attracts fused couples because of its acceptance of the warfare model. The court system buys into the fused couple's belief that each party is the cause of the other's misery. The court system sees the solution to their problem as an imposition of a decision about who is right and who is wrong, rather than requiring each party to individually take responsibility for his or her role. In mediation, personal responsibility is a requirement for any change to take place. A court-imposed solution finding one party right and the other wrong will not encourage both parties to take responsibility for their contributions to the dispute. A court decision may end the legal dispute, but it is unlikely to end the cycle of conflict between the parties. In mediation, the mediator's goal of bringing parties to awareness of their *individual* responsibility is a challenge, especially when the mediator is focused

---

[319] Id., 47.

on simply maintaining order. A mediator mindful of the importance of personal autonomy and responsibility in a high conflict case, can sometimes, rather simply, accomplish this goal.

The Case of the Angry Mom
A Case Study in Responding to Anger

Mom and Dad appeared for a mandatory custody mediation regarding their fourteen-year old daughter. The mediator appeared in the mediation center, and immediately noticed an air of tension in the waiting room. Approximately twelve people sat in the reception area waiting for their cases to be called, a few standing in line at the window attempting to file custody papers and ask questions of the receptionist at the "Kids First" court-connected custody and mediation center. The room was unusually quiet, and, the mediator noticed, as he walked into the area for employees only, even the staff was silent, and seemed to be glancing at him sideways. "Why are you looking at me that way?" he asked the receptionist. "Oh, Glenn, that's your client out there. She's mean, and she's fuming. Yelling at me two minutes ago until the sheriff threatened to handcuff and remove her if she said another word. She is not happy about being here. She just told everyone in the waiting room she had to miss two days of work because of her jerk loser ex. She keeps making a scene and everyone's afraid of her! Lucky you." Soon the mediator heard the angry Mom ranting again, probably not realizing that she was dangerously close to being evicted by the sheriff who stood guard to keep peace in the mediation center. "How many times do you have to ruin my life?" she was heard asking, her voice several decibels above what was needed. The mediator was prepared, as he picked up the file and walked into the hallway to call the case. After he called out the parties' first names, he saw the angry mom approaching him and asked her, "Are you ready?" Mom said, "I'll never be ready." The mediator did not react at all. As he led the parties to the mediation room, he pointed to the chairs and asked the parties to sit down. Mom said, brusquely, "You better get a sheriff in here." Mediator responded, deadpan, "Why is that?" Mom said, "'Cause I don't like him," referring to Dad. Mediator asked Mom, "Do you think you will have trouble controlling yourself?" At this, the angry Mom's demeanor changed entirely, as she responded, "Oh….me? No, no, not at all."

By focusing on Mom's responsibility for her own behavior and not reacting at all to Mom's anger (as everyone else in the entire center had by avoiding eye contact with her, talking about her, noticing her, focusing on her, and rolling their eyes to each other, as she subtly controlled the room) the mediator did the one thing no one else had yet done: placed responsibility on her. Mom was not taking responsibility for herself, but was blaming Dad for her problems, and, when that did not work, blamed the entire mediation center, controlling the waiting area with her anger. Everyone there was focused on her. By putting responsibility for her behavior squarely on her in a non-confrontational way, merely asking a question and merely responding to her, not even initiating the exchange, the mediator caused Mom to stop her antics. She immediately realized she could not control the mediator…she had met her match!

Questions for Discussion and Analysis

1. Was the mediator's question empowering for Mom?

Answer: Yes. Self-control is empowering, as is responsibility for one's feelings.

2. What else was the mediator saying with his one simple question, "Do you think you will have trouble controlling yourself?"

Try to guess at least seven messages the mediator conveyed to Angry Mom with the mediator's simple statement. Answers are on the next page.

The parties' daughter, tragically but not surprisingly, was self-destructive in the extreme. At age fourteen, she had recently jumped from a second-floor window and broken all of the bones in her left foot. Asked why she did it, she told the doctors in the emergency room, "I wanted to break my bones." Her parents reported she continued to want to hurt herself.

A Final Note On High Conflict Cases

In high conflict cases, the mediator's triage approach is to first provide safety and maintain order. If, after those interventions, there is any space left to provide other services, assessing the system for enmeshment, fusion, lack of differentiation (synonyms for a closed, dysfunctional family system) and intervening by promoting individual responsibility (differentiation) will lead the mediator to appropriate, and possibly helpful, interventions. The way the mediator maintains the proper mindset is through "reflective practice," the topic of the next chapter.

ANSWER TO QUESTION ABOUT THE ANGRY MOM

Name at least seven messages conveyed to the Angry Mom by the mediator's simple statement, "Do you think you will have trouble controlling yourself?"

1. I am okay with your anger. The mediator did not rebuke or judge Mom.

2. Being in divorce/custody litigation is not a license to be out of control. You need to behave yourself here.

3. You are responsible for your behavior- no one else is.

4. I will not be controlled or manipulated by your anger.

5. I am a powerful mediator. I am strong. (Possibly: I can act as a leader for you temporarily – in this system where there is no leader.)

6. I am not ignoring or avoiding your anger. I acknowledge your anger.

7. I am not judging your anger, your behavior, or your rudeness because I can deal with it and so can you.

8. I am willing to mediate your case, even though your behavior is unpleasant; I value this process enough to go forward with the belief that it may help you.

Chapter Ten

"It's an Inside Job."— Bill Eddy

Reflective Practice

In *The Making of a Mediator*[320] Lang and Taylor argue that it's not enough for a mediator to achieve mediocrity and mediators should strive for artistry in practice. To achieve artistry, the mediator must continuously engage in Reflective Practice, or "…think divergently, be unfettered by the limits of conventional wisdom, and accept the challenge of the novel circumstance to develop a new approach or analysis."[321] To get there, Lang and Taylor describe a process of continual self-evaluation and self-awareness. They suggest that practice decisions (strategies, techniques) are driven by the mediator's beliefs.[322] If theory drives practice, then a mediator's beliefs underlie every move the mediator makes. Regular self-examination, therefore, should be a useful tool for refining one's skills. Lang and Taylor encourage reflective practitioners to "engage in a continual process of self-reflection…[and] test their observations, perceptions, and formulations…."

Initially, a mediator might want to consider why they became, or wanted to become, a mediator. Knowing one's reasons for choosing the profession, perhaps stemming from childhood or family of origin, can be a starting point of self-reflection. Many, but not all, of the most gifted mediators find that their high threshold for conflict comes from experiencing conflict as a child, or in another impressionable setting. Many mediators began as attorneys, psychotherapists, or other professionals, and transformed themselves into mediators due, at least in part, to some dissatisfaction with the first profession. To know one's evolution as a professional is valuable information in the reflective practice process.

History aside, the reflective practitioner is called upon to reflect continuously throughout their career. Following is a sample Reflective Practice Quiz that is to be taken privately and repeated from time to time. Students can take the quiz as a baseline. Students should consider their impressions of mediation so far, and answer from their current beliefs about hypothetical practice, or role-play experience. Sharing answers in small groups and, if desired, when reconvening to the large group is an enjoyable course activity.

---

[320] Lang, M. & Taylor, A. (2000). *The making of a mediator*. San Francisco: Jossey-Bass.
[321] Id., 120.
[322] *See also* Lang, M., 2004, 218

REFLECTIVE PRACTICE QUIZ

A mediator's understanding of what is effective mediation drives the mediator's practice. How the mediator explains mediation to the unschooled and thinks about mediation dictate the mediator's actions in session. Understanding why the mediator does any chosen action in session (including unconscious actions) is important for developing a style that is authentically one's own.

Questions

1. List three personal values you hold. Do these values, or any of them influence your mediation practice, and, if so, how?

2. Do you subscribe to a system of belief? Most of us do. Examples are: Democracy, Capitalism, a religion or faith, theories of personality, negotiation, conflict, any philosophy, or even a personal motto or slogan? If so, how would or do these influence your approach to mediation?

3. Do you believe in mediation? Why? What is the value of mediation?

4. When someone asks you what mediation is, what is your answer?

5. How do you define conflict?

6. How do you define impartiality?

7. How do you as the mediator influence the mediation process?

8. How do you measure whether mediation is effective or not?

Chapter Eleven

"Much unhappiness has come into the world because of bewilderment and things left unsaid." -- Fyodor Dostoevsky

Communication and Mediation

Communication

No one would dispute that communication is vital to the mediation process. Since a lack of effective communication is often the cause of conflict, mediation, as the proposed solution, should offer a superior model for communication. Coogler recommended Transactional Analysis for dissecting faulty communication between parties and helping them understand their flawed communication. TA, as it is commonly called, assigns "ego states" of Parent, Adult, or Child to parties' communications, interpreting them through childhood experiences. TA was popularized in the sixties with two books, *Games People Play*[323] by Eric Berne and the very popular *I'm OK, You're OK*[324] by Thomas Harris. Berne coined the term "strokes" to denote a unit of human recognition, leading to the popular phrase "Different strokes for different folks." Although TA has had a following, it is not currently a visible one and few, if any, mediators have followed Coogler's TA prescription. Haynes's focus on the mediator's communication with clients prescribed open-ended questions followed by responses such as empathizing and mutualizing to communicate understanding and foster trust in the mediator.[325]

Morton Deutsch, whose work was studied by Coogler, addressed communication in his 1973 book *The Resolution of Conflict*,[326] but only peripherally. He studied parties' approaches to dispute resolution as either competitive, where individuals pursued self-interest, or cooperative, where they pursued mutually beneficial outcomes. He observed that in a competitive process, communication was either absent, deceptive, or threatening. He noted that communication in a cooperative exchange enhances trust because with each exchange of information, the parties increase trust, while communication can change a purely competitive negotiation into a cooperative negotiation if the parties are able to convince each other that they are both committed to the choice of cooperation over competition. Deutsch was particularly intrigued by his finding that not all parties choose communication even when it is available. A cooperative negotiation, requiring "complimentarity" of expectation and intention is all but impossible in the absence of communication. Deutsch proved his theories with subjects undergoing numerous trials and games such as the Prisoner's Dilemma in which two suspects are taken into custody and separately given two

---

[323] Berne, E. (1964). *Games people play: The basic hand book of Transactional Analysis.* New York: Ballantine Books.
[324] Harris, T. (1969). *I'm OK, you're OK.* New York: Harper & Row.
[325] Haynes, 1989, 32.
[326] Deutsch, 1973.

alternatives by the district attorney who suspects both are guilty, but secretly lacks sufficient evidence to convict them. Players are given two alternatives: to confess or not confess. If they both confess, they will be given light sentences. If they both refuse to confess, they will both go free. If one confesses and the other refuses, the one who confesses will receive a light sentence while the one who refuses to confess will receive the maximum harsh sentence. Clearly, communication would enable the prisoners to maximize their mutual benefit, while lack of communication forces them to act competitively, each looking out for his own interests and risking the harsher penalty. Rarely would an isolated prisoner trust the other to be cooperative without some communication. Yet, Deutsch repeatedly found that the opportunity to communicate was not utilized by most of his subjects. When communication was offered, it did not lead to greater cooperation in the tests. Deutsch concluded this was because the subjects often chose not to communicate, or, when they chose to communicate, the nature of the communication itself would discourage cooperation (i.e., by being threatening or intimidating). Deutsch then conducted an experiment in which subjects were required to communicate in order to find out whether compelled communication created cooperation and found that it did. He also found that third party intervention to help remove blocks and distortions in communication was helpful.

As validating as Deutsch's observations are to family mediators, he and others seem to take communication as a given. If Deutsch were to observe an actual family mediation, he would find the opposite. In fact, a family mediation session has the potential to be a study in the failure to communicate. Communication failure in mediation originates from three sources: (1) the mediator's failure to listen to the parties; (2) the parties' flawed communication with each other (and/or the mediator) or *interpersonal* communication, and (3) the parties' and mediator's flawed communication with themselves or *intrapersonal* communication.

The family mediator has many balls in the air. Minutes into the first session, the mediator is already multi-tasking on a grand scale. The following tasks are all "fundamental" tasks of the mediator:

1. Exploring positions to identify underlying interests

2. Looking for and noticing signposts that signal empowerment and recognition

3. Assessing for power imbalances, capacity to mediate, readiness issues, domestic abuse

4. Responding to parties' expressions of emotion

5. Maintaining impartiality, neutrality.

6. Maintaining a sense of balance- not talking to or listening to one party over the other

7. Managing the conflict

8. Ensuring the parties' and mediator's safety

9. Maintaining the mediator/client boundary

10. Refraining from giving legal advice or opinions

11. Clarifying the mediator role

12. Assessing for "sufficient knowledge and information" on behalf of the clients

13. Balancing power

14. Listening for parties' identity concerns

15. Responding to own emotions, checking gut

16. Reflecting and Summarizing. (Mediation 101)

17. Empathizing and acknowledging

18. Promoting awareness of unconscious thoughts, beliefs, actions

19. Observing behaviors, body language, expressions, patterns

20. Detecting story lines in the parties' narratives

21. Entering the parties' world; being culturally relative, "in sync"

The Mediator's Failure to Communicate

With all these balls in the air, it's no wonder that, occasionally, the mediator forgets to listen to the parties. In order for the mediator to be *in sync* with the parties and to be present in the mediation, the mediator must be listening and attentive to every single sound in the room. *In sync* simply means the mediator is present in the moment with the clients-- in effect, entering their world. The mediator never has an agenda in mediation but always has only the parties' agenda, except where the standards of practice require the mediator to meet ethical obligations. In the following examples, the mediator is unwittingly not listening to the parties, and is following his or her own agenda, missing opportunities to communicate. In most cases, the mediator reports being distracted by other tasks viewed as important; however, the examples demonstrate that all of the other mediator tasks combined do not compensate for a mediator's failure to listen.

The Mediator's Failure to Listen

Mediator's Agenda 1
Get an Agreement, Any Agreement

The Scene: Mediator gathered information to find out what the custody dispute involved. Mediator had a sense of the parties' attitudes about the dispute when he heard Mother say, "He has basically ignored his son for six years, didn't visit him in the hospital, doesn't have a clue how to give him his breathing treatments, and now just wants to step in and be Dad because he is getting married and his new wife wants to play house with my kid." Mediator rushed to judgment and imagined a solution from Mother's strong words, making up his mind about the outcome before actually mediating the case.

Mediator to Father: "Eric, would you be willing to get training from the hospital about how to do the breathing treatments?"

Father: "Of course."

Mediator: (Patting himself on the back for doing such a good job of getting an agreement on this issue) "Okay, now we have an agreement that Eric will receive this training, and Cindy, that satisfies your concern about Eric knowing how to do Zach's treatments."

The parties were unimpressed.

Describing his tactics in a debriefing session, the mediator explained that he was subscribing to the mediation school of thought that says, "Get an agreement on smaller issues, and you will build a foundation, and be able to work towards agreement on larger issues." This myth did not serve the mediator or the parties. Just because the mediator sees an opportunity to score one for the mediator and check off "agreement" on an issue, does not mean that issue is the one the parties want to focus on. Here, as seen in Father's easy reply, "Of course," this imagined issue was never in dispute. The issues to solve in mediation are those that exist for the parties—whether the parties identify them or the mediator recognizes them. The child's breathing treatments were not presented as an issue. Father never voiced any opposition to them. By stopping the flow of the conversation that would have led to the real issues, the mediator's detour into breathing treatments did not serve the process.

Mediator's Agenda 2

Get an Agreement the Mediator Likes-

Stay on Positions-Don't Get Into Interests

Mediator to Father: "Eric, do you have the proper facilities for your son?"

Father: "What do you mean?"

Mediator: "Well, do you have a room, a bed, and a comfortable home?"

Father: (offended): "Yes."

At this point the mediator has offended Father, primarily because instead of finding out from Father what he wants (listening) in terms of custody, Mediator is making the assumption that Father wants custody (not stated yet) and that Father may not be equipped to handle custody. When given the opportunity to explain, the mediator stated, "Well, he wants custody and I want to find out if he can handle it." Asked if he knew what schedule Father wanted, the mediator stated, "I am just assuming he wants full custody."

Mediator to Father: "Do you want full custody, sole custody, or six months with you and six months with Cindy?"

Father: "I want 6 months!"

Mediator: "Well, what is your work schedule?"

Father: (more offended) "What does that have to do with it? She works too!"

Mother: (interrupting) "There's no way I would ever agree to be away from my child for six months! Are you crazy?!"

Mediator: "Eric, would you consider a schedule that divided time between you and Cindy on a weekly basis?"

Father: "Sure, I want joint custody."

Mediator to Mother: "Cindy, Eric wants joint custody. Would you consider that?"

Mother: "What's that?"

Mediator: "Okay Eric, what do you mean by that?"

Father: "50/50."

Mediator: "Cindy, Eric wants 50/50, would you consider that?"

The mediator's failure to listen kept the parties at the level of positions, and unable to move on to a discussion of interests. Joint custody and 50/50 are positions. The mediator asked questions, seemingly to dig deeper, but failed to fully listen to the responses to the questions, which were simply more positions. The mediator's leading question to Father, suggesting alternative positions, was not helpful because it threw out alternatives that further polarized the parties before the mediator really knew what either party was looking for. In debriefing, Father offered that he was never interested in a six-month rotation, but chose it because it sounded like the best deal the mediator was offering. The mediator never did accomplish the first task in custody mediation, which is to find out what each party wants (exploring interests). An open-ended question such as "Eric, would you be willing to say specifically what parenting time you are looking for?" and then listening to Eric's answer, would have moved Eric from positions. Mother cannot respond to proposals of "50/50" or "joint custody" because they have no meaning to her except as generalities which she would likely reject. The mediator admitted in de-briefing that he had made up his mind early that Father should not have much custody time, having only seen the child a few times in six years, and that Mother should have custody, with occasional time for Father. The Mediator's agenda was to convince Father that he should not have custody and probably did not have the facilities, or an appropriate work schedule. These assumptions did a disservice to the parties, who, if the mediator had listened, in the end turned out to be ready for a true shared parenting arrangement after discussing numerous concerns and filling in the gaps created by six years of near estrangement.

Mediator's Agenda 3

Preempt Conflict by Prejudging It and Not Listening-

Deflect Parties' Negative Comments

The scene: The same case as above. Mother accused Father of not being there for her during the pregnancy and delivery of Zach, who was conceived during a very brief relationship that lasted only a few weeks. In retaliation for her accusation, Father responded:

Father: "Well, how could you expect me to step up when there was no way I could know if he was mine or one of the six other guys you slept with that month?"

Mediator: "Well, I don't think that kind of thing is helping the custody issue we are here to talk about."

Father: (offended) "What? She's allowed to say whatever she wants about me but I can't defend myself?"

By failing to listen, the mediator interrupted a valid exchange between the parties. The mediator attempted to preempt a potential conflict without knowing if there would be a conflict. The mediator guessed how Cindy might have responded if allowed instead of giving Cindy a chance to respond and see what happened. It is possible she may have expected this type of remark and welcomed the opportunity to explain herself. In debriefing, Father said that the mediator's comment made him feel the mediator was not impartial, was defending Cindy, and was biased. Father did not feel his comment was offensive because at that earlier point in their lives, he believed they were both with multiple partners. He felt the mediator was judging him for stating a mere fact of which the mediator had no knowledge. Here, the mediator needed to allow the exchange and observe whether or not Cindy had a reaction to Eric's remark. It was possible the remark would not have fazed her since it was, presumably, a true comment on their lives in the past. In fact, as the case continued, Cindy did not react, and the mediator had no reason to interrupt to stop the comment. The mediator's reaction served only to dilute his role by appearing weak and indirect, trying and failing to control the parties, as if to say, "We are only going to say nice things here," or, worse, "Eric is only allowed to say nice things here." If the remark had inflamed Cindy, then perhaps the mediator would need to intervene, but only if the parties are losing control of themselves and/or their discussion is deteriorating into a shouting match about something even they are not very interested in. If the mediator had allowed communication, and then found the conflict to be escalating, the mediator could regain control appropriately by saying, "Hold on. I'm not sure this is the direction you want to pursue right now. I thought you were beginning to make some progress talking about the schedule. I think you need to get back to that. We don't really have time to waste in here. I would like to see you resolve this and leave here with an agreement."

Mediator's Agenda 4
Fear of Failure

Get Agreement on a Small Issue- Ignore the Big Issue Because

It's Too Difficult to Resolve

The scene: A different case from above. Father is trying to reunite with a daughter he has not seen in eight years, since she was an infant. He has sent many cards and letters and a few pictures over the years, but not consistently. He missed holidays and birthdays altogether in some years. This infuriated Mother and reinforced her belief that Father would only disappoint their daughter with his inconsistency and lack of commitment to her. Mother began to withhold cards that came, becoming cautious about what information she shared with the daughter. As the parties discussed this, they seemed to believe it was relevant to the ultimate issue of whether Father would become a consistent parent. The mediator had another agenda, and decided, purely on her own, to mediate the issue of the cards, trying to get an agreement on what cards would be sent, when, and what Mother would do with them. The mediator was straying from the main goal of changing custody to something healthier for the child. By focusing on the cards (that were purely symbols), the mediator was distracting the parties from the issue they needed to address, physical custody. The parties, new to mediation, did not know they had the right to tell the mediator they weren't very worried about the cards and wanted to mediate the important issue of custody schedules, especially since Father came from out of town and was only available to mediate for one day.

In debriefing, the mediator stated she focused on this issue "because this seems like the easier, smaller issue and if I get agreement on this maybe they will see they can agree on something and it will be easier to get agreement on the bigger issues." With this statement, the mediator implicitly admitting she had no hope the parties would come to an agreement about custody and that Father would forever be tied to his daughter by cards alone. In fact, what seemed like "such an easy issue" should not have been addressed at all because it would not be an issue if the real issue of custody was resolved. The parties were wise enough to know that if they could work out the reunification issue, the cards and presents would take care of themselves. The mediator did not see the whole picture. The mediator needed to listen and pay attention to get a sense of what was important to the parties. Since this was a reunification case, the mediator needed to first find out if reunification was possible. If so, the issue of cards and presents would become irrelevant.

Mediator's Agenda 5
Be a Referee- Defend a Party- Don't Allow Conflict

The mediator who acts as a referee wants peace at all costs, even if it means choosing a side. This mediator is not comfortable listening to both sides and not comfortable being neutral. This tendency is sometimes seen in mediators with a legal background where choosing a side is learned.

Stepmother: "Jean can't get over the divorce—she makes everything about how terrible the divorce was; meanwhile everyone is over it except her. Jack and I have moved on."

Mediator to Stepmother: "No, I don't think Jean is doing that—she's just trying to make you see how it's affecting the kids."

Stepmother (offended) thinking, "This mediator has no clue what is going on here."

In debriefing, the mediator was proud of himself for not ignoring the stepmother's inflammatory remarks, which other mediators might have evasively done. Although this is true, a better way to respond to the inflammatory remarks would be, "Really? Because I didn't hear it that way. What I heard was Jean saying she wants to give the kids time to get used to the changes before introducing another change. Am I wrong about that?" Another possible response would be, "Really? I didn't hear it that way. (Pause) But I understand that that is the way you heard it." That response satisfies both parties, maintaining neutrality of the mediator. Jean will feel defended, even though the mediator stayed neutral, and Stepmother will not feel the mediator has taken Jean's side.

Mediator's Agenda 6
I Have a Beautiful Ending to Your Story-

If You Would Let Me Tell It Instead of You

In a tragic case, Father had just been released from prison and wanted to see his ten-year-old daughter who was being raised by her maternal grandmother. Dad was in jail for vehicular homicide in the death of his wife (his daughter's mother) while they were both very drunk. When clients have undergone a uniquely tragic and ironic event, such as losing a daughter (and wife and mother) by the negligence of the son-in-law, the mediator's response to this information should be more measured than merely to say, "I'm sorry for your loss." The mediator needs to assure the parties that she really gets what happened. The mediator role is sometimes an acting role, and it is okay to be dramatic if the situation calls for it, provided the feelings are genuine. A greater expression of sorrow might be appropriate, "I am so sorry," followed by a solemn silence. Appreciation for the irony or gravity of the misfortune indicates that the mediator notices the uniqueness of the events. A facial expression or shaking of the head or other body language shows that the mediator is moved by the experience and its profundity is not lost on him. An appropriate mediator response could even be an empathetic summarization such as, "I notice your family [a bonding term applied to a very fractured group of people who do not think of themselves as a family; the mediator is "reframing" here] has experienced multiple losses—this must be very hard for you—losing a daughter, losing a son-in-law, losing your wife, losing six years of your life in prison, losing the opportunity to see your daughter grow up." These moments of empathy are meaningful moments to the parties whose response to being understood and acknowledged will likely be favorable towards the mediator. This type of communication by the mediator, which begins with the mediator listening, creates a strong bond of trust. With bonding on this level, even a novice mediator can do little wrong. The parties' attitude towards such a mediator will always be, "You're doing a great job!"

Unfortunately, here the mediator did little empathizing or acknowledging of the parties' profound losses. The maternal grandmother was hesitant to allow Father to see his daughter, but eventually would likely have relented because it also unfolded that she was recently widowed, and now had cancer herself. The mediator, instead of allowing the parties to talk and share information to move towards a mutually beneficial solution, had a solution in mind (without the benefit of knowing the facts). The mediator felt that the father and grandmother should move in together and suggested it to the parties. Grandmother laughed, nervously. Father appeared very uncomfortable, and the parties quickly changed the subject. Nevertheless, the mediator continued along this vein, believing that his solution was the perfect fairytale answer to Father's living alone, grandmother's poor health, and the young daughter's need for both parental figures in her life. If the parties had chosen, or even shown any interest in this solution, the mediator's desires may have been fulfilled, but to impose the mediator's fantasy on the parties whose real lives have been shattered, was inappropriate and out of sync with the parties' needs due to the mediator's failure to listen.

Mediator's Agenda 7
I Can Be All Things to All People ("Mighty Mediator")

In the above scenario, the mediator's response to hearing about the family's tragedy was a blank facial expression as he merely said, "I understand." Parties often feel that no one can possibly understand their unique situations and that even suggesting that one understands is to minimize the party's experience. Grief is unique. It is much less risky and beneficial for the mediator to say, "I can only imagine."

The Parties' Flawed Communication

In addition to mediator failure to communicate, the parties may have faulty communication with each other. Interpersonal communication relies on conscious and unconscious messages. Beneath conscious communication, we all send out and pick up unconscious messages received by our senses. By recognizing an unconscious dimension to communication, a mediator is able to hear, see, and sense what is being said more accurately, and will be able to assist parties to hear each other in new ways.

Communication Theory

Communication is an elusive concept. To discuss communication is to discuss practically everything. Our cells communicate with each other in highly sophisticated processes using hormones, DNA, amino acids, and unknown media. In nature, all creatures communicate with their environment in some way. Communication theory[327] relates to epistemological (study of knowledge) foundations of intellectual thought and, more concretely, to the study of human interactions at the level of thought, language and cultures. Numerous approaches are taken to the study of human communication, and little consensus has been reached[328] because, according to Craig, there are so many theories, with little certainty. Various approaches have been taken to study communication in mediation, including examining parties' information processing styles and cultural differences,[329] noticing body language, intonation, inflection,

---

[327] Anderson, J.A. (1996). *Communication theory: Epistemological foundations.* New York: The Guilford Press.
[328] Craig, R.T. (1993). Why are there so many communication theories? *Journal of Communication, 43*(3), 26-33.
   Meierding, N. (2004). Managing the communication process in mediation. In Folberg, J. & Milne, A. (Eds.) *Divorce and family mediation: Models, techniques and applications* . New York: Guilford Press, 225-247.

stressing of words, voice, and nonverbal signals,[330] analyzing presupposed "conditions" of communication,[331] and comparing mediators' uses of words and nonverbal communication in their opening statements.[332] All of these are useful pursuits in gaining knowledge about communication in mediation. The problem with finding a theory for communication in mediation is that the communication theory literature, in general, proposes an abundance of theories from numerous perspectives, taking myriad approaches (i.e., cultural, empirical, internal). A simple, unified theory could be useful. I offer Gestalt theory as a straightforward, universal, and demonstrable framework that can be uniquely applied to communication in mediation.

Gestalt Therapy Approach to Communication

The beauty of Gestalt therapy is its simplicity. Gestalt therapy, a theory of personality, was introduced to psychology by Fritz and Laura Perls in 1951.[333] The term *Gestalt* refers to the whole, and the study of Gestalt therapy involves examining how man organizes his existence by examining his world holistically rather than in parts. The theory proposes that the whole is greater than the sum of its parts. "Therefore, the whole is a new event, as water is greater than two parts of hydrogen and one part of oxygen, and a hand is greater than four fingers and a thumb."[334]

A concrete way of demonstrating this fundamental principle of Gestalt therapy, that man organizes his existence with reference to the whole, is a blind spot exercise that is commonly used to describe optical illusions.

Instructions for Blind Spot Exercise:

Close your left eye and focus your right eye solely on the dark black cross on the left. Hold the page about twelve inches from your head and move the page slowly towards and then away from your head. You will notice that the black dot on the right disappears and then reappears in your visual field while you move the page. This is because there is a blind spot in your field of vision caused by a bundling together of the axons that form the optic nerve in each eye. Given the anatomy of the eye, it is not surprising that a blind spot can be found. What is surprising, however, is that the brain provides information that is *not there* where the blind spot fails to pick up information. This can be seen in the exercise, where the blind spot has a white background (the same color as the page) meaning that the eye "sees" the background color.

---

[330] Id., 244.
[331] Chilton, S., Cuzzo, M.S.W. (2005). Habermas's Theory of communicative action as a theoretical framework for mediation practice. *Conflict Resolution Quarterly*, 22(3), 325-348.
[332] Szamania, S. (2006). Mediators' communication in victim offender mediation/dialogue involving crimes of severe violence: An analysis of opening statements. *Conflict Resolution Quarterly*, 24(1), 111-127.
[333] Perls, F., Hefferline, R., Goodman, P. (1951). *Gestalt therapy: Excitement and growth in the human personality*. New York: Julian Press.
[334] Latner, J. (1986). *The Gestalt therapy book*. The Center for Gestalt Development, Inc.

Amazingly, when the background color is changed to yellow, pink, purple, or even polka dots or plaid, the eye "sees" the same background. Clearly, our brains see something that we know is not detected by the eye. Our brain is independently providing information to fill in the blind spot in a highly sophisticated way, and very quickly.

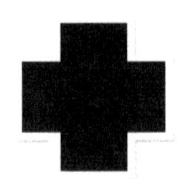

To observe different backgrounds and how the brain can fill in all of them, go to *Seeing More Than Your Eye Does* at https://serendipstudio.org/bb.blindspot1.html

Question for Discussion

How does the blind spot exercise demonstrate the tenet of Gestalt therapy that man organizes his existence with reference to the whole? If the answer is not clear yet, revisit the question at the conclusion of the chapter.

The Unconscious Mind in Communication

Clearly, no one is aware of making a conscious choice to fill in the appropriate background for the blind spot. The unconscious mind is at work, not subtly, but brazenly. This brash behavior of the unconscious mind is the subject of Malcolm Gladwell's book *Blink*.[335] According to Gladwell, the unconscious mind makes decisions the conscious mind is not aware of. "The only way humans could have survived as a species in a dangerous world is to have developed another kind of decision making apparatus that's capable of making very quick judgments based on very little information."[336] Gladwell calls this thought process the "adaptive unconscious" and believes it is what has kept us alive. As defenses go, humans had little else than their minds when they evolved in the wild, and, even today, Gladwell believes

---

[335] Gladwell, M. (2005). *Blink: The power of thinking without thinking*. New York: Little, Brown and Company.
[336] Id., 11, 12.

it is the unconscious thought process that saves us from being killed in traffic, just as it saved our ancestors from being consumed in the wilds.

The interesting thing is that the adaptive unconscious does much more than help with vital, snap decisions. According to experiments described by Gladwell, it serves as an information system on a much wider scale, helping humans to size up people and situations in milliseconds and processing huge amounts of data quickly using a process he calls "thin-slicing," or drawing conclusions about a whole based on a piece. "'Thin-slicing' refers to the ability of the unconscious to find patterns in situations and behaviors based on very narrow slices of experience." [337] According to Gladwell, humans thin-slice because they have to. Thin-slicing is not always accurate, but it is surprisingly accurate most of the time. "It is a central part of what it means to be human."[338] Gladwell describes an experiment done by a group of scientists at the University of Iowa where human subjects played a gambling card game in which they were being cheated. By the fortieth turn of the card, the gamblers had figured out the ruse and learned to change their behavior to protect themselves. However, when the subjects were hooked up to sensors, the gamblers began to reveal physical signs of stress and fear as reactions to being cheated as early as the tenth turn of the card. This is the unconscious mind at work, a source of "information" that is hidden from the conscious mind.

Gladwell calls the unconscious mind a "locked door" and expresses a wish to capture its powers and unleash them into the conscious world, something that would equate to a superpower. In the next breath, however, he reveals this is not possible because science does not understand how it works, or how to access or control it.[339] But science is studying it. The study, Project Implicit is divided into three Implicit Association Tests that work by having subjects make snap decisions between familiar pairs of ideas. The test is available at https://www.implicit.harvard.edu/. A participant's email address is identification as a subject in an ongoing study. Although participants do not choose the tests that are administered to them, they may take a seemingly unlimited variety of tests and results are reported based on responses. Results reveal partiality to vegetables or meat, for example, as well as racial or ethnic prejudices, political leanings, and numerous other preferences and thoughts.

Gladwell and others conclude that the door to the unconscious is likely not closed completely, and that the way to influence the unconscious mind is through the conscious mind. Although people do not seem to deliberately choose their unconscious attitudes, they do form, in part, from the conscious experience. "The giant computer that is our unconscious silently crunches all the data it can from the experiences we've had, the people we've met, the lessons we've learned, the books we've read, the movies we've seen and so on and it forms an opinion…the disturbing thing is that our unconscious attitudes may be utterly incompatible with our stated conscious values."[340] Of importance to the mediator is that people

---

[337] Id., 23.
[338] Id., 43.
[339] Id., 49.
[340] Id., 85.

behave out of their unconscious beliefs, and that in order to understand what parties communicate unconsciously, the mediator should be aware that everyone is also communicating unconsciously.

Gestalt theory holds that much of what happens in relationships (including the relationship with the self) is hidden from awareness. In mediation and in life, communication becomes faulty when the thinker is unaware of the thoughts. Such a thinker is not communicating effectively with himself or with others. A mediator who recognizes an unconscious dimension to communication is able to listen to what is said as well as what is unsaid.

Awareness

Gestalt theory holds that the organism is self-regulating.[341] Another way of saying this is the organism is self-correcting. Awareness is the mechanism by which the organism self-corrects. The mere attainment of awareness enables the organism to self-correct. This is a humanistic view and supports the classic mediation premise of client autonomy and self-determination. By merely becoming aware of one's behaviors, motives, and thoughts that were previously unrecognized, a person is set on the path of self-correction, without more.

Awareness means simply having knowledge or information about something. Fritz Perls is said to have believed that awareness is an aspect of all existence, organic and inorganic, along with time and space,[342] "I am sure that one day we will discover that awareness is a property of the universe—extension, duration, awareness." [343] Awareness, in Gestalt therapy is never-ending like onion layers or Chinese lacquer boxes.[344] Ubiquitous, awareness occurs naturally over the course of mediation. It is not unusual for clients to come to a second or third appointment for mediation with new realizations that just came to them.

Awareness comes to the conscious mind simply by being in the present,[345] a state that enables one to focus on what is, rather than the past or the future. Most people spend little time in the present, wanting to think about what happened or what will happen. Certain activities force presence, such as a crisis, danger, or more peaceful pursuits such as worship, prayer, meditation, reading or thinking. There is actually little a mediator can or should do to promote awareness, since it is the clients' own process. By creating an environment that is calm, comfortable, compassionate, and nonjudgmental, the mediator promotes awareness by offering an opportunity for clients to see what is and observe themselves. In listening, the mediator is focusing on the present moment (what is being said), modeling awareness. Being heard, hearing, and speaking are all ways of gaining awareness. When a mediator senses that a party's behavior or beliefs exist apart from awareness, it is often enough for the mediator to see this, and do nothing more. By waiting

---

[341] Latner, 1986, 4.
[342] Id., 12.
[343] Id.
[344] Id., 3.
[345] Id., 76

for the client to progress to awareness (or not) the mediator creates an open space for awareness to happen if it is going to happen.

At times, a client is ready for responses from the mediator that will assist the client in gaining awareness, as in the case of Susan and Joe (Chapter 5) where it was clear to the mediator that Susan was experiencing a conflict between what she was saying (conscious belief) and the unspoken awareness she had about her son and his father and their strong, positive relationship. Susan appeared to be "stuck" in a belief she could no longer sustain. The experienced mediator took the risk, obliquely, of asking Susan if she could *imagine* doing what Joe was asking her to do, in an effort to find out if Susan would come to a new awareness. However, often the mediator would not be proactive to elicit awareness because people are not ready to be aware of everything. Clearly, awareness is something that unfolds over an entire lifetime and it is not a mediator's province to decide when a party is ready for a particular realization. It is not always a mediator's (or even a therapist's) role to intrude on a person's lack of awareness. Unconscious behavior can be protective, as in denial. Awareness is a very powerful catalyst, according to Gestalt therapy, and allows people to "choose and/or organize ...existence in a meaningful manner."[346] More typical than the case of Susan and Joe are situations where the mediator (or almost anyone) can sense a party's lack of awareness about something. In the case of Darla and John, the mediator did very little to bring about awareness, but was able to observe the clients "self-correct" using their own awareness mechanisms.

The Case of Darla and John

A Case Study in Silently Supporting Awareness

Darla and John had not spoken in two months since their last mediation session. They were waiting for appraisals to come back in order to value several parcels of real estate they owned. They had been married for 24 years and had no children but lots of animals.

During the two months between mediations, Darla seethed with anger at John because she felt he ignored her needs during their long marriage. She ran their successful family business (she had the professional license enabling her to do so) while John "golfed' and "lived off of her labor." John wanted her to come back to their home, reconcile with him, and could not understand why "all of a sudden" she was so angry. Everything was fine. "We were happy." After 24 years, she must have some kind of problem to be acting this way now.

---

[346] Yontef, G. (1993). Gestalt therapy: An introduction. In *Awareness, dialogue, and process*. The Gestalt Journal Press. Retrieved October 7, 2009 from http://www.gestalt.org/yontef.htm

For the first five minutes of the mediation session the only thing they could do was yell at each other, loudly. They were having a big argument. The mediator could see that they were both so full of steam they could barely stick to one topic for longer than a few seconds before they were on to the next. The mediator hesitated to stop them because she could see they needed to let off some of the steam and wanted to let each other know how much they both hurt and how frustrated they were. John became so angry at what Darla was saying that he stood up and told the mediator he was leaving, "I'll still mediate," he said, "But it will have to be in separate rooms because I'm not listening to anymore of *this*." The mediator said, "Okay, but now I need to say something." The parties respectfully stopped. The mediator then said, "It's fine with me if this is how you guys want to spend your time here. It's fine with me if you want to mediate in separate rooms. But I can tell you that if you do that, you will reduce by about 90% your chances of resolving this. I haven't heard either one of you say anything that I haven't seen resolved in hundreds of cases. If you'll sit down and let me help you discuss the issues you came here to resolve, I think you'll be able to work this out."

The mediator wanted John to sit down and wanted the mediation to go on as planned. His anger and threat to leave imperiled the process. The mediator needed John to sit down, and, in an effort to spare his pride, used a made-up statistic to convince him that it was in his best interest to continue seated in the room. The mediator believed that Darla's anger probably was, as John observed, sudden and magnified. The mediator sensed that Darla was as angry, or angrier, at herself than she was at John. The injustices she recited apparently happened over a long period of time while she tolerated the situation. Perhaps someday Darla will benefit from seeing that much of her anger was at herself. (Certainly John would benefit from such awareness.) But the mediator did not believe that Darla would benefit from anyone pointing it out to her now. Extreme anger or agitation is a sign of fear, a clear signal to the mediator that a party's unconscious behavior is protective. Similarly, some clients misdirect anger at a spouse that really belongs with their family of origin, manifesting anger they adopted as children when they identified with the parent they saw as the "victim." Others bottle up anger that was originally directed at a parent they loved but felt forbidden from expressing. Still others manifest anger or hatred towards their spouse that is a disguise for shame felt as a result of rejection by the other and feelings of inadequacy and fear of not being good enough. These feelings are private, and it would be intrusive for a mediator to explore them, uninvited. By simply listening, empathizing and acknowledging the anger, the mediator is promoting awareness without soliciting it.

The Contact Boundary

The Gestalt study of human personality starts with the Contact Boundary, the fundamental concept that defines personality because a person exists by differentiating self from other and by connecting self to others.[347] The function of the boundary is two-fold: to allow contact and to protect from contact. Contact can be harmful, yet contact is wanted because contact equals survival and growth. The Contact Boundary is, literally, the skin, and figuratively, the mind, where communication occurs. More abstractly, the boundary is the figurative "place" where one person ends and another begins. The Contact Boundary is subject to disturbances, or interruptions. The two extremes of a dysfunctional Contact Boundary are fusion (also called confluence) and isolation.[348] Both are unhealthy and very common. Gestalt therapy is about regulating the Contact Boundary.

Interruptions (or Disturbances) of the Contact Boundary

How the Contact Boundary is Regulated

Interruptions of the Contact Boundary are unconscious ways in which the organism regulates the Contact Boundary. Babies and dogs interrupt the Contact Boundary by turning their eyes from a stare, overwhelmed with contact. The four main interruptions of the Contact Boundary below are practiced by everyone. They are unconscious, but not necessarily hidden. In each example, self-observation, introspection, or feedback from the outside can bring the disturbance into awareness. The behaviors described are performed instinctively without awareness, and typically under a mistaken belief about the behavior. It is the lack of awareness and the mistaken beliefs that affect communication between individuals and within the individual. The cycle suggested by Gestalt theory is unaware interruption of the contact boundary followed by awareness followed by self-regulation followed by more unaware interruption of the boundary and so on. The goal is responsibility or owning of one's behavior and feelings.[349] This sounds very much like mediation where individual responsibility, as opposed to blaming, is a goal and the responsibility for feelings belongs to the party.

Projection

In projection, a person attributes to the outside that which is self. The blind spot exercise is an example of projection. The mind fills in what is missing, thereby attributing to the outside (the page) that which is self (the brain's perception). People typically project qualities onto others they know to exist in themselves. A person who never lies (if there could be such a person) would probably not call others "liar." When people make unfounded or untested assumptions, have suspicions, or ascribe qualities onto another, projection is likely to be involved. This is why, in our culture, we say, "It takes one to know one." Sometimes there can be some truth to projection, but it is just as often inaccurate. Projection is innocent. Children project all the time as a way of learning about their environment. A child will make assumptions

---

[347] Id., 10.
[348] Id.
[349] Id., 12.

about the world based on his own world formed by the information he has. Nevertheless, projection obstructs communication by allowing potentially false information to be perceived as true. In projection, the self-accepts as true information about the outside that comes from the inside. Pathological projection is attribution of facts or ideas to a situation without awareness and without taking responsibility for the conclusions. This happens frequently when people add meaning to what others say without awareness. What seems to be most damaging to human relationships is when people project good or bad qualities onto one another as a substitute for actual information.

Retroflection

Retroflection is a split within the self. The self-substitutes self for the environment. The self does to the self what the self wants to do to the environment. There are many examples of retroflection. When a person is sitting and waiting impatiently for something to happen, fidgeting or shaking of a foot or hand are retroflection. The rapid movement of the foot or fingers is what the self wants from the environment, "Hurry up!" Babies learn, apparently in the womb, to self-soothe with thumb sucking. Excessive body piercing, excessive facial hair, or excessive makeup are retroflection, doing to the self (hiding, disguising, mutilating) what one wants to do to the environment. Retroflection can be functional as in resisting the impulse to express anger by biting one's lip or stomping one's foot. It can be destructive as in cutting or suicide. It is the doing to oneself what one wants to do to someone else (or the world). Retroflection can lead to isolation because by substituting the self for the environment, one is deprived of the environment and others. In couples, starting an argument to create intimacy is a form of retroflection—attacking the relationship (self) to get something (intimacy) wanted from the environment (the other). Fidgeting and awkward body movements are almost always a retroflection, which means there is meaning behind them. Retroflection is relevant to communication because it is a form of communication.

Introjection

Introjection is a "should." It is foreign material absorbed without discriminating or assimilating. When we swallow whole a value passed down from parents or teachers or taken in from the environment without realizing our uncritical acceptance of it, it is an introject, or a "should." Everyone operates by introjects without realizing it. All disturbances of the Contact Boundary are survival mechanisms, and introjection serves the purpose of allowing us to make judgments quickly. Even the most open-minded among us subscribe to introjected, unchallenged, and unexamined values without awareness. Introjection is the imposition of these values and their resulting behavior on the self. Introjection can be healthy. When one needs to absorb material uncritically (for instance, in order to regurgitate it for an "A" on a test), it is a skill that comes in handy. However, it is often unhealthy. Children and adults internalize their parents' values (which might be introjects) without judging the content for themselves. An example is a mother who harshly disciplined her daughter for lying, while the daughter's "lie" was a typical protective defense that made sense from a child's perspective. Although children should be taught the value of honesty, this mother placed not lying above all other values, even self-defense, in a way that did not appear to be thoughtful or protective of her child. In the Vince and Julie case (Chapter 3), Vince operated his entire life under an introject that in every family, one parent is always preferred over the other. It is not known where Vince came by this belief, but it did not appear that he had ever questioned it until it was gently and indirectly challenged by the mediator. Other destructive introjects seen by mediators are that children belong in service to their parents, that children's desires should not be considered, and that children should not be given deference or power, that a betrayal should never be forgiven, that children need to be punished with hitting or violence, that parents should yell or speak sternly to their children, and that the teacher or priest is always right.

Deflection

Deflection is the avoidance of contact. Being polite or tactful at the expense of being direct and entirely truthful are deflections. In some cultures, there is no word for "no" or "yes" because these words are considered to cause offense to the listener. In such languages, the listener must use context in order to detect a "no" or "yes" answer. With deflection, communication is indirect, avoiding eye contact and giving incomplete information. Placating, not tolerating silence and filling it up with meaningless chatter (verbosity), vagueness, understating facts, talking about someone rather than to them are other examples of deflection. Contact can feel uncomfortable. Adjusting the contact boundary with deflection makes contact bearable; however, communication is interrupted and compromised. Deflection can make communication difficult because the speaker is not saying what he is thinking or feeling, and is unaware that his discomfort is caused by beliefs about which he is unaware. Deflection is often detected by a gut feeling in the listener that the speaker is not being direct. It is, in itself, an unconscious communication of discomfort.

The Case of Tim and Marianne

A Case Study in Clarifying Deflective Communication

Tim and Marianne mediated custody of their three daughters, ages 10, 8, and 6. Their arrangement was primary physical custody with Mother and partial physical custody with Father. Four years went by and Tim contacted the mediator to request additional mediation but only wanted to mediate if the mediator would include the children, now 14, 12, and 10, in the mediation. Tim said he had remarried and had a baby son. Marianne remained single and was very close with their daughters. The mediator asked Tim why he felt the children should come to mediation. Tim was unable to answer the mediator's question directly. He revealed that he felt alienated from his daughters and had been thinking for about a year that he might "just give up the fight for custody and just concentrate on my new family." The mediator was alarmed because Tim was the only father his girls had, and father and daughters loved each other deeply. Marianne did not want the children to come to mediation. Tim insisted it was necessary saying he wanted to "give a voice to the children." The mediator's job at this point was to figure out what Tim was really trying to say. In caucus, the mediator explored Tim's thoughts and experiences around his daughters. Caucus was the chosen forum because Tim was already feeling "alienated" from

Marianne and the girls and felt judged and marginalized by Marianne. To ask him to discuss his feelings in joint session would have been an infringement of his privacy and might have caused him embarrassment. In caucus, Tim told the mediator that in four years he had never discussed the divorce or the custody situation with his daughters, although he wanted to initiate a conversation to explain to them how much he loved them and valued his (limited) time with them. He simply did not know how to speak to his daughters. The mediator was able to figure out that what Tim meant by "give a voice to the children" was give a voice to *himself* and learn to communicate with his daughters. His feelings were too painful to admit openly, "I don't know how to get close to these girls I love so much," so he deflected his communication by being vague. It can also be said that Tim was projecting (the first interruption of the contact boundary) his discomfort and inability to speak to his girls on the outside, in the form of stating the girls' needing "a voice" rather than his needing a voice.

A Final Note on Communication in Mediation

By recognizing the trouble spots in communication, the mediator becomes open to the possibility that communication is not only what is said, but what is unsaid, or said through nonverbal or unconscious means. The mediator can take responsibility for the mediator's role in faulty communication by taking the time and effort needed to listen and pay attention to everything that happens in session. Gestalt theory is a good fit as a mediation communication theory because it aligns with fundamental mediation principles. Both mediation and Gestalt therapy are based on personal responsibility, "owning" one's beliefs, feelings, and decisions, recognizing unconscious communication, and being introspective and self-correcting. The mediator cannot be responsible for the parties' communication, but, by being aware of unconscious communication as well as indirect communication in the form of the "interruptions" to the Contact Boundary, the mediator can be aware of possibilities for communication beyond the literal plane. In addition, the mediator can use his or her awareness of unconscious communication to promote awareness for clients about what they are experiencing inside, allowing them, if they choose, to bring such information into the open.

Chapter Twelve

"Skill is better than strength." -- Polish Proverb

Mediation Skills (Mediation 102)

The Mediator Toolbox

As artists, mediators constantly hone new skills, resurrect old skills, copy other mediator's skills, and share their skills. The following is a collection of skills, tools, techniques and reminders. Some have already been discussed in previous chapters, listed here for handy reference.

1. *Observe patterns, roles, consistent behaviors, words and themes.*

Patterns are habits—they are unconscious. By observing, the mediator helps parties become aware of actions they might not have noticed in a non-threatening way. Once aware of their actions, parties can then choose consciously if they want to continue such actions. This is an example of how the mediator uses conflict (his stock in trade) to resolve conflict.

The Case of Carol and Andrew

A Case Study in Patterns, Roles & Themes

Andrew and Carol were approaching their 25th anniversary when Andrew wanted out of the marriage. He was twenty years older than Carol, now in his seventies, and wanted to enjoy life without Carol. He explained that her depression placed a wedge in their marriage. Although he'd been married once before, his marriage to Carol bore him two children, and in their earlier years Carol was the "love of his life." He still cared for her, wanted to continue a friendship, but desired no intimate relationship with her. The case was complex financially because Andrew was a self-made business man and owned layers of business interests that had to be sorted out. Andrew was impatient with the pace of the mediation and seemed to believe that because he offered Carol a generous settlement and she would be "set for life," there should be no scrutiny or delay in reaching a quick settlement. Every time the parties appeared for one of nearly a dozen sessions needed to complete the case, Andrew would consume the first ten minutes complaining about how slow this was going, and if something decisive isn't done "today," he intends to quit mediation and go right to court.

Carol, on the other hand, felt exactly the opposite and similarly consumed mediation time complaining, but her complaints were about how fast the process was going, not giving her sufficient time to meet with her attorney, read and absorb all of the documentation, and obtain information and advice to help her make decisions.

The mediator was at a loss for how to reconcile their opposing viewpoints about the pace of the process. The mediator decided to comment on the paradoxical pattern she observed, and how it seemed to repeat itself every session. The mediator saw Carol struggling and did not see her as "passive/aggressive" and "procrastinating" as Andrew described her. Andrew's hurried demeanor and unreasonable deadlines made the mediator (and Carol) feel pressured. The mediator called a caucus, but that intervention only gave the parties an opportunity to reinforce their complaints and did not help. In joint session, the mediator decided to comment on what she observed as a pattern. "You have both shared your feelings with me and I am convinced that you, Andrew, genuinely feel that this is going at a snail's pace. You want this to be over yesterday and are very anxious to move on with your life. You, on the other hand, Carol, feel like you just stepped onto a rollercoaster against your will and it is taking you somewhere you don't want to go, fast! You feel pressured and hurried. I don't know how to resolve the difference in the way you both perceive this, but I do feel that you are working at cross-purposes and I am not surprised there is no agreement yet. In order to get an agreement, you are probably going to need to understand how the other person feels." The parties gained an increased awareness of what they were doing and how they were sabotaging the process, and were able to change their behavior and get an agreement.

2. *Use humor and ice breakers (carefully).*

If parties like and trust the mediator, it goes a long way towards getting an agreement. Humor in divorce mediation may sound like an oxymoron, and it often is. Most people will appreciate some comic relief, and a mediator who can pull it off can gain some good will with humor, preferably humor that is directed at the mediator (not the parties). On rare occasions, the parties are receptive to humor directed at them. An example occurred in a court-connected compulsory mediation between two teenage parents who were practically children themselves, but had grown up quickly in the last six months. The mediator noticed that they were acting infantile, calling each other names like two kids in a school yard. The mediator was half-expecting them to stick out their tongues. Impulsively, the mediator started to laugh. Both teenagers looked at the mediator quizzically. Then, they got it and also began to laugh. The mediator affectionately said, "Sorry I just laughed, but you guys reminded me of two little kids fighting. You're funny." The parties laughed too and decided they did not want to behave like children. They were committed to being good parents. This is also an example of getting "in sync" with clients and entering their world. Nevertheless, it is important to observe boundaries and use humor with humility and respect. If humor offends, trust is very hard to recover.

3.   Getting in sync with the parties

In addition to the example in 2 above, there are other ways to get "in sync" with parties. Using their words and phrases, even when they are unfamiliar to the mediator, gives parties a sense that the mediator is one of them and deserves their trust and respect. Without discussing the mediator's parenthood, it is possible, for instance, for a mediator to express understanding for behaviors of children at various ages. A mediator who understands that a seven year old boy is not likely to pick up the telephone to call the other parent, or that a teenage girl might not go out of her way to spend "quality time" with her parents gives parties a comfort level and trust in the mediator. Asking questions about the children to show interest, such as how they are doing in school, responding to their cute and clever stories about the children, and even asking to see the child's picture creates a bond of trust with parents.

4.   Reflection and Summarization (Mediation 101)

Reflection and Summarization (Chapter 5) are never out of style. If a mediator is sitting in a mediation with no clue what to do, even feeling awkward and embarrassed about her bewilderment, Reflection and Summarization are almost always an easy way out of the awkward silence. When Reflection and Summarization are not in order (because they have already been tried, exhaustively, refer to Skill No.11.

5.   Don't get on the bus.

This is mediator speak for "Don't buy in to the beliefs of either party." The mediator might find himself heartily agreeing with one side and mightily disagreeing with the other side. If the parties know this, they get the sense the mediator is not doing his or her job. Even the party whose side the mediator has taken will be disappointed in the mediator. After all, the parties paid for a neutral service, and if the case does not resolve, they may very likely blame the mediator for not appearing impartial.

6.   Climb over a brick wall.

Don't give up too quickly. If parties come to mediation, chances are they expect to be there for a while, and will respect a mediator who tries to revive a mediation that seems to be on life support. Unless both parties convincingly make it very clear that they both want to give up and leave, the mediator should be the last one standing. When it seems like all efforts have been exhausted, use transparency to express to the parties that there seem to be unsurmountable obstacles, but you believe there is a chance they can overcome them. Ask each party what they might do, individually, the close the gap if settlement is what they want to achieve.

7. Think of mediation as a game of Solitaire or Chess.

In solitaire, it is the deck against the player. There is no other player, or outside influence to affect the game. There is a rule against shuffling the deck. It is a closed system. The game is predestined once the deck is stacked. Every Solitaire player knows how it feels to reach the end of a losing game. One full turn of the deck without a play means game over. There is no way to refresh the game. In mediation, when it feels like "game over" there is no rule against changing the game. Nearly any change is like a reshuffling of the deck. The mediator has substantial power to alter the game. Taking a break, offering refills of drinks, ending the session early and rescheduling, changing the subject, talking about the process, commenting on how much the mediator would like to see the parties find a satisfactory outcome, are all ways to shuffle the deck. All of these interventions hold the possibility of effecting a change. For instance, a conversation could occur in the hallway on the way to the bathroom. A party alone could get away from the mediation room for a drink, and think a new thought at the water fountain or receive a phone call that could make a key difference for the conflict. As in an actual shuffling of a deck, there is no guarantee, only a chance that some change could lead to the way out. *Being open to the possibility* is part of the excitement of being a mediator (and playing Solitaire!)

8. Brainstorm—Make suggestions, share ideas, ask questions.

There are always ideas no one has considered. Often, an idea proposed by the mediator will sound impractical to the parties, but will lead to an idea that is perfect for them. When parties are stuck and searching for ideas, offer to help. "Here's an idea. Please don't feel like you ever have to do what I suggest- I merely offer it to get you thinking."

9. When in doubt, use time as a factor.

Time is an often-overlooked tool. When a proposed solution seems desirable, but impossible, see if time can help. "If you cannot afford it this year, would you consider trying to pay it in two years?"

10. Don't get caught up in the facts; externalize the facts and the law.

Don't see the facts as set in stone. The parties' experience belongs to them and it is as fluid as their perceptions. The facts can change. Be open to that possibility. When the facts are unpleasant or the law is unpalatable and "against" a party, externalizing is how the mediator separates the messenger from the message. Use of an easel or other board or screen upon which to project words, numbers, and images allows the mediator to place all of the bad news on an external surface. That surface, or the easel, becomes a separate force in the room. Similarly, the mediator can provide actual copies of the divorce or support laws where a particular law must be considered, but is not particularly appealing. The same goes for support guidelines in the form of grids or formulae. The objective is to figuratively separate the facts and/or the law from the mediator as the source so that the parties do not associate the mediator with the unpleasant reality they must face.

11. Comment on process.

Commenting on process is something the mediator can do when sensing a potential impasse to inspire parties to keep on trying. "In order to get to an agreement, you need to continue to talk about this. Would you like to leave this subject now and move on to something else; then we can return to this later? Maybe by then you will be able to think of something that works." Or, a comment on process can be pedestrian, such as, "I can tell you that this process does work, but only if you keep talking. Having done this for many years, I'm convinced the key to settlement is getting a true understanding of the other party's perspective, as strange as that might sound." Commenting on process is allowed anytime, especially if the mediator is at a loss for what to do next. It acts as a unifier. The process is something that everyone in the room is engaged in cooperatively, even if on opposite sides or roles. The process is something all parties have presumably agreed to. The process is the reason everyone is there. Commenting on process brings the focus to the present moment and takes the focus off the potential impasse, creating the possibility for fresh perspectives.

12. Mediator Language: Respectful, Considerate, and Euphemistic

Don't use this language with your adult children. It makes them angry. I say this tongue-in-cheek, but I know a mediator who use reflection with her adult kids, and they caught on immediately, "Mom, stop trying that mediator stuff on us." Mediator language is not the language you use with your friends or colleagues. You really are taking some of your words from a script.

Instead of saying this……	Say this….
Please explain what you want. Or, Okay, I'd like you to explain your side now.	Would you be willing to say what you are looking for? Or, Would you be comfortable responding?
Explain your position.	Would you be willing to tell me your perspective?
Would you like to set ground rules about name-calling?	I would prefer for there not to be name calling. Or, I am not comfortable with name-calling.
If you'd like to leave, there is nothing I can do about it. It is your choice.	I invite you to please sit down. The one thing I know about this process is that it can only work if you are here and participating.
Is that all?	Is there more?
Custody	Parenting
You two	Your family
Divorce	Changing family or Restructuring of your family
Home	Mom's House or Dad's House
Let Dad have time on weekends	Agree on a schedule to share parenting time
Compromise	Tweak it to meet both of your needs
I'm Confused	Help me understand
All right! That's enough. Stop!	I need to stop you. Or, Hold on. I need to speak. Or, I need to do my job.
We	I or You

Interrupting	I want to check in with you. Or, I'm wondering if this is helpful.
No, that's not what [other party] is saying. She is just saying [blank].	Really? Is that what you heard? Because I didn't hear it that way. I heard [something else]. Am I wrong about that?
How does that make you feel?	I can imagine you might be concerned about that. Or, I can imagine you might feel [sad, happy, worried] about that.
I notice you are crying.	Nothing. Hand over a Kleenex.
You said….	I heard you say….
Interviewing….	Ask open-ended questions.
Cross-examining	Reflect back and ask for feedback or clarification
You indicated (attorney speak)	I heard you say
Arguing	Reflect, ask questions
The past is over. I want to focus on the present.	If you want to talk about the past, that is fine. I just want you to be aware that you have been talking about what happened for 30 minutes, and you haven't been discussing the schedule, which you said you wanted to address.
Susan, John wants alternating weekends	Susan, would you be willing to respond? (Susan knows what John said. She heard it.)
Nothing when parties demonstrate cooperation, kindness, considerateness.	Say, "I appreciate that." or "Thank you," with affirming nod and appreciative eye contact and facial expression.

13. Keep it balanced.

The cardinal rule for a mediator is to maintain balance in attention to the parties. In a two party mediation, the mediator's attention is highly visible to the parties, and it occupies much of their attention. Parties are acutely aware of who is getting the mediator's attention. While speaking to and/or listening to one side, the mediator needs to make eye contact with the other side, as well as use body language signifying that the mediator's attention is also on the other party. This skill can feel nearly impossible for the novice mediator (it did for me in the beginning) but comes with practice. The mediator should be sensitive to any misperception that he appears to be more interested in one side than the other. Focus should be shifted from one side to another, never forgetting that there are two people who need attention.

14. Pay attention to body language.

Body language, often unconscious, is personal, and the mediator should be respectful towards it. Some body language can be embarrassing and the mediator should not call attention to it out of respect to the party. At other times, body language becomes a tool for the mediator. A client who appears shut down or reticent may be hard to approach. The mediator noticing such body language has an opportunity to approach the party with an icebreaker. "Glenn, I noticed you looking down at the table while Judy was talking and I was wondering what you think about all of this." The mediator has conveyed to Glenn that she has been giving him her attention, thinking about him, and making neutral observations, not assumptions.

15. Encourage parties to address each other.

It may feel more comfortable to the parties to talk to the mediator instead of each other. There is nothing wrong with this; after all, it is one of the functions of the mediator to be an intermediary, or go-between. However, if parties do not take the opportunity to have direct contact with each other, they miss experiencing powerful moments of empowerment and recognition of each other. *Always* remember that the key to peacemaking is to enable empathy for each other's perspective. This is never automatic. Each side's defenses prohibit that. The parties need to invest time into listening and understanding each other's point of view, and they come into the process strongly resisting it. When the mediator hears a party say something that the mediator senses needs to be said to the other party directly, he may say to the speaker, "I hear what you are saying, and you sound convincing, but the person who needs to believe you is Christy. Would you be comfortable explaining to Christy directly with me listening?"

16. Reframe

Reframing offers a new perspective for the parties. It can be a positive or neutral spin on a negative belief. For example, parties who see themselves as alienated, separated, or a "broken" family should be referred to by the mediator as "your family." The mediator knows they do not view themselves as "family" but offers this perspective in an indirect, non-threatening and powerful way because it is true. It's more than a mere device; it's the truth.

17. Give thanks and praise.

Recognition is not something that only takes place between the parties. The mediator can give recognition to parties. When parties do anything positive or productive, the mediator has an opportunity to offer recognition. Notice when a party cooperates, gives in on something, apologizes, admits something, agrees with something, and say "Thank you. I appreciate that," using lots of eye contact and positive facial expression. This can feel clumsy at first (it did for me), but it's well worth overcoming the clumsy feeling because recognition feels like a breath of fresh air to your client and will soon feel natural to the mediator.

18. Do not Include children in mediation.

In past editions, I addressed the strategy of including children in mediation. In fact, this is a process O.J. Coogler recommended "…if the mediator finds that their participation may facilitate settlement."[350] I have never included children in mediation because, although some of today's mediators do (see this part in the first and second editions of this book), I believe it does much more to hurt than to help children to include them in adult conflict. It puts them squarely in the middle of their parents' conflict, suggesting to them that they are the mediator. The children are not mediators! Do not be persuaded by parents who put their children in that untenable position. Even when the children are fully grown adults, I am of the opinion that it is rarely, if ever, helpful to them to become part of their parents' conflict or to even know the intimate details of it.

19. Explore the prospect of unilateral change.

The dance in which the parties have participated for years or decades is carefully choreographed by the parties, and the mediator can do little to inspire a change in even one small step. Any suggestion for improving their interaction is met with, "Yeah, but I tried that already and it didn't work. She just does the

---

[350] Coogler, 1978, pp. 111, 123.

same thing. I have tried everything and nothing works." When the parties have a rebuttal for every possible intervention known to man, it is time for the mediator to introduce the concept of unilateral change. This can be done in caucus or in joint session. The first step is to say to the party who has "tried everything" to change this unhealthy dynamic, "Do you know what? I think he is not ever going to change." This suggestion usually throws a party off-balance because it is not what she is expecting to hear. She is expecting to hear the mediator lecture about how both parties have to cooperate and change a little bit to meet somewhere in the middle. By surprising the client with this statement, the mediator primes her for the next suggestion, "Do you know that I believe that everything the two of you do and say to each other is a reaction? And I truly believe that if only one of you makes a permanent change it will ultimately change the whole system? I know it's hard to imagine, but go with me for a minute, because I have seen it happen dozens of times. Whenever you are ready to say 'enough' you do have the power to change this two-step that is going on here. Change your reaction and he will have no choice but to change his. Not right away. He'll keep trying to get you to go back to the old way. But be patient and you will find that you have some power here." This intervention does not always work because many interlocked couples want to continue the dance they know; however, some people are able to break free and find the possibility of "unilateral change" to be liberating.

20. Take the children's perspective

If parties are intractably combative, the mediator might wait for a pause and say something like, "I'm listening to you and imagining that this is how it feels to your child-- like a war is going on in here." Sometimes this perspective can be illuminating. Another perspective rarely seen by embattled parties is the child's perspective towards the *other party*. Each parent sees the child through a myopic lens that blurs the other party's existence from view. But this is never the child's true viewpoint. Offering the child's perspective on the other party goes something like this: "Hold on. I just want to remind you of something. This is the person your child loves more than anyone in the world except you. Am I wrong about that? This is the person you chose to be the mother for your child. Your child sees herself as one-half you and one-half you. Do you know that anything you do or say to each other you are doing or saying to your child? So, every time you disrespect Jen, you are disrespecting your daughter?" To the mediator's delight, the vast majority of combative clients respond very favorably to this type of intervention because they do not feel confronted. They see the mediator as advocating for their child, and do not react defensively. It is important to maintain balance and not direct the comment at only one party. Occasionally a party will inform the mediator that, "No. I did not choose her as the mother of my children." The mediator knows that a simple, unassailable biology lesson will refute this assertion. The mediator does not give a biology lesson at this point, but remains silent and uses only a facial expression and body language to make her point. A faint smile, a shrug of the shoulders, a nod of the head conveys that the mediator is not going to argue the point, but knows her biology. For the rare party who does not understand how a child feels when one parent disparages the other, I offer stronger language, "In my experience with families and kids, I have learned that when a child hears someone say something negative about one of their parents, it feels like a gut-punch." Kids do not like it when anyone, especially their other parent, denigrates their parent."

21. Responding to recalcitrant parents

Sometimes clients resist change by letting the mediator know that what is being suggested is just too much trouble. Driving twenty extra minutes in traffic every morning to take a kid to school instead of using a school bus, changing a longstanding work schedule, paying for airline tickets, buying a duplicate PlayStation, taking the time to email or text the other parent are examples of tasks parents will balk at. The mediator's response of "It's not easy. I agree. Welcome to parenthood!" is oddly persuasive. This response neutralizes the impact of a potentially intrusive request by affirming the parental role. Most parents respond with acceptance because, when it comes down to it, they love parenting, even when it is a burden.

22. Responding to "The judge will correct this injustice."

With genuine regret and sympathy, the mediator must correct the misperception that there is a judge sitting on a high pedestal with a robe and gavel, this very minute, just waiting for a dissatisfied parent to walk into the courtroom to correct all injustices with the wave of a pen. This intervention must be made with care not to misrepresent the courts and not to contravene legal advice. An example is parties who are deadlocked over a scheduling issue that involves, for instance, immutable time commitments, duties towards other children, or other immovable obstacles. Here is an opportunity for the mediator to offer a reality check about the court alternative. "You know, this is hard. It's really a puzzle that you need to take responsibility for. I wish I could tell you that someone else can do this for you. But, unfortunately, I don't think even a judge would solve this in a way that satisfies you. Most judges are too important to have to listen to every minuscule detail of your day—like where you are at 3:00 p.m. on a Thursday…..that's my job." (At this point, most people will laugh and get the point that no one but them can really tailor their custody order to their family's needs.)

23. Suggest a family meeting.

Some co-parenting parties will present unwieldy issues that involve family schedules, family spats, teenage and adolescent manipulations of playing a parent against the other, the failure to put up a "united front," or complicated logistical issues. By saying, "Have you guys had a family meeting lately?" the mediator offers hope of a whole new way of doing things. Rarely will parents balk at this suggestion. If they do, they can often be convinced if they are presented with the business model of parenting. "No business runs without meetings, and your family business is the most important thing to both of you." If there is continued opposition, try, "All people have co-workers they don't like at some point in their working lives, and work with them anyway because they have to." Often, parties will set up their family meeting during the mediation session. Keep in mind, however, that this strategy does not work for warring parents but only for parents who can observe boundaries. The meeting should be set up around a single topic on which parents are united.

24. Responding to sarcasm or rudeness.

I have been zinged by a client on occasion. It's startling to be the target of a zinger thrown directly at you. It is the mediator's choice whether or not she wants to continue to work with a party despite the rudeness or personal attacks. The mediator can ignore subtle rudeness and hope it changes; however, it is unlikely to change if ignored but, instead, likely to grow *less* subtle in search of a reaction from the mediator. Therefore, another option would be to confront it directly. The most important thing about the mediator's response is to check your gut. If the mediator feels defensive and agitated, care must be taken not to act out those emotions. The mediator needs to calm that feeling and address the client with words that are not threatening, such as, "You can go after me, but it doesn't help this process work better. I'm not part of your conflict. I understand this is hard, and I hope I didn't give you the impression it's easy. Mediation can bring out the worst feelings, and I can see how it might feel better to find someone to blame or target, but I am on your kids' side, and that's what motivates me to try to help you come to an agreement. Does that make sense?" The good news is that such behaviors do not tend to occur often, at least in my experience.

25. Normalizing

Normalizing is a mediator statement in which the mediator assigns universal application to a condition or situation the client perceives as uniquely personal. Normalizing is a reframing (see No. 16 above) of a party's statement that lets the client know the mediator does not see the situation as negatively, or as hopelessly, as the party does. An example is a mediator's response to a party who expresses anger at the "unfairness" of divorce laws that penalize the higher income earner by making him pay a larger share of support, or, in some cases, making him accept a smaller share of the marital property. The party could be thinking out loud and not attempting to make an issue of his complaint, or the party could be trying to use his complaint of "unfairness" to suggest that the law be ignored. This, of course, is possible if the parties ignore the law with informed consent, but for purposes of the example, assume the complainer is just trying to position himself as uniquely affected by this unjust law as a negotiating ploy. A mediator wanting to neutralize his move might "normalize" his statement by making a universal observation such as, "Yeah, I know. The divorce laws seem counterintuitive to many people. If you want, we can discuss the logic behind them." Most parties do not want to have this discussion. Haynes described normalizing in this way, "Everyone coming to mediation thinks that his or her problem is unique, and idiosyncratic problem definitions are not easily resolved. As long as the parties believe that theirs is a unique situation, they have defined it as difficult or impossible to resolve. Normal problems are solvable and are solved by people every day. Thus, as the mediator normalizes the clients' position, she enhances their belief that they can solve their problem."[351]

26. Be aware of being ethnocentric; instead be culturally relative

Ethnocentricity is when we see our own culture as superior to others, and cultural relativity is when we have a more open-minded view towards other cultures. Daniel Lieberman, an evolutionary biologist, views culture as a distinct evolutionary force. He defines culture as "a set of learned knowledge, beliefs, and values that cause groups to think and behave differently…." He believes that culture is Homo sapiens' most distinctive characteristic.[352]

There isn't anything inherently wrong with being ethnocentric; it's part of how we live within our own culture. Marilynn Brewer argues that humans' tendency to prefer their own group is perhaps the most well-established phenomenon is social psychology. She concluded that this preference (our natural "ethnocentrism") is based on the universal need for belonging and distinctiveness. Interestingly, she found that humans' attitudes towards out-groups are most positive when these needs are well satisfied within the in-group.[353] Therefore, the better-adjusted we are, the greater tendency we show towards open-mindedness about other cultures. Any conflict can involve culture even when parties have the same ethnicity. Cultural conflict can involve family values, a town, or even particular occupations. When different nationalities are involved, a mediator benefits from understanding cultural differences relating to language, customs, and social mores. For example, in some Asian cultures, the word "no" is considered offensive and when "no" is the answer, it may not be spoken, but only hinted at. My American friend related a story to me about his long stay in South Korea with his wife. They came to love the hot wings at one restaurant because they missed American food. One night the restaurant was out of hot wings, but the waitress could not tell them this because she felt it would disappoint and offend them. Therefore, the waitress simply told them the wings "would take a long time to be ready." When "a long time" turned out to be not at all, they figured out what the waitress meant, and that she did not want to offend them by saying "no."

---

[351] Haynes, 1989, p. 36.
[352] Lieberman, D. (2013). *The story of the human body: Evolution, health and disease.* New York: Random House.
[353] Brewer, M.B. (2007) The importance of being we: Human nature and intergroup relations. *American Psychologist,* 62(8), 728-738.

27. Use Systems Thinking

In Chapter 3 systems are discussed. A system is any group of individuals that works together. The purpose of the system is to benefit each individual separately, but also to keep the system together and functioning because without it, the individuals do not thrive. A system always tries to maintain balance and equilibrium because of its importance to the individual members. What does this have to do with mediation techniques? In any conflict, there may be a system involved. A good example of this is the workplace. Even if the conflict in front of you in an employment mediation involves only two of the members of the organization for which they work, the entire system is involved because these parties are a part of the system. This means the system can be used by the mediator as a tool. The system is a resource for the mediator and the party. The problem may be systemic. Perhaps the problem the parties are having is due to a malfunction in the system. If so, the parties can work to tweak the system to correct an imbalance, resulting in resolution of their conflict. This intervention often works where the problem involves schedules, lack of compliance with rules, missing links in the chain of command, etc. By addressing the systemic issue, the conflict between members of the system is solved. The mediator intervention using systems thinking can be as subtle as simply observing the system and commenting on it. The mediator doesn't have to analyze or try to fix the system. The mediator does have to, in some way, affect the elements of the system, but this can be as subtle as simply recognizing and commenting on it. Other examples of systems in conflict are the extended or immediate family, a business, a system of laws, a school, a church, or any institution or organization. The point of systems thinking is not to make conflict more complicated, but to simply think about whether a system is involved. If one is, then the mediator should think about how that system might be influencing the conflict. That is systems thinking. Once the mediator gains this awareness, simply noticing this possible tool becomes empowering.

Class Exercise

Pick one of the 27 Skills, Tips, Techniques and Reminders and create a scenario where the mediator uses the intervention, successfully or unsuccessfully. Students may perform the skill before the class using role players from the class, or simply narrate the scenario in a 5–10-minute presentation followed by the class's observations and comments on each student's use of the chosen skill. Alternatively, use the role plays in Chapter 14, conduct simulated mediations, and assign observers to identify the mediator's use of any of the 27 skills.

Chapter Thirteen

"Believing as I do in evolution, I merely believe that it is the method by which God created, and is still creating, life on earth." -- Rachel Carson

The Science of Mediation

Recently, mediation literature has extended the discussion of mediation from the art of mediation to the science of mediation. Mostly, the conversation merely confirms what we already knew about the art, but gives us insight into how biology causes mediation processes and theory to work the way they do. This is very encouraging to mediators because it tells us we are on the right track.

Neuroscience confirms existing theory on human negotiation behavior. Physical processes of the brain explain many of the behaviors observed in this book, specifically: human reaction to conflict first avoids it; the operation of the mind is largely unconscious; emotions are very important in decision-making; humans need autonomy; and identity concerns, particularly identifying with a social group, are important considerations. Knowing that these processes are based in physiology, mediators can use them to assist participants in maximizing opportunities to change perceptions, a necessary component of resolving conflict. Oddly, the evolutionary impetus for all of these phenomena has been found to be something quite surprising: **energy efficiency**. The high energy demands of the human brain dictated important evolutionary body changes to help the brain save energy. Daniel Lieberman states, "…life is fundamentally a way of using energy to make more life."[354] All of creation spends most of its time obtaining food and using it to survive, grow, and perpetuate life.

Body Changes

The application of neuroscience to negotiation begins with a simple physical premise: When the human brain began to grow in size relative to body size roughly 1.5 million years ago, the brain's demands for energy dictated other evolutionary changes that make modern man what he is today.[355] When *Homo erectus* initially broke off from chimpanzees about 6.5 million years ago, he habitually and effectively walked upright on two legs, although differently from modern humans because the ability to climb trees was retained.[356] Bipedalism led to many other important evolutionary changes culminating in modern man's computer-like brain.

Initially, bipedalism was driven by diet and climate change. Global cooling resulted in less fruit, the primary food for hominids, requiring them to travel farther to find food and to rely on additional food

---

[354] Lieberman, p. 95
[355] Id., p. 107
[356] Id., p. 37

sources such as leaves, stems, and herbs.[357] Bipedalism also conserved energy because it uses up to 5 times less energy than knuckle walking.[358] Around this time females evolved to have three wedged vertebrae in their lower spines versus men's two to accommodate pregnancy in an upright stance.[359] About 2.5 million years ago, during the Ice Age, the Australopiths in Africa evolved important characteristics that still exist in modern man. Fruit being rarer necessitated travel to farther distances for alternative foods to hunt for underground tubers, leaves, roots, seeds, nuts, herbs, and even insects.[360] Larger back teeth (molars) evolved along with large jaws. More importantly, the need to trek long distances brought about skeletal muscular changes in gait and increased economy of locomotion, requiring less energy to travel than is used by chimpanzees.[361]

The earliest members of the genus *Homo* (of which there were many species) evolved around this time as the Ice Age required its members to hunt and gather outside of Africa in search of food. One of these species, *Homo erectus,* evolved a slightly bigger brain and a body resembling modern humans. Calories available from plant sources were insufficient to accommodate individual caloric need to gather and extract food, especially for pregnant females. Hominids therefore began to consume meat, long before projectile weapons came on the scene.[362] Food sharing and cooperative group behavior within families, extended families, and groups evolved to provide adequate food for survival. Stone tools developed to process food. The need to trek long distances resulted in longer legs (with almost no tree climbing ability), larger bodies, and the ability to endurance run. Even in cold climates, endurance runners overheat, requiring evolutionary changes such as sweating, loss of fur, and an outward nose that moistens dry air before it reaches the lungs.[363]

Humans have smaller gastrointestinal tracts and larger brains than mammals of similar size. By eating meat and processing food, humans became able to spend less energy digesting food so that more energy could be expended developing a larger brain.[364] Hunting meat required cooperation and cognitive abilities to communicate, remember, suppress urges, lead, follow, and organize. These skills demanded a brain that consumed high quantities of energy. The cost of this unique brain was slower reproduction than lower order species that reproduce rapidly and in great numbers. Humans, similar to apes and elephants, mature at a slower pace, have few offspring, and devote great energy to raising their young. Yet, humans reproduce faster than apes that have long periods of infertility, with up to 6 years between offspring. *Homo erectus*, the most prolific and first intercontinental hominid, is said to have combined the low investment, fast reproduction of mice with the apes' skill of high investment in offspring and slow reproduction.

---

[357] Id., p. 40
[358] Id.
[359] Id., p.46
[360] Id., pp. 55, 56
[361] Id., p. 65
[362] Id., p. 74
[363] Id., p.81
[364] Id., p. 91

About one million years ago, it is believed that archaic humans first controlled fire, although its use does not appear widespread until 400,000 years ago. Also, sharp, thin stone tools (such as spear heads) appear around 500,000 years ago. Fire had important consequences. Cooked food yields more energy, is less likely to spread harmful bacteria, allowed humans to travel to colder locales, avoid predators, and to stay up late at night.[365] The brain size of early humans reached that of modern man's brain size about 500,000 years ago.[366] The fundamental reason for the increase in brain size is the number of neurons in the neocortex, the outer layer of the brain, where most cognitive functions such as memory, reasoning, language, and awareness, take place.[367] Modern humans evolved about 200,000 years ago.[368]

Such a brain is costly, consuming up to 420 calories a day[369], or nearly one-fourth of a day's calories. In addition, the brain's needs for blood supply, warmth, and protection are costly. To develop this big brain, humans began the process prior to birth, producing babies with relatively large heads, necessitating assistance at birth due to the tenuous way humans are born. The baby's head must be delivered first, requiring a 90-degree turn within the birth canal just so it can get out.[370] The brain then takes years to develop to full maturity, prolonging the human child's growth to full adulthood far beyond that of any other animal, due to the brain's large size and complex wiring.[371] The human brain reaches full size by about six years of age, but requires another nineteen years to reach full maturity at age 25.[372] Scientists believe that all of these costs are the reasons most other animals don't evolve large brains. They also believe that large human brains produced other intelligent behavior in addition to tool making and control of fire, not necessarily evident in the fossil record, such as working together to share food, raise the young, communicate, and create social networks.

Brain tissue cannot store energy and requires glucose from the bloodstream. Even a minute's interruption of this steady stream of energy can cause irreparable brain damage.[373] While the physical processes of the brain use up 30 percent of the brain's energy demands, fully 70 percent of the brain's energy is used up from brain activity, or thinking.[374] Fat bodies are one adaptation that humans evolved to accommodate this need. Humans store fat like no other species; even human infants are famously fatter than infants of other species. Nevertheless, the brain has adapted its own abilities to conserve energy, mainly by creating energy efficient neural pathways that save on energy consumption. These pathways

---

[365] Id., p. 104
[366] Id., p. 108
[367] Id.
[368] Id., p.125.
[369] Id., p. 109
[370] Id.
[371] Id., p. 114.
[372] Aamodt, S.& Wang, S. (2013) *Welcome to your child's brain*. New York: Bloomsbury.
[373] Id., p.116.
[374] Tomasi, D., Wang, G., Volko, N. (2013). Energy cost of brain functional connectivity. *Proceedings of the National Academy of Sciences of the United States of America, 110*(33), 13642-13647.

dictate the way people think. This "neuroscience" discovery is of use to mediators and negotiators because it dictates how people think.

The brain uses three operating systems simultaneously: social, emotional, and cognitive. These systems evolved at different times in human development. The reptilian brain located in the brain stem at the bottom of the brain is believed to have evolved 500,000 years ago. Its focus is survival, and it is responsible for fight or flight. It can take over the other areas of brain function when necessary. [375] The limbic system, also referred to as the mammalian brain, houses the emotions, and receives sensory stimuli.[376] It is able to filter out irrelevant information and consists of the thalamus and the amygdala. The thalamus is a filter station[377] and the amygdala stores traumatic and unconscious memories. The amygdala signals panic and fear.[378] The neocortex is the most recent layer of the mammalian brain and highly developed in humans. It is responsible for higher order thinking, logic, and coordination of motor and sensory function. The frontal cortex accounts for one-third of the human brain[379] and produces abstract thought, imagination, planning, and the "conscious appreciation of emotions."[380]

By filtering stimuli, the amygdala conserves energy, guarding against unnecessary panic reactions. This leads to the conclusion that all perception is first processed through the emotions, suggesting that once the emotional brain is triggered and glucose is delivered to that site, an angry person becomes angrier.[381] This information is of value to mediators when participants' emotions tend to get in the way of rational thinking and seem out of control. Unlike previous mediation theory that encouraged separating emotions from rational thought,[382] a neuroscience model affirms the importance of emotion as a means of perception. The neuroscience model of conflict resolution also asserts several other principles.[383]

Patterns and Neural Networks

To create efficiency, the brain uses patterns and neural networks to save energy. For example, a certain smell or sound will connect to a memory automatically. Memory is used to predict certain events. These patterns create personality because perceptions and predictions are based more on subjective beliefs than on reality. By observing individual behavior, a mediator can become familiar with a party's unique personality developed as the result of the brain's efficiency. For example, a party who appreciates a certain quality in another person may value that quality strongly because it fulfilled an important need in childhood.

---

[375] Lack, J. & Bogacz, F. (2013). The neurophysiology of ADR and process design: A new approach to conflict prevention and resolution? *Cardozo Journal of Conflict Resolution, 14.1, 6-53.*
[376] Id.
[377] Id
[378] Aschwanden, C. (2013). The curious lives of the people who feel no fear. (Cover story). *New Scientist, 217*(2907), 36-40

[379] Lack & Bogacz, 2013, Id.
[380] Id., p. 10
[381] Id., p. 11
[382] Fisher & Ury, 1991.
[383] Lack & Bogacz, 2013. The Ten "Neuro-Commandments," condensed here to four principles.

In the case of a couple battling over school choice for their child, the mediator observed that the father was highly appreciative of the mother's ability to help the child with his homework. Father's pattern of approval of this behavior by the mother seemed as automatic and unquestioned as it was strong. Ultimately, the parties resolved the school choice battle by father agreeing to mother's choice of school district, largely as the result of much conversation between them regarding the child's actual academic needs and the mother's skills at addressing those needs.

Fear and Reward

The perception of fear appears to be more powerful than attraction to reward.[384] Since humans assess everything through emotions, the result is either fear or reward. The mediator who understands this principle from neuroscience emphasizes reward over fear because a fear reaction almost always leads to a destructive process. To create a constructive process, the mediator creates an environment that feels safe. If fear is present, this mediator does not react with an instinctive, mirrored fear response. To do so would create more fear. Yet, some mediators try to capitalize on fear to motivate change. For example, BATNA and WATNA have elements of fear.[385] Use of such fear tactics can be productive, but only when tempered with positive, fear-reducing alternatives. Positive conflict intervention by the mediator can shift parties from fear-based thinking to rational thinking. An example is a competitive couple who both wanted primary custody of the children, and were unable to see any type of shared custody as an alternative. Their view made sense, since the father had recently moved an hour away from the mother and children. The mediator, wisely, sensed that father's behavior (moving so far away from his children to be with his girlfriend) was inconsistent with his stated desire for primary custody. The mediator sensed that father may not have been fully invested in his primary custody position. Nevertheless, the mediator did not try to impose a solution or steer the parties in that direction. The mediator's tactic was to diffuse fear and create positive feelings by exploring the possibilities for sharing time with the children cooperatively instead of reinforcing the parties' competitive positions on primary custody to the near exclusion of the other.

Social Stimuli

Because humans evolved as social animals, they are highly motivated by positive and negative social stimuli. These motivations powerfully dictate behavior. No human wants to be excluded from the group. As humans evolved, and today, exclusion is a threat to survival. Conversely, positive social stimuli engender feelings of pleasure. Being respected, being treated fairly, having status or belonging in the group, and having autonomy are incentives that flow from living in a group. Mediators can make use of these strong social needs by appealing to them. The most obvious example is the need to be treated fairly. If a party perceives that a mediator is deviating from the role of neutral and favoring the other party, the first

---

[384] Id. p. 14
[385] Best Alternative to a Negotiated Agreement and Worst Alternative to a Negotiated Agreement both place the consequences of not reaching agreement before the parties in an effort to convince them that going to court is risky and could bring about an unwanted result.

party will most surely react against the mediator. Being true to the promise of neutrality is a powerful tool for the mediator because it creates trust and good feelings with the parties. By going out of her way to show respect for parties, a mediator is appealing to parties' need for respect and social status. Therefore, a mediator should show respect for parties at almost all costs, even when a feeling of respect is hard for the mediator to summon. Being authoritarian and establishing arbitrary ground rules can seem disrespectful to parties. For example, the mediator who tells parties immediately upon meeting them that there will be no name-calling, no interrupting, and no yelling risks insulting parties who do not typically exhibit those behaviors. A respectful approach, on the other hand, reaps the reward of trust and makes the parties feel comfortable.

The Inability to Multi-Task

Humans can perform reflexive tasks without thinking. Driving sometimes fits into this category. A person can drive, arrive at the destination, deep in thought about something else the entire time, forgetting most of the mundane details of the driving experience. We call this auto-pilot. The opposite ability is called reflective mode[386] and requires concentration and more glucose.[387] It is thought that reflective mode thinking tends not to be used during conflict resolution negotiations or mediation[388] because parties retain a sense of fear, which creates a different neural pathway from safety, which allows more creativity and reflective thought. I have observed this phenomenon in my mediations where parties behave defensively, with their guards up, and engage in a back and forth of attack and defend dialogue. Many times, this behavior shifts to a more reflective mode after the parties have exhausted their need to attack and defend, if the conversation is allowed to shift to a higher level. This usually happens serendipitously and not by design. It explains the phenomenon often observed by mediators, where parties enter fighting, and, after a space of a few hours, are seen leaving the session enthusiastically chatting and continuing the conversation as they exit the building together. In the language of the neuroscience model, their interaction has shifted from the limbic system to the neocortex.

Conclusions from the Neuroscience Model

Mediators have always wished their clients would operate from the neocortex, be logical, rational, and less emotional. This wish has gotten them into trouble with mediation participants who have felt dismissed and judged for being too emotional. A mediator who tries to avoid emotion nearly always fails to reach a mediated resolution when parties don't want to be told how to think. Mediators have, therefore, instinctively allowed venting in the hope that rational behavior will follow if the venting process can cycle through to a rational process. The risk, of course, is that sometimes the venting process will become too emotional and destructive, leading nowhere. It's a delicate balance the mediator learns to modulate largely from instinct and experience. Knowing the science behind all we have learned from our experiences is

---

[386] Id., p. 19
[387] Id.
[388] Id.

possibly helpful, but mostly fascinating to those of us who have observed all of these now provable and explainable phenomena for many years.

Chapter Fourteen

"You can't make this stuff up." -- Anonymous

Role Plays and Case Scenarios

Mediation simulations performed in the classroom are only truly educational when two elements are present: realism and immediate feedback. To achieve realism, artificiality is avoided as much as possible given a simulated setting. No one, not even a master mediator, can effectively and consistently demonstrate authentic mediation skills in a setting that feels artificial. This is because a mediation session is greater than the sum of its parts. Mediation comprised of, for instance, a husband, a wife, and a mediator has other conditions present, including, but not limited to, the parties' relational history, the parties' current interpersonal dynamic, and the ineffable moments that occur between the lines. Each participant's motives, desires, hopes and fears are the unseen forces at work. In an artificial setting, a script can be created, but the intangible relational conditions and feelings will not manifest; therefore, effort needs to be made to create "genuine" conflict in the classroom. There are three recommended ways in which to do this.

Imagined Conflict

The first and most popular method to create a feeling of authenticity in a simulation is to ask students to invent a private scenario with as much detail as possible. Their story is not shared with anyone else in the class, especially the make-believe mediator. With the theoretical portion of the course already under their belts, students typically become surprisingly adept at creating these scenarios. By not knowing the scenario ahead of time (because it is not from a script circulated to the whole class) the student mediator is not distracted by prior knowledge of the facts and is more able to pay attention "in the moment" as the situation unfolds in real time, as a real mediator must do-- no matter how much advance preparation may have taken place-- because the mediator's job is to be present for the parties.

Actual Conflict

The second method for creating realism is to ask students days ahead of time to think of an actual conflict in their lives. In response to the blank stares that follow, the instructor reminds them that life is conflict, and all of us have several conflicts with others happening at any given time. Possibilities include conflicts with a landlord, a job, a roommate, a friend, or a retail establishment. Private personal conflicts are not encouraged if sharing them may cause embarrassment or discomfort to anyone in the class. The conflict should be something that is significant but not longstanding, deeply rooted, distressing, or of high importance. The conflict that is chosen should be one the student would be comfortable re-enacting, and the student should only share it if he or she is able to keep in mind that what happens on the classroom stage bears no relation to the real conflict. In a typical class, only a small handful of volunteers come forward with a real-life dispute, usually a landlord dispute or one related to a job or retail transaction. One attorney student brought up a conflict with his wife, who has always been (and probably always will be) chronically late for everything. If the instructor is fortunate enough to generate a simulation from this method, there are several benefits to using this "half-real" conflict. Because the conflict was actual, both parties (even the other student in the re-enactment who did not actually experience the conflict) are inclined to adopt some of the natural feelings that would accompany the conflict. Suddenly, a simulation includes real (or closer to real) passion, desires, feelings, resentments and concern. Because the actual conflict involved their classmate, the students also tend to adopt a degree of motivation to resolve the dispute. Since, in real mediations, participants come with varying levels of motivation to resolve their dispute, and mediators typically are motivated to resolve cases, this scenario plays out more realistically than a fictional rendering.

Scripted Conflict

The third and traditional method for creating realistic dispute scenarios is to ask the students playing the roles of disputants to use one of the scripted scenarios that follow in this chapter, encouraging them to change or add facts to make it their own. These role-players are also instructed to keep the story from the rest of the class so the mediator has the opportunity to be fully present for the evolving fact scenario.

Role-Play Feedback

Immediate feedback is the other vital element for effective teaching using mediation role-plays. Feedback is optimized in two ways. The first is to have all simulations take place in the presence of the entire class. Traditional basic mediation training involved breaking students into small groups to perform simulations; however, this proved to be of little didactic value (although it is a good way to encourage bonding between the students, or just give them a welcome break from the instructor). When the entire class observes the role-play, students have an opportunity to participate by watching and identifying with the mediator, observing interactions between participants, and mentally composing their own responses to the parties. Afterwards (or even during the simulation), the class can ask questions and make observations and thus learn from the role-play of another just by watching. I will offer the mediator the option to signal me if she wants a suggestion from me or classmates about what to do or say. I always remind the class that it's okay to role-play a technique even if it's a bad idea for the parties. This gives students an idea to see where an unwanted technique might lead.

The second way to optimize feedback is for the instructor to freeze-frame the mediation at critical points in the process and teach the class about what is going on at that moment in the laboratory of the simulated mediation. For instance, when the fledgling mediator dwells on facts to "get to the truth" or tries to resolve tangential bickering, the instructor can call a break in the action and ask the mediator, "What are you thinking right now?" After the mediator answers, the class can be addressed, "Is there something else you think the mediator should be doing?" After a brief class discussion, the mediation resumes. Often, a student mediator will pause and look at the instructor to ask, "What should I do now? I have no idea." The student should first be asked why she feels uncertain about what to do and what options she might consider.

Then the class makes suggestions. If those questions do not lead to an appropriate answer, the instructor has an opportunity to demonstrate and give a brief lecture.

The Scenarios

The "scripts" that follow cover a panoply of scenarios. In addition, non-family law cases are included. This is because shifting to another substantive area besides family law is encouraged in basic mediation training because it sharpens the mediator's ability to be present and "ready for anything." As a basic mediation training text, this book serves as a foundation for mediation of any other substantive area, when supplemented with training in that substantive area. In other words, the fundamental skills of a mediator are what guides the process and, while a mediator's knowledge of subject matter in a dispute can be important, the ability of the mediator to apply the numerous skills and techniques that comprise the craft (or art) of mediation are the same regardless of the subject matter. Some would say that so long as the parties know what they need to know about the subject matter, a mediator could theoretically facilitate negotiations and manage conflict without knowledge of the subject matter. The benefits of knowing the subject matter are, primarily, to gain the confidence and trust of the parties, and to assist the parties in understanding their options and alternatives, if needed. If the parties themselves do not understand the subject matter, then the mediation should not take place until they gain the needed understanding. Although the overwhelming majority of scenarios in this text are from family settings, students should be exposed to other types of mediation in their family mediation training. This breaks up the monotony and exhaustion of having to focus on too many (often-heartbreaking) family disputes. It also prepares students to consider mediation as a career.

THE CASE SCENARIOS

Custody

Cindy and Eric

Cindy is 29 and Eric is 30. They have a 7-year-old son Tyler who was conceived during a brief relationship between Cindy and Eric. At the time of Cindy's pregnancy and Tyler's birth, Eric was alienated from Cindy and he denied paternity or any interest in Tyler. They had to undergo genetic testing before Eric would accept a parental role.

When Tyler was three, he developed a serious medical condition that required hospitalization and many tests before a diagnosis was reached. He was finally diagnosed with a rare disease that leaves him vulnerable to a stroke attack at any time. During the onset of Tyler's illness, Eric did not visit him in the hospital or show any interest in him or his condition.

Cindy is now happily married and has a two year old daughter and a three year old son, who adore their older brother Tyler. Eric is in a relationship with a woman he is considering marrying. Eric has had sporadic contact with Tyler. He states that he wants a written court-ordered schedule so that he can be a regular father with established partial custody rights. He has not been able to obtain such an order for one reason or another, e.g., lacking funds for attorneys, a demanding and time-consuming new job, and Cindy's insistence that they not involve the courts but agree amicably on a schedule for Tyler. They have had an unwritten schedule, but Eric states that when he tries to follow it, Cindy always has some excuse for why he cannot see Tyler.

Cindy is now hesitant to agree to a sudden strict schedule because she says that she really does not know Eric and that Tyler barely knows him either and has only seen him about fifteen times in his whole life. Eric did not acknowledge Tyler's recent birthday with a card or phone call. Cindy concedes that when Eric and Tyler do get together they have great affection for each other, lots of fun, and a surprisingly close bond. When he was 5, Eric even taught Tyler to tie his shoes, which is quite an accomplishment. She credits their relationship to Eric's innate kindness and Tyler's loving nature. She states that in spite of everything, she has always told Tyler that his dad is a good person and loves him. Eric states that the reason he has been sporadic in contact and sparing in his efforts to acknowledge birthdays is that he feels it is unfair to Tyler to act like a dad when he doesn't spend regular time with Tyler. He sees the situation as "all or nothing."

Cindy and Eric begin mediation to create a written schedule and agreement. They agree that it is important to establish a schedule of contact. Cindy is reserved and fearful, though, because she believes Eric is untrustworthy and may not follow through on a commitment to Tyler, which could hurt Tyler deeply. Eric feels that Cindy is trying to control his contact with Tyler and tell him what he can do, when, where, and for how long. He wants a free and liberal schedule or he'll go to court.

Beth and Larry

Beth and Larry were never married but lived together for 12 years. Larry is an elected state official and Beth is a homemaker. They have an eight-year-old son Anthony. About six months ago they decided to end their relationship, but neither party was willing to leave their home until a complete agreement could be made regarding custody of Anthony.

Recently, the tension in their home came to a head and Beth attacked Larry in the second floor hallway while Anthony was taking a bath in the first floor bathroom. Larry lashed back to restrain her and bumped her head into the wall, causing soft tissue damage to her neck. Larry called the police and he was charged with assault and battery.

Larry filed for custody and the parties have been ordered to mediation. Larry recognizes the close relationship between Anthony and Mother and is requesting alternating weekends and one evening every week, to gradually increase (after a year or two) to a shared 50/50 custody arrangement. Beth is requesting only supervised custody, as she believes Larry's violent behavior (which never exhibited itself physically before this incident, but has seethed "underneath" for years, according to Beth) is causing Anthony's angry outbursts at school. Beth is considering home schooling Anthony because of his behavior problems at school. She is adamant that Larry should not have overnights ever, and will only agree to Larry seeing Anthony in their home.

Gregory and Cheryl

Gregory and Cheryl were married for ten years and have two children, Chelsea 7 and Micah 9. Gregory and Cheryl met in graduate school where they both received Master's degrees in business. Gregory has been a high-level manager for a successful overseas company with offices in the U.S. His job has required constant travel, late hours, and weekends away from home. Cheryl stayed at home with the children until two years ago when Chelsea began school. For the last two years, Cheryl has worked for a financial services company three days a week. Recently, her employer has allowed her to work one of the three days from home. Recently, as well, Gregory's employer filed for bankruptcy and laid off Gregory and hundreds of other employees worldwide. Gregory is now collecting unemployment, severance pay, and attempting to cultivate a private consulting practice because he never again wants to go back to working at such a demanding and all-consuming position.

Cheryl is worried about money. Gregory is somewhat relieved to have lost his job and relishes the thought of spending more time with his family. Gregory has also made a decision to leave the marriage. This is something he has been mentioning to Cheryl for the past year, and thinking about privately for as long as three years. Cheryl is extremely angry at Gregory's behavior and "crazy" decisions. She wants life to return to the economic security she knew when Gregory was a highly paid business executive. She wants him to find another job identical to the one he lost. She does not want divorce and believes she and Gregory can "work on the marriage" if he would just agree to go to counseling. She doesn't understand his need to be "happy" and thinks he should do whatever it takes to hold the family together. Gregory has moved into his own apartment and has had the children overnight several times a week. He wants to have shared (50/50) custody and wants to work on all issues relating to parenting in mediation. Cheryl is opposed to 50/50 custody because she thinks it shuffles the kids around too much. She wants them to have the same stability she feels she is losing. Gregory is adamant about his plan and will agree to a gradual schedule that builds up to 50/50 over a year's period, but will not back down in any other respect.

Donna and Daniel—Grandparents

Donna and Daniel are the grandparents of Meredith, age three. Their son Danny was Meredith's father. Danny died suddenly eight months ago from a work-related traffic accident at the age of 25. Marcy is Meredith's mother. Although Marcy and Danny were never married, they did live together in an apartment owned by Donna and Daniel. They received a good deal of financial support from Donna and Daniel, and Donna provided daily care for Meredith so that Marcy could go to school to receive a certificate as a pharmacy assistant. Marcy is 21 years old. Since Danny died, she has been thinking about moving from the apartment provided by Donna and Daniel into public housing. She is entitled to social security benefits of $1,200 per month for Meredith (due to Danny's death) but Donna and Daniel are discouraging her from claiming the benefits. They say she will "fritter" the money away. They prefer to pay for Marcy's apartment, car and anything else she needs until she can finish her schooling.

When Donna and Daniel learned of Marcy's attempts to go on welfare and move into a housing project, they filed for custody. They believe that they can provide a much better environment for their granddaughter (who is their only living descendant) and that Marcy's choice to raise Meredith in the projects shows bad judgment. They are seeking shared legal custody and have tried to have Marcy sign a paper prepared by their lawyer so that they have legal custody rights. This will give them control over Meredith's social security benefits. They are only proposing two weekends a month for physical custody, but have stated that they will not hesitate to seek full physical custody if they do not get what they want. Marcy is fearful that Donna and Daniel are trying to take her child away from her. She is grateful to them for the support they have provided for her, but feels there are strings attached and wishes they would back off. Marcy cannot afford a lawyer or to fight a custody battle, but she did receive a free consultation from a lawyer who told her that Donna and Daniel are seeking legal custody so that they can control the social security claim as well as a worker's compensation claim that is pending.

Caleb and Sereta

Sereta: Sereta is 43 years old. She has three sons, Jordan, 22; Ryan, 17, and Sean, 12. She was married to Caleb from age 20 until about five years ago when they divorced. She is now remarried to Robert. She works fulltime as a school bus driver. She has summers off. She and her husband Robert enjoy gambling and often take weekend trips to the casinos. Since divorcing Caleb, Sereta has allowed him to see his sons much more than every other weekend and Wednesday evenings, as their "custody agreement" states (entered into five years ago). In fact, she has enjoyed many weekends to go on vacation without having to pay a babysitter due to Caleb's intense desire to spend time with his sons. Now that Caleb is attempting to modify the custody order to formally obtain primary custody of Sean and shared custody of Ryan (to match the actual custody schedule they have been following), she has had to cut back on his time for fear that he might attempt to reduce child support.

Caleb: Caleb is 45 years old. He is engaged to and lives with Melissa. Five years ago, when he was divorced from Sereta, he began attending AA meetings and has not had a drink since. He is very committed to his life of sobriety and recovery. He had been estranged from his oldest son Jordan, with whom he has now reconciled. He sees Jordan often, although Jordan chooses to live fulltime with his Mother. His two younger sons have stated a preference to live with Caleb. This has caused Caleb to hire an attorney to seek primary custody. He has many concerns, among them the lifestyle of Sereta and her husband Robert. Caleb feels that their drinking and gambling have a negative impact on the children and that both Ryan and Sean are too familiar with gambling vocabulary terms and gambling in general.

Custody action: Caleb has just filed his petition for primary custody and the parties are attending mandatory mediation.

George and Lydia

George: George is 45 years old and separated from Lydia, his wife of 18 years. They have two children, Alex, 13 and Amanda, 15. George continues to live in the parties' suburban marital residence and Lydia lives in a rented house one block down the street, on the same street. The parties have agreed to share custody of the children equally and are attempting to follow an alternating weekly schedule with exchanges taking place every Friday evening. The children have numerous extra-curricular activities to which they need to be transported almost daily. George travels frequently in his job, and, as much as he has tried to schedule trips around his weeks without the children, he often has to travel during his weeks with the children and relies on Lydia to take the children during his time. He then offers Lydia make-up time as often as possible to give her a break. He is very worried about money and does not want to reduce his custody time at all, even though he is having a hard time following the established schedule and actually using the time allotted to him.

Lydia: Lydia is 41 years old and the mother of two teenagers. She and George are separated and going through a divorce. Although she has a college degree and 16 years ago was a licensed stockbroker, she now works as a waitress because it provides her with flexible hours to be available for her children and their busy schedules. She struggles financially and has seen herself go into debt since the separation because George is very tightfisted about money and is unwilling to pay for the children's expensive activities including Alex's hockey and Amanda's cheerleading. Her attorney has suggested that she take George back to court to get more support, but she doesn't have enough money to pay the attorney.

Custody action: Lydia has filed a complaint for full custody. She does not have the money to pursue this action to its completion, but is hoping to get George's attention and to settle amicably. Her primary interest is in changing the formal schedule so that it matches what is actually being done, with George having the children a few nights a week when he is home. She then wants to obtain more child support. She sees the solution to the problem to be: more custody time for her (formally and informally) and more money from George. George's solution is to keep things as they are. He believes he can get his work travel schedule under control so that he does not have to be away during his custody time, yet, to date, he has not done this.

Roger and Karen

Roger is a 45 year old single man who has been divorced from Karen for four years. He works fulltime for a gas company, mostly on the road making repair calls to residents. He lives with his mother (his father is deceased) and has his children Katie, 11 and Anthony, 8, every Wednesday night overnight and every Friday or Saturday overnight. Roger is seeking shared custody because he wants to be more involved in his children's lives and believes it is his right to have his kids at least 50% of the time. He says would like to have them 100% of the time but knows that is not possible. Roger says that the children love being with him in his mother's house, love seeing their grandmother, and want to stay with him more often. He states that both children are a joy to care for, their time together is very beneficial, and that both children are thriving.

Karen is a 41-year-old single woman, divorced from Roger. Karen has earned her college degree since she and Roger divorced and works fulltime at a job that allows her flextime, telecommuting from home, and has a liberal policy for paid parental leave. Karen says that Roger can see the children "any time he wants" and that she never denies him the ability to see the children for additional time. She refuses, however to add any more overnight time to Roger's schedule because she says he left the marriage because he couldn't handle their son who has PDD (pervasive developmental disability, similar to autism). She says she is the one who has gotten Anthony help and wrap-around services, while Roger denied there was a problem. Anthony has tantrums and is a challenge to care for. Karen states that Roger spends most of his time riding his motorcycle and drinking beer at a local tavern on the days he does not have the children, and that when he has the children he is at home, but makes his mother do the cooking and child care. She says that Roger has the right, under their current custody order, to have the children two full weeks in the summer for "vacation" whether or not he goes away, but has never exercised the additional time. She says she has often offered him additional days on the weekends to spend a Sunday afternoon with the children but he would rather ride his motorcycle.

The parties agree to try mediation but both feel it offers little hope because neither is willing to budge. Roger will not settle for anything less than 50% physical custody. He states that Karen is exaggerating and that he has taken part in plenty of trips to doctors, dentists, and school field trips for Anthony. Karen states that the time he has with the children is plenty and he could spend more time (not overnights) already if time was what he really wanted. She says that Roger's mother smokes, and that places both children at a health risk, especially Katie who has asthma. Roger says his mother has a bad heart and now limits her smoking to three cigarettes a day, in the basement.

Mary and Tom- Relocation

Mary, the 29 year-old mother of Jaden, age 8, was accused of abusing her daughter Jaden when Jaden was six. At the time, Mary was living in the state of Maryland with Jaden. The abuse allegation was made by Jaden herself who told a school guidance counselor she was abused after a school assembly on child abuse. Jaden was possibly confused by what was said at the assembly. It described abusive hitting, while, at the same time, Jaden heard her friends routinely talk about being "slapped" by a parent without concern. The guidance counselor had a two- hour discussion with Jaden using dolls, pictures, and a chalkboard. The result was a child abuse report called in by the guidance counselor alleging Jaden was punched in the stomach and hit near the eye by her mother. The investigation that followed resulted in an "unfounded" conclusion. In the meantime, Jaden was placed with her father Tom who lived in Virginia. She has now been with Tom for a little over a year and Mary is trying to get Jaden back. Mary is pleading with Tom to let her little girl live with her Mommy. She says Jaden has been with her mother all of her life and should not be raised by her father and his new wife. Under the current arrangement, Mary has Jaden virtually every holiday, the entire summer, and every other weekend when the parties each drive half of the 5-hour drive between Mother and Father's houses. Mary desperately wants to reunite with her daughter. She states that Tom never took much interest in Jaden and did not see her very often before she was placed with him. She feels that the only reason he is refusing to change the custody arrangement back to the way it was is because he is now married to a woman who cannot have children and Jaden is all they have. Mary says that Jaden cries when she is with her and begs her to fight to get her back.

Tom, a 35 year-old man who was never married to Mary, was recently married to Cynthia. He states that he is willing to let Mary have Jaden for the lion's share of all vacations, summers, and holidays but feels strongly that Jaden should live with him. He says that Jaden did poorly in school when she lived with Mary and that now Jaden is doing better, participates in more sports and extracurricular activities and is part of a close-knit suburban community that provides her with a lot of love and support. He is unrelenting in his decision that he will fight to keep Mary from taking Jaden to Maryland. He says that Jaden loves his new wife Cynthia and that they have fun together and an affectionate, close relationship. He is the "house-husband" with a home internet business that earns some money, while Cynthia is a university professor. Tom says that Jaden has never said she wants to live with her mother.

The parties are very bitter about the past. Mary feels falsely accused, framed, misunderstood, and defensive. Tom feels that Mary judges him, does not know him, judges his lifestyle, his new wife (whom she does not know) and is untrustworthy. They are in compulsory mediation and the mediator would like to help them reach an agreement.

Roy and Nancy

Roy is a 37-year-old man living in Wisconsin. Today he has traveled to Youngstown, Ohio to attend mandatory custody mediation with Nancy, the mother of his six-year-old daughter Julia.

Roy owns a working farm in Wisconsin and is self-employed. He has not seen Julia in over five years. He was shattered emotionally when Nancy left their home in Wisconsin to relocate to Ohio, taking Julia (an infant) with her. He received divorce papers in the mail. He later found out they contained custody provisions, but he hadn't read them. He remembers signing them and returning them to Nancy's lawyer. Apparently, they said he would have contact with Julia "as the parties agreed." Unfortunately, they never agreed. He sporadically sends cards and presents to Julia (although he somehow missed her most recent birthday altogether). He has cultivated a relationship with a new woman who moved in with him four years ago. He now feels strong enough to pursue a real father/daughter relationship with Julia. His desire is to reunite with Julia (on this trip, briefly) and establish some kind of regular contact with her that would lead up to her spending summers on his farm in Wisconsin. Although Julia is his only child, he teaches horseback riding on his farm to students Julia's age and feels that he relates very well to those children. He has high hopes that he and Julia will form a close and loving bond.

Nancy thinks Roy is incapable of being a father. She is not 100 percent against his seeing Julia; however, she has grave reservations because she thinks Roy will revive Julia's hopes of having a "real dad" and then abandon her once again. Over the years, she has been truthful with Julia about her dad. She has explained that she does have a father, but that he lives very far away and is not able to see her much. She showed Julia his picture and gave her some (not all) of the cards and presents he sent. Julia is now eight years old and an honors student in school. She has an intense interest in her father and wants to pursue a relationship with him. Roy has called several times over the years trying to see Julia but Nancy rejected his requests each time and rarely told Julia that he called. She is very afraid of the legal action he has recently taken and, more than anything, wishes he would fade away into the background. She cannot imagine ever allowing Julia to go to Wisconsin or even to be alone with him.

Shannon and William

Shannon and William are attending a mandatory custody mediation session. They have three children, William Jr., 17; Amanda, 9, and Addison, 7. Currently the oldest son William lives with Father and the two girls live with Mother. Father is filing for "full custody" because Mother refuses to share any school or medical information with him. He says that Shannon refuses to speak to him about anything and that he recently went a whole month without seeing his daughters because Shannon has been so avoidant of him.

Shannon: After William filed for custody, Shannon became somewhat more cooperative about returning phone calls and allowing William to see the girls. For the past two months, he has had them at his house every weekend and sees them during the week occasionally, but not overnight. She proposes that William have them every other weekend during the school year and for three hours 2 nights per week to do homework, take them to activities, have dinner, but not overnight. She is also agreeable to alternating weeks during summer only. Her feeling about school night overnights is that it is too disruptive for the girls and too difficult for Father to get them to school in the morning because he might not have their backpacks, books, and other things they need for school. She is upset that her oldest son refuses to spend time in her home and that Father does not encourage him to spend time with his Mother. She wants William Jr. to spend two weekends a month in her home so that she can heal their relationship and he can spend time with his sisters.

William: William has a new girlfriend who lives with him. She has four children who live with them. He knows he hurt Shannon by leaving her but would like to have an amicable parenting relationship with her now. She blames him for ruining her family, making selfish choices, and hurting her deeply. He feels punished by her in her refusal to work with him to see the girls or to even return his phone calls. He is willing to share custody but thought going for "full custody" would be a better way to deal with Shannon, who has always been unwilling to listen to him or to hear his feelings on any issue. He is not willing to spend only every other weekend with his daughters and is offended by Shannon's refusal to allow him school night overnights.

The Unkempt Mom

The parties are Mom, "Cindy," Dad, "Dave," and 2 family friends Shelly and Pete who have gained standing to file for custody due to their strong *in loco parentis* status in caring for the child of Cindy and Dave, Skylar, age 8. The current court order gives primary custody to Father, Dave, who has cancer. The order states that if Dave dies or becomes hospitalized, partial custody shall go to Shelly and Pete, not to Mom. The Mother Cindy currently has every other weekend with the child, but often the child will not go.

Mother Cindy is seeking primary custody. She says that since Father began to use his friends to help with their daughter, the friends Shelly and Pete have pushed Mom away and alienated her from her daughter Skylar. Shelly and Pete claim that Mother is incapable of caring for Skylar any more than the small amount of time she currently has, and that, if it weren't for them, Skylar would not have anyone to raise her, help with school work, feed and clothe her, and take her to activities. Father, as weak and sick as he was, chimed in. He told the mediator, "I'd like to respond. The problem here is Cindy isn't clean. She's dirty. She can't cook and doesn't know how to clean. She can't do laundry. She doesn't keep herself clean. A month ago I had to give her $300 to go to a beauty shop and get the mats out of her hair. I'm passing away from terminal incurable cancer." Mom agreed that her lack of cleanliness is a problem and she is trying to change. Her parents have begun to help her more. Shelly asked to speak, and asked Cindy, "How am I pushing you out? I am only trying to help here. Cindy responded that Shelly and Pete are not intentionally pushing her out but that they do everything and don't communicate with Cindy at all. "You guys don't tell me anything."

The Mediator asked Mother what she is able to do now, "Do you attend your child's school events?" Mother stated, "No." The Mediator asked, "Who gets Skylar at school if she's sick?" Mother stated, "I don't know." Shelly stated, "That would be me. Pete and I have a daughter Lilly who is 9. Skylar thinks of her as family. She loves her mom, and I want her to spend time with her mom, but our home is her home. She and Lilly are sisters. Skylar loves having a clean house." Mediator asked who goes to Skylar's parent-teacher conferences. Shelly responded, "That's me. I do everything for Skylar." Mom stated, "That's because I'm not allowed." Shelly said, "That's not true. You are free to attend all school events. You just don't. No one is stopping you." Dad chimed in, "Well, she shows up filthy and that embarrasses Skylar." Mother, sobbing, said, "I just feel like no one tells me anything. When I call Dave, he says he doesn't know what's going on." Shelly asked, "Do you call me?" Mom admitted she does not. The Mediator identified 2 issues and was able to settle the case with a parenting agreement.

Support

Robin and Benjamin

Robin and Benjamin were married for fifteen years. They have three children, Craig, now 23; Steve, 21; and Amy 17. Craig and Steve are living on their own. Amy has lived with Robin (Mother) since the parties separated six years ago. Benjamin is now married to Diane (Stepmother) and lives in a neighboring community. Recently, Amy decided to leave her mother's residence and moved in with Father. Although the parties had a custody order granting primary physical custody to Amy, Mother did not contest Amy's choice to live with her Father.

Benjamin is requesting a termination of the support he now pays Robin in the amount of $256 per month. He is also requesting that Robin begin paying him support for Amy. Robin has always provided health insurance coverage for the children through her employer. Coverage is provided for her at no cost; however, in order to include a child, coverage costs $36 per month. Robin's income is $43,000 per year. For the last twelve years she has received a monthly bonus equal to one month's pay. Benjamin's income is $26,000 per year. His wife Diane earns $28,000 per year. Although Amy turns 18 on February 28, she will not finish high school until May of next year.

Benjamin is requesting guideline child support. Robin thinks the guidelines are unreasonable nd states that she should not have to pay any more than Benjamin paid her when she was the one receiving support. She also thinks that Benjamin has an advantage since he is married and has a working spouse.

Lorena and Paul

Lorena and Paul are separated after thirty-one years of marriage. Their grown children are 26 and 22 and live on their own. They filed a joint tax return last year. Lorena recently filed a complaint for spousal support and a hearing is scheduled in two months. The parties want to resolve the support issue as well as the other issues in their divorce prior to the hearing so they do not have to attend.

Lorena works in an orthodontist's office as an office manager. Her gross earnings are $33,000 per year. Paul is a heavy equipment operator. His gross earnings are $65,000 per year. They both belong to a union. Coincidentally, both have settled grievances brought by their unions for overtime pay and received lump sums for two years' back overtime pay. Lorena's lump sum was $643 received in January of this year. Paul's was $932 received in March of this year.

Prior to bringing the complaint for spousal support, Lorena and Paul had signed a separation agreement they prepared by themselves that required Lorena to pay the first mortgage of $524 per month (she lives in the marital residence) and all of her utilities. It required Paul to pay the second mortgage of $425 per month, both parties' car insurance, and the parties' MasterCard credit card.

Lisa and Sam

Lisa and Sam were never married to each other but did produce a daughter, Aliyah, who is now 11 years old.

Aliyah lives with her mother who has a fulltime job as a billing supervisor in a major metropolitan hospital. Lisa (Mother) earns $15 per hour and works 40 hours per week. Sam has never had the same job for more than 9 or 10 months. He has done odd jobs, traveled some, and now works fulltime as a security guard earning $9 per hour. He works five days a week for 7 hours per day or 35 hours per week. For the last six months, he has been given overtime resulting in an additional five hours per week at the $9 rate, plus an average of five hours per week at $13.50 per hour. His total additional work hours, including overtime, for the last six months, have yielded an additional $2,795. He has told Lisa that he does not expect to have any overtime again because the company has hired a new security guard to handle the overflow.

Sam wants Aliyah to attend an expensive private school in the city. Lisa is tempted to agree because Aliyah is a gifted child; however, upon reviewing the application materials Lisa knows they cannot afford to send their daughter to the school. The nonrefundable application fee alone is $500. Sam states that he has a friend (a man he used to work for) who is willing to pay Aliyah's tuition. The friend is affluent, is fond of Sam, and loves to hear Sam talk about his gifted daughter Aliyah. The friend has been a benefactor for minority children (of which Aliyah is one) in the past. Lisa is hesitant to accept the friend's generosity because there is no guarantee it will continue and she and Sam alone cannot afford it without assistance. Sam believes that once they get Aliyah into the school, she would not be turned away even without assistance because scholarship funds are available and the school has an affirmative action policy of attracting diversity among its student body.

Property Division, Alimony

Louis and Marilyn

Louis, 46, and Marilyn, 45, separated after 16 years of marriage. Marilyn is now living with her parents and Louis remains in the marital residence (their "dream house") built 10 years ago. When they married, Louis was 30 years old and well established as the owner of a successful and popular pet and pet supply business called "Seascapes." Marilyn has worked with Louis throughout the marriage keeping the business organized, ordering supplies, doing the bookkeeping, and taking inventory. Marilyn knows the business up and down and is fearful that the separation will cause Louis to remove her as an employee because all of the stock is in his name, since he started the business from his garage before they were married. During the marriage she managed the business alone for months at a time during periods when Louis was overtaken by depression that prevented him from leaving their home.

The couple has a daughter Kristi, age 14. Marilyn and Kristi have not been getting along for the last year, which is the same length of time Marilyn has been telling Louis she wants a divorce. Marilyn believes that Louis has alienated Kristi from her by blaming Marilyn for their problems and by inappropriately making Kristi his confidante and friend. One Friday evening, Marilyn found Louis in Kristi's room lying on her bed whispering and giggling with her, and suddenly becoming silent when Marilyn knocked on the door and entered. Marilyn fears that Louis is burdening Kristi with his emotional needs and is violating her boundaries by trying to be her intimate friend and confidante. Even though she knows Louis is a responsible parent, she fears that he has allowed his resentments toward her to interfere with what he knows Kristi needs now-- a loving father, not a needy, dependent father who reverses the parent/child role and burdens Kristi with his problems. Kristi's behavior towards Marilyn is becoming increasingly hostile and rude and Marilyn is certain that if she attempts any custody action, Kristi and Louis will strongly oppose any structured contact between Kristi and her mother.

Marilyn knows she is entitled to spousal support because the salary she receives from the business as a secretary ($25,000 per year) is one-fourth what Louis receives as president of the company ($100,000). Louis has asked Marilyn to quit her job at the pet shop but she does not believe she can make a comparable salary anywhere else. She has no education or other skills and any job available would pay considerably less. Louis says he cannot stand to see her at work and it is disruptive to the employees to be exposed to their obvious hostilities. Marilyn agrees that one of them should quit, but she thinks it may just as well be Louis. In addition, Louis wants child support from Marilyn because she "abandoned" Kristi and he is now her sole support. The guidelines state that Marilyn would receive only $2,000 per month for her support due to the fact she also owes child support payable to Louis. Louis resents having to pay her anything because she was the one who chose to leave. Marilyn feels that she cannot live on $2,000 per month (in addition to her salary) because any place to live costs at least that much to rent if she is to live in a style comparable to the marital residence.

Harold and Anne

Harold and Anne have been married 11 years. They have two children, Myriah, age 6; and Jonathan, age 9. They have decided to separate (although they currently still live together) and share physical custody of their children by alternating weeks, exchanging the children every Friday after school. They have also agreed that Harold will pay child and spousal support to Anne in the amount of $1,600 per month for three years. After three years, the spousal support (alimony) portion will end and they agree he will then pay guideline support using their incomes at that time.

They own a house with a fair market value of $275,000 and a mortgage balance of $210,000. Their monthly mortgage payment is $1,400. This does not include property taxes and insurance. Harold has a pension with the state that employs him as a counselor worth $75,000 per year when he retires. Of this amount, $40,000 was contributed in the last three years due to the larger salary ($80,000 per year) he has earned in recent years. The parties have no other assets. Anne has been a homemaker during the marriage and is anxious to get back into the workforce, even though her training and education are limited. She has no college degree but is very resourceful and handy and feels that she is capable of earning a living. Harold's annual income is $95,000.

Harold feels that Anne's decision to leave the marriage occurred three years ago and that she should not benefit from the last three years of increase in his retirement account because he has not felt married to her for those years. Anne is willing to give in somewhat on this demand because she feels it is the only way Harold can afford to keep the marital residence (where the children are comfortable) and "make the divorce work." Her plan is to move into a rented house a couple of blocks away.

Ian and Gail

Ian and Gail are separating. Ian has been disabled for the last 10 of their 20-year marriage. He receives social security disability in the amount of $1,500 per month for himself. In addition, the children receive $450 each from social security as a result of his disability.

Gail works as a legal assistant in a law firm. She earns $33,000 gross per year. They have three children, Corey, age ten and twin girls, Ashley and Erica, age eight.

Ian is addicted to pain pills and spends most of his time relaxing in front of the television and sleeping. He does some cooking but states he is in constant pain. He does not want a divorce but the tension in their home is unbearable and he has recently agreed to Gail's demand that he leave. He sleeps at his parents' house but stays all day every day at the marital residence to watch the children while Gail works, and also to have something to do during the day.

Ian thinks the most practical thing is for Gail to leave while he stays in the house with the children. Gail wants Ian to leave, but still provide free day care for the kids after school and during the summer. She wants all of the social security disability payments of $450 per child to be paid to her and for Ian to live at his parents' house on the $1,500 he receives.

Bridget and Tony

Bridget's Perspective

Bridget is 35 years old and works as a supervisor for a utility company. She met Tony in high school when she was 17 and he was 27. Her parents objected to their dating but there wasn't much they could do when they eloped and married a year later. Their early years of marriage were happy. Tony was already established as an engineer and they were able to afford a modest 4-bedroom home that was much nicer than the apartments her friends could afford. Tony was a traditional man who expected her to provide him with a hot meal every night, and he did not object to her working outside the home. She loved to cook and loved making their home comfortable and peaceful. Money was important to both of them and they saved and saved. Bridget had no education, but lots of smarts and worked her way up to supervisor in the customer service office. Four years into their marriage she became pregnant with their first child. The couple was ecstatic when Anthony Sr. was born and Bridget quickly became pregnant again the following year and every consecutive year until they had 5 children, each barely a year apart. Six years ago, she became pregnant for the last time with twins. After the twins were born, they both decided they did not want to have any more children. The last six years have been a nightmare for Bridget. She has seen Tony become more and more isolated from the family. He seems to do nothing but work. His job has provided them with a nice income and lots of overtime pay, but shift work has taken its toll and her pleas to Tony to turn down overtime always fall on deaf ears. She manages the household all alone. When Tony comes home, he expects the children to be seen and not heard. He is a kind man and loves the children, but has never spent any time with them. He has never once taken the children anywhere. The family does not do any activities as a family. Even though Tony is a religious man, Bridget attends church with the children while he stays home and sleeps. The children have outside interests and friends, and all of the driving and organizing has fallen on Bridget. Tony is very proud of himself for having paid off their mortgage. They are debt free. He is an excellent provider. He is also a chain smoker and drinks daily, but never to excess. For the last five years, he has become verbally abusive toward her, calling her a bitch whenever she brings up issues she believes need to be addressed. He has gained 40 lbs. and is on high blood pressure and high cholesterol medication at the age of 45. Tony and Bridget have not had sex in 5 years. Bridget told him 5 years ago she did not want to get pregnant again, but the truth was she found Tony's excess weight, smokers' breath and overall appearance and bad health unappealing. She was surprised that Tony never objected to her single refusal to have sex. It seems she feels nothing for him now except resentment. He expects her to keep total order in the household, which she skillfully does, yet she also works a fulltime job. She wishes he would handle family responsibilities and show some interest in the children besides kissing them good night at bedtime. She is beginning to resent him intensely. Recently, she befriended the bus driver she met on her bus ride home from work every day. They are just friends, but he recently divorced, and she has been leaning on him for support, while she considers divorce herself. She also recently told Tony that this is her plan. She worries that it will destroy him because he relies so heavily on her for everything, yet the thought of spending her whole life being unappreciated, verbally picked on, taken for granted, and overwhelmed with household responsibilities is unacceptable. She knows Tony will never change.

Tony's Perspective

Tony is 45 years old and recently received divorce papers from his wife of 17 years, Bridget. He can't believe she is serious about divorcing. He knows they can't afford to divorce. He has worked hard all his life so he could retire and they could enjoy retirement and grandchildren together. He has diligently paid off their mortgage and made sure they have always been debt free and had a hefty savings account in the bank. He can't understand why she would do this when he has been such a good husband. He feels very guilty that he has been verbally abusive to her for the last 5 or 6 years, since she became pregnant with twins, bringing the number of children in their family to six. He couldn't seem to help himself for resenting her for getting pregnant so often, and then twins. Yes, he loves his children completely, would give his life for them. Each and every one is adorable and special to him. When Bridget told him she was considering divorce, he pleaded with her to change her mind. He told he would do anything if he could rewind the last 5 years and take back the mean words he said to her, calling her awful names. He doesn't know what made him treat her that way. He wants her to see all the good things he has done as a husband, providing for the family better than any of the other couples they know. He has never looked at another woman, even though Bridget does not like sex and prefers to be left alone. He made that sacrifice for her out of respect for all the work she does every day taking care of the kids, cooking, working, and keeping house. She's a good woman and he can't believe he is losing her. He continues to try to convince her that she is causing them to lose everything he has worked for. He wants her to see that she will never have an easy life again. She will have to struggle financially without him. He is worried that she may be leaving him for someone else- he has noticed that she receives a lot of text messages and phone calls on her cell phone from a guy she met on a bus. Bridget insists they are just friends and Tony does not believe she would lie. He feels that maybe she is suffering from a hormonal imbalance or mental problems- why else would she throw away everything he has worked for and destroy the perfect family they have had? Tony is ready to tell his lawyer what he wants to do--- if Bridget can't be convinced to stay. He has seen the support guidelines and cannot possibly pay the amount set by the courts for 6 children. That will destroy him financially. He has talked to Bridget about what will work for him, and she said she will agree to what he wants. He will pay a maximum of $1,000 child support even though it is less than what those guidelines state. He will keep the house and she will use her half of their savings to buy herself a house. She will have full custody and he will see the kids every weekend for one day. He cannot handle overnights with six kids, and Bridget agrees that he would not be able to do that. His work schedule has never been family-friendly and he will not have any more time than that to spend with his kids. He is pretty sure that his job is probably the main reason for the divorce- he is simply in a career that does not allow a person to have much of a family life. Tony has lost 40 lbs. He is back to the weight he was 20 years ago. He has been taken off of his medications, but does need to think about quitting smoking. He is very sad and does not believe that Bridget is going to be happy or that she will ever find someone who will take her with her six kids, or take care of her the way he did.

Civil Cases

Employment Discrimination Case—Pregnancy

Tammy is a 19-year-old single woman who has filed a complaint with a government agency claiming that her employer "The Dew Drop Inn," a large hotel chain, has discriminated against her for her pregnancy.

Tammy began working as a front desk clerk for $15.75 per hour in August. Over Labor Day weekend she discovered for the first time she was four months pregnant. She became somewhat panicked, aggravating the nausea and vomiting she had already been experiencing. She saw a physician who gave her a doctor's excuse to miss work. She called off of work September 3. On September 4 and 5, she still did not feel well enough to go back to work. She called her employer but was unable to speak with a manager. She was only able to tell the front desk clerk on duty that she would not be in. When she called in for the third sick day, the front desk clerk told her that the manager said that if Tammy calls to tell her she must have a doctor's excuse or she would be fired. Tammy obtained a doctor's excuse from an agency called "Bright Beginnings," a known pregnancy clinic.

Tammy returned to work September 6 and was told to gather her belongings and that she was fired for failure to show up to work and to call off sick.

Tammy filed her complaint for pregnancy discrimination after speaking to a lawyer. She is attending the mediation without her lawyer. Her employer has sent Tammy's manager, Mary Sue, who has been the manager of the front office for 20 years and has full settlement authority to complete the mediation. In her entire career, Mary Sue has never had any type of discrimination complaint filed against her and has never been involved in such an action. She is appalled that she is being accused of improper discrimination. She vehemently denies that she fired Tammy for pregnancy. She states she has two grown children of her own and wouldn't think of ever discriminating against a pregnant woman. She believes that Tammy is just an immature "child" who is not responsible enough to hold down the position of front office clerk. During Tammy's absences, Mary Sue had to leave her family celebrations and fill in for Tammy. She resents Tammy for this and for filing the complaint.

Tammy was denied unemployment compensation because the hotel fought it, stating she failed to show up for work. She was able to get another comparable job at a department store after being unemployed for three months. She is asking for lost wages and some compensation for the pain and suffering she has endured. She comes to the mediation very prepared with telephone records showing she did call off for each absence.

Commercial Transaction

Amanda Jones borrowed $15,000 from River City Bank so that she could purchase a wedding gown and clothing to wear on her honeymoon. After her wedding, she and her husband purchased a jointly titled home worth $150,000, with a $30,000 mortgage balance. Amanda had several other debts, including three credit cards totaling roughly $8,000, but was afraid to tell her husband until after they were married. Amanda does not have any solely owned property that could be attached by creditors; however, she lives in a state where wages can be attached to pay judgments, and she has requested mediation with River City Bank in an attempt to settle the lawsuit the bank has filed against her to collect $25,000, the current amount due on the original $15,000 loan, including principal, interest, late fees, collection charges, and attorneys' fees.

In mediation, the mediator, a lawyer, notices that River City Bank has violated usury laws, charging Amanda Jones excessive interest, penalties, late fees, and overstating attorneys' fees. The parties have come to mediation without attorneys.

Medical Malpractice

Marcia Smith, age 52, had plastic surgery at Hillview Hospital as an outpatient, including a face lift and rhinoplasty. She signed a release, required of her surgeon Dr. Howell by all plastic surgery patients, relieving the doctor of any liability whatsoever. While receiving general anesthesia prior to surgery, a nurse anesthetist injected Marcia's left wrist with lidocaine. Marcia was still awake at the time of the injection and felt a sudden, sharp, tingling pain at the injection site. Within seconds, Marcia was put under and did not awaken until she was in the recovery room. Within a few hours, Marcia was home recovering and being taken care of by her husband, Will.

The day after surgery, when most of the general anesthesia had worn off, Marcia noticed her left arm was black, blue, and green and she could hardly move it. She noticed a bandage on her left wrist and then vaguely recalled the injection in her left wrist. Removing the bandage, Marcia noticed a large bruise and scab. She remembered that the anesthesiologist spoke to her prior to administration of general anesthesia, explaining every step of the procedure. She was sure that an injection into her left wrist was not part of his explanation, and began to worry that the nurse had harmed her by administering an injection into her wrist that was not necessary or wanted, and not explained. Marcia began to notice that when she did resist the pain and move her arm, her hand had a hot, tingling sensation with intermittent sharp pains. She decided to wait a few days, hoping her arm and wrist would heal, and that she could put this disturbing "problem" behind her.

Unfortunately, after two months, Marcia's wrist and arm still had not recovered. Marcia felt continuing pain, heat, and tingling sensations in her arm. She could no longer scratch her back or reach back to pull up a zipper when putting on clothes. Getting dressed and cooking, activities she needed to perform daily, were painful. Marcia had never been involved in any kind of lawsuit, did not want to sue anyone, and was worried that she had already lost all of her rights by signing a release for Dr. Howell.

Marcia decided to handle this herself and wrote a detailed letter to Hillview Hospital explaining the situation and her current condition. She felt particularly angry at the nurse, and felt physically violated. She pointed out to the hospital that she had been under general anesthesia numerous times in her life, having had three caesarean section operations to give birth, and prior plastic surgery. She had never before been injected directly into her wrist, and felt certain that the nurse who injected her damaged a nerve, and did not know what she was doing. In response to Marcia's letter, the hospital called Marcia and told her the call was being recorded. The hospital asked her questions, and after about the fourth question, Marcia began to feel that the hospital had no concern for her, was not calling to apologize or make amends, but was taking advantage of an opportunity to try to get her to say things on record and to confuse her, in an effort to protect itself from any lawsuit she might file. After 6 months of stewing over how badly the hospital treated her, Marcia obtained an attorney who reviewed the release Marcia signed and determined that no release was made of the hospital or its employees. Marcia then consulted with a neurologist who assessed nerve damage that could be permanent. If so, the current symptoms were unlikely to go away.

The parties have appeared for mediation to resolve Marcia's claim for medical malpractice against the nurse anesthetist and the hospital.

References

Aamodt, S.& Wang, S. (2013) *Welcome to your child's brain.* New York: Bloomsbury.

Ahmad, F., Hogg-Johnson, S., Stewart, D., Skinner, H., Glazier, R., Levinson, W. (2009). Computer-assisted screening for intimate partner violence and control. *Annals of Internal Medicine, 151* (2), 93-115.

Amadei, R.N., Lehrburger, L.S. (1996). The world of mediation: A spectrum of styles. *Dispute Resolution Journal, 51*(4), 62-86.

American Bar Association. 41 FAM. L. Q. 711 (2008).

Aderson, J.A. (1996). *Communication theory: Epistemological foundations.* New York: The Guilford Press.

Applewhite, Ashton. (1997). *Cutting loose: Why women who end their marriages do so well.* New York: Harper Collins.

Arbuthnot, J., Kramer, K. (1998). Effects of divorce education on mediation process and outcome. *Mediation Quarterly, 15(3),* 199-213.

Arkowitz, H., Lilienfeld, S.O. (2009). Road rage. *Scientific American Mind, 22*(2), 64-65

Aschwanden, C. (2013). The curious lives of the people who feel no fear. (Cover story). *New Scientist, 217*(2907), 36-40

Ballard, R.H., Holtzworth-Munroe, A., Applegate, A.G., & Beck, C.J.A. (2011). Detecting intimate partner violence in family and divorce mediation: A randomized trial of intimate partner violence screening. *Psychology, Public Policy, and Law, 17*(2), 241-263.

Barsky, M. (1983). Emotional needs and dysfunctional communication as blocks to mediation. *Mediation Quarterly, 7*(2), 55-66.

Bartunek, J.M. & Bowe, B.E. (1988). The transformational management of conflict: A perspective from the early Christian Church. *Employee Responsibilities and Rights Journal,1*(2), 151-162.

Bauserman, R. (2002). Child adjustment in joint custody versus sole custody arrangements: A meta-analytic review. *Journal of Family Psychology, 16*(1), 91-102.

Benjamin, R.D. (1998). Negotiation and evil: The sources of religious and moral resistance to the settlement of conflicts. *Mediation Quarterly, 15*(3), 245-266.

Benjamin, R.D. (2007). Jim Melamed is 2007 recipient of ACR John Haynes Distinguished Mediator Award: A tribute and lament on the field of mediation. Retrieved from http://www.mediate.com/mobile/article.cfm?id=3147

Benjamin, R. (2012). The natural history of negotiation and mediation: The evolution of negotiative behaviors, rituals, and approaches (Updated). Retrieved from: http://www.mediate.com/articles/NaturalHistory.cfm

Berne, E. (1964). *Games people play: The basic handbook of Transactional Analysis.* New York: Ballantine Books.

Brewer, M.B. (2007). The importance of being we: Human nature and intergroup relations. *American Psychologist, 62*(8), 728-738.

Bush, R.A.B. & Folger, J.P. (1994). The promise of mediation: Responding to conflict through empowerment and recognition. San Francisco: Jossey Bass

Bush, R. & Pope, S. (2004). Transformative mediation: Changing the quality of family conflict interaction. In Folberg, J., Milne, A., Salem, P. (Eds.) *Divorce and family mediation: Models, techniques, and applications*. New York: Guilford Press, 67.

Carnegie, D. (1936). How to win friends and influence people. New York: Simon & Schuster.

Chilton, S., Cuzzo, M.S.W. (2005). Habermas's Theory of communicative action as a theoretical framework for mediation practice. *Conflict Resolution Quarterly, 22*(3), 325-348.

Clemants, E., Gross, A. (2007). "Why aren't we screening?" A survey examining domestic violence screening procedures and training protocol in community mediation centers. *Conflict Resolution Quarterly, 24(4),* 413-431.

Coltri, L. (2010). *Alternative Dispute Resolution: A Conflict Diagnosis Approach.* Upper Saddle River, NJ: Pearson Education.

Coogler, O.J. (1978) *Structured mediation in divorce settlement*. Lexington, MA: D.C. Heath and Company.

Craig, R.T. (1993). Why are there so many communication theories? *Journal of Communication, 43*(3), 26-33.

Crawford, S., Dabney, L., Filner, J., Maida, P. (2003) From determining capacity to facilitating competencies: A new mediation framework. *Conflict Resolution Quarterly, 20* (4), 385-401.

Cullen, L. (2003). Unleashing an era of dread. *Time, 161*(13), A24.

Danois, Diane L. (2012). The cost of mediation versus litigation in family law. *The Huffington Post.* Retrieved from: http://www.huffingtonpost.com/diane-l-danois- jd/post_4201_b_2318483.html

Darnell, Douglas. Workshop on Parental Alienation: Its Impact on Children and Managing High Conflict Families, Rivers Club, Pittsburgh, PA (2003).

Darnell, D. (1998). *Divorce casualties: Protecting your children from parental alienation.* Lanham, MD: Taylor Trade Publishing.

Deutsch, M. (1973). *The resolution of conflict.* New Haven: Yale University Press

Divorce bill 11 million so far. *Sunday Tasmanian* (Australia), *November 1, 2009, 5.*

Donohue, W.A., Allen, M., Burrell, N. (1985). Communication strategies in mediation. *Mediation Quarterly,10,* 75-89.

Dunn, J., Davies, L., O'Connor, T., Sturgess, W. (2001). Family lives and friendships: The perspectives of children in step-, single-parent, and non-step families. *Journal of Family Psychology, 15(2),* 272-287.

Ehmke, R. (2010). Helping children deal with grief. Retrieved from http://www.childmind.org/en/posts/articles/2010-10-12-helping-children-deal-grief

Ellis, D., Stuckless, N. (2006). Separation, domestic violence, and divorce mediation. *Conflict Resolution Quarterly, 23*(4), 461-485.

Ellis, D.(2008) Divorce and the family court: What can be done about domestic violence? *Family Court Review,46*(3), 531-536.

Emery, R.E., Lauman-Billings, L., Waldron, M.C., Sbarra, D.A., Dillon, P. (2001). Child custody mediation and litigation: Custody, contact, and co-parenting 12 years after initial dispute resolution. *Journal of Consulting and Clinical Psychology, 69*(2), 323-332.

Expert offers advice on how to pick the right mediator for your case. (April 3, 2000). *Journal of Commerce, p. 10.* Retrieved September 9, 2009, from ABI/INFORM Global. (Document ID: 52162676).

Fabricius, W.V. & Hall, J.A. (2000). Young adults' perspectives on divorce living arrangements. *Family and Conciliation Courts Review, 38(4),* 446-461.

Fine, G.A. (1997). Scandal, social conditions and the creation of public attention: Fatty Arbuckle and the problem of Hollywood. *Social Problems, 44* (3), 297-323.

Fisher, R. & Ury, W. (1991). *Getting to yes: negotiating agreement without giving in.* (2nd ed). New York: Penguin Books.

Folberg, J., Milne, A., Salem, P. (Eds.). (2004). *Divorce and family mediation: Models, techniques, and applications.* New York: Guilford Press.

Folger, J.P. & Bush, R.A.B. (1996). Transformative mediation and third-party intervention: Ten hallmarks of a transformative approach to practice. *Mediation Quarterly, 13* (4), 263-278.

Freeh, L. (2012). The Freeh report on Pennsylvania State University. Retrieved from http://progress.psu.edu/the-freeh-report

Gale, J., Mowery, R., Herrman, M. & Hollett, N. (2002). Considering effective divorce mediation: Three potential factors. *Conflict Resolution Quarterly, 19* (4), 389-420.

George, A.L. (2003). *Awaiting Armageddon: How Americans faced the Cuban Missile Crisis.* Chapel Hill: University of North Carolina Press.

Gerencser, A. (1995). Family mediation: Screening for domestic abuse. *Florida State University Law Review,* Retrieved September 22, 2009 from http://www.law.fsu.edu/Journals/lawreview/issues/231/gerencse.html#FNT2

Gershoff, E. T., & Bitensky, S. H. (2007). The case against corporal punishment of children: Converging evidence from social science research and international human rights law and implications for U.S. public policy. *Psychology, Public Policy, And Law, 13*(4), 231-272.

Gilbert, R. (1992). *Extraordinary relationships: A new way of thinking about human interactions.* Minneapolis: Chronimed Publishing

Gjelten, E.A. (2022). How much will my divorce cost? Nolo.

Gladwell, M. (2005). *Blink: The power of thinking without thinking*. New York: Little, Brown and Company.

Glenn, C. (2013). Introduction to Symposium on the legal implications of the Sandusky scandal. *Widener Law Journal, 22,* 551.

Gordon, T. (1975). *Parent effectiveness training.* New York: New American Library, Inc.

Gray, C., Koopman, E., Hunt, J. (1991). The emotional phases of marital separation. American Journal of Orthopsychiatry, *61(1)*, 138-143.

Grebe, S. (1988). Structured mediation and its variants: What makes it unique. In Folberg, J. & Milne, A. (Eds.) *Divorce mediation: Theory and practice.* New York: Guilford Press.

Grebe, S. (1989) Ethical issues in conflict resolution: Divorce mediation, *Negotiation Journal, April 1989,* 179-190.

Harris, T. (1969). *I'm OK, you're OK.* New York: Harper & Row.

Harrison, K. & Hughes, M. (2013). Mushroom clouds in the Arctic. *History Today, 63*(8), 18-20.

Hart, Stuart N. (1991). From property to person status: Historical perspective on children's rights. *American Psychologist, 46 (1).* 53-59.

Haynes, J. (1981). *Divorce mediation: A practical guide for therapists and counselors.* New York: Springer Publishing Co.

Haynes, J. (1988). Power balancing. In Folberg, J., & Milne, A. (Eds.). *Divorce mediation theory and practice.* New York: Guilford Press, 277-296.

Haynes, J., Haynes, G. (1989). *Mediating divorce: Casebook of strategies for successful family negotiations.* San Francisco: Jossey-Bass.

Haynes, J., Haynes, G., Fong, L. (2004). *Mediation: Positive conflict management.* SUNY Press.

Hedeen, T. & Coy, P. (2000). Community mediation and the court system: The ties that bind. *Mediation Quarterly,17*(4), 351-367.

Holland, E. (2020). Understanding the top 3 styles of mediation with ADR Times. https://www.adrtimes.com/styles-of-mediation/

Holtzworth-Munroe, A., Applegate, A.G., D'Onofrio, B., Bates, J. (2010). Child Informed Mediation Study (CIMS): Incorporating the children's perspective into divorce mediation in an American pilot study. *Journal of Family Studies,16,* 116-129.

Horowitz, R.M. & Davidson, H.A. (Eds.). (1984). *Legal rights of children.* New York: McGraw Hill.

Huffer, K. (1995). *Overcoming the devastation of legal abuse syndrome.* Retrieved November 12, 2009 from http://www.legalabusesyndrome.org.

Illinois Coalition Against Domestic Violence, *Mediation and Domestic Violence,* http://www.ilcadv.org/legal/mediation_n_DV.htm

Jessani, A.D. (2009). Dealing with objections to mediation along the continuum of case complexity. *American Journal of Family Law, 23* (2), 85-89.

JFK Library (2014) Retrieved from http://microsites.jfklibrary.org/cmc/oct22/doc5.html

Kelly, J.B. (2000). Children's adjustment in conflicted marriage and divorce: A decade review of research. *Journal of the American Academy of Child & Adolescent Psychiatry,39 (8),* 963-973.

Kelly, J., Emery, R.E. (2003). Children's adjustment following divorce. *Family Relations, 52*(4), 352-362.

Kelly, J.B., Johnston, J.R. (2005). The alienated child: a reformulation of parental alienation syndrome. *Family Court Review, 39, 3,* 249-266.

Kitson, G.C., Babri, K.B., Roach, M.J. (1985). Who divorces and why: A review. *Journal of Family Issues, 6,* 255-293.

Klick, J., Avraham, D., & Stratmann, T. (2003). The effect of abortion legalization on sexual behavior: Evidence from sexually transmitted diseases. *Journal of Legal Studies, 32*(2), 407-433.

Kline, M., Tschann, J., Johnston, J., Wallerstein, J. (1989). Children's adjustment in joint and sole physical custody families. *Developmental Psychology, 25 (3),* 430-438.

Kressel, K. (2007). The strategic style in mediation. *Conflict Resolution Quarterly, 24*(3), 251-283.

Kruk, E. (1998). Deconstructing family mediation practice via the simulated client technique: The case of unresolved marital attachment. *Mediation Quarterly, 15(*4), 321-332.

Kubler-Ross, E. (1973). *On death and dying.* Routledge.

Kuttner, R. (2011). Conflict specialists as leaders: Revisiting the role of conflict specialist from a leadership perspective. *Conflict Resolution Quarterly, 29*(2),101-126.

Lack, J. & Bogacz, F. (2013). The neurophysiology of ADR and process design: A new approach to conflict prevention and resolution? *Cardozo Journal of Conflict Resolution, 14.1, 6-53.*

Lang, M. & Taylor, A. (2000). *The making of a mediator.* San Francisco: Jossey-Bass.

Lang, M. (2004). Understanding and responding to power in mediation. In Folberg, J., Milne, A., Salem, P. (Eds.). *Divorce and family mediation: Models, techniques, and applications.* New York: Guilford Press, 209-224.

Lannin, D.G., Bittner, K.E., Lorenz, F.O. (2013). Longitudinal effect of defensive denial on relationship instability. *Journal of Family Psychology,27*(6).

Lansky, D. Swift, L., Manley, E., Elmore, A., Gerety, C. (1996). The role of children in mediation. *Mediation Quarterly, 14*(2), 147-154.

Latner, J. (1986). *The Gestalt therapy book.* The Center for Gestalt Development, Inc.

LeBaron, M. (2003). *Bridging cultural conflicts: A new approach for a changing world.* San Francisco: Jossey Bass.

Lefkowitz, J. (2005). Movement outcomes and movement decline: The Vietnam War and the anti-war movement. *New Political Science, 27*(1), 1-22.

Lieberman, D. (2013). *The story of the human body: Evolution, health, and disease.* New York: Random House.

Lind, D. (1992). On the theory and practice of mediation: The contribution of seventeenth-century jurisprudence. *Mediation Quarterly, 10* (2), 119-128.

MacBeth, L. (2010). *The art of family mediation: Theory and practice, 1st edition.* Lake Mary, FL: Vandeplas Publishing, p. 38.

Mason, M.A. (1994). *From father's property to children's rights: The history of child custody in the United States.* New York: Columbia University Press.

Mathis, R. (1998). Couples from Hell: Undifferentiated spouses in divorce mediation. *Mediation Quarterly, 16*(1), 37-49.

Mayer, B. (1987). The dynamics of power in mediation and negotiation. *Mediation Quarterly, 16,* 75-85.

Mazor, A., Baptiste-Hamel, P., Gampel, Y. (1998). Divorcing spouses' coping patterns, attachment bonding and forgiveness processes in the post-divorce experience. *Journal of Marriage and the Family, 29*(3/4), 65-81.

Mazur, A., Michalek, J. (1998). Marriage, divorce, and male testosterone. *Social Forces, 77(1), 315-330.*

McDermott, E.P. & Obar, T. (2004). What's going on in mediation: An empirical analysis of the influence of a mediator's style on party satisfaction and monetary benefit. *Harvard Negotiation Journal, 9,* 75-113.

McIntosh, J. (2000). Child-inclusive divorce mediation: Report on a qualitative research study. *Mediation Quarterly, 18*(1), 55-69.

Meierding, N. (2004). Managing the communication process in mediation. In Folberg, J. & Milne, A. (Eds.) *Divorce and family mediation: Models, techniques and applications* . New York: Guilford Press, 225-247.

Nelson, S.D. (2011). The posttraumatic growth path: An emerging model for prevention and treatment of trauma-related behavioral health conditions. *Journal of Psychotherapy Integration, 21*(1), 1-42.

Oliver, R.E. (2004). *What is transparency?* NY: McGraw Hill, 3.

Pappalardo, J. (2008). Ever-present arsenals. *Popular Mechanics, 185*(11), 24.

Pearson, J., (1997). Mediating when domestic violence is a factor: Policies and practices in court- based divorce mediation programs. *Mediation Quarterly, 14*(4), 319-335.

Peck, M. Scott. (1978). *The road less traveled: A new psychology of love, traditional values and spiritual growth.* New York: Simon and Schuster.

Perls, F., Hefferline, R., Goodman, P. (1951). *Gestalt therapy: Excitement and growth in the human personality.* New York: Julian Press.

Portnoy, S.M. (2006). The psychology of divorce: A lawyer's primer part I—the effects of divorce on adults. *American Journal of Family Law,* 20(2), 73-79.

Retzinger, S., Scheff, T. (2000) Emotion, alienation, and narratives: Resolving intractable conflict. *Mediation Quarterly, 18*(1), 71-85.

Rhoades, H., Boyd, S. B. (2004) Reforming custody laws: A comparative study. *International Journal of Law, Policy and the Family, 18,* 119.

Richardson, D. (2012). Lessons from Hiroshima and Nagasaki: The most exposed and the most vulnerable. *Bulletin of the Atomic Scientists, 68*(3), 29-35.

Rifkin, J. (1984) Mediation from a feminist perspective: Promise and problems. *Law and Inequality, 21,* 330-342.

Rimelspach, R. (2001). Mediating family disputes in a world with domestic violence: How to devise a safe and effective court-connected mediation program. Retrieved September 22, 2009 from http://www.mediate.com/articles/rimelspach.cfm

Ringstad, A. (2012). The evolution of American civil defense film rhetoric. *Journal of Cold War Studies, 14*(4), 93-121.

Rodriguez, M., Bauer, H., McLoughlin, E., Grumbach, K. (1999). Screening and intervention for intimate partner abuse. *Journal of the American Medical Association, 282*(5), 468-474.

Saposnek, D. (1991). The value of children in mediation: A cross-cultural perspective. *Mediation Quarterly, 9*(4), 325-342.

Saposnek, D. (2004). Working with children in mediation. In Folberg, Milne, & Salem, 2004, 155-208.

Schneider, C.D. (2010). The works of John Haynes. Retrieved from http://www.mediationmatters.com/review_the_works_of_john_haynes.php

Scott, C. & Jaffe, D.T. (1989). *Managing personal change: Self-management skills for work and life transitions.* Los Altos, CA: Crisp Publications.

Shapiro, D. (2002). Negotiating emotions. *Conflict Resolution Quarterly, 20* (1), 67-82.

Silberman, L. (1982). Professional responsibility problems of divorce mediation. *Family Law Quarterly, 16* (2), 107.

Sternheimer, K. (2008). Hollywood does not threaten family values. *Contexts,7* (4), 44-48.

Szamania, S. (2006). Mediators' communication in victim offender mediation/dialogue involving crimes of severe violence: An analysis of opening statements. *Conflict Resolution Quarterly, 24*(1), 111-127.

Tauber, M., Nahas, A., Cedenheim, P., Dodd, J., Jones, O., Garcia, J., et al. (2012) Desperate and alone. (Cover Story) *People, 77*(6), 64-70.

Tauber, M., McNeil, E., Morrisey, S., et al. (2014). Gwyneth and Chris: The truth about their split. *People,81*(15), 64.

Terebelo, S. (2006). Practical approaches to screening for domestic violence. *Journal of the American Academy of Physician Assistants, 19* (9), 30-35.

The Hive Law. (2021). Divorce rate in America. https://www.thehivelaw.com /blog/divorce-statistics-us-divorce-rate-in-america/

Tolle, E. (1999). *The power of now*. Novato, CA: New World Library.

Tolman Screening Model mandated by court rule in York County, Pennsylvania, Pa. Bulletin, Doc. No. 00-1156 (July 7, 2000).

Tomasi, D., Wang, G., Volko, N. (2013). Energy cost of brain functional connectivity. *Proceedings of the National Academy of Sciences of the United States of America, 110*(33), 13642-13647.

Tower, L.E. (2003). Domestic violence screening: Education and institutional support correlates. *Journal of Social Work Education, 39 (*3), 479-494.

Twenge, J., Catanese, K., Baumeister, R. (2002). Social exclusion causes self-defeating behavior. *Journal of Personality and Social Psychology, 83*(3), 606-615.

Vaughan, Diane (1986). *Uncoupling: Turning points in intimate relationships*. New York: Oxford University Press.

Ver Steegh, N., Dalton, C. (2008). Report from the Wingspread Conference on Domestic Violence and Family Courts. Retrieved September 22, 2009 from http://www.mediate.com/pdf/Report%20from%20the%20Wingspread%20Conference%20on%20Domestic%20Violence%20and%20Family%20Courts.pdf

Vestal, A. (2007). Domestic violence and mediation: Concerns and recommendations. Retrieved September 22, 2009 from http://www.mediate.com/articles/vestalA3.cfm

Vital Statistics of the United States, 1975, Volume III, Marriage and Divorce. Retrieved from http://www.cdc.gov/nchs/data/vsus/mgdv75_3.pdf

Vital Statistics of the United States, 2014, National Marriage and Divorce Rate Trends. Retrieved from http://www.cdc.gov/nchs/nvss/marriage_divorce_tables.htm

Wall, J. Chan-Serafin, S. (2014). Friendly persuasion in civil case mediation. *Conflict Resolution Quarterly.* 285-304.

Wall, J.A., Dunne, T.C., Chan-Serafin, S. (2011). *Conflict Resolution Quarterly, 29*(2), 127-150.

Warshak, R. A. (2014). Social science and parenting plans for young children: A consensus report. *Psychology, Public Policy, And Law, 20*(1), 46-67

Webster's encyclopedic unabridged dictionary of the English language. (1996). New York, Gramercy Books.

Well, G.L., Olson, E. A., Charman, S.D. (2003). Distorted retrospective eyewitness reports as functions of feedback and delay. *Journal of Experimental Psychology: Applied, 9*(1), 42-52.

Weller, C. (2014). Parental alienation isn't in DSM yet, but it's in plenty of arguments. *Newsweek.* Retrieved from http://www.newsweek.com/2014/07/18/parental-alienation-syndrome-isnt-dsm-yet-its-plenty-arguments-258079.html

Whitehurst, D.H., O'Keefe, S.L., & Wilson, R.A., (2008). Divorced and separated parents in conflict: Results from a true experiment effect of a court mandated parenting education program. *Journal of Divorce and Remarriage, 48 (3/4),* 127-134.

Widiger, T. A. (2013). A postmortem and future look at the personality disorders in DSM-5. *Personality Disorders: Theory, Research, and Treatment, 4*(4), 382-387. doi:10.1037/per0000030

Willen, H., Montgomery, H. (2006). From marital distress to divorce: the creation of new identities for the spouses. *Journal of Divorce and Remarriage, 45(*1/2), 125-147.

Williams, K.R. (2012). Family violence risk assessment: A predictive cross-validation study of the Domestic Violence Screening Instrument-Revised (DVSI-R). *Law and Human Behavior, 36*(2), 120-129.

Wilmot, W., Hocker, J. (2001). *Interpersonal conflict, 6th ed.* New York: McGraw Hill.

Wissler, R. (2002). Court-connected mediation in general civil cases: What we know from empirical research. *Ohio State Journal on Dispute Resolution, 17,* 641-680

Yontef, G. (1993). Gestalt therapy: An introduction. In *Awareness, dialogue, and process.* The Gestalt Journal Press. Retrieved October 7, 2009 from http://www.gestalt.org/yontef.htm

Zubok, V. (2007). A failed empire: The Soviet Union in the Cold War from Stalin to Gorbachev. University of North Carolina Press.

Index

5

5/2/2/5 schedule, 262

A

abuse, 7, 45, 51, 63, 75, 89, 97, 102, 103, 117, 120, 122, 123, 124, 125, 126, 127, 128, 132, 133, 157, 169, 174, 210, 211, 259, 260, 263, 272, 274, 283, 284, 294, 295, 296, 297, 298, 299, 300, 301, 303, 310, 330, 379, 395, 398
Acceptance, 20
Acknowledgment, 205
Active Listening, 194, 196
adaptive style, 15
addictions, 25, 26, 27
ADVANCEMENT OF MEDIATION PRACTICE, 87
advertisement, 65, 76, 77, 98
affair, 47, 316
AGREEMENT TO MEDIATE, 211
alimony, 12, 15, 90, 94, 96, 147, 148, 154, 160, 162, 170, 195, 209, 224, 226, 229, 231, 235, 236, 238, 249, 250, 278, 283, 289, 290, 291, 318, 385
Alimony, 226, 235, 241, 283, 290
Allowing conflict, 177
amygdala, 366
anger, 25, 26, 31, 36, 37, 38, 53, 55, 97, 184, 187, 191, 199, 273, 296, 310, 311, 312, 313, 315, 321, 323, 343, 344, 346, 360
Anger, 20, 321
anxiety, 37, 44, 45, 46, 47, 48, 60, 250
Apologizing, 191
arbitration, 3, 7, 85, 100, 101, 168
Arbitrator, 152, 167, 168
artist, 15, 192
assertive, 12, 13, 15
Assertive, 12, 16, 17
Association for Conflict Resolution, vii, 6, 7, 63, 79, 98, 133
Association of Family and Conciliation Courts, 3, 7, 63
attack and defend, 32, 368
attorneys' fees, 4, 208, 213, 289, 290, 389
authenticity, 371

autonomy, 19, 45, 47, 48, 178, 194, 299, 315, 320, 321, 342, 363, 367
awareness, 49, 163, 166, 190, 196, 198, 291, 293, 314, 315, 320, 325, 342, 344, 345, 346, 348, 350
Awareness, 23, 342, 343, 400

B

balance, 41, 44, 45, 46, 48, 59, 60, 80, 186, 187, 224, 225, 226, 227, 233, 235, 250, 287, 288, 294, 302, 330, 335, 356, 358, 362, 368, 385, 389
Bargaining, 20
beneficiaries, 291
Benjamin, 36, 204, 382, 391
best interests of children, 64, 65, 72, 95, 96, 258
blame, 27, 31, 48, 197, 214, 310, 320, 351
Blame, 22
Blind Spot Exercise, 339
body language, 52, 56, 179, 188, 189, 190, 199, 200, 331, 337, 338, 356, 358
boundaries, 39, 45, 156, 160, 173, 178, 181, 184, 210, 294, 320, 350, 384
Boundaries, 17, 183
boundary, 91, 177, 178, 179, 180, 181, 182, 186, 196, 209, 210, 345, 347, 348
Bowen, 43, 44, 48, 60, 61
Bowen Systems Theory, 43
brain, 33, 339, 340, 345, 363, 364, 365, 366, 391, 399
bully, 185, 186, 294

C

capacity to mediate, 20, 22, 24, 26, 64, 68, 90, 91, 166, 294, 298, 299, 330
caucus, 4, 12, 57, 58, 91, 97, 146, 147, 148, 157, 158, 160, 161, 162, 163, 205, 207, 209, 211, 300, 301, 347, 350, 358
certified mediator, 140, 141, 143
change, 15, 16, 20, 21, 22, 23, 25, 36, 37, 39, 40, 42, 46, 48, 49, 51, 52, 55, 56, 58, 85, 156, 166, 173, 175, 176, 178, 180, 186, 189, 190, 192, 193, 194, 196, 199, 200, 209, 235, 237, 253, 263, 264, 267, 268, 275, 281, 293, 311, 312, 313, 320, 329, 336, 341, 350, 352, 353, 357, 359, 360, 363, 367, 372, 379, 387, 398

Change, 175, 219, 255, 358
character assassination, 30, 310
child, 31, 35, 36, 39, 40, 41, 42, 43, 48, 49, 51, 63, 64, 65, 67, 72, 74, 76, 89, 94, 96, 97, 99, 128, 146, 153, 159, 169, 179, 187, 193, 195, 197, 199, 200, 205, 207, 208, 217, 219, 223, 226, 231, 235, 236, 237, 241, 243, 244, 245, 246, 250, 253, 254, 255, 256, 257, 258, 259, 260, 261, 262, 263, 264, 265, 267, 268, 269, 270, 271, 272, 273, 274, 275, 277, 281, 282, 283, 290, 291, 293, 295, 316, 317, 325, 332, 333, 334, 345, 346, 351, 358, 376, 377, 378, 379, 380, 382, 383, 384, 385, 386, 388, 395, 397
child abuse, 63, 64, 65, 67, 74, 96, 99, 128, 277, 295, 379
Child Abuse Reporting, 102, 128
Child support, 281
child's perspective, 28, 31, 42, 258, 358
children, 26, 31, 36, 37, 39, 40, 41, 42, 46, 48, 67, 73, 75, 89, 94, 95, 126, 148, 153, 162, 169, 183, 184, 185, 196, 199, 200, 204, 214, 221, 242, 243, 245, 246, 248, 249, 250, 253, 254, 255, 256, 258, 260, 261, 262, 263, 264, 266, 267, 269, 272, 275, 277, 278, 281, 286, 288, 289, 291, 293, 301, 302, 316, 318, 319, 320, 343, 344, 346, 347, 349, 350, 351, 353, 357, 358, 359, 375, 377, 378, 379, 380, 381, 382, 383, 385, 386, 388, 393, 395, 396, 397, 398
Chinese symbol for conflict, 176
Client Readiness, 27
clients' rights, 181
cognitive, 364, 365, 366
Cold War, 1, 398
college, 1, 56, 96, 219, 262, 289, 291, 318, 377, 378, 385
Commitment, 21, 23, 27, 55
common goals, 45
communication, 43, 49, 51, 57, 65, 77, 79, 86, 100, 195, 196, 198, 200, 221, 296, 313, 315, 320, 329, 330, 335, 337, 338, 339, 342, 345, 346, 347, 348, 392, 397, 399
communication techniques, 6
Communication theory, 338, 391
community property, 284, 286
compensation, 64, 70, 93, 284, 312, 318, 376, 389
COMPETENCE, 82
competitive, 54, 329, 367
confidentiality, iv, 7, 63, 64, 68, 69, 72, 73, 83, 84, 91, 95, 97, 99, 101, 102, 126, 128, 130, 132, 145, 157, 162, 163, 167, 169, 210, 211, 213, 254, 296
CONFIDENTIALITY, 83
conflict, 17, 37, 39, 41, 42, 46, 47, 55, 58, 63, 64, 67, 69, 70, 73, 80, 81, 82, 88, 92, 93, 94, 96, 98, 156, 158, 160, 161, 167, 173, 175, 176, 177, 178, 181, 189, 190, 193, 194, 196, 200, 201, 203, 205, 260, 262, 275, 277, 293, 294, 300, 310, 311, 314, 315, 320, 322, 325, 326, 327, 330, 335, 343, 349, 371, 373, 392, 394, 395, 398, 400
conflict of interest, 3, 6, 64, 69, 81, 92, 134, 176
conflicts, 36, 64, 69, 70, 79, 80, 82, 92, 208, 371, 391
CONFLICTS OF INTEREST, 81
conscious mind, 340, 341, 342
Contact Boundary, 344, 345, 346, 348
contempt, 269, 272, 310, 312
contextually bound, 29
Coogler, 3, 4, 5, 6, 9, 10, 14, 158, 329, 392
cooperative, 166, 198, 261, 310, 329, 380
co-parenting, 34, 42, 50, 183, 198, 200, 312, 359, 393
costs of mediation, 134
counsel fees, 224, 229, 231, 238, 290
Court-Connected Mediation Programs, 129, 144
credibility, 32, 35, 144, 206, 294
culture, 1, 40, 43, 60, 65, 67, 73, 77, 176, 277, 345, 361
cultures, 43, 176, 338, 347, 361
custody, 25, 36, 37, 38, 40, 41, 42, 50, 54, 94, 96, 144, 146, 147, 151, 153, 155, 158, 161, 166, 169, 172, 183, 184, 187, 189, 192, 193, 197, 198, 199, 200, 201, 205, 207, 208, 215, 228, 237, 241, 242, 243, 244, 245, 246, 247, 248, 249, 253, 254, 255, 256, 257, 258, 261, 263, 264, 267, 268, 269, 270, 272, 273, 275, 278, 283, 301, 304, 312, 316, 317, 321, 323, 329, 332, 333, 334, 336, 347, 373, 374, 375, 376, 377, 378, 379, 380, 381, 382, 384, 385, 391, 393, 396, 397, 398
Custody, 36, 217, 228, 237, 242, 244, 245, 246, 247, 248, 256, 257, 258, 275, 354, 373, 377, 393
custody arrangements, 34, 41, 241, 253, 261, 268, 391

D

Danger and Opportunity, 176
Daniel Lieberman, 60, 361, 363, *See* Lieberman, D.
decision making, 79, 257, 340
Deflection, 347
Denial, 20, 21, 26, 27, 55
dependent, 259, 283, 319, 384
depression, 20, 25, 37, 349, 384
Depression, 20
designated patient, 44, 48, 60
destructive behavior, 22, 30, 177
differentiation, 44, 45, 46, 47, 49, 320, 322
directive, 10, 13, 39, 89, 94, 160, 190, 194, 200, 250
disrespect, 179, 210, 312, 358
distributive, 15, 230, 239
divorce culture, 28, 29, 32
domestic abuse, 64, 65, 67, 74, 75, 86, 96, 277, 294, 295, 299, 300, 303, 394

domestic violence, 74, 91, 96, 98, 144, 146, 159, 293, 294, 295, 296, 298, 299, 300, 302, 303, 392, 393, 397, 398, 399
Douglas Darnell, 19, 272
duty to assess power, 186
dyads, 45

E

effective communication, 4, 329
effective mediation, 84, 178, 326
emotion, 26, 151, 166, 191, 293, 311, 315, 317, 330
emotional, 4, 5, 6, 15, 19, 20, 24, 39, 43, 44, 48, 52, 58, 65, 206, 266, 272, 293, 296, 311, 312, 315, 319, 366, 368, 384, 394
emotional needs, 6, 384
empathize, 177, 194
Empathizing, 331
empathy, 14, 53, 177, 190, 337
empower, 188, 189, 190, 201
empowering, 14, 15, 23, 38, 187, 189, 190, 192, 313, 322, 362
empowerment, 5, 13, 14, 15, 16, 190, 192, 193, 196, 200, 201, 205, 310, 330, 356, 392
Empowerment, 14, 17, 190
energy, 22, 51, 55, 206, 363, 364, 365, 366
enforceability, 216, 240, 249
enmeshment, 46, 322
ethical concerns, 7
Ethics, 145, 157
ethnocentrism, 361
evaluative, 10, 13, 94
Evaluative, 10, 13, 16, 17
evidence, 26, 32, 34, 35, 89, 100, 101, 142, 143, 212, 266, 330, 394
evolutionary, 60, 361, 363, 364
expert, 34, 35, 54, 93, 160, 222, 282, 289
Expert Forensic Testimony, 35
Exploration, 21, 22, 23, 27, 55
externalizing, 353

F

facilitation, 13
facilitative, 10, 13
failed mediation, 25
Family, 36, 37, 41, 49, 56, 61, 63, 64, 65, 67, 69, 77, 88, 256, 261, 262, 273, 277, 279, 298, 299, 300, 304, 391, 393, 394, 395, 396, 397, 398, 399

family mediation, vii, 2, 3, 5, 7, 12, 15, 19, 23, 29, 46, 63, 65, 66, 67, 68, 77, 89, 94, 95, 133, 141, 180, 205, 208, 278, 329, 330, 338, 373, 392, 393, 396, 397
Family Mediation Association, 5
Family Systems, 49, 56, 61
fear, 19, 22, 29, 39, 44, 48, 179, 184, 185, 186, 191, 209, 273, 296, 298, 299, 300, 303, 314, 315, 341, 344, 366, 367, 368, 376, 391
fee, 70, 71, 87, 93, 206, 207, 211, 213, 215, 298, 383
FEES, 87
Flawed Communication, 338
freedom, 6, 10, 15, 16, 32, 69, 81, 317
frontal cortex, 366
full disclosure, 7, 229, 236, 238, 240, 284, 295
functional self, 45
fundamental task, 291, 311, 314
fusion, 46, 49, 320, 322, 345

G

Gestalt, 339, 340, 342, 343, 344, 345, 396, 398, 400
Gestalt theory, 339, 342, 345
Gestalt therapy, 339, 340, 342, 343, 345, 396, 398, 400
gifts, 81, 92, 284, 285
Gilbert, 43, 44, 45, 46, 49, 394
Gladwell, 340, 341, 394
glucose, 365, 366, 368
Grandparents, 259, 260, 376
gray area, 89, 147, 160, 209, 249, 273
Grebe, 3, 7, 394
grief, 20, 27, 28, 42, 91, 179, 191, 393
growth, 14, 22, 23, 30, 47, 48, 176, 339, 345, 365, 397, 398
Guidelines, 281

H

Harvard Negotiation Project, 11
Haynes, 5, 6, 7, 186, 190, 197, 329, 360, 361, 395
health insurance, 227, 236, 246, 282, 290, 296, 382
high conflict, 293, 310, 315, 321
High conflict, 310
high-conflict, 39, 46, 151, 166
higher order thinking, 366
Hollywood, 28, 29, 32, 33, 90, 393, 399
humor, 191, 350

I

identities, 19, 43, 400
identity concerns, 315

imbalance, 44, 132, 185, 186, 300, 362, 387
immunity, 128, 310
impartial, 64, 65, 68, 69, 79, 81, 87, 92, 173, 209, 251, 335, 351
impartiality, 3, 64, 69, 70, 71, 76, 81, 82, 87, 92, 97, 145, 181, 182, 205, 299, 327, 330
IMPARTIALITY, 81
impasse, 91, 154, 155, 171, 172, 211, 249, 251, 288, 311, 313, 315, 317, 353
in loco parentis, 259
in sync, 331, 350, 351
income, 7, 35, 90, 94, 97, 148, 162, 195, 207, 208, 214, 223, 229, 231, 235, 236, 238, 241, 278, 281, 282, 283, 284, 285, 289, 290, 360, 382, 385, 386
Income, 281
inheritances, 284
initial client contact, 203, 204, 205
inner conflict, 176
inquiry, 82, 143, 175, 264, 298, 299
insecurity, 186
interests, 11, 26, 34, 38, 39, 40, 54, 64, 65, 67, 72, 79, 89, 91, 93, 94, 95, 97, 134, 169, 171, 228, 251, 253, 254, 255, 258, 260, 264, 265, 268, 269, 279, 284, 288, 330, 334, 349, 386
Interim Agreement, 146, 159
internal power, 14, 187
Internal Revenue Code, 283
Internal Revenue Service, 281
Interruptions, 345
intimate partner violence, 293, 294, 297, 298, 391
intimate relationships, 19, 399
intractable, 14, 175, 310, 311, 315, 398
Introjection, 346
introspection, 14, 177, 178, 192, 293, 313, 345
IRS, 281, 283, 289

J

Jim Lange's Tax Planning Card, 281
John Haynes, 3, 5, 34, 392, 398
joint, 27, 41, 58, 79, 97, 154, 162, 170, 205, 207, 209, 214, 219, 226, 228, 237, 241, 244, 245, 246, 255, 256, 257, 258, 261, 263, 286, 289, 291, 333, 334, 348, 350, 358, 382, 391, 396

K

Kelly and Emery, 41

L

language, 43, 53, 56, 130, 140, 144, 158, 169, 178, 181, 182, 187, 188, 191, 196, 215, 216, 241, 255, 273, 313, 338, 353, 356, 361, 365, 400
leader, 2, 15, 177, 320, 323
legal advice, 4, 65, 71, 94, 131, 134, 158, 160, 185, 208, 209, 211, 213, 249, 278, 290, 303, 331, 359
legal information, 208, 211, 213
legal labels, 249
Legislation, 129, 303
limbic system, 366, 368
Listening, 196, 204
litigation model, 198, 200
logic, 33, 265, 360, 366

M

magic, 192
Maintenance, 241, 280, 281
mammalian brain, 366
Managing, 17, 177, 273, 330, 338, 393, 397, 398
marital assets, 284, 288, 290
marital attachment, 20, 23, 396
Marital property, 284
marital residence, 153, 168, 180, 183, 225, 226, 229, 234, 235, 241, 288, 289, 377, 383, 384, 385
mediation in a nutshell, 204
Mediation style, 10
Mediator compensation, 136
mediator role, 90, 160, 177, 208, 209, 213, 331, 337
mediator's responsibilities, 135
mediator's rights, 181
mediator/client boundary, 91, 160, 208, 330
mediator-client boundary, 177, 178
Memorandum of Understanding, 25, 26, 131, 135, 136, 153, 168, 169, 211, 215, 216, 240, 284
Mental illness, 24
mental states, 20
misbehave, 29, 30
misbehavior, 29
Model Standards for Family and Divorce Mediation, 88
Model Standards of Conduct for Mediators, 63, 79
modeling respect, 210
modeling respectful behavior, 16
modification, 236, 246, 268, 290, 312
Morton Deutsch, 314, 329
Murray Bowen, 43
myth, 30, 32, 36, 40, 42, 175, 264, 294, 295, 299, 312, 332
Myths, 28, 40

N

narrative, 200, 311, 313, 314
Negative Emotions, 17
neglect, 64, 67, 74, 96, 128, 259, 277, 295
neocortex, 365, 366, 368
Neuroscience, 363, 368
neutral, 13, 39, 85, 91, 96, 131, 147, 160, 168, 181, 194, 207, 213, 336, 337, 351, 356, 367
neutrality, 24, 39, 89, 93, 145, 157, 178, 181, 196, 249, 330, 337, 368
No-Fault Divorce, 3
Non-Parents, 258
normal life passage, 42
Normalizing, 24, 360

O

O.J. Coogler, 3, 10
opening statement, 24, 39, 91, 208, 210, 211
Opening Statement, 213
opinion, 35, 56, 89, 147, 160, 161, 190, 208, 213, 249, 250, 260, 341
orientation, 144, 203

P

paradox, 61, 350
parent education, 42, 94, 199, 320
Parent Education, 42
Parental Alienation, 272, 273, 393
parenting, 3, 37, 39, 40, 42, 50, 53, 72, 73, 75, 192, 198, 244, 246, 249, 253, 255, 257, 260, 261, 273, 275, 279, 316, 334, 335, 354, 359, 375, 381, 400
Parenting, 217, 260, 354
partiality, 24, 70, 81, 86, 92, 196, 341
past, 5, 14, 17, 21, 22, 28, 34, 53, 58, 81, 132, 169, 183, 187, 189, 190, 220, 230, 239, 267, 297, 316, 317, 318, 335, 342, 355, 375, 379, 380, 383
Patterns, 349
pension, 90, 282, 289, 385
people problem, 11
personal responsibility, 21, 30, 31, 178, 320, 348
persuasion, 11, 16, 49, 61, 194, 400
Ping-Pong ball, 41, 261
positions, 2, 11, 12, 38, 55, 175, 180, 288, 295, 330, 334, 367
power, 6, 7, 14, 15, 33, 41, 54, 132, 144, 159, 168, 179, 184, 185, 186, 187, 189, 190, 253, 268, 274, 294, 295, 300, 317, 319, 320, 330, 331, 340, 347, 352, 358, 394, 396, 397, 399
power dynamics, 6
powerless, 186, 187, 319, 320
predictable life event, 42
pressing, 6, 12
prima facie right, 258
Prisoner's Dilemma, 329
privilege, 7, 63, 95, 99, 100, 101, 103, 129, 130, 132, 157, 169, 171, 174, 213, 271, 293
Privilege, 99, 101
problem-solving, 13, 14, 190
process, 27, 42, 45, 49, 54, 61, 63, 64, 65, 66, 67, 68, 69, 71, 72, 73, 74, 75, 76, 79, 80, 85, 86, 89, 90, 91, 92, 94, 95, 96, 97, 99, 100, 101, 144, 158, 166, 167, 169, 177, 178, 180, 181, 189, 191, 192, 201, 203, 204, 205, 206, 207, 208, 211, 213, 251, 253, 255, 277, 278, 282, 291, 293, 294, 295, 297, 298, 299, 301, 303, 314, 325, 328, 329, 332, 338, 340, 342, 343, 344, 350, 352, 353, 354, 360, 372, 373, 391, 397, 400
projection, 211, 345
Promoting awareness, 331
property division, 25, 96, 249, 283, 284, 288
Props, 207
Psychotherapists, 180
psychotherapy, 43, 177

Q

QDRO, 218, 289
Qualified Domestic Relations Order, 240
QUALITY OF THE PROCESS, 84

R

real estate, 90, 235, 240, 241, 278, 284, 285, 290, 343
reality testing, 24, 27, 184
recognition, 5, 6, 13, 14, 15, 16, 19, 38, 39, 190, 192, 193, 196, 200, 201, 205, 254, 310, 329, 330, 356, 357, 392
recognizes, 94, 149, 163, 177, 191, 192, 253, 332, 342, 375
red flags, 25
Reflection, 192, 193, 194, 196, 351
reflective, 322, 325, 368
reflective practice, 322, 325
Reframing, 194, 196, 357
Reinforcing the boundary, 182
relative balance of power, 186, 295
Religion, 266
religious freedom, 267
religious liberty, 267

relocating, 253, 264, 265
relocation, 255, 264
report suspected child abuse, 126
Reporting abuse, 310
Resistance, 21, 22, 27, 55
resourceful, 187, 385
resources, vii, 31, 44, 45, 73, 75, 97, 134, 176, 179, 186, 195, 261, 291, 303
responsibility, 42, 48, 51, 52, 55, 97, 99, 144, 166, 177, 178, 179, 180, 191, 193, 214, 228, 237, 253, 272, 294, 299, 313, 320, 321, 322, 345, 346, 348, 359, 398
responsible, 37, 60, 78, 178, 180, 186, 187, 208, 220, 225, 226, 227, 234, 236, 237, 254, 257, 260, 262, 268, 323, 348, 384, 388
restructured, 32, 42
retirement benefits, 240, 290
Retroflection, 346
revenge, 30, 260
reward, 269, 315, 367, 368
Rigidity of roles, 48
Rigidity of Roles, 46, 48
Robert Benjamin, 5, 204
rudeness, 323, 360
rules, 3, 4, 16, 30, 32, 33, 57, 58, 63, 66, 80, 84, 85, 88, 91, 94, 95, 96, 129, 130, 136, 137, 142, 144, 145, 152, 154, 166, 167, 169, 170, 210, 249, 261, 289, 354, 362, 368

S

safety, 41, 75, 76, 84, 97, 200, 299, 303, 310, 317, 322, 330
Sample Memoranda, 223
Sarah Childs Grebe, 6, 9
sarcasm, 360
satisfaction, 11, 12, 13, 33, 36, 145, 397
Scapegoating, 46, 48
schedule, 36, 50, 179, 183, 192, 193, 196, 214, 217, 243, 245, 246, 247, 248, 257, 260, 261, 262, 263, 264, 269, 316, 317, 333, 334, 335, 354, 355, 359, 374, 375, 377, 378
school, 36, 57, 176, 183, 193, 195, 214, 221, 228, 237, 244, 247, 248, 253, 254, 257, 261, 264, 265, 271, 272, 318, 319, 332, 350, 351, 359, 375, 376, 378, 379, 380, 381, 382, 383, 385, 386
screening, 294, 295, 296, 297, 298, 299, 301, 303, 391, 392, 399
Screening, 296, 297, 298, 299, 300, 303, 394, 398, 399, 400
Section 10, Article I of the U.S. Constitution, 6
self-destructive, 30, 185, 322
Self-Determination, 17
SELF-DETERMINATION, 80

self-reliance, 190
serendipitously, 13, 15, 368
settlement, 3, 11, 12, 13, 14, 16, 24, 25, 26, 36, 68, 71, 77, 80, 85, 87, 89, 91, 93, 98, 100, 102, 152, 153, 154, 167, 168, 170, 201, 207, 216, 222, 233, 240, 242, 249, 264, 278, 279, 284, 349, 391, 392
shadow of the law, 253
shame, 31, 41, 48, 55, 311, 312, 313, 314, 344
shaming, 27
shared custody, 41, 42, 246, 256, 263, 264, 268, 367, 376
shuttle mediation, 12
siblings, 253, 264
signposts, 191, 192, 330
simulations, 371, 372
skills, 58, 63, 77, 82, 83, 194, 198, 203, 282, 290, 296, 325, 349, 371, 373, 384, 398
social security, 281, 290, 376, 385, 386
social stimuli, 367
spiritual growth, 176
stage, 11, 20, 22, 23, 24, 26, 28, 80, 179, 296, 371
Standards of Conduct for Mediators, 63
Standards of Practice, 63, 64, 65, 99
structure, 5, 10, 28, 64, 71, 94, 291
Style Continuum, 10, 16
sub-myth, 42
subpoena, 72, 95, 155, 156, 172
substance abuse, 7, 22, 24, 91, 135, 299
sufficient information and knowledge, 64, 71, 94, 291
sufficient information and knowledge., 64, 71, 94, 291
Summarization, 192, 196, 351
support, vii, 3, 15, 20, 25, 30, 40, 44, 45, 49, 50, 90, 94, 96, 146, 148, 156, 159, 162, 173, 177, 195, 207, 208, 215, 224, 226, 229, 230, 231, 234, 235, 236, 237, 238, 239, 241, 242, 243, 250, 253, 260, 269, 273, 281, 282, 283, 286, 289, 290, 291, 297, 304, 316, 351, 353, 360, 376, 377, 379, 382, 383, 384, 385, 387, 399
support guidelines, 207, 208, 253, 353
systems, 39, 43, 44, 46, 48, 54, 61, 261, 362, 366
Systems thinking, 43

T

"I" statements, 30, 179, 180, 181
tax, 90, 195, 216, 234, 236, 243, 278, 281, 282, 283, 289, 382
tax consequences, 216
taxability, 241
techniques, 190, 192, 194, 325, 338, 349, 373, 392, 393, 396, 397
terminate the mediation, 64, 69, 76, 97

406

Termination of Mediation, 135
thalamus, 366
The Do-It-Yourself Movement, 6
The peace movement, 1
The Style Continuum, 17
therapeutic process, 177, 258
therapist, 36, 43, 48, 149, 163, 177, 180, 183, 184, 185, 203, 343
thin-slicing, 341
togetherness, 44
Tolman Screening Model, 296, 297, 399
Transactional Analysis, 4, 329, 392
transformative, 94, 190, 192, 196, 205, 249
transformative mediation, 6, 14, 201
Transformative mediation, 10, 13, 14, 392, 394
Transformative Mediation, 201, 208
transformative style, 13
Transition, 21
transparency, 314, 320
Transparency, 27, 314, 315
transparent, 311, 314
trial, 29, 32, 34, 36, 37, 38, 268, 297, 391
Triangulation, 46, 47
trust, 29, 52, 99, 160, 181, 182, 183, 189, 193, 196, 199, 278, 291, 314, 315, 317, 329, 337, 350, 351, 368, 373

truth, 22, 28, 32, 33, 35, 40, 144, 184, 185, 186, 296, 319, 345, 372, 386, 399

U

unallocated, 235
unauthorized practice of law, 6, 158, 171
unconscious, 48, 178, 273, 326, 331, 338, 340, 341, 342, 344, 345, 347, 348, 349, 356, 363, 366
Unconscious behavior, 343
unconscious communication, 347, 348
unconscious mind, 340, 341
undifferentiated, 45, 319, 320
unilateral change, 357, 358
unseen power, 186

V

victimhood, 30

W

warfare model, 32, 34, 36, 320
Wingspread Conference on Domestic Violence, 298, 299, 399